The Myth of Racial Color Blindness

The Myth of Racial Color Blindness

Manifestations, Dynamics, and Impact

Edited by

Helen A. Neville, Miguel E. Gallardo,
and Derald Wing Sue

American Psychological Association

Washington, DC

Published by
American Psychological Association
750 First Street, NE
Washington, DC 20002
www.apa.org

To order
APA Order Department
P.O. Box 92984
Washington, DC 20090-2984
Tel: (800) 374-2721; Direct: (202) 336-5510
Fax: (202) 336-5502; TDD/TTY: (202) 336-6123
Online: www.apa.org/pubs/books
E-mail: order@apa.org

In the U.K., Europe, Africa, and the Middle East, copies may be ordered from
American Psychological Association
3 Henrietta Street
Covent Garden, London
WC2E 8LU England

Typeset in Goudy by Circle Graphics, Inc., Columbia, MD

Printer: Edwards Brothers, Inc., Ann Arbor, MI
Cover Designer: Minker Design, Sarasota, FL

The opinions and statements published are the responsibility of the authors, and such opinions and statements do not necessarily represent the policies of the American Psychological Association.

Library of Congress Cataloging-in-Publication Data

The myth of racial color blindness : manifestations, dynamics, and impact / [edited by] Helen A. Neville, Miguel E. Gallardo, and Derald Wing Sue. — First edition.
    pages cm
  Includes bibliographical references and index.
  ISBN 978-1-4338-2073-1 — ISBN 1-4338-2073-0 1. Post-racialism—United States—Philosophy. 2. Post-racialism—United States. 3. Race awareness—United States.
4. Racism—United States. 5. Ethnicity—United States—Psychological aspects.
6. United States—Race relations—Psychological aspects. 7. Ethnicity—United States—Philosophy. 8. United States—Race relations—Philosophy. I. Neville, Helen A.
II. Gallardo, Miguel E. III. Sue, Derald Wing.
  E184.A1M98 2016
  305.800973—dc23
                                        2015013050

British Library Cataloguing-in-Publication Data
A CIP record is available from the British Library.

Printed in the United States of America
First Edition

http://dx.doi.org/10.1037/14754-000

CONTENTS

CONTRIBUTORS

Hadiya A. Adams, MA, Department of Counselor Education and Counseling Psychology, Marquette University, Milwaukee, WI

Germine Awad, PhD, The College of Education, The University of Texas at Austin

Laura G. Babbitt, PhD, Department of Economics, Tufts University, Medford, MA

Lee Anne Bell, EdD, Department of Education, Barnard College–Columbia University, New York, NY

Caryn J. Block, PhD, Department of Organization and Leadership, Teachers College, Columbia University, New York, NY

Eduardo Bonilla-Silva, PhD, Sociology Department, Center for Latin American and Caribbean Studies, Duke University, Durham, NC

Alan W. Burkard, PhD, HSPP, Department of Counselor Education and Counseling Psychology, College of Education, Marquette University, Milwaukee, WI

Sheri A. Castro-Atwater, PhD, PPS, Department of Educational Support Services, School of Education, Loyola Marymount University, Los Angeles, CA

Hether R. Cook, MA, Department of Psychology, University of Akron, Akron, OH

John F. Dovidio, PhD, Department of Psychology, Yale University, New Haven, CT

Lisa M. Edwards, PhD, Department of Counselor Education and Counseling Psychology, Marquette University, Milwaukee, WI

Miguel E. Gallardo, PsyD, Graduate School of Education and Psychology, Pepperdine University, Irvine, CA

Phillip Atiba Goff, PhD, Malcolm Wiener Center for Social Policy, John F. Kennedy School of Government, Harvard University, Cambridge, MA

Lindy Gullett, PhD Candidate, Department of Social Psychology, New York University, New York

Margaret Ann Hagerman, PhD, Department of Sociology, Mississippi State University, Mississippi State, MS

Amber A. Hewitt, PhD, Department of Psychology, University of Akron, Akron, OH

Karen Moran Jackson, PhD, Institute for Urban Policy and Research Analysis (IUPRA), The University of Texas at Austin

Matthew C. Jackson, PhD, California State University, Long Beach

James M. Jones, PhD, Department of Psychology, University of Delaware, Newark

Cyndi Kernahan, PhD, Department of Psychology, University of Wisconsin—River Falls

Amanda E. Lewis, PhD, Department of African American Studies and Department of Sociology, University of Illinois at Chicago

Helen A. Neville, PhD, Department of Educational Psychology, Department of African American Studies, University of Illinois at Urbana-Champaign

Louis A. Penner, PhD, Department of Oncology, Population Studies and Disparities Research Program, Karmanos Cancer Institute, Wayne State University, Detroit, MI

Margaret Shih, PhD, UCLA Anderson School of Management, University of California, Los Angeles

Samuel R. Sommers, PhD, Department of Psychology, Tufts University, Medford, MA

Suzette L. Speight, PhD, Department of Psychology, University of Akron, Akron, OH

Derald Wing Sue, PhD, Teachers College, Columbia University, New York, New York

Sharon Y. Tettegah, PhD, Beckman Institute for Advanced Science and Technology, University of Illinois at Urbana-Champaign

Negin R. Toosi, PhD, Technion-Israel Institute of Technology, Haifa, Israel

Jonathan Warren, PhD, Henry M. Jackson School of International Studies, University of Washington, Seattle

Tessa V. West, PhD, Department of Social Psychology, New York University, New York

Vera Katelyn Wilde, PhD, Malcolm Wiener Center for Social Policy, John F. Kennedy School of Government, Harvard University, Cambridge, MA

Maia J Young, PhD, UCLA Anderson School of Management, University of California, Los Angeles

The Myth of Racial Color Blindness

INTRODUCTION: HAS THE UNITED STATES REALLY MOVED BEYOND RACE?

HELEN A. NEVILLE, MIGUEL E. GALLARDO, AND DERALD WING SUE

Many people in the United States believe that the country has moved beyond race and racism, especially after the 2008 election of Barack Obama as president and his reelection in 2012. The logic of this position is that the United States could not be racist if a Black man was twice elected into the nation's highest office. Others counterargue that race and racism persist in the United States, as evidenced by a range of disparities in education, income, health, and incarceration rates between people of color and Whites as well as by the attacks and killings of unarmed Black and Latino men and women by police officers. The 2014 killing of Michael Brown symbolizes these later abuses. On August 9 of that year, Michael Brown, an unarmed African American teenager, was shot and killed by a White officer, Darren Wilson, in Ferguson, Missouri. The African American community erupted in protest after the shooting and the subsequent disrespectful and shameful handling

http://dx.doi.org/10.1037/14754-001
The Myth of Racial Color Blindness: Manifestations, Dynamics, and Impact, H. A. Neville, M. E. Gallardo, and D. W. Sue (Editors)

of the situation: Brown's lifeless body was left by law enforcement personnel in the street for more than 4 hours, and community members reported that the police desecrated the impromptu memorial site. Police responded to the mostly peaceful demonstrators in riot gear and with military-grade weapons. They even patrolled the neighborhood in armored vehicles and brandished tear gas, a chemical weapon that has been banned in war by most nations, including the United States, since the Chemical Weapons Convention of 1993 (Organisation for the Prohibition of Chemical Weapons, 1993). Cities throughout the nation protested again after the acquittal of Wilson by a grand jury; for some, the acquittal symbolized the mounting injustice of the killing of unarmed Black and Latino people by police officers that have gone unpunished. These incidents provided impetus for the development of the Black Lives Matter movement and other calls to action to affirm the humanity of Black people in the face of racial oppression.

Not surprisingly, peopled differed markedly in their interpretations of the killing of Michael Brown; some maintained a view that race and racism did not play a role even in this specific tragedy, whereas others believed Brown's death provided evidence of the persistence of racism in law enforcement and the criminal justice system. These varied positions reflected a stark racial divide both in initial perceptions of Brown's killing and in the later acquittal of Wilson. According to a Pew Research Center (2014b) poll, about 80% of the Black Americans compared with 37% of White Americans polled believed that the Brown killing raised important issues about race in the United States. Moreover, nearly five of 10 (47%) of the White Americans polled believed that race was getting more attention than it deserved. There were also racial differences in the perception of the grand jury decision acquitting officer Darren Wilson: About six of 10 White individuals polled agreed with the decision to acquit, whereas about the same proportion of Black adults believed the verdict was wrong and that Wilson should have been indicted (Pew Research Center, 2014a). Early in 2015, the U.S. Department of Justice (2015) released an investigative report on the Ferguson Police Department, which described the prevalence of racial bias on the force:

> Ferguson's approach to law enforcement both reflects and reinforces racial bias, including stereotyping. The harms of Ferguson's police and court practices are borne disproportionately by African Americans, and there is evidence that this is due in part to intentional discrimination on the basis of race. (p. 5)

The killings of unarmed boys and men of color by police around the United States, including Eric Garner (Bronx, New York), Michael Brown (Ferguson, Missouri), Ezell Ford (Los Angeles, California), and Darrien Hunt (Salt Lake City, Utah)—all of which occurred in the summer of 2014—speak to potential police misconduct directed at communities of color. These were followed by two more deaths in early 2015—those of Walter Scott (Charleston, South Carolina) and Freddie Gray (Baltimore, Maryland); in both cases, police were charged with murder. Although the killing of unarmed girls and women of color by police are less frequent and does not receive attention, they occur and further highlight police misconduct. For example, within a span of 3 months, Tanisha Anderson (37) was killed by Cleveland police in November 2014 and Jessica Hernandez (17) was killed by Denver police in February 2015; both killings were ruled homicides.

The divergent views of community members in assessing the role that race and racism played in the incidents highlight the varying racial worldviews in society. Some people—mostly Whites but also a few people of color—argue that as a society we have moved beyond race and racism. For such individuals, race did not play a role in the killing of unarmed men of color by police; instead, these incidents were either justified or an unfortunate turn of events. Those who argue that race and racism played a role in the killings argue that men of color are stereotyped as violent and aggressive, there are racial tensions between the police and communities of color (particularly Black and Latino communities) primarily because of police misconduct and harassment, and society is organized in such a way that creates and perpetuates racial inequality. Ferguson offers a case in point. At the time of Brown's death, approximately 67% of Ferguson residents were Black, but the city council was 83% White, and the police force was about 94% White; it is not surprising, then, that the overwhelming majority of the traffic stops in Ferguson involve Black motorists (85%) and that 92% of those searched by police are Black, even though few illegal articles are found in such searches (Leber, 2014). The systematic practices in Ferguson were part of a larger system of policing that failed to protect the members of the community from harm and instead exploited the community for financial gain (U.S. Department of Justice, 2015).

This edited volume is designed to provide an interdisciplinary exploration of the concept of color-blind racial ideology (CBRI)—the widely held belief that skin color does not play a role in interpersonal interactions and institutional policies/practices. In this collection, scholars in psychology, education, sociology, and related fields provide a probing analysis deconstructing racial color blindness; all of the contributors point out the problems with the concept as it is currently practiced in society. These scholars deconstruct the theoretical and empirical literature on the definitions and manifestations of racial color blindness, point out major flaws in the myth of racial color blindness, and reveal its harmful impact on the lives of people of color. Moreover, the contributors provide new conceptual frameworks to understand the clash of racial realities that occur between people of color and White Americans and why such highly publicized killings of unarmed Blacks and Latinos are viewed so differently. As long as the philosophy of color blindness maintains its role as a dominant belief in our society, not only will people of color continue to suffer individually, but it will perpetuate inequities in health care, education, and employment. The balanced strength of the text is that all authors provide useful research, practice, and policy implications for anyone interested in reducing racial inequalities in society and thus challenging so-called racial color-blind discourse and policies. The volume thus is intended to serve as a resource for students, researchers, and practitioners interested in understanding contemporary expressions of racism and race relations.

As a way to contextualize the topic, we first outline the varying perspectives on racial color blindness; there are multiple approaches to the concept, and there is not one agreed-on definition. We then debunk the myth of a racial color-blind society by outlining current national racial disparities and by unpacking three key arguments used to assert a racial color-blind position. This is followed by the organization of the collection and a summary of each chapter. We conclude with a discussion of future directions for researchers and practitioners, together with the need to increase the sophistication of empirical studies in this area and to disrupt the faulty logic of racial color blindness.

DEFINING CBRI

A color-blind racial perspective embodies the view that the United States has moved beyond race and racism and that the color of someone's skin does not matter in today's society. People arguing that "race" was made too much of an issue in the Brown killing reflect a certain type of racial color blindness. There are debates in the field about the definition of racial color blindness that include whether the term is best captured through the denial of the color of someone's skin, through the denial of institutional racism, or both. These varied positions are outlined in Neville, Awad, Brooks, Flores, and Bluemel (2013) and Sue (2015); they also correspond to the sociologist Ruth Frankenberg's (1993) articulation of color- and power-evasion approaches. Frankenberg defined *color evasion* as the emphasis on "sameness as a way of rejecting the idea of white racial superiority" (p. 14). From this standpoint, researchers explore the development and implications of someone adopting the belief that "I do not see race." In contrast, power evasion can be captured by the sentiment that "racism is not a big deal today" or rather that everyone has the same opportunities to succeed and consequently "any failure to achieve is therefore the fault of people of color themselves" (Frankenberg, 1993, p. 14).

Because the contributors of this collection represent varying ideological and disciplinary approaches to the topic, most authors provide a brief definition of racial color blindness in their chapter. These definitions provide a context in which to understand the perspectives of the authors and subsequently the arguments they present.

RACISM PERSISTS: THE UNITED STATES HAS NOT MOVED BEYOND RACE

The persistence of racial disparities in education, health, wealth, poverty, and incarceration supports the notion that we live in racially hierarchical society, which affords unearned benefits to White Americans and unfairly burdens people of color. The very existence of these disparities challenges claims that race does not matter in U.S. society. Although a handful of people of color have been elected to political offices, confirmed to sit on the U.S. Supreme Court, or earned millions of dollars, these individuals are the exceptions. The reality is that people of color are disproportionately represented among many indicators of poor quality of life broadly defined.

People of color are overrepresented among the poor and those who are unemployed (U.S. Department of Labor, 2012), and consequently, they have lower wealth compared with White Americans (Kochar & Fry, 2014). The poverty rates for American Indians and Alaskan Natives (27%) and Black Americans (25.8%) are nearly twice the national average (14.3%); specific Latino ethnic groups such as Mexican Americans and Dominican Americans also have high rates of poverty (upward of 23%; Macartney, Bishaw, & Fontenot, 2013). The unemployment rates of Black Americans is consistently at least two times higher than those of their White American counterparts; for example, in 2014, Black American unemployment for persons aged over 20 years was about 9.7% compared with 4.2% for White Americans; the unemployment rates for Latinos and Asian Americans were 5.9% and 4.5%, respectively (U.S. Department of Labor, 2015). Furthermore, the gap in wealth between Whites and Black and Latinos is growing. In 2014, the average wealth of White Americans was $141,900 compared with only $11,000 for Black Americans, and $13,700 non-Black Latinos (Kochar & Fry, 2014).

There are mounting data documenting the racial disparities in all aspects of the criminal justice system (Alexander, 2010). The Department of Justice report on Ferguson highlights the nature and extent of the disparities in one American town. These disparities reflect national trends. For example, in 2013, Black (38%), Latino (21%), and other races (6%) constituted the majority of those incarcerated during the year, and although Whites make up about 63% of the U.S. population, they comprised only 35% of those incarcerated during that time (Carson, 2014). Black Americans suffer the largest disparity. Nationally, the racial and ethnic disparity in incarceration is 5.6 Black

Americans to 1.0 White American and for Latinos it is 1.8:1; felony disenfranchisement for Black Americans is 7.7% compared with 2.5% nationally (Sentencing Project, n.d.).

Many people of color experience health inequalities, primarily due to limited access to quality health care or living in neighborhoods with higher concentrations of poverty. For example, the infant mortality rates for Black women are twice that of White women, and Blacks are more likely to die from a stroke or coronary heart disease before age 75 compared with their White counterparts. They also have the highest rates of diabetes. Blacks and Latinos have greater rates of tuberculosis, HIV infection, and preventable hospitalization compared with Whites (Centers for Disease Control and Prevention, 2013).

DEBUNKING THE MYTH OF RACIAL COLOR BLINDNESS

Even when confronted with government statistics documenting the disparities in a range of quality-of-life indicators between people of color and White Americans, some individuals maintain their viewpoint that race does not matter in a person's life experiences or day-to-day reality. This edited volume provides cogent retorts to three commonly held interrelated assertions we hear from people who continue to argue for the virtues of a racially color-blind perspective.

"Racial color blindness is a good thing." This comment is often associated with a vague reference to Martin Luther King's (1963) "I Have a Dream" speech delivered on the steps of the Lincoln Memorial more than 50 years ago. King eloquently stated, "I have a dream that my four little children will one day live in a nation where they will not be judged by the color of their skin but by the content of their character" (para. 16). The quote is commonly decontextualized in these lay discussions because the speaker does not take into consideration the context or entirety of the comments. King never intended for people to ignore the realities of racial inequalities. To live in a society in which race does not matter and that people are judged solely on the content of their character is ideal and assumes a level playing field; unfortunately, as King noted in his speech, we did not then—nor do we now, for that matter—live in an ideal society in terms of race. The United States remains a racially hierarchical society in which people of color face individual and institutionalized discrimination. Race matters in terms of social indicators and peoples' lived experiences. Thus, to deny race and ignore the existence of racism actually causes harm to people of color because it (a) falsely perpetuates the myth of equal access and opportunity, (b) blames people of color for their lot in life, and (c) allows Whites to their lives in ignorance, naiveté, and innocence.

The idea of a living in a world in which the color of someone's skin does not matter in terms of social relationships and lived experiences is especially attractive to some. For example, for White individuals who benefit from racial privilege, not seeing race or racism provides an opportunity to maintain a positive sense of self: "I am a good, moral, and decent human being and do not discriminate. I do not think about someone else's race." On the surface, it may seem like "good people" do not consider race when interacting with others. The assumption here is that by not noticing race, the individual does not treat people differently based on racial group membership. As we shall see in future chapters, engaging in strategic color blindness is nearly impossible because it has been shown that we begin to distinguish race and gender differences early in life.

Unfortunately, "good people" with the notable goal of ignoring race actually do harm in interracial interactions. There are multiple theories and emerging research documenting the problems with "ignoring" race in interpersonal interactions. Jones (Chapter 2, this volume), Gullett and West (Chapter 4), and M. C. Jackson, Wilde, and Goff (Chapter 7) review the research that examines this question, primarily from the color-evasion perspective. Findings overwhelming suggest that when White individuals do not pay attention to race (e.g., "I don't see race"), there is often a negative effect on people of color, such as feeling less motivated and engaged in the workplace. Part of the issue is that because the United States is racialized, to say one does not see the color of someone's skin is similar to not acknowledging the proverbial elephant in the room.

Researchers adopting a power-evasion perspective argue and provide empirical data indicating that by ignoring the reality of institutional racism, people rationalize or explain away racial inequality that exists in terms of, for example, income, housing, education, and criminal justice. Often underneath the color-blind racial discourse is antipathy toward people of color and justification for policies that, in the end, create race problems. For example, the implementation of stop-and-frisk policing was intended to create safe neighborhoods regardless of race. However, because of racial stereotyping, the actual implementation of this policy in places such as New York City has created racial disparities. In 2013, District Judge Shira Scheindlin ruled in *Floyd, et al. v. City of New York, et al.* that the "stop-and-frisk" practices of the New York Police Department violated the constitutional rights of racial and ethnic minorities in the city and reflected a form of racial profiling of Blacks and Latinos.

"Race(ism) isn't as relevant today as it was before the civil rights movement." The assumption here is that the United States has moved beyond racism,

as exemplified by the election of Barack Obama as president. However, a number of the authors in this collection argue that contemporary forms of racism have morphed from the publicly sanctioned vitriol and corresponding racial policies of the Jim Crow era to public discourse that masks covert forms of racism that may on the surface appear more "civil" (see Chapter 1 by Bonilla-Silva, Chapter 2 by Jones, Chapter 5 by Warren, and Chapter 6 by Bell, all in this volume). After the election of President Obama in 2008, membership in hate groups rose about 60% over a 5-year period (Chiles, 2013). On average, the unemployment rate for Blacks is consistently double that of their White counterparts (Desilver, 2013). Asian American teenagers experience bullying at significantly higher rates than other racial and ethnic groups (DeVoe & Murphy, 2011). Together with the death of Michael Brown and other unarmed people of color by police officers, these facts all point to the persistence of racial inequality.

"Talking about race makes things worse." Some people claim that talking about race promotes racism or is racist in and of itself. By claiming that the discourse is the problem, people are able to evade the real culprit—that is, racist acts or behavior. The following example exemplifies our point. "Laura," a Latina freshman living in a predominantly White residence hall, was given the nickname "Taco Lover." She told her residence hall coordinator about the incident and mentioned that she found the joke racially offensive. The coordinator told Laura that everyone was given nicknames and that she was making things worse by implicating racial insensitivity to a harmless moniker. In situations like these, the spotlight is shifted from the perpetrator to the person (or people) harmed by the racial insensitivity. Shining the light on racism is not racist, nor does it heighten racial tension. What is made worse in such situations is the comfort level of Whites who want to ignore race. By noticing race and naming racism, one calls into question racial privilege and unequal treatment of people of color. For some, this causes anxiety and discomfort. On a larger scale, claims that discussions about race and racism cause racial problems provides people and institutions with a convenient rationale not to explore policies and practices that create inequalities, either intentionally or unintentionally.

FRAMING CBRI: ORGANIZATION OF THIS EDITED VOLUME

This book is organized around answering three main questions:

1. What is CBRI?
2. How is CBRI measured or assessed?
3. What are the manifestations of CBRI?

We organized the book to appeal to the varied interests of the targeted audience. The first question has the broadest appeal, and answering this question is essential to ensuring a common language in which to understand the nature of the problem. The second question is of primary concern to people interested in researching racial beliefs, particularly racial color blindness. We end by describing the multiple ways in which racial color blindness manifests in everyday interactions at the intrapsychic, interpersonal, group, institutional, and societal levels. Delineating these manifestations is of special concern to practitioners and others committed to identifying policies and practices that will counter the ill effects of racial color blindness and promote more racial equity.

What Is CBRI?

In Part I, "Theoretical and Methodological Foundations," the contributors provide a review of the theoretical perspectives of CBRI. The chapters differ in their theoretical standpoint (e.g., color and power evasion) and in their (sub)disciplinary approach (e.g., sociology, social psychology, counseling psychology, education, international studies); they also differ in their foci. Included in this section is a broad sociological view of the issues, consideration of racial color blindness on individual and interpersonal levels, and consideration of alternative perspectives. To understand what CBRI is, it is important to conceptualize what it is not. Chapters incorporate alternatives to CBRI, specifically multiculturalism (i.e., appreciation of cultural diversity) and race consciousness (i.e., critical awareness of policies and actions that serve to disrupt racial inequality). Although most of the chapters center on the dynamics within the United States, Warren's chapter includes a multinational analysis, with an emphasis on Brazil. This chapter was included in the text as a case study in the ways in which racial color blindness operates in a multiracial country outside the United States. Warren's analysis helps to bring perspective on the boundaries of racial color blindness and whiteness in racially hierarchical societies.

Sociologist Eduardo Bonilla-Silva (2001) popularized contemporary articulations of color-blind racism in his seminal text, *White Supremacy and Racism in the Post-Civil Rights Era*. He builds on his earlier work in the first chapter of the current volume. Bonilla-Silva sets the stage for first the conversation by defining color-blind racism as the new racism that emerged after the civil rights era and that has deepened since the 2008 election of President Obama. Color blindness from his standpoint represents the dominant racial ideology of the contemporary moment in which people—individually or collectively—use racial frames, styles, and stories to minimize or justify racial inequalities in society. While Obama for some represents a definitive end to racism in the United States, Bonilla-Silva argues against this stance, citing the continued persistence of racism in all sectors in society. He further argues that Obama himself contributed to the racial narrative minimizing race and racism through the "raceless" persona he adopted during the campaign, his distancing himself from dominant civil rights era leaders, and his lack of consideration of structural racism in his public talks on race issues in the United States. Bonilla-Silva argues that what is needed to counteract the dominant racial perspective that denies the existence of racism, and ultimately to transform society, is new social movements that will raise critical racial consciousness of people of color.

In Chapter 2, Jones asks a central question that seems to undergird much of our ambivalence, confusion, and fear about acknowledging race: Does it really matter? He reviews the social psychological literature on social categorization, stereotyping, reaction time studies to racial stimuli, correlation of Afrocentric features to criminal justice outcomes, and the impact of color-blind policies in organizations to build a case that ignoring race is impossible. He addresses the myth of color blindness while outlining how it provides cover for many Whites: (a) It prevents Whites from critically examining their racial beliefs and behaviors, (b) it exonerates them from complicit responsibility for obstructing the rights of groups of color, and (c) it allows them to continue their lives in innocence and naiveté. Jones concludes that color blindness has major detrimental consequences to people of color because it perpetuates the myth of meritocracy and denies their racial reality. Similar to Bonilla-Silva's critique of President Obama's adoption of "racelessness," Jones presents an interesting new perspective to color blindness by asserting that racelessness (when people of color downplay or minimize their own race) is another side of the same coin as "color blindness." Like color blindness, he concludes that racelessness is self-protective, self-delusional, and also not possible for people of color. Although racelessness may have functional value in limited situations, it has major harmful consequences for the holder.

In Chapter 3, Babbitt, Toosi, and Sommers explore the various motivations that people have for endorsing color blindness as a racial ideology. The authors provide a useful discussion of how White individuals who perceive zero-sum competition between racial groups may endorse color blindness as a way to preserve their own privileged status. This is one of the few discussions in the literature that explores in depth "why" people find CBRI attractive from the perspective of White individuals. They discuss the psychological mechanisms through which individuals may harbor apprehension about being labeled a racist simply for mentioning race, may believe that racial categorization is to blame for racism, and thus endorse color blindness as a way to avoid this label and because they believe it to be beneficial to people of color.

In Chapter 4, Gullett and West examine the anticipatory tensions that arise in interracial relationships and how entering an interracial interaction with a color-blind or multicultural mind-set influences the cognitive and affective processes that unfold during interracial interactions. The authors use an actor partner interdependence model framework to discuss how individuals' color-blind or multicultural mind-sets influence not only their own outcomes but their partners' as well. The authors compare the effectiveness of color-blind and multicultural approaches to interracial interactions with alternative methods for cultivating interracial relationships.

Warren broadens the discussion of CBRI in Chapter 5 by presenting a scholarly rationale on the theoretical and heuristic value of critical race studies in other parts of the world, especially Brazil. He adeptly illustrates how the study of race in Brazil helps to push back against attacks on black counterpublics, teach how racial literacy is learned, and delegitimize liberal forms of racism. In his analysis of Brazilian worldviews on race, Warren concludes that White supremacist consciousness is defined by color blindness, race evasiveness, and whitening narratives. In short, an international perspective is useful to the tasks of undermining color blindness and universalizing color consciousness in the United States. He concludes with a seldom spoken truth: "To move closer toward full emancipation, cultures will have to be violated rather than respected." In other words, to move from color blindness toward color consciousness necessitates upending White identities and worldviews.

In the final chapter in this part, Bell builds on Warren's conclusions by presenting an insightful discussion of race consciousness as an alternative to CBRI. Bell provides a critique of CBRI for its failure to understand racial inequality in society. A race conscious perspective, she argues, is essential to deconstruct race and dismantle racism. She outlines the stories we tell ourselves and others to reinforce a CBRI perspective, which she refers to as *stock stories*; there are also stories that counter racism and uncover the ways in which race matter as well as stories of resistance, the latter of which Bell characterizes as race-conscious stories. Bell provides concrete strategies to develop race consciousness. Some of these strategies include recognizing stock or dominant stories that support CBRI, working to uncover ways in which Whiteness and race are hidden, exploring the root causes of current disadvantages, creating opportunities to interrupt stock stories through rehearsal or role-play, and working to increase racial literacy.

How Is CBRI Measured or Assessed?

Understanding and synthesizing the literature on CBRI in the social sciences requires an exploration of the conceptual framework of the researchers and also the methodology used to empirically investigate the topic. Part II,

"Context and Costs," consists of three chapters that cover the most common methodological approaches in the social sciences (i.e., experimental, survey, and qualitative or ethnographic). Each of these methods provides researchers with the tools to answer different types of interrelated questions.

In Chapter 7, M. C. Jackson, Wilde, and Goff review the social psychological research methods used to assess the causes and consequences of CBRI. The authors frame the various methodology into two broad groups. They discuss first the research that illustrates the consequences when CBRI is the norm and, second, the research that investigates which contexts motivate individuals to endorse CBRI. They further discuss that predominate research methodologies in social psychology laboratory experimental methods. The authors discuss that results from this body of research indicate that CBRI often has drawbacks even when implemented with egalitarian motivations. Finally, they discuss how future CBRI research could benefit from mixed-method approaches.

Whereas M. C. Jackson and colleagues' discussion centers on assessing racial color blindness through experimental designs, Awad and K. M. Jackson review the primary CBRI measures used in survey research. Their review focuses on five published measures with psychometric information, but they also identify a handful of other measures that have limited information about the validity of the measure. A summary of the scale purpose, sample items, and psychometric information for the scales are part of the review. This type of information is especially helpful to researchers who may be interested in measuring CBRI in future studies. In their identification of future directions, Awad and K. M. Jackson encourage researchers to develop additional psychometrically sound measures that assess both color- and power-evasion dimensions of CBRI; to date, measures only assess one or the other dimension but not both.

In Chapter 9, Lewis and Hagerman identify the limitations in quantitative explorations of CBRI. Racial color blindness is complex, and the nuances of how race and racism are enacted in systems are not easily captured through experimental or survey methods. Instead, they argue that ethnographic research designs and in-depth interviews are essential in uncovering the hidden ways in which CBRI is practiced in institutional settings and in interpersonal relationships. The authors provide three research case examples to illustrate the benefits of and methodological strategies used in ethnographic and interview studies in the schools.

What Are the Manifestations of CBRI?

In the final section, "Manifestations of Color-Blind Racial Ideology," contributors document the multiple ways in which CBRI operates on individual and interpersonal levels and within various contexts. We intentionally selected three large contexts in which CBRI operates to produce racial disparities: education, the workplace, and health care–related settings. We have included two chapters on each of these broad settings to capture the complexities in the manifestations while honoring the diversity represented in the broad context categories. The chapters in this section bring to life the damaging effects of the denial of race and racism on individuals and within institutions. As a way of acknowledging human agency, authors also provide concrete strategies that researchers, educators, and applied psychologists can use to disrupt CBRI and promote color- or race-conscious practices as a means of reducing racial inequalities. We include two chapters that focus on the individual manifestation of racial color blindness, one primarily centering on White individuals and the other on people of color. We also include chapters that outline the broader manifestation of CBRI on contexts in which social scientists have collected data and have intervened to promote increased race or color-conscious policies designed to disrupt disparities.

Tettegah weaves together research from psychology, philosophy, and neuroscience to connect CBRI to expressions (or lack of) empathy in Chapter 10. A chapter on empathy was included to better capture an underlying dimension of racial color blindness that remains underdeveloped in the literature. Tettegah argues that people are wired to see group differences; thus, although people may believe they "don't see race," denial of race in our society is unrealistic. Drawing on the interdisciplinary research, Tettegah raises thought provoking questions about our moral obligation as humans to find appropriate ways to understand differences to develop compassion and perspective taking, which are critical dimensions of empathy. Tettegah critiques White people's use of "preferential" or strategic color blindness; people articulate a vision of themselves as being color-blind with respect (and therefore "good") in some situations but many times inadvertently fall back on racial assumptions when judging situations that are racialized, such as the killing of Michael Brown or the 2012 murder of Trayvon Martin by George Zimmerman, a neighborhood watch volunteer. The manifestation of racial color blindness is thus lack of empathy. In this novel exploration of CBRI, Tettegah holds the concept of inclusive empathy—empathy built on context and cultural understanding—as a desired goal.

Both White people and people of color can adopt a color-blind racial perspective; however, the frequency and consequences of this endorsement differ by race. Endorsement of CBRI among White people helps protect the individual from "appearing" racially intolerant and moreover perpetuates racial privileges through inaction (and thus maintenance of the racial status quo). People of color who adopt a racial color-blind perspective may work against their individual and group interest by supporting policies and practices that unfairly discriminate against people of color. We have included a chapter in the collection to explicate the manifestation of CBRI among people of color. In Chapter 11, Speight, Hewitt, and Cook provide a thought-provoking discussion of the link between internalized racism and expressions of CBRI among people of color. They provide a sharp analysis that conceptualizes CBRI as existing within the context of structural racism and as an attitude that people of color may, to their detriment, adopt. Writing from a power-evasion perspective, Speight and her colleagues identify the underlying core dimensions of CBRI as being the denial of racism. This denial serves to legitimize racial inequality and thus suppresses action to remedy the social maladies. According to Speight et al.'s review, CBRI and internalized racism go hand in hand among people of color. They offer the development of critical consciousness (similar to Bell's conceptualization of race consciousness in Chapter 6, but Speight and colleagues draw more on the work of liberation education and psychology scholars) as a way to guard against internalized racism and CBRI. Speight et al. conclude by urging scholars to focus their work on critiques of systems of oppression to eliminate inequality.

Racial disparities are well documented in educational settings, and there is growing research on the ways in which color–blind racial beliefs create or maintain these disparities. We included two chapters on the manifestations of CBRI in the school context to capture the different expressions in the kindergarten through Grade 12 (K–12) context compared with the higher education. In Chapter 12, Castro-Atwater provides compelling data about the detrimental effect of CBRI on learning outcomes for K–12 students of color and on teachers' effectiveness among these children. She unpacks the ways in which race matters in schools. For example, teachers' (inadvertent) biased attitudes and behaviors can lead to lower expectations of students of color and to lower student achievement. In addition, teachers' indifference or inadvertent biases may lead youth to ignore or dismiss their own experiences with discrimination. Castro-Atwater reviews a set of teacher variables that promote CBRI in the schools, primarily through a restricted worldview or cultural lens that they bring to the classroom. The hopeful news is that teachers can and do provide counternarratives and practices that promote a color- or race-conscious school climate. Schools can encourage these narratives and practices by promoting the inclusion of cultural pedagogy in the classroom and incorporating color- or race-consciousness training in teacher education.

In Chapter 13, Kernahan extends the discussion of CBRI to the context of higher education. She specifically focuses on the role of higher education in challenging CBRI, which is consistent with many colleges' and universities' goal to promote inclusivity. Kernahan evaluates the research on the role of courses and extracurricular activities in disrupting CBRI. Overwhelming empirical data support the effectiveness toward this goal of courses with significant "diversity-related" content. Emerging research also centers on uncovering the active ingredients in the courses that promote the desired learning outcomes. On the basis of Kernahan's review, lectures plus intergroup dialogue and learning from other students appear to be key pedagogical tools. Kernahan also weaves in the long-standing empirical research on the "contact hypothesis" to illustrate the need of institutions of higher education to provide students with meaningful opportunities to promote intergroup friendships. Kernahan suggests faculty development around these issues be provided as one way to better prepare teachers for the difficulty in incorporating these types of experiences and information in the classroom.

We balance our discussion of color blindness in the workplace by including a chapter on the effects it has on organizational contexts, such as in the hiring, retention, and promotion of people of color and on the individual adaptive strategies employees of color use to deal with an institutional culture that professes not to see color. Block, in Chapter 14, provides an eye-opener on how CBRI in institutional policies, practices, and structures contributes to inequities in workplace outcomes. Reviewing the large body of literature on the workplace, she reveals how disparities for people of colors in the labor force exist in every step of the process: entering the job market, the type of job an individual is assigned, career advancement, and the associated wages that accompany each of these areas. Using the two-component analysis of color blindness (power evasion and color evasion) proposed by Neville et al. (2013), Block reveals how they manifest in the sociocultural organizational context. When organizational philosophy operates from a color-blind philosophy, it places the blame on employees of color for their lack of success and also perpetuates the threat of stereotype. Countering CBRI in organizational settings means that movement toward awareness of diversity dynamics must be instituted. Block takes issue with some who profess that multiculturalism alone offers an alternative to combatting injustices in organizational settings. Although many aspects of appreciating cultural diversity in employees and highlighting the value of different cultures may contribute to a positive climate for employees of color, it is not enough. She believes that these programs do not adequately address the systems that create and maintain the disparities and focus primarily on individuals. Block provides alternative goals to enhance systemic change.

In Chapter 15, Shih and Young extend the discussion of CBRI to understand policies and practices in the workplace. The authors define *organizational color blindness* as possessing a policy that emphasizes an overarching organizational identity while ignoring differences in race, culture, and ethnicity. Although misguided, a CBRI is intended to eliminate discrimination by treating everyone the same and preventing one group from being advantaged over another. The problem, as the authors point out, is that a default standard to White norms and values become the criteria from which policies and practices are created. The downside is that instead of eliminating bias, it actually promotes and perpetuates inequities toward socially devalued groups in the workforce. It forces assimilation and acculturation and uses White prototypical norms to judge performance and the worth of employees of color. If color-blind workplaces are detrimental to women and employees of color, what does research tell us about how they cope in such an environment? The authors identify two major identity management strategies used by employees from socially devalued groups: (a) identity switching that involves deemphasizing a negatively valued identity and (b) identity regeneration or replacing a negative identity with a positively regarded one. Both are complex methods of dealing with color blindness and surviving in an organization that fails either to acknowledge or value differences. For those who use identity management strategies, there may be benefits such as helping individuals control how they experience discrimination, protect their self-esteem, increase performance outcomes, reduce anxiety, and increase interpersonal comfort. The authors point out however, that there are major psychological costs associated with these strategies: backlash effects, failure to accurately perceive important feedback, being placed in a double bind, and alienation from one's group. Again, the key for solution and major responsibility seems to lie with organizations and their recognition of the harmful consequences of CBRI.

We conclude the book with two chapters on the manifestations of CBRI in health-related contexts. Hospital settings and the provision of health care are additional contexts in which CBRI operates and unfortunately perpetuates inequality on indicators of physical health. In Chapter 16, Penner and Dovidio provide a focused discussion on how racial color blindness can negatively affect the quality of health care that Black patients, relative to White patients, receive. The authors focus primarily on Black patients, and primarily non-Black physicians, in the United States, considering the historical and continued disparities in health care that have dominated the literature for Black relative to White patients. Although the authors focus on Black patient–White physician relationships in the United States, they believe their discussions about the causes of disparities in health and health care between races would generally apply to other racial and ethnic minorities in the United States and in many other countries around the world.

In Chapter 17, Burkard, Edwards, and Adams address the manifestation of CBRI in mental health settings, particularly in the contexts of counseling and supervision. They invite readers to consider the advantages of implementing a racially conscious and inclusive perspective as a way to increase opportunities for deeper exploration and understanding within counseling and supervisory relationships. The authors review conceptual associations between CBRI and other multicultural counseling constructs that are specific to counseling practitioners and trainees and examine empirical findings specific to color blindness in counseling and supervision processes.

CONCLUSION

The authors in this edited volume provide a rich discussion of the racial color blindness literature in terms of theoretical perspectives, research methods, and the manifestations that shape individuals' and groups' experiences. The insights offered in the chapters provide students, scholars, and practitioners with information to identify the ways in which race is still present in U.S. society, the reasons some people endorse CBRI, and the harmful effects of CBRI on in interracial interactions and in policies that intentionally or unintentionally create racial disparities. The authors' critical analysis of the theory and empirical research on CBRI reveals several gaps in our current thinking. Of particular note is the lack of interdisciplinary research that incorporates both color- and power-evasion dimensions of CBRI and how they may potentially affect interpersonal interactions and organizational practices differentially.

These chapters offer a number of consistent recommendations for reducing CBRI. A particularly noteworthy strategy is to provide educators, researchers, and practitioners with professional development opportunities to learn how to increase their critical awareness about racism and to develop efficacy and skills to identify and implement race-conscious actions. Such actions would reduce anxiety in interracial interactions and promote inclusive policies that increase racial equity in a given setting. In addition to covering information on theories and research on race and racism in these development opportunities, it may be helpful to offer training in how to talk about and facilitate difficult dialogues about race and inequality. Being racially color-blind is to be racially color mute, so we must begin to help one another address nondefensively issues of race, racism, Whiteness, and White privilege. On an individual level, talking about race or helping others talk about it requires a firm sense of who we are as racial and cultural beings and a willingness to acknowledge and explore racial biases. On institutional and societal levels, several educational goals seem important. First, we must make the "invisible" visible by identifying the manifestation, dynamics, and harmful impact of racially color-blind policies or practices that create racial inequality in specific settings. Second, we must learn to work within systems and organizations to advocate and implement race-conscious policies and practices that will help to create equal access and opportunities for all.

REFERENCES

Alexander, M. (2010). *The new Jim Crow: Mass incarceration in the age of colorblindness*. New York, NY: New Press.

Bonilla-Silva, E. (2001). *White supremacy and racism in the post-civil rights era*. Boulder, CO: Lynne Rienner.

Carson, E. A. (2014). *Prisoners in 2013*. Washington, DC: Bureau of Justice Statistics, Office of Justice Programs, U.S. Department of Justice. Retrieved from http://www.bjs.gov/content/pub/pdf/p13.pdf

Centers for Disease Control and Prevention. (2013). *CDC Health Disparities & Inequalities Report 2013*. Retrieved from http://www.cdc.gov/minorityhealth/CHDIReport.html#CHDIR

Chiles, N. (2013, March 5). In the age of Obama, hate groups on the rise in America. *Atlanta BlackStar*. Retrieved from http://atlantablackstar.com/2013/03/05/in-the-age-of-obama-hate-groups-on-the-rise-in-america

Desilver, D. (2013, August 13). *Black unemployment rate is consistently twice that of Whites*. Washington, DC: Pew Research Center. Retrieved from http://www.pewresearch.org/fact-tank/2013/08/21/through-good-times-and-bad-black-unemployment-is-consistently-double-that-of-whites

DeVoe, J., & Murphy, C. (2011). *Student reports of bullying and cyber-bullying: Results from the 2009 School Crime Supplement to the National Crime Victimization Survey*. Retrieved from http://nces.ed.gov/pubs2011/2011336.pdf

Floyd, et al. v. City of New York, et al. 959 F. Supp. 2d 540 (2013).

Frankenberg, R. (1993). *White women, race matters: The social construction of Whiteness*. Minneapolis: University of Minnesota Press.

King, M. L., Jr. (1963). *I have a dream*. Speech by the Reverend Martin Luther King Jr. at the March on Washington. Retrieved from http://www.archives.gov/press/exhibits/dream-speech.pdf

Kochar, R., & Fry, R. (2014, December). *Wealth inequality has widened along racial, ethnic lines since end of Great Recession*. Retrieved from http://www.pewresearch.org/fact-tank/2014/12/12/racial-wealth-gaps-great-recession

Leber, R. (2014). Ferguson's police force is 94 percent White—And that's basically normal in the U.S. *New Republic*. Retrieved from http://www.newrepublic.com/article/119070/michael-browns-death-leads-scrutiny-ferguson-white-police

Macartney, S., Bishaw, A., & Fontenot, K. (2013, February). *Poverty rates for selected detailed race and Hispanic groups by state and place: 2007–2011* (American Community Survey Briefs, 11-17). Retrieved from http://www.census.gov/prod/2013pubs/acsbr11-17.pdf

Neville, H. A., Awad, G. H., Brooks, J. E., Flores, M. P., & Bluemel, J. (2013). Color-blind racial ideology: Theory, training, and measurement implications in psychology. *American Psychologist, 68*, 455–466. http://dx.doi.org/10.1037/a0033282

Organisation for the Prohibition of Chemical Weapons. (1993). Article 1(5). *Convention on the prohibition of the development, production, stockpiling, and use of chemical weapons and on their destruction*. Retrieved from http://www.opcw.org/index.php?eID=dam_frontend_push&docID=6357

Pew Research Center. (2014a). *Sharp racial divisions in reactions to Brown, Garner decisions: Many Blacks expect police–minority relations to worsen*. Retrieved from http://www.people-press.org/2014/12/08/sharp-racial-divisions-in-reactions-to-brown-garner-decisions

Pew Research Center. (2014b). *Stark racial divisions in reactions to Ferguson police shooting*. Retrieved from http://www.people-press.org/2014/08/18/stark-racial-divisions-in-reactions-to-ferguson-police-shooting

Sentencing Project. (n.d.). *Interactive map*. Retrieved from http://www.sentencing-project.org/map/map.cfm#map

Sue, D. W. (2015). *Race talk and the conspiracy of silence: Understanding and facilitating difficult dialogues on race*. Hoboken, NJ: Wiley.

U.S. Department of Justice. (2015). *Investigation of the Ferguson Police Department*. Retrieved from http://www.justice.gov/sites/default/files/opa/press-releases/attachments/2015/03/04/ferguson_police_department_report.pdf

U.S. Department of Labor. (2012). *Employment status of the civilian population by race, sex, and age*. Retrieved from http://www.bls.gov/news.release/empsit.t02.htm

U.S. Department of Labor. (2015). *Labor force statistics from the current population survey*. Retrieved from http://www.bls.gov/web/empsit/cpsee_e16.htm

I

THEORETICAL AND METHODOLOGICAL FOUNDATIONS

1

DOWN THE RABBIT HOLE:
COLOR-BLIND RACISM IN OBAMERICA

EDUARDO BONILLA-SILVA

Forty plus years after the Kerner Commission (1968)[1] issued the statement that "our nation is moving toward two societies, one black, one white—separate and unequal," race still divides the nation profoundly, and we may in fact have more than two nations. The evidence for this is "clear and convincing." Data on income (in 2011, Black household income was 59% of White household income, Hispanic household income was 60% of White income, and Asian[2] income was 102% of White income), wealth (in 2011,

---

This chapter is derived from a 2013 presentation given at the National Conference on Race and Ethnicity in American Higher Education in New Orleans.

[1]The Kerner Commission, or the National Advisory Commission on Civil Disorders, was an 11-member commission established in 1967 by President Lyndon B. Johnson to investigate the causes of the race riots of that year and provide recommendations for the future.

[2]The data on Asian income are problematic because Asians have, on average, significantly more education than Whites, are concentrated in expensive urban areas, and have more people on average contributing to the household income than Whites. For a silly perspective on Asian success, see the recent book by Chakravarty and Chua (2012). For careful analyses on this matter, see Kitano and Daniels (2001) and Takaki (1990).

http://dx.doi.org/10.1037/14754-002
The Myth of Racial Color Blindness: Manifestations, Dynamics, and Impact, H. A. Neville, M. E. Gallardo, and D. W. Sue (Editors)

Latinos had one 12th of the wealth of Whites and Blacks had one 20th), housing (Blacks and Latinos are one third less likely to own their houses), and educational and occupational inequality show huge racial disparities (Alonso-Villar, Del Rio, & Gradin, 2012; Everett, Rogers, Hummer, & Krueger, 2011; Pew Research Center, 2013). How can this be the case if racism presumably ended in the 1960s? Moreover, how can this be the case when we elected in 2008 and reelected in 2012 a Black man to the White House?

Far too many Americans have lived an Alice in Wonderland–like reality since 2008 where nothing is what it seems. The election of Barack Obama as the 44th president of the United States led them to believe that a fundamental change had occurred in the nation's racial trajectory. Yet this postracial view soon faced trouble as traditional racism resurfaced with a vengeance evidenced by the growth of racist groups (a general increase from 2008 to the present), the emergence of the Tea Party and the Birther movement (Coates, 2012), and the racist efforts of the Republican Party to disenfranchise minority voters (Daniels, 2013; Mock, 2012).

Thus, America today seems to be at a racial crossroads. Will we return to a crude version of racial domination or move forward and become a postracial society? My answer in this chapter is that America's likely path is neither. I argue that the United States has been transitioning from the Jim Crow racial regime of the past to a new racial order (the "new racism") for some time and that Obama's election was not a game changer (Bonilla-Silva & Ray, 2009). In fact, Obama's election may represent a deepening of the "new racism." After all, across the world, racial domination works best when "people of color" are in charge, particularly while claiming to be "racial democracies" (Bonilla-Silva, 2013).

To address this perplexing fact will require me to do four things in this chapter: first, define what racism is and argue for the need to conceptualize the phenomenon in structural or systematic ways; second, explain how the collapse of Jim Crow in the late 1960s did not mean the end of "systemic racism" (Feagin, 2006) but instead led to the new racial regime I label the "new racism"; third, identify the new prejudice (new racial ideology) that organizes the racial views of Whites and, increasingly, of many non-Whites—color-blind racism; and last, make the controversial claim that Obama's presidency did not represent a break with our racial history.

WHAT IS RACISM?

Most social analysts recognize that race matters in all sorts of social affairs, yet when non-Whites try to talk about it, average Whites tell them, "Here you go again" or "Come on, man, stop playing the race card!" This disconnect can be explained by the fact that "racism" is conceived differently by Whites compared with most non-Whites. For Whites, racism is prejudice, whereas for Blacks and other racial and ethnic minorities, racism is not mere prejudice but, above all, institutional practices and mechanisms that form a system of racial domination (Hutchings, 2009; Schuman, 1998). Most Whites regard racism as the Ku Klux Klan, neo-Nazis, and, lately, the Birthers and their Tea Party cousins. Thus, the folk definition of racism is the *irrational beliefs some people have about the presumed inferiority of others,* which is almost the same as the standard definition we social scientists give our students: "a *doctrine* of racial supremacy, that one race is superior" (Schaefer, 1990, p. 16, emphasis added). This view does not allow us to conceive of racism as a systemic, national problem and leads us to think about racism as a matter of good versus bad people, of the racists versus the nonracists.

I have argued that racism should be conceptualized, first and foremost, as a systemic, societal, or structural problem (Bonilla-Silva, 1997, 2001). Racism is foundational in America (Feagin, 2000), and indeed it is as American as apple pie. Racism during slavery and Jim Crow was not about some bad people, but about a society partially organized around race. And once the *logic* and the *practice* of race became part of the structure of the nation, all members of the polity have participated in systemic racism—some as beneficiaries (Whites) and some as victims (non-Whites). Racism has always been about providing what McIntosh (1988) called "White privilege" to the social group recognized as "Whites" in all areas of life—social, economic, political, and psychological. Therefore, racism exists today not as a remnant from the past or as the behavioral expression of prejudiced (bad) people as so many analysts believe. Instead, racism remains in place because it benefits Whites as a social group.

The second problem with conceiving racism as a psychological quirk or as the overt behavior (discrimination) of some individuals against (mostly) people of color is that analysts miss most of the racial affairs happening in contemporary America. Nowadays, as I argue later in the chapter, most racial events and practices tend to be subtle, institutionalized, and apparently nonracial (Bonilla-Silva & Dietrich, 2011). Therefore, by focusing attention on overt racial events for moral judgment and political action, analysts (a) legitimate an erroneous conceptualization of racism; (b) cloud efforts to bring to the fore discussions about how race matters in the everyday life; and (c) help sustain the notion of the United States as a nation that is no longer "racist" because racially motivated incidents are, as we love to say in universities and colleges, "isolated incidents."

This conceptual matter is extremely important because until Whites and non-Whites agree on the basic term being debated, the debate will go nowhere. Yet I caution readers that this conceptual impasse between Whites and non-Whites is not the product of mere misunderstanding but a reflection of the groups' positions in the racial order. As I have stated elsewhere,

> Generally, then, stereotypes are reproduced because they reflect the group's distinct position and status in society. As a corollary, racial or ethnic notions about a group disappear only when the group's status mirrors that of the dominant racial or ethnic group in the society. (Bonilla-Silva, 2013, p. 476)

"RACISM ENDED IN THE 1960s!" ON THE NEW RACISM

In discussions about the significance of racism in contemporary America, people of color are in a corner because they can no longer say they routinely face the odious practices associated with slavery and Jim Crow. Therefore, Whites tell them things such as, "Come on, folks, slavery and Jim Crow are long gone, so if you are not doing well today, it is your own darned fault!" In a recent survey, Parker (2010) found that 58% of Whites disagreed with the proposition that "generations of slavery and discrimination have created the conditions that make it difficult for Blacks to work their way out of the lower class." But there is an answer for this simplistic view, too. Social analysts must state vigorously that the end of Jim Crow did not imply the end of "systemic racism" (Feagin, 2000). Instead, racial domination was reorganized into a new regime I have labeled in my work the *new racism* (Bonilla-Silva, 2001; Bonilla-Silva & Dietrich, 2011). I have defined the new racism as the post–Civil Rights era set of arrangements, mechanisms, and practices (the *racial structure*) responsible for the reproduction of White privilege at all levels. These practices tend to be covert, institutionalized, and, for the most part, seemingly nonracial (Bonilla-Silva, 2001).

Let me give you a few specific examples of new racism practices. Because the practices associated with residential segregation in the Jim Crow period (e.g., housing covenants, racial terrorism) became illegal and the normative climate of the post–Civil Rights era disallows the open and public exercise of racist behavior (Picca & Feagin, 2007), one would expect residential segregation to have dwindled. Yet this is not the case. Today residential segregation remains almost as high as in the 1960s (Massey & Denton, 1993), and new forms of residential exclusion not captured by the traditional index of dissimilarity have emerged (Bonilla-Silva & Baiocchi, 2008). How can this be? Residential segregation is still a big problem today because discrimination in the housing and lending markets remains.

Report after report document how little we have improved in this area and how new racism practices of steering by realtors, disproportionate rates of subprime loans, and a lack of action by cities are behind our current levels of residential segregation (Orfield & McArdle, 2006). The 2005 report by the Fair Housing Center of Greater Boston indicated that its African American, Latino, Asian, and Caribbean testers experienced discrimination in 45% of cases. The report also indicated that the exclusionary tactic most often used was providing differential information to minority applicants about availability of housing units.

Racial practices in housing and banking exemplify new style discrimination because they are hard to detect and even harder to label "racial" unless one has the smoking gun. How can one prove discrimination by banks or realtors or renters? In both cases, analysts would need either a whistleblower (Savage, 2012) to uncover these operations within the industry or systemic data from the U.S. Department of Housing and Urban Development showing not only differential treatment but also the kind of practices used to maintain people of color at bay. Similar practices have been documented in other venues and areas of life (Bonilla-Silva & Dietrich, 2011). Accordingly, given the character of contemporary discrimination, people of color must bring along a White friend to go shopping (Schreer, Smith, & Thomas, 2009), buy a car (Ayres, 1995), get a loan (Pager & Shepherd, 2008), rent an apartment or buy a house (Bayer, Casey, Ferreira, & McMillan, 2012), drive a car (Walker, Spohn, & DeLone, 2000), or walk in the streets (Coviello & Persico, 2013) to prove discrimination!

THE (WHITE) COLOR OF RACIAL COLOR BLINDNESS

Alongside the new racism regime, a more seemingly suave, strategic type of racial ideology[3] has emerged. I call it *color-blind racism*, but other scholars refer to the same phenomenon as *laissez-faire racism* (Bobo, Kluegel, & Smith, 1996), *competitive racism* (Essed, 1991), or *symbolic racism* (Kinder & Sanders, 1996). It is imperative that analysts understand the nature of this new racial ideology because the crass, direct Jim Crow racial prejudice and racial language of the past are no longer the primary ideological tools used to defend the status quo. Although occasionally people of color have to contend with Jim Crow–like actions and practices from Whites, racial domination in postracial America is mostly accomplished in a more refined and, thus, much more dangerous manner, in terms of both behaviors and justifications for the racial status quo.

---

[3]I have argued that the term *racial ideology* is the most fitting to explain the "prejudice" of any period. Racial ideology refers to the dominant views of a racial group and gets us away from the individualistic reading of the concept of prejudice (Bonilla-Silva, 2003).

I have labeled the new, dominant racial ideology *color-blind racism* and contend that it has all but replaced the nasty racial discourse of yesteryear. This ideology (Bonilla-Silva, 2013) is anchored on the abstract extension of the principles of liberalism to racial matters that furnishes apparently non-racial explanations for all sorts of race-related matters. Hence, if Whites want to justify (in contemporary America) segregated schools, they say things such as, "Schools are about *choice*. No one should be forced to attend a school. Besides, folks should send their kids to *neighborhood schools*." If they wish to oppose affirmative action, they say things such as, "I am all for equal opportunity; that's why I'm against affirmative action because it is *reverse discrimination*."

In my book *Racism Without Racists* (2013), I deconstruct the three component parts of this ideology (*frames, style,* and *racial stories*) and explain how each element helps justify the racial order of things. Due to space limitations, I provide here just one example of the frames and one example of the racial stories of color-blind racism. The central frames (set paths for interpreting information) or themes of color-blind racism are *minimization of racism, cultural racism, naturalization,* and *abstract liberalism*. I illustrate only the abstract liberalism frame because it is the core of this ideology. This frame incorporates tenets associated with the notion of liberalism in an abstract and decontextualized manner. By framing race-related issues in the language of liberalism, Whites can appear "reasonable," even "moral" while opposing all practical approaches to deal with de facto racial inequality. For instance, Jim, a 30-year-old computer software salesperson from a privileged background, explained his opposition to affirmative action as follows:

> I think it's unfair top to bottom on everybody and the whole process. It often, you know, discrimination itself is a bad word, right? But you discriminate every day. You wanna buy a beer at the store and there are six kinda beers you can get from *Natural Light* to *Sam Adams*, right? And you look at the price and you look at the kind of beer, and you . . . *it's a choice*. And a lot of that you have laid out in front of you, which one you get? Now, should the government sponsor *Sam Adams* and make it cheaper than *Natural Light* because it's brewed by someone in Boston? That doesn't make much sense, right? Why would we want that or make *Sam Adams* eight times as expensive because we want people to buy *Natural Light*? (Bonilla-Silva, 2013, p. 81)

Because Jim assumes hiring decisions are like market choices (choosing between competing brands of beer), he embraces a laissez-faire position on hiring. The problem with Jim's view, a view shared by most Whites, is that labor market discrimination is alive and well and affects black and Latino job applicants 30% to 50% of the time (Pager, 2003). Furthermore, although Jim believes, as do most Whites, that jobs in the United States are awarded in a meritocratic fashion, researchers have documented that most jobs (as many as 80%–85%) are obtained through informal networks (McDonald, 2011). This finding applies to "good" as well as "bad" jobs as the work of Deidre Royster (2003) shows. Therefore, by upholding a strict laissez-faire view on hiring while ignoring the significant impact of discrimination in the labor market, Jim can safely voice his opposition to affirmative action in an apparently race-neutral way.

Racial stories are an important component of color-blind racism because we all narrate or tell stories to explain our views on things, racial or otherwise. But the stories of color-blind racism are ideological in that they are *collective* (Durkheim, 1912) or *social representations* (Moscovici, 1982). They represent in narrative forms actors' interests in the racial order. In my work, I have identified three types of stories: storylines, testimonies, and a residual, sui generis category (see Bonilla-Silva, 2013). For illustrative purposes, I examine one of the storylines.

Storylines are "socially shared tales that are fable-like and incorporate a common scheme and wording" (Bonilla-Silva, 2013, p. 124). The dominant storylines of contemporary America are: "The past is the past," "I did not own any slaves," "If Jews, Irish, and Italians made it, how come Blacks have not?" and "I did not get a job, or a promotion, or was admitted to college because of a Black man." All these stories are used to rationalize racial matters such as not supporting affirmative action or not doing well in life. For Whites, as the work of Nancy DiTomaso (DiTomaso, Parks-Yancy, & Post, 2011) and of Tom Shapiro (2005) shows, seldom have to think they are not good enough for a job or promotion because they can always resort to the excuse of the "Black man took my job."

Andy provides a perfect example of how students use a storyline to answer the question "Do you believe that the history of oppression endured by minorities merits the intervention of the government on their behalf?"

> I almost—I think that the past is kind of the past and so, history of oppression? I don't know if anyone [is] owed anything because of the, like, past [is] really past history, but to look at things, the way things are right at this moment and to try to move forward from there. Then I support some things, maybe affirmative action, so long as it wasn't a runaway sort of. (Bonilla-Silva, 2013, p. 125)

Andy expressed his view that by dwelling on the past, we are in fact keeping the storyline alive. Andy, like other Whites, interpreted this question to ask about slavery, although this is not explicitly stated. This ambivalence toward any current forms of racial oppression allows Whites to maintain their opposition to race-based compensatory programs.

RACE MATTERS IN POSTRACIAL OBAMERICA

Since 2008, most Americans have not seen what has been in front of their noses. Whites have seen confirmation of their belief that the United States is indeed a racially color-blind nation, and Blacks and other people of color have seen in Obama the impossible dream come true. But there is a more fitting, historically accurate, and sociologically viable explanation for Obama's so-called miracle—one I advanced 6 months before he was elected in 2008. The fact that race matters in America in every aspect of our lives yet we elected a Black person means our president is but an apparent contradiction. Obama's campaign and "success" are the outcomes of 40 years of racial transition from the Jim Crow to the new racism regime or the new face of White supremacy. In Obamerica,[4] racism has remained firmly in place and, even worse, is becoming a more formidable obstacle as Obama's so-called post-racial stand and persona bolster the racial regime. Obama never represented "change we can believe in" (the famous slogan of his 2008 campaign) but more of the same in the racial terrain.

What is Obama's connection to the new racism? An important component of the post–Civil Rights racial regime is the process of selecting and vetting minority politicians developed by Republicrat operators in the past 30 years. After the Democratic Party co-opted many old Civil Rights leaders (John Lewis, Andrew Young, and the like) and made them shadows of themselves, both parties forged a new kind of minority politician. Today's minority politician (a) is electorally oriented, (b) is not the product of social movements, (c) joins the party of choice while in college, and (d) moves up quickly through the party ranks. Not surprisingly, plutocrats love these minority politicians because, whether Republican or Democrat, neither threatens the "power structure of America" (Gillespie, 2012). Therefore, post-Civil Rights minority politicians like Obama are not truly about deep change but about compromise; they are "accommodationist" and teach the "wretched of the earth" the wrong political lesson: that electoral, rather than social-movement, politics is the vehicle for achieving social justice (Persons, 2009). If Republican, these politicians are conservative antiminority people such as Nikki Haley (South Carolina governor) or Susana Martínez (New Mexico governor), and if Democrat, a neoliberal politico such as Cory Booker (New Jersey senator) and, of course, Barack Obama.

---

[4]I have used the term *Obamerica* since 2008 to refer to the fact that Obama was elected president without the backing of a real social movement, a fact that explains in part why "the masses" have not derailed him even when he has not delivered on most of his basic campaign promises (Bonilla-Silva & Dietrich, 2011).

Obama reached the level of success he did in large measure because he made a *strategic* (not tactical) move toward racelessness and adopted a post-racial persona and political stance. He distanced himself from most leaders of the Civil Rights movement, from his own good (and now much maligned) reverend, from his church, and from anything or anyone who made him look "too Black" or "too political." Throughout his first term, he always tried to avoid seeming "too Black," said less about race than any president since 1961, and took all sides on affirmative action in a 2008 interview with George Stephanopoulos (Coates, 2012; Kantor, 2012). When Obama talked about race in that infamous Philadelphia speech, or more recently in his 2013 speech at Morehouse College, he talked about racism the wrong way! In the Philadelphia speech, he claimed that both Whites and non-Whites have a legitimate beef on race matters, thus validating Whites' views on affirmative action and their nonsense "reverse racism" mentality. Thus, racism for Obama is just prejudice, a stand that ignores the power differential in which Whites maintain the institutional power to implement their agenda (Obama, 2006). In the 2013 speech, he chastised Blacks (particularly young Black men) for not working hard enough, talked about "no excuses," and minimized the significance of racism in contemporary America; in short, he talked like a White man to this Black audience. When asked in press conferences about racism—which no longer happens—he answered by pointing out he was dealing with America's "deep and real problems" and facing "two wars" (Obama, 2009).

I made a prediction that Obama was going to continue the American path in foreign and domestic policies (Bonilla-Silva, 2001), and, in general, he has done so. He has followed U.S. imperial policies in Iraq, Iran, Pakistan, and Afghanistan as well as in Latin America. After a brief period of reversing Bush's so-called counterterrorist policies, he has become "Bush light": Guantanamo is still open, we are still doing renditions, and Obama has increased exponentially drone attacks all over the world (5 times more than Bush). On the domestic front, his stimulus package did not target workers and folks of color and has been, for the most part, a failure. By this I mean that Obama's universalist position and his decision to give control to localities on how to distribute funds are quite problematic. Localities have historically distributed funds unevenly, preserving existing inequities (Katznelson, 2005). Unless these funds are distributed through "targeted universalism," a perspective that takes into consideration that people are differently situated in the social order and, thus, that some may need more resources than others, "universal" efforts such as this one will not reduce racial inequities (Kirwan Institute, 2009; Powell, 2008). His health care reform did not deal with the central issues at hand: controlling costs and trying to make the system universal or close to it. The financial reform bill he passed added a few positive things for consumers but did nothing to control Wall Street's gambling and to downsize "too big to fail" corporations; hence, the new regulations will not do much to prevent another economic meltdown. (For a longer discussion on his policies, see Chapter 10 in *Racism Without Racists*.)

So what is to be done in this peculiar moment in America? I have urged people of color and their allies to get back to basics. We are indeed, as Obama says again and again in his speeches, in a defining moment—a moment of racial retreat and reactionary politics—and we need to revitalize and retool our politics and political organizations if we wish to survive it. We need specifically new social movements to inspire, unite, and raise the consciousness of people of color because racial color blindness has affected their views too. Of course, this is not surprising; all dominant ideologies affect the views of all members of a polity (Bonilla-Silva, 2013). But we also need new organizations with new strategies to deal not with the enemies of the past but with the new enemy we face—that is, with the new racism and its accompanying monster of racial color blindness nonsense. Second, we must work hard to see that the antiracist White community (Cushing, 2010; Hughey, 2012; O'Brien, 2001) grows so that its members challenge racial color blindness among their fellow Whites. We also need to work with all vulnerable Whites (poor and White workers). The only way to persuade vulnerable Whites of our shared struggle is for researchers and activists to develop counterideological arguments to each of the frames of color-blind racism and explain why we all would be better off in a nonracialized society.

And we as researchers must go beyond the White racial structure of academia and identify important scholarly works that were erased from discipline-specific memory, be willing to sacrifice White (mainstream) validation in exchange for research that is heavily self-directed and unapologetically critical of mainstream research, speak up in class to counter racist assumptions and comments of peers, refuse to give in to assimilation pressures and normativity in race research, decolonize our sociological imagination, and maintain participation in community and political organizations (Hordge-Freeman, Mayorga, & Bonilla-Silva, 2011).

Therefore, to do what we must do, we need to summon up the spirit of Malcolm X (1970), who rightly told us,

> We declare our right on this earth . . . to be a human being, to be respected as a human being, to be given the rights of a human being in this society, on this earth, in this day, which we intend to bring into existence by any means necessary! (p. 56)

For those who still want "change we can believe in," it is time to realize that "we the people" must force that change to happen. The historical record clearly shows that major structural transformations are always the product of social protest (Piven, 2006). It is time for us to make frontal demands on the

Obama administration, on future Democratic or Republican administrations, and on the country at large. It is time for us to realize that only by demanding what seems impossible to attain now will we be able to get out of the rabbit hole we have been in since 2008.

REFERENCES

Alonso-Villar, O., Del Rio, C., & Gradin, C. (2012). The extent of occupational segregation in the United States: Differences by race, ethnicity, and gender. *Industrial Relations: A Journal of Economy & Society, 51*, 179–212. http://dx.doi.org/10.1111/j.1468-232X.2012.00674.x

Ayres, I. (1995). Further evidence of discrimination in new car negotiations and estimates of its cause. *Michigan Law Review, 94*, 109–147. http://dx.doi.org/10.2307/1289861

Bayer, P., Casey, M. D., Ferreira, F., & McMillan, R. (2012, May). *Price discrimination in the housing market* (NBER Working Paper 18069). Cambridge, MA: National Bureau of Economic Research. Retrieved from http://www.nber.org/papers/w18069

Bobo, L., Kluegel, J. R., & Smith, R. A. (1996). Laissez–faire racism: The crystallization of a kinder, gentler, anti-Black ideology. In S. A. Tuch & J. K. Martin (Eds.), *Racial attitudes in the 1990s: Continuity and change* (pp. 15–42). Westport, CT: Greenwood.

Bonilla-Silva, E. (1997). Rethinking race: Towards a structural interpretation. *American Sociological Review, 62*, 465–480.

Bonilla-Silva, E. (2001). *White supremacy and racism in the post-Civil Rights era.* Boulder, CO: Lynne Rienner.

Bonilla-Silva, E. (2003). Racial attitudes or racial ideology? An alternative paradigm for examining actors' racial views. *Journal of Political Ideologies, 8*, 63–82. http://dx.doi.org/10.1080/13569310306082

Bonilla-Silva, E. (2013). *Racism without racists* (4th ed.). Lanham, MD: Rowman & Littlefield.

Bonilla-Silva, E., & Baiocchi, G. (2008). Anything but racism: How sociologists limit the significance of racism. In T. Zuberi & E. Bonilla-Silva (Eds.) *White logic, White methods: Racism and methodology* (pp. 137–152). Lanham, MD: Rowman & Littlefield.

Bonilla-Silva, E., & Dietrich, D. (2011). The sweet enchantment of color-blind racism in Obamerica. *Annals of the American Academy of Political and Social Science, 634*, 190–206. http://dx.doi.org/10.1177/0002716210389702

Bonilla-Silva, E., & Ray, V. (2009). When Whites love a Black leader: Race matters in Obamerica. *Journal of African American Studies, 13*, 176–183. http://dx.doi.org/10.1007/s12111-008-9073-2

Chakravarty, V., & Chua, S. G. (2012). *Asian mergers and acquisitions: Riding the wave*. Singapore: Wiley.

Coates, T. (2012, September). Fear of a Black president. Retrieved from http://www.theatlantic.com/magazine/archive/2012/09/fear-of-a-black-president/309064

Coviello, D., & Persico, N. (2013, February). *An economic analysis of Black–White disparities in NYPD's Stop and Frisk Program* (NBER Working Paper 18803). Cambridge, MA: National Bureau of Economic Research. Retrieved from http://www.nber.org/papers/w18803

Cushing, B. (2010). *Accountability and White anti-racist organizing*. Roselle, NJ: Crandall, Dostie & Douglass Books.

Daniels, G. R. (2013). Unfinished business: Protecting voting rights in the twenty-first century. *The George Washington Law Review, 82*(1), 1928–1965.

DiTomaso, N., Parks-Yancy, R., & Post, C. (2011). White attitudes toward equal opportunity and affirmative action. *Critical Sociology, 37*, 615–629. http://dx.doi.org/10.1177/0896920510380070

Durkheim, E. (1912). *The elementary forms of religious life*. London, England: Allen & Unwin.

Essed, P. (1991). *Understanding everyday racism: An interdisciplinary theory*. Thousand Oaks, California: Sage.

Everett, B. G., Rogers, R. G., Hummer, R. A., & Krueger, P. M. (2011). Trends in educational attainment by race/ethnicity, nativity, and sex in the United States, 1989–2005. *Ethnic and Racial Studies, 34*, 1543–1566. http://dx.doi.org/10.1080/01419870.2010.543139

Fair Housing Center of Greater Boston. (2005). *You don't know what you're missing: A report on discrimination in the greater Boston home sales market*. Retrieved from http://bostonfairhousing.org/DontKnow.pdf

Feagin, J. R. (2000). *Systematic racism: A theory of oppression*. New York, NY: Routledge.

Feagin, J. R. (2006). *Racist America: Roots, current realities, and future reparations*. New York, NY: Routledge.

Gillespie, A. (2012). *The new black politician: Cory Booker, Newark, and post-racial America*. New York, NY: New York University Press.

Hordge-Freeman, E., Mayorga, E., & Bonilla-Silva, E. (2011). Exposing Whiteness because we are free: Emancipation methodological practice in identifying and challenging racial practices in sociology departments. In J. H. Stanfield (Ed.), *Rethinking race and ethnicity in research methods* (pp. 95–122). Walnut Creek, CA: Left Coast Press.

Hughey, M. W. (2012). *White bound: Nationalists, antiracists, and the shared meanings of race*. Stanford, CA: Stanford University Press.

Hutchings, V. L. (2009). Change or more of the same? Evaluating racial attitudes in the Obama era. *Public Opinion Quarterly, 73*, 917–942. http://dx.doi.org/10.1093/poq/nfp080

Kantor, J. (2012, October 20). For President, a complex calculus of race and politics. *New York Times*. Retrieved from http://www.nytimes.com/2012/10/21/us/politics/for-president-obama-a-complex-calculus-of-race-and-politics.html?_r=0

Katznelson, I. (2005). *When affirmative action was White*. New York, NY: Norton.

Kerner Commission. (1968). *Report of the National Advisory Commission on Civil Disorders*. Washington, DC: U.S. Government Printing Office.

Kinder, D. R., & Sanders, L. (1996). *Divided by color*. Chicago, IL: University of Chicago Press.

Kirwan Institute. (2009, February). *Preliminary report of the impact of the economic stimulus plan on communities of color*. Retrieved from http://www.kirwaninstitute.osu.edu/reports/2009/02_2009_StimulusandCommunitiesofColor.pdf

Kitano, H. H. L., & Daniels, R. (2001). *Asian Americans: Emerging minorities*. Upper Saddle River, NJ: Prentice Hall.

Malcolm X. (1970). *By any means necessary: Speeches, interviews, and a letter by Malcolm X* (pp. 35–67). New York, NY: Pathfinder Press.

Massey, D. S., & Denton, N. A. (1993). *American apartheid: Segregation and the making of the underclass*. London, England: Harvard University Press.

McDonald, S. (2011). What's in the "old boys" network? Accessing social capital in gendered and racialized networks. *Social Networks, 33,* 317–330. http://dx.doi.org/10.1016/j.socnet.2011.10.002

McIntosh, P. (1988). *Race, class, and gender in the United States: An integrated study* (P. S. Rothenberg, Ed.). New York, NY: Worth.

Mock, B. (2012). Voting rights. Retrieved from http://colorlines.com/brentin-mock

Moscovici, S. (1982). The coming era of social representations. In J. P. Codol & J. P. Leyens (Eds.), *Cognitive approaches to social behavior* (pp. 115–150). The Hague, The Netherlands: Nijhoff.

Obama, B. (2006). *The audacity of hope: Thoughts on reclaiming the American Dream*. New York, NY: Crown.

Obama, B. (2009, March 24). Transcript: President Obama's press conference. CT Transcripts Wire. *Washington Post*. Retrieved from http://www.washingtonpost.com/wp-dyn/content/article/2009/03/24/AR2009032403036.html

O'Brien, E. (2001). *Whites confront racism: Antiracists and their paths to action*. Lanham, MD: Rowman & Littlefield.

Orfield, G., & McArdle, N. (2006). *The vicious cycle: Segregated housing, schools and intergenerational inequality*. Cambridge, MA: Joint Center for Housing Studies, Civil Rights Project of Harvard University.

Pager, D. (2003). The mark of a criminal record. *American Journal of Sociology, 108,* 937–975. http://dx.doi.org/10.1086/374403

Pager, D., & Shepherd, H. (2008). The sociology of discrimination: Racial discrimination in employment, housing, credit, and consumer markets. *Annual Review of Sociology, 34,* 181–209. http://dx.doi.org/10.1146/annurev.soc.33.040406.131740

Parker, C. (2010). *Multi-state survey on race & politics*. Seattle: University of Washington Institute for the Study of Ethnicity, Race, and Sexuality.

Persons, G. (2009). *Dilemmas of Black politics: Issues of leadership and strategy*. New York, NY: HarperCollins.

Pew Research Center. (2013, August 22). King's dream remains an elusive goal [press release]. Retrieved from http://www.pewsocialtrends.org/files/2013/08/final_full_report_racial_disparities.pdf

Picca, L. H., & Feagin, J. R. (2007). *Two-faced racism: Whites in the backstage and frontstage*. New York, NY: Routledge.

Piven, F. F. (2006). *Challenging authority: How ordinary people change America*. Lanham, MD: Rowman & Littlefield.

Powell, J. A. (2008). Post-racialism or targeted universalism. *Denver University Law Review, 86*, 785–806.

Royster, D. A. (2003). *Race and the invisible hand: How White networks exclude Black men from blue-collar jobs*. Berkeley: University of California Press.

Savage, C. (2012, July 12). Wells Fargo to settle mortgage bias charges. *New York Times*. Retrieved from http://www.nytimes.com/2012/07/13/business/wells-fargo-to-settle-mortgage-discrimination-charges.html

Schaefer, R. T. (1990). *Racial and ethnic groups* (4th ed.). Glenview, IL: Scott Foresman/Little Brown Higher Education.

Schreer, G. E., Smith, S., & Thomas, K. (2009). "Shopping while Black": Examining racial discrimination in a retail setting. *Journal of Applied Social Psychology, 39*, 1432–1444. http://dx.doi.org/10.1111/j.1559-1816.2009.00489.x

Schuman, H. (1998). *Racial attitudes in America: Trends and interpretations*. Cambridge, MA: Harvard University Press.

Shapiro, T. M. (2005). *The hidden cost of being African American: How wealth perpetuates inequality*. New York, NY: Oxford University Press.

Takaki, R. T. (1990). *Strangers from a different shore: A history of Asian Americans*. New York, NY: Penguin Books.

Walker, S., Spohn, C., & DeLone, M. (2000). *The color of justice: Race, ethnicity, and crime in America*. Belmont, CA: Wadsworth Thomson Learning.

2

THE COLOR-BLIND RACIAL APPROACH: DOES RACE REALLY MATTER?

JAMES M. JONES

What do people mean when they say they are color blind? Medically speaking, *color blindness* is "a deficiency—an abnormal condition characterized by the inability to clearly distinguish different colors of the spectrum" (The Free Dictionary, n.d.). But if color blindness is a deficiency, why is it lauded as a virtue of character when it comes to perceiving racial differences?

Consider the following examples of color-blind approaches:

> "Wow, you really don't look Japanese at all. You look White." He smiled. . . . He was telling me that I looked White, and he meant it as a compliment. (Kohei Ishihara, college student, May 10, 2011)

> I don't think that ignoring differences is good, either. You're Black, or you're German, or you're whatever you are. Me saying, "I don't see color," that is absolutely—pardon my French—bullsh*t. That's absolutely ridiculous because it exists, and stuff happened. (Undergraduate Teacher Education major, University of Delaware, October 14, 2013)

http://dx.doi.org/10.1037/14754-003
The Myth of Racial Color Blindness: Manifestations, Dynamics, and Impact, H. A. Neville, M. E. Gallardo, and D. W. Sue (Editors)

I am colored and
America's colorblind
So, do you see me? (Jones, 1997, p. 134)

I have a dream that my four little children will one day live in a nation where they will not be judged by the color of their skin but by the content of their character. (Martin Luther King, Jr., "I Have a Dream" speech, August 28, 1963)

These quotes reveal several issues regarding racial color blindness. For example, Whiteness appears to be a default preference—somehow it is better to look White than Japanese. The University of Delaware student recognizes that "not" seeing race is "not" an option. Things happen and race matters; failing to see that is problematic. Or, in the haiku I wrote for my 1997 book, how can you ignore a person's color when it defines and summarizes their experiences and identity? What does a color-blind approach take from people of color; what becomes "invisible" and at what cost? Finally, Martin Luther King's 1963 speech is often hailed as the signature endorsement of the color-blind approach to race. The eager adoption of this King quote signals a retreat from an affirmative attention to continued and expanding racial inequality. Each of these quotes identifies a troublesome aspect of the color-blind approach.

A color-blind approach to race consists of four beliefs: (a) skin color is superficial and irrelevant to the quality of a person's character, ability, or worthiness; (b) in a merit-based society, skin color is irrelevant to merit judgments and calculations of fairness; (c) a corollary of (b)—judgments of merit and fairness are flawed if race is included in their calculation; and (d) ignoring skin color when interacting with people is the best way to avoid racial discrimination. These beliefs conflate *White* with *American* and *good* (Devos & Banaji, 2005). The result is an artificial and illegitimate racial hierarchy that assigns superior qualities to Whites and inferior qualities to Blacks and other people of color. I use *Black* generically as the exemplar of race, or any other salient social category that is marginalized, nonnormative, and perceived and judged against mainstream standard.

A color-blind approach to race is heralded because the racialized hierarchy is subverted if there are no racial categories. The outcome, then, is uncategorized *individuals* who rise and fall on their own individual characteristics. The insidious biases that create the hierarchical categories in the first place go unexamined, and any correspondence of skin color and status is a byproduct of the individual's own makeup. A color-blind approach to race exonerates the holder from complicit responsibility for obstructing the rights of racial and other groups to opportunity, liberty, and equality.

Color-blind beliefs about race offer their holder neutrality, a putative objectivity, and immunization against the charges that they, products of a racist America, are de facto racists themselves. Neville, Awad, Brooks, Flores, and Bluemel (2013) suggested that these beliefs constitute an ideology of racial color blindness that consists of two interrelated domains: *color evasion* (denial of racial differences) and *power evasion* (denial of racism). This ideology provides specific mechanisms through which immunization against racism may be sought, but as I argue later in the chapter, not attained.

Martin Luther King's speech also provides cover—content of their character matters, not the color of their skin. Embracing a "color doesn't matter" philosophy is a way to feel good about yourself—to be part of the solution, not part of the problem. But what if race *does* matter? What then? A color-blind society, in this view, is one that reflects the consequences of holding these beliefs and implementing them in policies and practices. However, when racism is embedded in the institutions that govern this country and in the psyches of the citizens, and when it is entrenched over a long period of time, a racially color-blind society does not result from a color-blind approach. A color-blind approach does not eliminate discrimination, does not promote fairness, and is not meritocratic; instead, it contributes to racial inequality without addressing the means to alleviate it.

There is a flip side as well: *racelessness*—that is, the belief that one's own race does not and should not matter. If one's accomplishments are prefaced by their racial designation, they are, in many eyes, diminished. For example, Harlem Renaissance poet Countee Cullen proclaimed that

> if I am going to be a poet at all, I am going to be POET and not NEGRO POET. This is what has hindered the development of artists among us. Their one note has been the concern with their race. (http://www.english. illinois.edu/maps/poets/a_f/cullen/life.htm)

Suzette Charles, the "first" Black person to occupy Miss America (occupying the crown Vanessa Williams was forced to vacate in 1984), offered a similar sentiment: "I am not a Black Miss America, I am just Miss America." When he was appointed to anchor the seven o'clock evening news on ABC television in 1981, Max Robinson became the first Black network news anchor in the United States. His boss, Roone Arledge, avowed that his stature at ABC was unrelated to his race. According to Robinson (as cited in Fordham, 1988, p. 59), Arledge told him, "I told you when I hired you, I didn't think you were Black, or I didn't think of you as a Black man." What he meant, Robinson felt, was "I am going to give you credit. I admire you greatly, so therefore, I will not think of you as Black" (as cited in Fordham, 1988, p. 59). To discount one's race is to relegate a significant aspect of oneself to insignificance. Fordham (1988) raised the specter that "the practice of becoming raceless appears to have emerged as a strategy both to circumvent the stigma attached to being black, and to achieve vertical mobility" (p. 59).

Racelessness, too, offers a kind of existential neutrality. If one minimizes race (*deracinated* according to Cross, 1991), then perhaps the oppressive stereotypes of Blacks will not stick—one will be somehow be liberated from the damaging effects of racism. And, perhaps, the *double-consciousness* (DuBois, 1903) will be reduced to a single coherent consciousness. The net result is that a color-blind approach to race may have psychic benefits to its holder regardless of which side of the racist divide one is on. But those psychic benefits mask other subversive effects: Whites' feelings of superiority and Blacks' feelings of inferiority.

A color-blind approach to race is not possible and may even be detrimental. In this society with its racial history, race matters! In the first section of this chapter, I explore race matters, reviewing research that demonstrates the subtle ways in which awareness of and response to race affects judgments, behavior, and emotions. The basic argument is that ignoring race is not an option. However, paying attention to race provides an opportunity to confront unconscious feelings that are activated when race becomes salient. The second section explores the flip side, that is, how ignoring race for racial people can have adverse effects on psychological well-being. The final section provides a summary of what these foregoing analyses may mean for race relations and psychological well-being.

WHY A COLOR-BLIND APPROACH TO RACE IS BOTH NOT POSSIBLE AND DETRIMENTAL

What happens when a person holds color-blind racial beliefs but race really matters? Empirical evidence supports the idea that race does matter in overt and explicit ways, but more critically in a covert and implicit fashion. The resulting implication is that believing oneself to be racially color blind is a self-enhancing illusion. This illusion is detrimental because (a) it prevents a person from critically examining his or her racial beliefs and subsequent actions and (b) it alienates those whose race is being discounted.

WHY A COLOR-BLIND APPROACH TO RACE IS NOT POSSIBLE

Race is intricately woven into the culture, institutions, and psyche of America. Its presence has been overt, intentional, self-aggrandizing, and instrumental at times and covert, subtle, and unconscious at others. Whether overt or covert, conscious or unconscious, race is there, waiting for a drop of animus or fear to ignite its destructive potential. This is the offspring of our racial and racist history as a nation.

Yet those who profess to follow a color-blind approach view it as a good thing, a fair thing, a righteous thing. They do not mean literally that they do not see race; they mean, I think, they "choose to ignore it." Former Secretary of Education William Bennett articulated this view of a color-blind approach to race in a 1985 speech on Martin Luther King's birthday in Atlanta, Georgia:

> People of good will disagree about the means [but] I don't think anybody disagrees about the ends.... I think the best way to achieve the ends of a colorblind society is to proceed as if it were a colorblind society.... *I think the best way to treat people is as if their race did not make any difference.* (as cited in Sawyer, 1986, p. A8, emphasis added)

Is viewing the world with color-blind eyes really the best way to achieve a society that is color blind to race? Is a color-blind society really what we want to achieve?

Categorizing People by Race Is Natural

First, we have found that categorizing others into socially meaningful groupings is a hardwired tendency of the human species (Wilson, 1992). We have, furthermore, convincingly demonstrated that once categorization takes place, a variety of consequences ensue, including favorable treatment of others within your group and less favorable treatment of others outside of your group (Brewer, 1979). Categorization processes occur automatically, in the same way that we discriminate between and among any set of objects in our visual field—that tree is tall, that tree is short; that car is red, that car is blue. However, social category groups have psychological, motivational, emotional, and even neurobiological consequences that affect what we think and feel and how we behave. In short, we perceive race automatically, and it affects us fundamentally.

Race Activates Processes in the Brain

The brain center that guides processing of faces responds differently to faces of our own racial group than to those of other racial groups. The amygdala, the area of the brain that reacts to threat and triggers a fear response, is also sensitive to race. People who have been found to harbor subtle and unconscious racial biases show greater amygdala reaction to images of Black men, a finding based on studies with U.S. samples. In addition, they show stronger startle responses to quick, sudden, and unanticipated strong stimuli—loud noise, a puff of air, and so forth. In other words, amygdala activation—triggered by fear—causes generalized reactivity and hypervigilance (Phelps et al., 2000). These far-reaching effects are beyond the conscious awareness of those who proclaim race does not matter.

Racial Stereotypes Affect Our Judgments

Research by Stanford professor Jennifer Eberhardt and colleagues (Eberhardt, Davies, Purdie-Vaughns, & Johnson, 2006) shows that among Black males convicted of murder in Philadelphia between 1979 and 1999, the probability of being sentenced to death or life in prison depended on how prototypically Black they looked, over and above other factors known to influence sentencing like aggravating or mitigating circumstances, severity of the murder, the defendant's and the victim's socioeconomic status, and the defendant's attractiveness. The more Black they looked (Figure 2.1, right)—hair texture, facial features, skin tone—the more likely they were to face a death sentence (58% for Black-looking men, 24% for those less prototypically black looking—Figure 2.1, left). The critical variable, however, was the race of the victim. These disparities were only found when the victim was White; when the victim was Black, racial features bore no relationship to the sentence: About 46% received a death penalty sentence regardless of how Black they looked.

Mr. A–less typical   Mr. B–more typical

Figure 2.1. Two faces that vary in racial prototypicality. From "Looking Deathworthy: Perceived Stereotypicality of Black Defendants Predicts Capital-Sentencing Outcomes," by J. L. Eberhardt, P. G. Davies, V. J. Purdie-Vaughns, and S. L. Johnson, 2006, *Psychological Science, 17,* p. 384. Copyright 2006 by SAGE Publications. Reprinted with permission.

A clever research paradigm, labeled the *shooter bias*, assesses the different probabilities of shooting an unarmed suspect based on his or her race (Correll, Park, Judd, & Wittenbrink, 2002). Participants are shown a person on a computer screen who is holding an object. Their task is to shoot the person if he has a gun but to refrain from shooting if he does not. These decisions are made rapidly. The target person is either Black or White, and the participant's accuracy (shooting if he has a gun, not shooting if he doesn't) indicates whether there is bias as a function of the target's race. The results show a systematic racial bias: The correct decision to *shoot an armed target* is made more quickly when the target is Black, but the correct decision *not to shoot an unarmed target* is made more quickly when the target is White. Research shows these shooter biases are related to the cultural stereotype of Black men as dangerous and to the prototypicality of how Black they look.

WHY A COLOR-BLIND APPROACH TO RACE IS DETRIMENTAL

Adopting a color-blind approach to race may make the holder of that belief feel better about his or her own sense of fairness, objectivity, and lack of bias. However, research suggests that it only masks their bias and also has adverse effects on people of color about whom they claim to have no bias. Following are some reasons why.

Color-Blind Approaches to Race May Alienate Those Whose Color Matters to Them

The idea that a color-blind racial approach is the best approach to take to promote favorable interracial interactions and outcomes is challenged by Plaut, Thomas, and Goren's findings (2009). They administered a web-based diversity climate survey to 3,758 employees (79% White and 21% racial/ethnic minorities) at a health care organization. The survey included, in addition to demographic information, measures of Whites' multiculturalism, racial color blindness, and indicators of psychological disengagement among the ethnic and racial minority employees. Results showed that the stronger the color-blind racial attitudes of White employees, the more psychologically disengaged the minority employees were. Conversely, minorities were more psychologically engaged in their work the more their White coworkers endorsed multicultural attitudes. The disengagement of minorities resulted because racial color blindness correlated with minorities' perception of bias in the workplace, and it was the perception of bias that directly produced their disengagement.

A similar conclusion can be drawn from research by Purdie-Vaughns, Steele, Davies, Ditlmann, and Crosby (2008). These researchers created authentic looking corporate brochures that were distributed at a corporate booth at a job fair. The brochures pictured either a diverse workforce or a mostly White one, and either a color-blind corporate philosophy to race or one that espoused the value of diversity. When brochures depicted a low minority representation and a color-blind diversity philosophy (a negative identity contingency), African American professionals were unmotivated to work for the company and reported little institutional trust.

A Color-Blind Approach to Race Often Leads to More, Not Less, Prejudice

Richeson and Nussbaum (2004) presented White American college students with one-page essays that advocated either a racially color-blind or multicultural ideology. They found that the color-blind messages, relative to the multicultural messages, led to more negative attitudes on race, both explicitly and in more unobtrusive ways (e.g., in an implicit association test measure).

Even When Color-Blind Approaches to Race Are Favorable, They Produce Negative Effects

We should acknowledge, however, that favorable outcomes sometimes result from a color-blind approach to race. For example, in high-conflict situations, it may lessen outgroup bias (Apfelbaum, Norton, & Sommers, 2012; Correll, Park, & Smith, 2008). Believing that we can and do ignore race in human judgments does not necessarily produce a fairer, more equitable society, but it may promote more tolerance in certain situations. Sasaki and Vorauer (2013) reviewed the large and expanding literature on racially color-blind and multicultural effects on interracial attitudes and behavior and concluded that although racial color blindness can have positive effects in the short term, the mental efforts it takes to inhibit and suppress negative responses to race undermines executive mental functions and is difficult to sustain. This, they argued, is because a color-blind approach to race tends to emanate from a self-focus that consumes mental capacity. It also originates in a *prevention approach*—the desire to avoid loss and to be safe. Research has shown that a prevention focus tends to produce avoidance of outgroup members, and when that is not possible, leads to greater agitation (Shah, Brazy, & Higgins, 2004).

RACELESSNESS IS SELF-PROTECTIVE, SELF-DELUSIONAL, AND . . . NOT POSSIBLE

There is a long-standing literature on the harmful effects of stereotyping and discrimination on racial targets (for a review, see Pascoe & Smart Richman, 2009). Targets of discrimination may react to their victim status by downgrading their stigmatized attributes—race, in this analysis. Here I refer to *racelessness* as rejecting the relevance of race in determining outcomes in one's life. In this way, racelessness is the obverse of a color-blind approach to race: Both presume that race is irrelevant and that invoking it is to stigmatize the target.

Among the responses to being a target of racial discrimination are justifying the basis of racial inequality (system justification; O'Brien & Major, 2005), diminishing the importance or even relevance of race in one's life (deracination and miseducation; Cross, 1991), adopting nonracial personal identity (assimilation or humanistic perspective on race; Sellers et al., 1997), and adopting a nonracial impression management strategy (racelessness; Arroyo & Zigler, 1995; Fordham, 1988). In each of these cases, one minimizes one's race as a way to cope with or avoid racial stigma and its negative effect on self-worth. This section expands on each of these effects.

Justifying One's Unequal Status May Be Detrimental to Well-Being

O'Brien and Major (2005) examined the relationship between endorsing system-justifying beliefs—that status in society is fair, deserved, and merited—and psychological well-being among individuals from racial and ethnic groups of varying social statuses. Examples of system-justifying beliefs in the United States include the beliefs that hard work pays off and that anyone can get ahead regardless of their group membership. O'Brien and Major (2005) found that endorsing system-justifying beliefs was negatively related to psychological well-being among members of low-status groups but only when they were highly identified with their group. When they did not identify with their group, holding system-justifying beliefs conferred greater psychological well-being. The implication of this reproach is that accepting the status quo as merited, even if you are low status, can produce positive feelings of psychological worth if you adopt a racelessness orientation.

Racelessness May Be a Precursor to Miseducation and Self-Hatred

Cross's theory of *Nigresence*—the process of becoming Black—describes an evolution from a raceless to a race-conscious self-awareness and identity

(Cross, 1991). The themes are (a) *preencounter*, a raceless stage; (b) *immersion–emersion*, a hyper racialness followed by a retreat to a more balanced racial awareness; and (c) *internalization*, adopting a broader perspective that includes other similarly situated oppressed groups.

The preencounter raceless stage is characterized by *assimilation* (I am not so much a member of a racial group as I am an American), *miseducation* (Blacks place more emphasis on having a good time than on hard work), and *self-hatred* (privately, I sometimes have negative feelings about being Black). According to Nigrescence theory, personal identity and reference group orientation can be separated, and only personal identity has direct bearing on psychological well-being. Consistent with this thesis, only self-hatred was linked directly to lowered self-esteem (Vandiver, Cross, Worrell, & Fhagen-Smith, 2002). This work offers additional support for the negative consequences of ignoring the relevance of race for racialized people.

Humanism Provides Rose-Colored Glasses on Race

The Multidimensional Inventory of Black Identity (Sellers, Rowley, Chavous, Shelton, & Smith, 1997) proposes that racial identity consists of ideologies about the best way for Blacks, individually and as a group, to approach race in the United States, in addition to self-referent evaluations of one's racial group and the salience of one's group for personal identity and esteem. Among the four ideologies Sellers et al. (1997) identified—assimilation, oppressed minority, nationalism, and humanism—subscribing to a humanistic ideology was associated with believing that others perceived their racial group more favorably and with a lesser likelihood of reporting experiences with racial discrimination in the past year. The net result may be more positive psychological well-being, but also less preparedness for discrimination when it occurs.

Racelessness Enhances Academic Achievement but Undermines Psychological Well-Being

Students who adopt a raceless orientation have been accused uncharitably of "acting White" (Fordham, 1988). Unfortunately, striving to be academically successful in certain contexts is perceived by some as an affinity for White culture and standards and as distancing oneself from Black culture. Arroyo and Zigler (1995) examined the relation between racial identity and personal psychological functioning within the framework of the racelessness construct. They developed a Racelessness Scale (RS) and assessed the extent to which higher RS scores were associated with higher grade point averages in a sample of African American public school students (mean age 16.7 years). Racelessness consists of two factors: Achievement Attitudes/Alienation (e.g., Doing well in school helps you do better later in life; I don't hang out in places where most of the other people in school go) and Impression Management/Stereotypical Beliefs (e.g., I feel I must act less intelligent than I am so other students will not make fun of me). They found a significant relationship as predicted. However, when they examined the identity and psychological well-being characteristics, they found that high-achieving African American students scored significantly higher in anxiety and depression and believed that others held more negative views of Blacks as a group than those low in racelessness.

Cose (2011) explored how race figured into ideas about how people of color approach success in the United States. He asked an open-ended question to Harvard Business School students: "Could you sum up what you consider to be the most important factors contributing to individual success in America?" He distilled their collective responses into 10 rules, the last of which was *Never talk about race (or gender) if you can avoid it, other than to declare that race (or gender) does not matter.* In a subtle way, Cose has distilled the main points of my argument: Color-blind approaches to race obscure or challenge the relevance of race, and people of color have to steer a tight course to success in a racially color-blind world.

WHAT HAVE WE LEARNED, AND WHAT DOES IT MEAN?

Ignoring race is neither possible nor desirable. Although there may be short-term psychic benefits for both Whites and persons of color, the research strongly suggests that the long-term negative consequences are greater both for individuals and society. Race is complicated and deeply embedded in our nation's history and our collective psyches (see Jones, 1997).

A color-blind approach to race is problematic as a strategy for improving intergroup relationships and creating a more just and fair society. Color-blind racial ideologies have been shown to have adverse effects on both Whites and persons of color who adopt them. Although categorizing by race may be natural, it activates processes in the brain that often adversely affect judgments, emotions, and behavior. Evidence shows that we categorize people even if we are unaware of dong it. Believing oneself to be color-blind with regard to race prevents a person from acknowledging or acting on the unconscious biases that emerge. Color-blind approaches to race may alienate those for whom their color matters by disregarding salient and important identities that comprise their sense of belonging and self-worth. Finally, color-blind approaches to race are linked directly to increase in bias.

The more effective approach to reducing intergroup bias is not to attempt to be color-blind but, rather, to pay attention to race and be open to discussing and exploring how it affects one's judgment, emotional responses, and the experiences of others. Just paying attention is clearly not sufficient, however; one must also work at engaging, understanding, and responding meaningfully to race. Sue and colleagues (Sue, 2010; see also American Psychological Association, Presidential Task Force on Preventing Discrimination and Promoting Diversity, 2012) provide useful concepts, principles, and strategies for taking human differences into account with significant positive benefits.

Adopting a color-blind racial ideology is detrimental to people of color. The color-blind approach to race emerges as a racelessness ideology for people of color. When people adopt this ideology, they may rationalize unequal status as normative, internalize the beliefs that sustain their own marginalization, misperceive the degree to which others value their racial group, and perceive that distancing themselves from race will enhance their opportunities for success despite evidence that it undermines their psychological well-being.

The lessons are clear: A color-blind approach to race is not the avenue to a more just and fair society and improved intergroup relations. A growing body of research and intervention strategies chart a course to avoid the pitfalls of a color-blind approach to race and suggest ways to embrace and benefit from paying attention to race and other important human differences. I am confident that this work will gain prominence, and our progress toward a better society will continue at an accelerated rate.

REFERENCES

American Psychological Association, Presidential Task Force on Preventing Discrimination and Promoting Diversity. (2012). *Dual pathways to a better America: Preventing discrimination and promoting diversity.* Washington, DC: Author.

Apfelbaum, E. P., Norton, M. I., & Sommers, S. R. (2012). Racial color blindness: Emergence, practice, and implication. *Current Directions in Psychological Science, 21,* 205–209. http://dx.doi.org/10.1177/0963721411434980

Arroyo, C. G., & Zigler, E. (1995). Racial identity, academic achievement, and the psychological well-being of economically disadvantaged adolescents. *Journal of Personality and Social Psychology, 69,* 903–914. http://dx.doi.org/10.1037/0022-3514.69.5.903

Brewer, M. B. (1979). In-group bias in the minimal intergroup situation: A cognitive motivational analysis. *Psychological Bulletin, 86,* 307–324. http://dx.doi.org/10.1037/0033-2909.86.2.307

Correll, J., Park, B., Judd, C. M., & Wittenbrink, B. (2002). The police officer's dilemma: Using ethnicity to disambiguate potentially threatening individuals. *Journal of Personality and Social Psychology, 83,* 1314–1329. http://dx.doi.org/10.1037/0022-3514.83.6.1314

Correll, J., Park, B., & Smith, J. A. (2008). Colorblind and multicultural prejudice reduction strategies in high-conflict situations. *Group Processes & Intergroup Relations, 11*, 471–491.

Cose, E. (2011). *The end of anger: A new generation's take on race and rage*. New York, NY: HarperCollins.

Cross, W. E., Jr. (1991). *Shades of Black: Diversity in African American identity*. Philadelphia, PA: Temple University Press.

Devos, T., & Banaji, M. R. (2005). American = White? *Journal of Personality and Social Psychology, 88*, 447–466. http://dx.doi.org/10.1037/0022-3514.88.3.447

DuBois, W. E. B. (1903). *The souls of Black folk*. Chicago, IL: A. C. McClurg.

Eberhardt, J. L., Davies, P. G., Purdie-Vaughns, V. J., & Johnson, S. L. (2006). Looking deathworthy: Perceived stereotypicality of Black defendants predicts capital-sentencing outcomes. *Psychological Science, 17*, 383–386. http://dx.doi.org/10.1111/j.1467-9280.2006.01716.x

Fordham, S. (1988). Racelessness as a factor in Black students' school success: Pragmatic strategy or pyrrhic victory? *Harvard Educational Review, 58*, 54–84.

The Free Dictionary. (n.d.). *Definition of color blindness*. Retrieved from http://medical-dictionary.thefreedictionary.com/color+blindness

Jones, J. M. (1997). *Prejudice and racism* (2nd ed.). New York, NY: McGraw-Hill.

King, M. L., Jr. (1963). *I have a dream*. Speech by the Reverend Martin Luther King at the March on Washington. Retrieved from http://www.archives.gov/press/exhibits/dream-speech.pdf

Neville, H. A., Awad, G. H., Brooks, J. E., Flores, M. P., & Bluemel, J. (2013). Colorblind racial ideology: Theory, training, and measurement implications in psychology. *American Psychologist, 68*, 455–466. http://dx.doi.org/10.1037/a0033282

O'Brien, L. T., & Major, B. (2005). System-justifying beliefs and psychological well-being: The roles of group status and identity. *Personality and Social Psychology Bulletin, 31*, 1718–1729. http://dx.doi.org/10.1177/0146167205278261

Pascoe, E. A., & Smart Richman, L. (2009). Perceived discrimination and health: A meta-analytic review. *Psychological Bulletin, 135*, 531–554. http://dx.doi.org/10.1037/a0016059

Phelps, E. A., O'Connor, K. J., Cunningham, W. A., Funayama, E. S., Gatenby, J. C., Gore, J. C., & Banaji, M. R. (2000). Performance on indirect measures of race evaluation predicts amygdala activation. *Journal of Cognitive Neuroscience, 12*, 729–738. http://dx.doi.org/10.1162/089892900562552

Plaut, V. C., Thomas, K. M., & Goren, M. J. (2009). Is multiculturalism or color blindness better for minorities? *Psychological Science, 20*, 444–446. http://dx.doi.org/10.1111/j.1467-9280.2009.02318.x

Purdie-Vaughns, V., Steele, C. M., Davies, P. G., Ditlmann, R., & Crosby, J. R. (2008). Social identity contingencies: How diversity cues signal threat or safety for African Americans in mainstream institutions. *Journal of Personality and Social Psychology, 94*, 615–630. http://dx.doi.org/10.1037/0022-3514.94.4.615

Richeson, J. A., & Nussbaum, R. J. (2004). The impact of multiculturalism versus color blindness on racial bias. *Journal of Experimental Social Psychology, 40*, 417–423. http://dx.doi.org/10.1016/j.jesp.2003.09.002

Sasaki, S. J., & Vorauer, J. D. (2013). Ignoring versus exploring differences between groups: Effects of salient color blindness and multiculturalism on intergroup attitudes and behavior. *Social and Personality Psychology Compass, 7*, 246–259. http://dx.doi.org/10.1111/spc3.12021

Sawyer, K. (1986, January 15). King scholars steal Bennett's lines. *The Washington Post*, p. A8.

Sellers, R. M., Rowley, S. A. J., Chavous, T. M., Shelton, J. N., & Smith, M. A. (1997). Multidimensional inventory of Black identity: A preliminary investigation of reliability and construct validity. *Journal of Personality and Social Psychology, 73*, 805–815. http://dx.doi.org/10.1037/0022-3514.73.4.805

Shah, J. Y., Brazy, P. C., & Higgins, E. T. (2004). Promoting us or preventing them: Regulatory focus and manifestations of intergroup bias. *Personality and Social Psychology Bulletin, 30*, 433–446. http://dx.doi.org/10.1177/0146167203261888

Sue, D. W. (2010). *Microaggressions in everyday life: Race, gender, and sexual orientation.* New York, NY: Wiley.

Vandiver, B. J., Cross, W. E., Jr., Worrell, F. C., & Fhagen-Smith, P. E. (2002). Validating the cross racial identity scale. *Journal of Counseling Psychology, 49*, 71–85. http://dx.doi.org/10.1037/0022-0167.49.1.71

Wilson, E. O. (1992). *The diversity of life.* Cambridge, MA: Harvard University Press.

3

A BROAD AND INSIDIOUS APPEAL: UNPACKING THE REASONS FOR ENDORSING RACIAL COLOR BLINDNESS

LAURA G. BABBITT, NEGIN R. TOOSI, AND SAMUEL R. SOMMERS

I have a dream that my four little children will one day live in a nation where they will not be judged by the color of their skin but by the content of their character.

—Reverend Dr. Martin Luther King, Jr.

Dr. King's call for a nation in which people are judged not "by the color of their skin but by the content of their character" seems straightforward: His words describe an ideal society in which color is not used as a basis for discrimination. Yet this ostensibly simple idea has been interpreted in starkly different ways. For example, Roger Clegg, president of a conservative think tank focused on race and ethnicity, used the speech to argue against race-conscious policies: "King gave a brilliant and moving quotation, and I think it says we should not be treating people differently on the basis of skin color" (as cited in Washington, 2013). In contrast, Michael Eric Dyson, a professor of sociology who has written extensively about King, maintained that race must be considered to reach the more equitable society of which King dreamed:

> Martin Luther King, Jr., hoped for a color-blind society, but only as oppression and racism were destroyed. Then, when color suggested neither privilege nor punishment, human beings could enjoy the fruits of our

http://dx.doi.org/10.1037/14754-004
The Myth of Racial Color Blindness: Manifestations, Dynamics, and Impact, H. A. Neville, M. E. Gallardo, and D. W. Sue (Editors)

common life. Until then, King realized that his hope was a distant but necessary dream. (Dyson, 2000, p. 29)

In this chapter, we examine the many interpretations and motivations behind the ideology of racial color blindness.

Color blindness as a racial ideology is one of the dominant approaches to race relations in the contemporary United States (Apfelbaum, Norton, & Sommers, 2012; Firebaugh & Davis, 1988; Plaut, 2010). The basic concept underlying colorblindness is that all people are fundamentally the same, and thus we should ignore racial differences and treat everyone as an individual. The implication is that acknowledging the existence of racial groups is inherently problematic because it is as a result of categorization that prejudice and discrimination occur (Brewer & Miller, 1984; Tajfel & Turner, 1979; Wolsko, Park, Judd, & Wittenbrink, 2000). Avoiding or ignoring racial categories in interpersonal interactions and barring them from consideration in institutional decisions would, according to this reasoning, decrease racism and potentially lead to increased equality (for reviews, see Apfelbaum et al., 2012; Markus, Steele, & Steele, 2000; Peery, 2011; Rattan & Ambady, 2013). However, the practice of ignoring race may obscure the real impact of inherited and ongoing inequality, leading the proponents of racial color blindness to claim or believe they are behaving fairly while they are actually reifying injustice (Hirsch, 1996; Markus et al., 2000; Sleeter, 1991).

Thus, the question that we address in this chapter is as follows: Why do so many people (primarily racial majority group members) endorse racial color blindness as an approach to diversity? We propose that racial color blindness is a malleable ideology that appeals to people across a spectrum of motivations and perspectives:

- Some individuals may truly believe that not discussing race advances racial harmony and equality by preventing people from being judged by their race (Goff, Jackson, Nichols, & Di Leone, 2013).
- For others, racial color blindness may be a way to ignore racial inequalities and thus preserve the status quo to their own benefit (Saguy, Dovidio, & Pratto, 2008). It might appeal to these individuals because they see other groups' progress as a loss for their own racial group (Norton & Sommers, 2011).
- Some may avoid any mention of race to ensure that they do not inadvertently say something offensive and risk being labeled a racist (Apfelbaum, Sommers, & Norton, 2008).
- Racial color blindness may be a response among White people to feeling excluded in situations where ethnic diversity is valued; they might believe their identity as racial majority group

members leaves them unable to contribute in these contexts (Plaut, Garnett, Buffardi, & Sanchez-Burks, 2011).

- Racial color blindness may also simply be a default approach, picked up through social norms but not consciously chosen or carefully examined (Apfelbaum, Pauker, Sommers, & Ambady, 2010).

- Finally, although many of the reasons already listed apply primarily to White people or members of a racial majority, racial minority group members may have their own reasons to endorse color blindness—for example, to avoid conflict in daily interactions with White people (Rattan & Ambady, 2013).

Thus, racial color blindness functions across racial boundaries and motivations, becoming a default panacea for the tensions of a diverse but not yet harmonious society. Indeed, it may appeal to some for a combination of the reasons just cited. In this chapter, we explore all of these reasons and review the associated literature.

STRIVING TO FULFILL KING'S DREAM

Racial color blindness holds appeal for some people as a way to prevent the kind of blatant discrimination that accompanied Jim Crow segregation—separate water fountains, separate schools, abusive governance, and vastly unequal job opportunities, for example. In 1963, when Dr. King called for people to be judged by the content of their character rather than by the color of their skin, this type of discrimination was rampant.

Individuals who hope to use racial color blindness to achieve King's dream of racial equality might try to ignore race altogether to prevent discrimination based on race. Importantly, in this conception of racial color blindness, inequality is recognized, but ignoring group difference is believed to be the best way to remedy that inequality. Because people are believed to be fundamentally equal to each other (different outcomes notwithstanding), they are also assumed to be similar to each other. Any group differences are considered superficial and not worth attention (Shweder, 1991), and acknowledging differences is seen as akin to stereotyping (Markus et al., 2000). In some cases, White people who are egalitarian (i.e., lower in social dominance orientation) are actually more likely to endorse racial color blindness, which suggests that they have good intentions in doing so (Knowles, Lowery, Hogan, & Chow, 2009). Furthermore, when discussing race, some White people spontaneously invoke the idea that racial color blindness protects minorities from harm (e.g., "Looking at their race demeans them"), particularly when participating in interracial (vs. all-White) discussion groups (Goff et al., 2013). Although it is not clear whether these participants were motivated by a genuine concern for racial minorities or were simply justifying their own discomfort in talking about race, the researchers found in a second study that White participants who were told that racial categorization has harmful effects on minorities were more likely to endorse racial color blindness (Goff et al., 2013).

Unfortunately, racial color blindness has limited power to address discrimination, even when endorsed with the best of intentions. One of the first things that we notice about other people is their racial background. Within a matter of milliseconds, our brains have done the work of categorizing and classifying the people we encounter using physical cues to race, gender, and age (Allport, 1954; Fiske, Lin, & Neuberg, 1999; Ito & Urland, 2003). Racial stereotypes are activated automatically as well. For example, seeing a Black man makes Whites more likely to mistake a tool for a gun; Blacks with more Afrocentric features (e.g., broad noses and thick lips) are more likely to be given the death penalty; and Blacks are more easily associated with negative concepts than positive concepts, even by those who profess to be egalitarian (Dovidio, Kawakami, & Gaertner, 2002; Eberhardt, Davies, Purdie-Vaughns, & Johnson, 2006; Payne, 2006). This means that ending bias requires paying attention to race and understanding its effects on our behavior, not claiming that we do not see race and are not affected by it.

In sum, the conception of racial color blindness as a means to prevent discrimination is endorsed by people who acknowledge inequality but believe that the best way to address that inequality is to stop paying attention to race: "the desire to remedy group prejudice by not seeing group difference" (Markus et al., 2000; p. 234). It should be noted that there are also some people who endorse racial color blindness with a distributive justice interpretation—that is, a focus on ensuring equitable outcomes, even if the process required to reach those outcomes does not involve equal treatment (as in affirmative action policies; Knowles et al., 2009). Importantly, this distributive justice approach to racial color blindness is fundamentally different than all of the others described in this chapter because it recognizes a role for the discussion and consideration of race and aims for color-blind (i.e., racially equitable) outcomes through this acknowledgment of race (see Knowles et al., 2009, for a more thorough discussion of this approach). By recognizing and addressing the role of race in race-based inequality, the distributive approach has the potential to reduce discriminatory outcomes.

Not everyone who endorses racial color blindness recognizes inequality or aims to reduce discrimination, however. The appeal of racial color blindness as a way of enforcing the status quo and protecting privilege is discussed next.

CAMOUFLAGING PRIVILEGE

Racial color blindness may also be endorsed by people with antiegalitarian beliefs and those in privileged positions. These individuals may see racial color blindness as a way to protect their privilege by ignoring racial inequalities and preserving the status quo, which typically works in their favor. Indeed, one study showed the importance of one's status within a given context in predicting color blindness. Black students at predominantly Black universities were more likely than Black students at predominantly White universities to endorse assimilation at the campus level, a concept that overlaps with color blindness, with items such as, "There is no point emphasizing our different racial identities when we are all just students at this university" and "I prefer to regard all students at this university simply as students rather than as Black students or White students" (Hehman et al., 2012). One interpretation of this finding is that the risk of discrimination and marginalization is lower at a predominately Black institution, creating a relatively safe space where Black students can be less concerned about race—that is, less vigilant about facing prejudice and less likely to be asked to explain racial issues. Alternatively, the finding could be evidence of a functional role of racial color blindness in protecting privilege—that is, Black students were more likely to endorse racially color-blind ideas when they were in the majority because they were more likely to perceive a benefit from protecting the status quo. This does not suggest that racial color blindness would actually benefit Black students, however; ignoring race may have detrimental effects for Blacks even within a predominantly Black environment. Being in the majority on campus does not make Black students immune to institutional and interpersonal bias, and remedying this bias will require attention to race.

Additional evidence comes from Saguy and colleagues' work on members of privileged groups. When given a choice between discussing differences or commonalities between privileged and disadvantaged groups, those with privilege preferred not to talk about the differences, choosing instead to focus on commonalities. This allowed them to feel positive about intergroup relations without actually feeling obligated to redress disparities (Saguy et al., 2008; Saguy, Tausch, Dovidio, & Pratto, 2009). Racial color blindness as a racial ideology focuses on commonalities rather than differences and thus allows those who are so inclined to ignore blatant and harmful racial disparities.

Other racial ideologies can contribute to this interpretation of color blindness: Members of the racial majority tend to view bias as a zero-sum system (Norton & Sommers, 2011). Zero-sum beliefs emerge from the following suppositions: first, that there are (usually two) discrete groups; second, that these groups are in competition with each other in such a way that gains for one group necessarily result in losses for the other (Hartstone &

Augoustinos, 1995). Therefore, any effort that is intended to benefit members of a racial minority is interpreted as an attack on the racial majority. Programs such as affirmative action, minority-focused scholarships, equal opportunity employment, and even a reduction in explicit bias against racial minorities are viewed not as pathways to achieving racial equality but rather as active discrimination against racial majorities (Wilkins & Kaiser, 2014). The resulting sense of threat results in attachment to the (unequal) status quo and opposition to any equalizing policies.

This is exacerbated by the related phenomenon demonstrated by Norton and Sommers (2011): Many White people believe that over the past few decades, as bias against Black people has decreased, bias against White people has simultaneously increased, to the point that White people now experience more discrimination than Black people. This belief is not supported by objective indicators of educational, financial, or health status (see Plaut, 2010). Nevertheless, in the eyes of these individuals, racial prejudice against minorities is in the past, so any policies that favor racial minority groups give them an unearned boost, leading to better outcomes for racial minorities than Whites. For example, some attacks on affirmative action portray individual White people as victims of unfair racial policies that prevent them from gaining a coveted spot, while ignoring the group's overrepresentation due to legacy admission policies and other structural and historical factors. In these cases, racial color blindness is evoked to argue against considering race in candidate selection, with the suggestion that policies intended to correct for structural discrimination against racial minorities are harmful to the majority. Ignoring race protects the racial majority from the perceived threat to their status. Other research has shown a correlation between White participants' belief that racism is largely in the past and their endorsement of racial color blindness (Mazzocco, Cooper, & Flint, 2012). Thus, racial color blindness is used as a justification for opposing equalizing policies.

As such, racial color blindness is framed as a mandate of procedural justice (Knowles et al., 2009). Adopting this procedural interpretation of racial color blindness means that the process through which decisions are made must be bereft of information about race or ethnicity, even if the outcome is consistently biased. Racial color blindness can therefore serve as a justification for eliminating or preventing race-conscious attempts to reduce inequality. For example, racial color blindness was invoked in a U.S. Supreme Court ruling striking down school integration efforts: "The way to stop discrimination on the basis of race is to stop discriminating on the basis of race" (*Parents Involved in Community Schools v. Seattle School District No. 1*, 2007, pp. 40–41). (Because there is also an egalitarian interpretation of racial color blindness, as discussed earlier, the dissenting opinion also invoked color blindness—using the distributive justice interpretation to argue for equitable outcomes over equal treatment.) Antiegalitarian Whites who have been primed with a subtle intergroup threat are more likely to interpret even Dr. King's famous quote in line with a procedural view of color blindness; after reading the quote and being asked how Americans can create a color-blind society, they were more likely to give procedural responses such as, "Get rid of affirmative action. Judge people on what they do, not how they look," rather than distributive responses such as, "Make more laws against prejudice and discrimination" (Knowles et al., 2009).

CAMOUFLAGING REAL OR LATENT PREJUDICE

A meta-analysis on dyadic interracial interactions showed that both implicit and explicit prejudice have declined over the past half-century, but self-reports of heightened anxiety and discomfort in interracial interactions have remained consistent (Toosi, Babbitt, Ambady, & Sommers, 2012). This anxiety was higher for racial majority members than for racial minorities and seems to be related to concerns about appearing prejudiced (e.g., Shelton, 2003; Stephan & Stephan, 1985). Therefore, for some individuals, part of the motivation for endorsing racial color blindness as a racial ideology may not necessarily be directly tied to their interest in protecting the broader status quo but rather to a preoccupation with not appearing prejudiced.

Anxiety about how others see them leads people to engage in strategic racial color blindness, an attempt to avoid the taboo of being labeled a racist by avoiding mention of race altogether. For example, in one series of studies, Whites played a photo-identification game in which they were given an array of photos and required to determine which of the photos their partner held by asking a series of yes–no questions (Apfelbaum, Sommers, et al., 2008; Norton, Sommers, Apfelbaum, Pura, & Ariely, 2006). Half of the photos were of White people, and half were of Black people, meaning that participants could quickly eliminate half of the array by asking their partner about the race of the person in the target photo. Whites were less likely to ask about race when paired with a Black partner than when paired with a White partner, a tendency that not only hampered their performance in the game but was also associated with reduced eye contact and appearing less friendly to their partner (Norton et al., 2006). This strategy—attempting to appear color blind by not mentioning race—was more common in Whites who were externally motivated to appear unprejudiced (i.e., those who avoid prejudiced behavior out of concern about others' reactions), but it proved counterproductive: Whites who adopted this color-blind strategy actually appeared *more* biased to Black observers, not less (Apfelbaum, Sommers, et al., 2008).

In sum, this research indicates that although racial color blindness is an intuitively appealing strategy for Whites who want to appear unbiased during social interaction, it tends to backfire. Because race is processed automatically within a matter of milliseconds (Ito & Urland, 2003), pretending not to notice it takes mental effort, and expending this effort in the course of an interracial interaction can lead to negative nonverbal behavior (Apfelbaum, Sommers, et al., 2008). Furthermore, the goal of appearing unbiased is not achieved.

Stranger in a Multiethnic Land

Anxiety about one's role and fit within a given context can also influence endorsement of racial color blindness as a racial ideology. Plaut and colleagues compared the reactions of White individuals to color blindness, defined in their studies as a view of diversity that "stresses that racial, ethnic, and cultural differences are superficial and emphasizes the similarity of all people" (Plaut et al., 2011, p. 341), versus multiculturalism (an approach that values racial, ethnic, and cultural differences). They presented evidence that White people did not feel excluded in the construct of color blindness, whereas they perceived multiculturalism as focused on the contributions of ethnic minorities to the exclusion of Whites. This may be due to the perception that Whiteness represents the absence or lack of a cultural heritage (McDermott & Samson, 2005). Because multiculturalism is focused on recognizing and appreciating the various cultures present in a setting, it is therefore interpreted as focusing only on minority cultures and is seen as exclusionary to White people. Plaut et al. (2011) found that in an implicit association task, White people were faster to associate multiculturalism with exclusion (and racial color blindness with inclusion), whereas racial minorities did not show similar associations. This sense of exclusion mediated Whites' lower support for diversity initiatives. If, however, the description of multiculturalism explicitly included a reference to European Americans, the strength of the association between multiculturalism and exclusion was reduced. In a further demonstration that support for these ideologies is tied to one's own sense of inclusion, White people who scored high on a need-to-belong scale showed more interest in working for a company that espoused color-blind policies than a multicultural one, whereas those with less need to belong did not show a preference between the two policies (Plaut et al., 2011).

These findings indicate another reason why members of racial majority groups may support racial color blindness. To the extent that alternative ideologies such as multiculturalism are perceived as excluding one's group, racial color blindness seems to provide a more inclusive approach because it purports to overlook all group memberships. However, saying that a setting subscribes to a racially color-blind ideology may be another way of saying that it is regulated by White cultural norms. In any setting, interactions are shaped by a set of cultural norms, expectations, and values. Unless these norms are the focus of deliberate attention and design, the default norms will tend to reflect those of the racial majority. In the United States, the concept of "American" is strongly associated with Whiteness (Devos & Banaji, 2005), and organizations that purport to treat everyone equally by not considering race or culture can often result in workplaces that are deeply uncomfortable to people of color (Ely & Thomas, 2001).

Inherited Silence

Racial color blindness may also simply be a default approach, picked up through social norms but unexamined in its implications. As noted earlier, racial color blindness tends to be the prevailing ideology in America. In workplaces, social gatherings, and educational settings, the default approach to race is to ignore it and focus instead on commonalities or individualizing traits (Apfelbaum et al., 2012; Rattan & Ambady, 2013). The consistency of this message influences mind-frames and trickles down to family-level interactions. In a study of racial socialization of children, White parents were videotaped while reading two race-themed books to their children, and their comments about the books were coded. Nearly all of the 84 parents took color-blind approaches, and some even ignored direct questions about race asked by their children (Pahlke, Bigler, & Suizzo, 2012). Avoiding the topic of race does not mean that children do not notice it. Rather, the lack of explanation about visible racial cues combined with manifest racial divisions, such as residential and occupational segregation, a lack of diversity among parents' social networks, or parents' negative nonverbal behavior toward people of other races, may lead children to infer that race is indeed a meaningful distinction between people, albeit one that is not appropriate to discuss. Furthermore, these environmental cues may foster feelings of racial superiority in children, without providing an opportunity for parents to explicitly disavow racial bias (Bigler & Liben, 2007).

The impact of color-blind social norms on children is evident in several ways. As early as age 10, children understand that some topics are inappropriate to speak about, and they desist from doing so, even in settings in which it would help them to do so (Apfelbaum, Pauker, Ambady, Sommers, & Norton, 2008). Even more troubling, children who were exposed to a racial color blindness message compared with a multiculturalism message avoided the topic of race even when encountering an incident of blatant racial prejudice between students; in one study, they were significantly less likely to identify the act as discrimination and to report the incident in a way that would bring about the teacher's intervention (Apfelbaum et al., 2010). Hearing a multicultural message did not make children more attuned to discrimination than they would be normally: Those who were not exposed to any diversity message were just as likely to identify discrimination as children who received the multiculturalism message. Only when they heard the racial color blindness message were children less likely to report that discrimination had occurred. Perhaps they were concerned that teachers would react negatively or were simply attempting to follow a social norm that prohibits acknowledging race (see Apfelbaum, Pauker, et al., 2008).

Whether learned through direct messages or subtle cues, color-blind attitudes can, if unexamined, persist into adulthood and lead to a general avoidance of, ignorance about, and complicity in race-based disparities that effectively leads to their continuation (e.g., Nelson, Adams, & Salter, 2013).

Eyes on the Prize

Although members of racial minorities tend to endorse racial color blindness less than Whites do (Ryan, Hunt, Weible, Peterson, & Casas, 2007), there are some reasons that they might favor color blindness. For one, color-blind policies are certainly preferable to policies that are explicitly designed to exclude minorities; for example, a color-blind mortgage-backing policy would be preferable to one that redlines integrated or minority neighborhoods. Additionally, members of racial minority groups may emphasize that skin color does not matter and that everyone is equal to gain inclusion and respect in mainstream institutions (Purdie-Vaughns & Ditlmann, 2010) and to avoid conflict in daily interpersonal interactions with Whites, although this latter strategy could entail negative consequences, including cognitive depletion (Rattan & Ambady, 2013; see also Holoien & Shelton, 2012). Similarly, emphasizing common struggles and goals can be a strategy to achieve racial progress in a polarized society—one that Barack Obama demonstrated in his 2008 speech about race: "Let us find that common stake we all have in one another . . . we want to talk about the crumbling schools that are stealing the future of Black children and White children and Asian children and Hispanic children and Native American children" (Obama, 2008). And although corporations that endorse color-blind diversity policies are viewed with suspicion by members of minority groups, those concerns can be allayed when minority representation at those corporations is high: Racial color blindness then becomes less threatening, and the organization seems more trustworthy (Purdie-Vaughns, Steele, Davies, Ditlmann, & Crosby, 2008).

DISCUSSION

Racial color blindness has become entrenched in our society. Since Dr. King's famous speech was seared into our collective consciousness, racial color blindness has become the language that we use to talk about race, but its meaning has splintered. We argue that it is precisely because racial color blindness has so many interpretations that it has become the prevailing ideology: Racial color blindness not only shifts to suit one's own beliefs, it acts as a mirror, reflecting back what each person wants to see. Individuals who endorse racial color blindness come from a wide range of backgrounds—they may be passionate about social justice or unapologetically racist; they may be privileged or oppressed; they may be Black or White or any other race. These individuals define racial color blindness differently depending on their overall goals. For example, someone who wants to protect the status quo may invoke a procedural interpretation of racial color blindness and call for ignoring race in decisions and policies, even if that leads to inequitable outcomes; someone who wants to ensure equitable outcomes may invoke a distributive interpretation and call for eliminating the role of race in determining outcomes, even if that means race is considered in determining rules and treatment. A White person talking with a Black person may avoid race to prevent appearing biased; a Black person may avoid race to prevent conflict. A child may be taught racial color blindness as part of an overall message to treat others equally regardless of external appearance, but as the child grows up, she may come to think of race as a forbidden topic; when the child reaches adulthood, her reasoning for avoiding race may take one (or more) of the many forms listed here, depending on her beliefs (Levy, West, & Ramirez, 2005).

In the absence of a national conversation about race, racial color blindness has become a refuge. Even when we do talk about race, it is tinged with color blindness; for example, while there was a broad and impassioned debate in the media and among the general public about the role of race in George Zimmerman's shooting of Trayvon Martin, explicit discussion of race was strangely absent from the courtroom during Zimmerman's trial: The judge prohibited the use of the term *racial profiling* (allowing only *profiling*) in opening statements, and the prosecutors insisted that the trial had nothing to do with race (Bloom, 2013). Moreover, the first juror to speak publicly after the trial made the difficult-to-fathom declaration that race had not been addressed in any way during the jury's deliberations: "I think all of us thought race did not play a role. We never had that discussion" (Ford, 2013). The pervasiveness of contemporary claims of racial color blindness can be seen in the emergence of such an assertion even when adjudicating a high-profile case that served as a flashpoint for contemporary American race relations.

It is clear that despite such protestations to the contrary, race continues to play a role in nearly every aspect of our lives. It shapes where we live, the schools we attend, the quality of the education we receive, the support systems that allow us to persist through higher levels of education, and the networks we build while in those institutions. Race is a factor in employment opportunities, salary offers, promotions, and the day-to-day work experience, as well as the extent of family wealth and financial resources. Race plays a role in physical and mental illness, access to competent and caring medical professionals, the type of medical treatment received, and how medical bills are paid. Race influences political representation and media portrayals. Race determines interactions with law enforcement and the criminal justice system. In all of these interpersonal and institutional contexts, bias still exists. If our goal is true racial justice and unity, we must address these disparities. Thus, racial color blindness is problematic not simply because it infuses the American approach to race while meaning different things to different people, so that the strategic intent behind it is not apparent at face value, but also because at a more basic level, endorsement of racial color blindness for any reason in a society in which race matters in so many domains will be harmful at worst and insufficient at best. Whether racial color blindness is invoked in a malevolent attempt to perpetuate inequity or in an idealistic attempt to make race not matter, it falls short of the promise it once seemed to hold.

Fortunately, racial color blindness is not the only approach to diversity. Alternative approaches include multiculturalism (Chapter 4, this volume), color consciousness (Chapter 6, this volume), all-inclusive multiculturalism (Stevens, Plaut, & Sanchez-Burks, 2008), identity safety (Purdie-Vaughns & Walton, 2011), and others. Each of these proffered ideological approaches to race relations may have its own strengths and drawbacks.

One step, then, is to carefully investigate these alternative ideological approaches as potential solutions to the present challenges of race relations and to continue to develop new approaches to diversity. Furthermore, when designing and interpreting research on intergroup relations, we can consider the multiple rationales underlying support for colorblindness and keep in mind that these rationales may shape people's responses to other ideologies as well. Finally, we should strive to effectively contribute what we learn to the public discourse, beginning by explaining why the intuitively appealing idea of racial color blindness can do more harm than good, and then offering better alternatives in hopes of changing attitudes and policies.

REFERENCES

Allport, G. W. (1954). *The nature of prejudice*. Reading, MA: Addison-Wesley.

Apfelbaum, E. P., Norton, M. I., & Sommers, S. R. (2012). Racial colorblindness: Emergence, practice, and implications. *Current Directions in Psychological Science, 21*, 205–209. http://dx.doi.org/10.1177/0963721411434980

Apfelbaum, E. P., Pauker, K., Ambady, N., Sommers, S. R., & Norton, M. I. (2008). Learning (not) to talk about race: When older children underperform in social categorization. *Developmental Psychology, 44*, 1513–1518. http://dx.doi.org/10.1037/a0012835

Apfelbaum, E. P., Pauker, K., Sommers, S. R., & Ambady, N. (2010). In blind pursuit of racial equality? *Psychological Science, 21*, 1587–1592. http://dx.doi.org/10.1177/0956797610384741

Apfelbaum, E. P., Sommers, S. R., & Norton, M. I. (2008). Seeing race and seeming racist? Evaluating strategic colorblindness in social interaction. *Journal of Personality and Social Psychology, 95*, 918–932. http://dx.doi.org/10.1037/a0011990

Bigler, R. S., & Liben, L. S. (2007). Developmental intergroup theory: Explaining and reducing children's social stereotyping and prejudice. *Current Directions in Psychological Science, 16*, 162–166. http://dx.doi.org/10.1111/j.1467-8721.2007.00496.x

Bloom, L. (2013, July 15). Zimmerman prosecutors duck the race issue. Retrieved from http://www.nytimes.com/2013/07/16/opinion/zimmerman-prosecutors-duck-the-race-issue.html?_r=0

Brewer, M. B., & Miller, N. (Eds.). (1984). *Groups in contact: The psychology of desegregation*. Orlando, FL: Academic Press.

Devos, T., & Banaji, M. R. (2005). American = White? *Journal of Personality and Social Psychology, 88*, 447–466. http://dx.doi.org/10.1037/0022-3514.88.3.447

Dovidio, J. F., Kawakami, K., & Gaertner, S. L. (2002). Implicit and explicit prejudice and interracial interaction. *Journal of Personality and Social Psychology, 82*, 62–68. http://dx.doi.org/10.1037/0022-3514.82.1.62

Dyson, M. E. (2000). *I may not get there with you: The true Martin Luther King, Jr.* New York, NY: Free Press.

Eberhardt, J. L., Davies, P. G., Purdie-Vaughns, V. J., & Johnson, S. L. (2006). Looking deathworthy: Perceived stereotypicality of Black defendants predicts capital-sentencing outcomes. *Psychological Science, 17*, 383–386. http://dx.doi.org/10.1111/j.1467-9280.2006.01716.x

Ely, R. J., & Thomas, D. A. (2001). Cultural diversity at work: The effects of diversity perspectives on work group processes and outcomes. *Administrative Science Quarterly, 46*, 229–273. http://dx.doi.org/10.2307/2667087

Firebaugh, G., & Davis, K. E. (1988). Trends in antiblack prejudice, 1972–1984: Region and cohort effects. *American Journal of Sociology, 94*, 251–272. http://dx.doi.org/10.1086/228991

Fiske, S. T., Lin, M., & Neuberg, S. L. (1999). The continuum model. In S. Chaiken & Y. Trope (Eds.), *Dual process theories in social psychology* (pp. 231–254). New York, NY: Guilford Press.

Ford, D. (2013, July 16). Juror: "No doubt" that George Zimmerman feared for his life. Retrieved from http://www.cnn.com/2013/07/15/justice/zimmerman-juror-book

Goff, P. A., Jackson, M. C., Nichols, A. H., & Di Leone, B. A. (2013). Anything but race: Avoiding racial discourse to avoid hurting you or me. *Psychology, 4,* 335–339.

Hartstone, M., & Augoustinos, M. (1995). The minimal group paradigm: Categorization into two versus three groups. *European Journal of Social Psychology, 25,* 179–193. http://dx.doi.org/10.1002/ejsp.2420250205

Hehman, E., Gaertner, S. L., Dovidio, J. F., Mania, E. W., Guerra, R., Wilson, D. C., & Friel, B. M. (2012). Group status drives majority and minority integration preferences. *Psychological Science, 23,* 46–52. http://dx.doi.org/10.1177/0956797611423547

Hirsch, E. D. (1996). *The schools we need: And why we don't have them.* New York, NY: Doubleday.

Holoien, D. S., & Shelton, J. (2012). You deplete me: The cognitive costs of colorblindness on ethnic minorities. *Journal of Experimental Social Psychology, 48,* 562–565. http://dx.doi.org/10.1016/j.jesp.2011.09.010

Ito, T. A., & Urland, G. R. (2003). Race and gender on the brain: Electrocortical measures of attention to the race and gender of multiply categorizable individuals. *Journal of Personality and Social Psychology, 85,* 616–626. http://dx.doi.org/10.1037/0022-3514.85.4.616

Knowles, E. D., Lowery, B. S., Hogan, C. M., & Chow, R. M. (2009). On the malleability of ideology: Motivated construals of color blindness. *Journal of Personality and Social Psychology, 96,* 857–869. http://dx.doi.org/10.1037/a0013595

Levy, S. R., West, T. L., & Ramirez, L. (2005). Lay theories and intergroup relations: A social-developmental perspective. *European Review of Social Psychology, 16,* 189–220. http://dx.doi.org/10.1080/10463280500397234

Markus, H. R., Steele, C. M., & Steele, D. M. (2000). Colorblindness as a barrier to inclusion: Assimilation and nonimmigrant minorities. *Daedalus, 129,* 233–259.

Mazzocco, P. J., Cooper, L. W., & Flint, M. (2012). Different shades of racial colorblindness: The role of prejudice. *Group Processes & Intergroup Relations, 15,* 167–178. http://dx.doi.org/10.1177/1368430211424763

McDermott, M., & Samson, F. L. (2005). White racial and ethnic identity in the United States. *Annual Review of Sociology, 31,* 245–261. http://dx.doi.org/10.1146/annurev.soc.31.041304.122322

Nelson, J. C., Adams, G., & Salter, P. S. (2013). The Marley hypothesis: Denial of racism reflects ignorance of history. *Psychological Science, 24,* 213–218. http://dx.doi.org/10.1177/0956797612451466

Norton, M. I., & Sommers, S. R. (2011). Whites see racism as a zero-sum game that they are now losing. *Perspectives on Psychological Science, 6,* 215–218. http://dx.doi.org/10.1177/1745691611406922

Norton, M. I., Sommers, S. R., Apfelbaum, E. P., Pura, N., & Ariely, D. (2006). Color blindness and interracial interaction: Playing the political correctness game. *Psychological Science, 17,* 949–953. http://dx.doi.org/10.1111/j.1467-9280.2006.01810.x

Obama, B. (2008). *A more perfect union.* Retrieved from http://constitutioncenter.org/amoreperfectunion

Pahlke, E., Bigler, R. S., & Suizzo, M. A. (2012). Relations between colorblind socialization and children's racial bias: Evidence from European American mothers and their preschool children. *Child Development, 83,* 1164–1179. http://dx.doi.org/10.1111/j.1467-8624.2012.01770.x

Parents Involved in Community Schools v. Seattle School Dist. No. 1, No. 05–908 (U.S. June 28, 2007).

Payne, B. K. (2006). Weapon bias: Split-second decisions and unintended stereotyping. *Current Directions in Psychological Science, 15,* 287–291. http://dx.doi.org/10.1111/j.1467-8721.2006.00454.x

Peery, D. (2011). Colorblind ideal in a race-conscious reality: The case for a new legal ideal for race relations. *Northwestern Journal of Law and Social Policy, 6,* 473.

Plaut, V. C. (2010). Diversity science: Why and how difference makes a difference. *Psychological Inquiry, 21,* 77–99. http://dx.doi.org/10.1080/10478401003676501

Plaut, V. C., Garnett, F. G., Buffardi, L. E., & Sanchez-Burks, J. (2011). "What about me?" Perceptions of exclusion and Whites' reactions to multiculturalism. *Journal of Personality and Social Psychology, 101,* 337–353. http://dx.doi.org/10.1037/a0022832

Purdie-Vaughns, V., & Ditlmann, R. (2010). Reflection on diversity science in social psychology. *Psychological Inquiry, 21,* 153–159. http://dx.doi.org/10.1080/1047840X.2010.486758

Purdie-Vaughns, V., Steele, C. M., Davies, P. G., Ditlmann, R., & Crosby, J. R. (2008). Social identity contingencies: How diversity cues signal threat or safety for African Americans in mainstream institutions. *Journal of Personality and Social Psychology, 94,* 615–630. http://dx.doi.org/10.1037/0022-3514.94.4.615

Purdie-Vaughns, V., & Walton, G. M. (2011). Is multiculturalism bad for African-Americans? Redefining inclusion through the lens of identity safety. In L. R. Tropp & R. K. Mallett (Eds.), *Moving beyond prejudice reduction: Pathways to positive intergroup relations* (pp. 159–177). Washington, DC: American Psychological Association. http://dx.doi.org/10.1037/12319-008

Rattan, A., & Ambady, N. (2013). Diversity ideologies and intergroup relations: An examination of colorblindness and multiculturalism. *European Journal of Social Psychology, 43,* 12–21. http://dx.doi.org/10.1002/ejsp.1892

Ryan, C. S., Hunt, J. S., Weible, J. A., Peterson, C. R., & Casas, J. F. (2007). Multicultural and colorblind ideology, stereotypes, and ethnocentrism among Black and White Americans. *Group Processes & Intergroup Relations, 10,* 617–637. http://dx.doi.org/10.1177/1368430207084105

Saguy, T., Dovidio, J. F., & Pratto, F. (2008). Beyond contact: Intergroup contact in the context of power relations. *Personality and Social Psychology Bulletin, 34,* 432–445. http://dx.doi.org/10.1177/0146167207311200

Saguy, T., Tausch, N., Dovidio, J. F., & Pratto, F. (2009). The irony of harmony: Intergroup contact can produce false expectations for equality. *Psychological Science, 20,* 114–121. http://dx.doi.org/10.1111/j.1467-9280.2008.02261.x

Shelton, J. N. (2003). Interpersonal concerns in social encounters between majority and minority group members. *Group Processes & Intergroup Relations, 6,* 171–185. http://dx.doi.org/10.1177/1368430203006002003

Shweder, R. A. (1991). *Thinking through cultures: Expeditions in cultural psychology.* Cambridge, MA: Harvard University Press.

Sleeter, C. E. (Ed.). (1991). *Empowerment through multicultural education.* Albany, NY: SUNY Press.

Stephan, W., & Stephan, C. W. (1985). Intergroup anxiety. *Journal of Social Issues, 41,* 157–175. http://dx.doi.org/10.1111/j.1540-4560.1985.tb01134.x

Stevens, F. G., Plaut, V. C., & Sanchez-Burks, J. (2008). Unlocking the benefits of diversity: All-inclusive multiculturalism and positive organizational change. *Journal of Applied Behavioral Science, 44,* 116–133. http://dx.doi.org/10.1177/0021886308314460

Tajfel, H., & Turner, J. C. (1979). An integrative theory of intergroup conflict. In W. G. Austin & S. Worchel (Eds.), *The social psychology of intergroup relations* (pp. 33–47). Monterey, CA: Brooks-Cole.

Toosi, N. R., Babbitt, L. G., Ambady, N., & Sommers, S. R. (2012). Dyadic interracial interactions: A meta-analysis. *Psychological Bulletin, 138,* 1–27. http://dx.doi.org/10.1037/a0025767

Washington, J. (2013, January 20). King "content of character" speech inspires debate. Retrieved from http://bigstory.ap.org/article/king-content-character-quote-inspires-debate

Wilkins, C. L., & Kaiser, C. R. (2014). Racial progress as threat to the status hierarchy: Implications for perceptions of anti-White bias. *Psychological Science, 25,* 439–446. http://dx.doi.org/10.1177/0956797613508412

Wolsko, C., Park, B., Judd, C. M., & Wittenbrink, B. (2000). Framing interethnic ideology: Effects of multicultural and color-blind perspectives on judgments of groups and individuals. *Journal of Personality and Social Psychology, 78,* 635–654. http://dx.doi.org/10.1037/0022-3514.78.4.635

4

UNDERSTANDING RACIAL COLOR BLINDNESS AND MULTICULTURALISM IN INTERRACIAL RELATIONSHIPS: COGNITIVE AND EMOTIONAL TENSIONS AND THEIR IMPLICATIONS

LINDY GULLETT AND TESSA V. WEST

Even though minorities comprise 37% of the U.S. population (U.S. Census Bureau, 2012), an astounding 30% of Americans interact exclusively with family members, friends, and coworkers who are of their own race (Reuters, 2013). Given these statistics, it is perhaps not surprising that despite increasingly favorable views of racial integration, interracial interactions in the United States continue to be anxiety provoking (Plant, 2004; Plant & Butz, 2006; Toosi, Babbitt, Ambady, & Sommers, 2012; Trawalter, Richeson, & Shelton, 2009). Even for the most well-intentioned individuals—those who actively make an effort to have positive cross-race contact experiences—interactions with a member of a racial or ethnic outgroup can be awkward and threatening (Blascovich, Mendes, Hunter, Lickel, & Kowai-Bell, 2001; Mendes, Blascovich, Lickel, & Hunter, 2002; Mendes & Koslov, 2013). As such, cross-race peers have more difficulty building rapport and developing relationships than same-race peers, even under optimal conditions of contact

http://dx.doi.org/10.1037/14754-005

(Shook & Fazio, 2008a, 2008b; Trail, Shelton, & West, 2009; West, Shelton, & Trail, 2009).

In response to the difficulties that Whites and minorities face in forming relationships across the racial divide, scholars and lawmakers have attempted to develop interventions that improve interracial interactions by targeting the psychological and interpersonal processes that undermine interracial relationship development. In this review chapter, we focus on two conceptual frameworks that influence the way people think about race and, subsequently, how they interact with others of a different race: racial color blindness and multiculturalism.

We begin with a review of the evidence regarding each approach's effectiveness at fostering the formation and development of interracial relationships, touching on the unique costs and benefits associated with both. We explore the psychological mechanisms through which these approaches influence Whites' and minorities' behaviors and perceptions of their partners during interracial interactions, as well as potential downstream consequences of entering interracial interactions with a racially color-blind or multicultural mind-set (e.g., increased prejudice and being disliked by cross-race interaction partners). We conclude by briefly comparing the effectiveness of color-blind and multicultural approaches to interracial interactions with alternative methods for cultivating interracial relationships.

Because interracial relationships necessarily involve at least two people, throughout this review, we take an *actor–partner interdependence model* approach (Kashy & Kenny, 2000) in which we consider how having a color-blind or multicultural mind-set might influence both members of dyadic interracial interactions. Specifically, we consider how individuals' color-blind or multicultural mind-set influences not only their own outcomes (e.g., their liking for and desire to interact with their interaction partner in the future, termed the *actor* effect) but also their partner's (e.g., their partner's liking for and desire to interact with them, termed the *partner* effect). We also consider how these two mind-sets differentially influence Whites and minorities as actors and partners. Before a review of the extant research on how color-blind and multicultural mind-sets influence interracial relationship formation, we begin with a brief definitional overview of racial color blindness and multiculturalism.

WHAT ARE COLOR BLINDNESS AND MULTICULTURALISM?

Although they share the same ultimate goal of facilitating positive interracial experiences, color-blind and multicultural mind-sets are quite different in how they propose individuals think about race and racial diversity within interracial contexts. Proponents of a color-blind approach to race argue that to reduce prejudice and discrimination, people must act as if they are "blind" to race (see Gotanda, 1991; Neville, Lilly, Duran, Lee, & Browne, 2000; *Parents Involved in Community Schools v. Seattle School District No. 1*, 2007). Historically, endorsing a color-blind mind-set to race meant embracing a world in which race cannot be used as a foundation for inequality. As the plaintiffs argued in *Brown v. Board of Education* (1954), "That the constitution is color-blind is our dedicated belief." Proponents of a color-blind approach claim that if people do not recognize and acknowledge one another's race, then prejudice and discrimination based on race will not have the opportunity to emerge. Given the straightforward and intuitive appeal of the color-blind approach to race, it is unsurprising that it is a popular method for reducing prejudice and discrimination in a number of social contexts, including organizational (Ely & Thomas, 2001; Thomas & Ely, 1996), educational (Apfelbaum, Pauker, Ambady, Sommers, & Norton, 2008; Pollock, 2004; Schofield, 2007), and legal (Kang & Lane, 2010; Peery, 2011; Sommers & Norton, 2008) settings.

In contrast to the color-blind approach, the multicultural approach stems from the notion that it is important to acknowledge and empower all races by celebrating each other's diverse backgrounds (Markus et al., 2000; Plaut, 2002; Wolsko, Park, Judd, & Wittenbrink, 2000). The United States is growing in racial diversity—racial minorities make up more than half of the population in California, Hawaii, New Mexico, and Texas (U.S. Census Bureau, 2012)—and within the next 50 years, minorities will begin to outnumber Whites (Ortman & Guarneri, 2009). In direct contrast to the color-blind perspective of ignoring race, multiculturalism seeks to celebrate the importance and harness the power of the perspectives and experiences that come with each individual's unique background. In the context of interpersonal interactions, the multicultural approach can help people accurately gauge the individual motivations and perspectives of one's cross-race interaction partners.

EFFECTS OF A RACIALLY COLOR-BLIND MIND-SET IN INTERRACIAL INTERACTIONS

How does harboring a racially color-blind mind-set influence interpersonal interactions? Despite the good intentions behind this approach, being color blind to race going into an encounter does not facilitate positive experiences for both partners; rather, it can impair communication, lead people to appear avoidant through displays of negative nonverbal behaviors, and lead to cognitive depletion (Apfelbaum, Sommers, & Norton, 2008; Norton, Sommers, Apfelbaum, Pura, & Ariely, 2006).

Individuals, especially Whites, often feel concerned about appearing prejudiced when interacting with a racial outgroup member (Bergsieker, Shelton, & Richeson, 2010; Plant & Devine, 1998; Richeson & Shelton, 2007). Attempting to appear color blind to race is one way to manage the concern of trying to appear unprejudiced. Indeed, acknowledging race is a necessary precursor to racism, and so individuals who do not want to appear racist might say to themselves, "If I do not notice race, then I cannot be a racist" (Norton et al., 2006, p. 949). However, race is encoded automatically and without conscious effort (Ito & Urland, 2003), and this incongruity between trying to appear as if one has not noticed race while still automatically noticing race can lead to a host of negative downstream consequences during interpersonal interactions.

Like other strategies in which individuals try to manage self-presentational concerns of trying to appear unprejudiced (e.g., Shelton, West, & Trail, 2010), individuals who try to appear color blind to race also appear more uncomfortable, more anxious, and less friendly during interracial interactions. In the first investigation of how attempts to appear color blind backfire during interracial interactions, Norton, Sommers, Apfelbaum, Pura, and Ariely (2006, Study 2) asked White participants to work with a partner (a Black or White confederate) on a cooperative task. Participants were given 32 photographs of Black and White targets while their partner (the confederate) was given one photograph at a time. The participants' goal was to ask their partner questions to figure out which of the 32 photographs their partner was given. In this task, race is a diagnostic tool, and mentioning the race of the target in the photograph would help one's partner identify the correct photograph.

When the confederate was White, participants asked about the race of their partner's photo 94% of the time. However, when the confederate was Black, participants suppressed their race-related questions and only mentioned the race of the person in the photo 64% of the time. Further, these color-blind behaviors during interracial interactions were associated with participant's negative nonverbal behaviors. When White participants interacted with a Black confederate, the less they mentioned race, the less eye contact they made with their partners and the less friendly they appeared. In addition, extensions of Norton et al.'s (2006) research revealed that trying to act color blind to race during interactions with an interracial partner can lead to more negative nonverbal behaviors in general (Apfelbaum, Sommers, et al., 2008).

Like Norton et al. (2006), Apfelbaum, Sommers, et al. (2008) had White participants interact with White and Black confederates while completing a race-relevant person identification task; however, Apfelbaum and colleagues manipulated the behavior of the participants' interaction partner (the confederate). To cue participants to suppress or acknowledge race during their interaction, confederates either acted color blind (i.e., did not voluntarily ask questions about the race of targets shown in the person identification task) or acknowledged the race of the targets shown in the person identification task. In response to their interaction partner's behavior, participants with a racially color-blind interaction partner mentioned race only 26% of the time, whereas participants with a race acknowledging interaction partner mentioned race 91% of the time. Most important, an investigation of participant's nonverbal behaviors during the interaction revealed that interacting with a color-blind interaction partner led to more negative nonverbal behaviors for those in interracial interactions. Thus, while Norton et al.'s findings suggest that Whites' own attempts at racially color-blind behavior can result in the individual exhibiting negative nonverbal behaviors, Apfelbaum, Sommers, et al.'s research shows that minorities' refusal to acknowledge race can lead their White partners to exhibit racially color-blind verbal behaviors and negative nonverbal behaviors. Taken together, these findings indicate both actor and partner effects of being color blind on behaviors. Individuals who espouse a racially color-blind mind-set engage in more negative nonverbal behaviors (e.g., anxiety), indicating an actor effect, and engaging in an interaction with a partner who acts in a racially color-blind fashion also leads one to engage in more negative nonverbal behaviors, indicating a partner effect.

These findings add to a growing body of literature demonstrating the effects that impression management concerns have on nonverbal behavior within interracial encounters. But how might interacting with someone who *displays* negative nonverbal behaviors affect the relationship? Within interracial interactions, having a partner who appears anxious might be particularly problematic because the meaning underlying nonverbal anxious behaviors is ambiguous and open to interpretation (Dovidio, Kawakami, & Gaertner, 2002), and Whites and minorities in interracial interactions are especially prone to interpreting anxious nonverbal behaviors, such as averting the gaze, as indicative of dislike and unfriendliness (Dovidio, West, Pearson, Gaertner, & Kawakami, 2007; Trail et al., 2009). In same-race encounters, these same behaviors are not interpreted negatively and have been shown even to be interpreted positively (e.g., as signs of genuine interest and attempts to make a good impression; West, 2011). For example, Trail et al. (2009) used a daily diary method to measure new roommate relationships over several weeks and found that perceptions of roommates' anxious behaviors (e.g., avoidance of eye contact, shifting attention), above and beyond people's own anxious experiences, predicted lower levels of intimacy and a weaker desire to develop a friendship with a cross-race, but not same-race, roommate. Shelton et al. (2010) further showed that within the first 2 weeks of living together, among people who felt anxious when interacting with their cross-race roommate, once those roommates were able to pick up on their anxiety (around Day 10 of the study), they were less interested in forming a friendship with them. These findings suggest that anxious behaviors resulting from attempts to act racially color-blind might serve as a roadblock for interracial relationship formation, leading to greater assumed disinterest by the partner and contact avoidance. Future research could explicitly examine these outcomes in both one-shot interactions and relationships that develop over time.

Because exhibiting anxious behavior can be deleterious to the formation and development of interracial relationships, research has also considered *why* attempting to be racially color-blind leads to negative nonverbal behaviors for White actors in particular. Apfelbaum, Sommers, et al. (2008, Study 2) demonstrated that trying to act color blind results in cognitive depletion (i.e., taxes cognitive resources) for Whites, thereby limiting their ability to suppress negative nonverbal behaviors. Using the same photo identification task as Study 1, Apfelbaum, Sommers, et al. (2008, Study 2) again had White participants interact with White and Black confederates, but rather than prompting participants to act color blind, researchers measured participants' innate tendency to act color blind, after which they measured cognitive depletion with the Stroop task (Richeson & Shelton, 2003). Results indicated that avoiding the topic of race with a cross-race partner was associated with cognitive depletion, and cognitive depletion mediated the relationship between color-blind behavior and nonverbal unfriendliness in interracial interactions, such that increases in cognitive depletion due to avoidance of race-based target descriptions led to more negative nonverbal behaviors among White participants. These finding suggest that because active attempts to suppress unwanted behaviors tax Whites' cognitive resources, Whites no longer have sufficient resources to successfully control their negative nonverbal behaviors.

Consistent with findings from Apfelbaum, Sommers, et al. (2008), Vorauer, Gagnon, and Sasaki (2009) found that attempts to suppress negative behaviors lead to expressions of negative affect for Whites. The authors asked White and minority participants to interact with one another and manipulated both partners' approach to the interaction by asking them to read a news article that promoted a racially color-blind approach, promoted a multicultural approach, denounced racism, or did not promote a specific approach. The authors found that during interracial interactions, adopting the racially color-blind approach led Whites to focus on suppressing negative behaviors, and this focus mediated the relationship between color-blind ideology and the behavioral expressions of negative affect. These results suggest that Whites in interracial interactions who attempt to appear color blind do not have sufficient resources to monitor the negativity of their own nonverbal behaviors, and that these negative behaviors can "leak out" (see also Shelton et al., 2010). It is also worth noting that, in line with research showing that interacting with interaction partners who exhibit subtle signs of racism can be cognitively taxing for minorities (Murphy, Richeson, Shelton, Rheinschmidt, & Bergsieker, 2013; Richeson, Trawalter, & Shelton, 2005), interacting with racially color-blind White interaction partners can lead to cognitive depletion for minorities (Holoien & Shelton, 2012). These findings reveal both actor and partner effects of racial color blindness on cognitive depletion. Depletion of cognitive resources is important when one considers the interactional contexts in which color-blind approaches to race are often implemented: schools and organizations. If interracial interactions in these settings are cognitively taxing, students and workers may not have sufficient cognitive resources to complete difficult or complex tasks, and as a result, those working together in diverse settings will underperform relative to those in more racially homogeneous settings.

Thus far, we have focused on how being racially color-blind influences White actors and their minority partners, raising the following question: Are racial minorities also affected by embracing a racially color-blind mind-set? To compare the effects of adopting a racially color-blind strategy on Whites and minorities, Vorauer et al. (2009) found that being instructed to adopt a racially color-blind mind-set did not have a significant effect on a desire to prevent negative behaviors or expressed behaviors for minority participants, suggesting that the inhibitory effects of the color-blind approach to race only apply to Whites. These findings may be attributed in part to evidence indicating that minorities' impression management concerns center around being the target of prejudice, rather than being perceived as prejudiced (Richeson & Shelton, 2007). However, future research should more fully explore how adopting a color-blind perspective of race affects minorities, given the paucity of research on the topic.

Despite continuing support for racially color-blind ideology among White Americans (Ryan, Hunt, Weible, Peterson, & Casas, 2007), the research presented herein depicts a dark picture of the consequences of entering interracial interactions with a racially color-blind mind-set. Research consistently shows that attempts to act racially color blind lead to expressions of negative nonverbal behaviors and cognitive depletion for Whites in interracial interactions (Apfelbaum, Sommers, et al., 2008; Holoien & Shelton, 2012; Norton et al., 2006), and interacting with Whites who exhibit negative behaviors is taxing for their minority interaction partners (Holoien & Shelton, 2012). Furthermore, research on the relational consequences of expressing negative nonverbal behaviors during interracial interactions suggests that exhibiting negative nonverbal behaviors disrupts rapport between interaction partners in both the short (Pearson et al., 2008) and long (Shelton et al., 2010; Trail et al., 2009) term.

EFFECTS OF A MULTICULTURAL MIND-SET IN INTERRACIAL INTERACTIONS

Unlike findings regarding the consistently negative consequences of racially color-blind mind-sets, research on how adopting a multicultural mind-set influences interpersonal processes during interracial interactions is more mixed. Some research on the influence of a multicultural mindset on behaviors during interracial interactions demonstrates positive effects. For example, Vorauer et al. (2009) found that relative to a control condition, participants who adopted a multicultural mind-set made more positive other-oriented remarks (i.e., statements directly referencing their partner in a positive light) during written exchanges with a future interaction partner (Study 1) and during actual interactions with an interracial interaction partner (Study 2), relative to a control condition. Furthermore, the positive behavioral effects associated with multiculturalism were observed for both White and minority members of the interaction (Vorauer et al., 2009, Study 2), showing that multiculturalism can lead to positive interpersonal consequences. Similarly, Holoien and Shelton (2012) found that when asked to interact with a minority partner, Whites primed to take a multicultural approach to the interaction exhibited more positive behaviors that were less indicative of prejudice than Whites primed to act racially color blind.

When considered from an actor–partner interdependence model perspective, the positive behaviors that people engage in during interracial interactions are just as important as the negative nonverbal behaviors in shaping interracial rapport and relationship formation. Just as negative nonverbal behaviors can hinder relationship building, research shows that positive behaviors (e.g., perceptions that a partner smiles and appears engaged and interested) play a large role in fostering the development of interracial relationships (Trail et al., 2009). For interracial roommates, Trail et al. (2009) found that being perceived as engaging in positive intimacy-building behaviors was just as important as being perceived as engaging in anxiety-related behaviors in predicting relational outcomes, such as a greater desire to live with their roommate in the future for both the actor (the person perceiving the behaviors) and their partner (the person whose behaviors were perceived).

At first glance, the multicultural approach appears to be an ideal intervention for improving interracial interactions. It enhances perspective taking (Todd & Galinsky, 2012), promotes positive other-oriented remarks (Vorauer et al., 2009), and increases positive behaviors without taxing interaction members' cognitive resources (Holoien & Shelton, 2012). However, research on how multiculturalism influences behaviors during interracial interactions suggests that the relationship between multiculturalism and interracial rapport is not simple and straightforward, and investigations into the importance of context and individual differences present a more nuanced picture of how multicultural ideology may shape interracial interactions.

One important question that recent research has examined is: For whom is a multicultural perspective most likely to effectively promote positive interracial contact? Multiculturalism can be threatening to Whites' values and identities, and for right-wing authoritarians (i.e., people who value respecting authority and societal norms and who view challenges to their social structure and values as threats; Asbrock et al., 2010; Jost, 2006), adopting a multicultural perspective can even lead to more rather than less bias (Kauff, Asbrock, Thörner, & Wagner, 2013). Because right-wing authoritarians are threatened by nonconformity (Duckitt, 2001), they find multiculturalism's emphasis on disrupting current social dynamics by taking power away from Whites (i.e., the current social norm) and redistributing it to empower all races to be extremely threatening. As a result, exposure to multicultural messages leads to decreased acceptance of diversity.

In addition to threatening right-wing authoritarians, adopting a multiculturalism perspective might also lead Whites to feel excluded by the focus on culture and individuality that is espoused by multiculturalism, to the extent that they not feel that their White identity contributes to multiculturalism (Plaut, Garnett, Buffardi, & Sanchez-Burks, 2011). As a result, Whites who feel a strong need to belong show less interest in working for an organization that endorses a multicultural rather than a color-blind approach to race (Plaut et al., 2011), and if White Americans strongly identify with their ethnicity, priming multiculturalism can increase their prejudice toward racial minorities (Kauff et al., 2013; Morrison, Plaut, & Ybarra, 2010).

The potential for negative effects of multiculturalism has also been observed in the context of interracial interactions. In the only study to our knowledge that has examined the moderating factors that can influence the relationship between multiculturalism and behavior during interracial interactions, Vorauer and Sasaki (2010) asked participants to exchange notes with an interracial partner with whom they believed they would have the opportunity to interact at the end of the study. Focusing on multiculturalism before writing to their partner allowed low-prejudice people to relax and exhibit more warmth toward their interracial partner in the written exchange, but for high-prejudice people, multiculturalism was threatening and led them to demonstrate less warmth toward their future interracial partner. As previously reviewed, to the extent that the partner in turn picks up on these behaviors, they will be less likely to want to engage in long-term contact with their White partner (Trail et al., 2009).

Although the research discussed here introduces a potential "dark side" to multiculturalism, it does not preclude the use of multiculturalism as an intervention to foster interracial relationships. Instead, research suggests that it is important to enact multicultural approaches in appropriate settings, where it will help rather than hinder rapport in burgeoning interracial relationships. If, for example, multiculturalism was fostered in settings where Whites are low prejudice and have a tendency to endorse color-blind approaches to race, the advancement of a multicultural approach to interracial interactions could potentially override the negative behavioral effects of color-blind ideology. Although multiculturalism is a potentially effective tool for improving interracial interactions for Whites who are well intentioned and motivated to appear unprejudiced, in contexts in which Whites are high in right-wing authoritarianism or prejudice, multiculturalism may harm rather than help interracial interactions. As discussed in the following section, we suggest that researchers must consider: (a) ways in which the message underlying multiculturalism could be reframed to reduce threat to specific White populations and (b) alternative interventions that benefit a wider range of populations.

SEEKING ALTERNATIVE METHODS FOR IMPROVING INTERRACIAL INTERACTIONS

We presented evidence of how racially color-blind and multicultural mind-sets can influence both partners in interracial interactions. For Whites, adopting a racially color-blind approach can result in cognitively taxing attempts to suppress negative behaviors that ultimately backfire, resulting in ironic increases in negative nonverbal behaviors. For minorities, interacting with these racially color-blind Whites can be cognitively taxing and unpleasant. However, in contrast to color-blind approaches to race, multicultural approaches can have both positive and negative effects on interracial interactions. When Whites in interracial interactions are low in prejudice, multiculturalism can promote positive behaviors that facilitate relationship development, but for Whites who find multiculturalism threatening—like those who are prejudiced, those who are threatened by the idea of change to societal values and structure, or those who fear racial exclusion—multiculturalism can lead to increases in bias and negative behaviors during interracial interactions.

Despite its good intentions, racially color-blind ideology backfires during interracial interactions, and because multiculturalism only fosters positive interracial interactions for low-prejudice individuals, it cannot be blindly applied to any situation. As such, neither can be broadly applied to all interracial interaction contexts, raising the question of whether there exists a panacea for interracial interactions. Although research has yet to uncover this perfect intervention for improving interracial interactions, we present in this section several alternative approaches to interracial interactions that show promise.

Unlike the color-blind approach to race, which seeks to deemphasize group membership, and the multicultural approach, which highlights everyone's unique group membership, dual-identity models emphasize both people's shared (e.g., students at a university, employees at a company) and unique (e.g., racial) identities. Similar to findings from research on multicultural approaches to reducing bias, allowing people to have dual identities (i.e., a common identity and subordinate identities) can be problematic when an interactions partner's subordinate identities are threatening to the values or identities of the other member of the interaction (Crisp, Stone, & Hall, 2006; de la Garza, Falcon, & Garcia, 1996; Hornsey & Hogg, 2000; Smith & Tyler, 1996). However, recent research from Scheepers (2009) and Alter, Aronson, Darley, Rodriguez, and Ruble (2010) suggests that it may be possible to reframe threats into challenges (i.e., making participants feel like they have the resources to handle a frightening or overwhelming situation), providing a promising future avenue for research on how both multiculturalism and dual-identity approaches can improve interracial interactions. Scheepers (2009), for example, found that framing status differences among groups as *stable* (i.e., suggesting that groups will maintain their current status) leads members of high-status groups to frame an intergroup competition in a positive, challenge-oriented rather than negative, threat-oriented light. If researchers, for example, reassure White members of interracial interactions that Whites are and will remain higher status than minority racial groups, Whites should feel less threatened by their minority interaction partner. However, researchers must use caution because framing status differences as stable, rather than in flux, increases threat felt by low-status groups, and as a result, it is possible that the suggested reframing may negatively affect perceptions or behaviors of minority members of interracial interactions. Moreover, framing inequality as stable and increasing social threat for minorities may perpetuate social inequality by worsening the psychological and physical health of minorities (Cole, Kemeny, & Taylor, 1997; Major & O'Brien, 2005), worsening minority performance on stereotype relevant tasks (Steele, 1997) and causing minorities to avoid stereotype-relevant situations (Major, Spencer, Schmader, Wolfe, & Crocker, 1998; Steele, Spencer, & Aronson, 2002)

The option just presented suggests supplementing multiculturalism with additional messages to improve its effectiveness. However, because the effects of modified versions of multiculturalism are not yet known, research must also explore other avenues for fostering interracial relationship development. We see promise in two such avenues: (a) interventions that increase perceptions of outgroup variability and (b) interventions that make people feel similar to outgroup members on nonthreatening dimensions. Recent research shows that increasing individuals' perceptions of variability in outgroup members' traits (e.g., showing people that members of the outgroup are different from each other and have different personalities and traits) can decrease prejudice and discriminatory behaviors toward the outgroup (Brauer & Er-rafiy, 2011; Brauer, Er-rafiy, Kawakami, & Phills, 2012), and Brauer et al.'s (2012) research shows that manipulations of perceived outgroup variability are most effective at reducing prejudice when participants are exposed to the outgroup's negative and positive traits rather than just positive traits of the outgroup. Manipulations of perceived outgroup variability have also been shown to be effective outside of the laboratory. Er-rafiy, Brauer, and Musca (2010) exposed people in the real world (e.g., students and clients seeing a physical therapist) to posters that showed Arabs who varied in age, gender, facial expression, and descriptors accompanying their photo. They found that exposure to the posters not only reduced prejudice toward Arabs but also increased participants' willingness to sit in close proximity to an Arab stranger.

A second promising intervention comes from West, Magee, Gordon, and Gullett (2014). In this work, we manipulated perceived interpersonal similarity between cross-race partners as they entered interactions. Our manipulation of similarity focused on two key attributes. First, the similarities should be *peripheral* to the goals of the interaction and be perceived to have no relationship to any given interaction context. Second, the dimensions must be perceived as self-revealing in that they communicate something important about the self while having no clear valence. Importantly, people need not actually be similar across these dimensions; they just need to think that they are. Participants responded to a series of seemingly trivial dilemmas (e.g., "Would you rather fly or be invisible?"). In cross-race encounters, those who perceived similarity (above and beyond actual similarity) experienced less anxiety, greater interest in sustained contact, and greater accuracy in reading their partner's interest in contact. In small task groups, manipulating perceived similarity bettered communication between partners and subsequently bettered performance on a group task. This work demonstrated one successful approach for promoting positive contact experiences across racial lines that focuses on the importance of improving interpersonal dynamics, rather than racial dynamics, between partners. Although this research has been successfully applied to interracial interactions, researchers have yet to specifically explore whether interaction members' level of prejudice moderates the relationship between perceived similarity and the outcomes we explored. Moreover, explicitly examining whether similarity manipulations are successful for promoting positive interracial interactions in contexts in which race may be seen as threatening (e.g., interactions with the police) would also be an interesting avenue for future research.

CONCLUSION

In sum, although this chapter touched on many promising avenues for improving interracial interactions, scholars must continue to work on improving existing tools and developing new methods for fostering interracial relationships. Despite their popularity across many settings (Apfelbaum, Pauker, et al., 2008; Ely & Thomas, 2001; Kang & Lane, 2010; Peery, 2011; Pollock, 2004; Schofield, 2007; Sommers & Norton, 2008; Thomas & Ely, 1996), color-blind approaches to interracial interactions worsen actors' nonverbal behaviors (Apfelbaum, Sommers, et al., 2008; Norton et al., 2006), cognitively deplete actors (Apfelbaum, Sommers, et al., 2008), and cognitively deplete their interracial partners (Holoien & Shelton, 2012). Although multicultural mind-sets promote positive behaviors during interracial interaction for well-intentioned individuals (Vorauer et al., 2009; Vorauer & Sasaki, 2010), multiculturalism can be threatening to White Americans' identities and values, and as a result, threatened actors behave less warmly toward their minority interaction partners (Vorauer & Sasaki, 2010).

Going forward, researchers should explore not only methods for improving the effectiveness of interventions based on multiculturalism but also alternative tools for cultivating interracial relationships. Interventions promoting a multicultural mind-set must consider ways in which evoked feelings of threat can be reduced by either: (a) modifying the underlying message of multiculturalism in so that Whites no longer feel that their identity or status is being threatened or (b) pairing multiculturalism messages with other tools that reduce the threat by Whites with strong racial identities and Whites who are right-wing authoritarians. In conjunction with developing tools based on multiculturalism, researchers must also explore new methods for improving interracial interactions by investigating whether tools, like those presented here, effectively promote positive interracial interactions for populations susceptible to feeling threatened by minority populations, such as Whites with strong identities and right-wing authoritarians.

REFERENCES

Alter, A. L., Aronson, J., Darley, J. M., Rodriguez, C., & Ruble, D. N. (2010). Rising to the threat: Reducing stereotype threat by reframing the threat as a challenge. *Journal of Experimental Social Psychology, 46*, 166–171. http://dx.doi.org/10.1016/j.jesp.2009.09.014

Apfelbaum, E. P., Pauker, K., Ambady, N., Sommers, S. R., & Norton, M. I. (2008). Learning (not) to talk about race: When older children underperform in social categorization. *Developmental Psychology, 44*, 1513–1518. http://dx.doi.org/10.1037/a0012835

Apfelbaum, E. P., Sommers, S. R., & Norton, M. I. (2008). Seeing race and seeming racist? Evaluating strategic color blindness in social interaction. *Journal of Personality and Social Psychology, 95*, 918–932. http://dx.doi.org/10.1037/a0011990

Asbrock, F., Sibley, C. G., & Duckitt, J. (2010). Right-wing authoritarianism and social dominance orientation and the dimensions of generalized prejudice: A longitudinal test. *European Journal of Personality, 24*, 324–340.

Bergsieker, H. B., Shelton, J. N., & Richeson, J. A. (2010). To be liked versus respected: Divergent goals in interracial interactions. *Journal of Personality and Social Psychology, 99*, 248–264. http://dx.doi.org/10.1037/a0018474

Blascovich, J., Mendes, W. B., Hunter, S. B., Lickel, B., & Kowai-Bell, N. (2001). Perceiver threat in social interactions with stigmatized others. *Journal of Personality and Social Psychology, 80*, 253–267. http://dx.doi.org/10.1037/0022-3514.80.2.253

Brauer, M., & Er-rafiy, A. (2011). Increasing perceived variability reduces prejudice and discrimination. *Journal of Experimental Social Psychology, 47*, 871–881. http://dx.doi.org/10.1016/j.jesp.2011.03.003

Brauer, M., Er-rafiy, A., Kawakami, K., & Phills, C. E. (2012). Describing a group in positive terms reduces prejudice less effectively than describing it in positive and negative terms. *Journal of Experimental Social Psychology, 48*, 757–761. http://dx.doi.org/10.1016/j.jesp.2011.11.002

Brown v. Board of Educ., 347 U.S. 483 (1954).

Cole, S. W., Kemeny, M. E., & Taylor, S. E. (1997). Social identity and physical health: Accelerated HIV progression in rejection-sensitive gay men. *Journal of Personality and Social Psychology, 72*, 320–335. http://dx.doi.org/10.1037/0022-3514.72.2.320

Crisp, R. J., Stone, C. H., & Hall, N. R. (2006). Recategorization and subgroup identification: Predicting and preventing threats from common ingroups. *Personality and Social Psychology Bulletin, 32*, 230–243. http://dx.doi.org/10.1177/0146167205280908

de la Garza, R. O., Falcon, A., & Garcia, F. C. (1996). Will the real Americans please stand up: Anglo and Mexican-American support of core American political values. *American Journal of Political Science, 40*, 335–351. http://dx.doi.org/10.2307/2111627

Dovidio, J. F., Kawakami, K., & Gaertner, S. L. (2002). Implicit and explicit prejudice and interracial interaction. *Journal of Personality and Social Psychology, 82*, 62–68. http://dx.doi.org/10.1037/0022-3514.82.1.62

Dovidio, J. F., West, T. V., Pearson, A. R., Gaertner, S. L., & Kawakami, K. (2007, October). *Racial prejudice and interracial interaction*. Paper presented at the annual meeting of the Society of Experimental Social Psychology, Chicago, IL.

Duckitt, J. (2001). A dual-process cognitive–motivational theory of ideology and prejudice. *Advances in Experimental Social Psychology, 33*, 41–113. http://dx.doi.org/10.1016/S0065-2601(01)80004-6

Ely, R. J., & Thomas, D. A. (2001). Cultural diversity at work: The effects of diversity perspectives on work group processes and outcomes. *Administrative Science Quarterly, 46*, 229–273. http://dx.doi.org/10.2307/2667087

Er-rafiy, A., Brauer, M., & Musca, S. C. (2010). Effective reduction of prejudice and discrimination: Methodological considerations and three field experiments. *Revue Internationale de Psychologie Sociale, 2*, 57–95.

Gotanda, N. (1991). A critique of "Our constitution is color blind." *Stanford Law Review, 44*, 1–68. http://dx.doi.org/10.2307/1228940

Holoien, D. S., & Shelton, J. N. (2012). You deplete me: The cognitive costs of color blindness on ethnic minorities. *Journal of Experimental Social Psychology, 48*, 562–565. http://dx.doi.org/10.1016/j.jesp.2011.09.010

Hornsey, M. J., & Hogg, M. A. (2000). Subgroup relations: A comparison of mutual intergroup differentiation and common ingroup identity models of prejudice reduction. *Personality and Social Psychology Bulletin, 26*, 242–256. http://dx.doi.org/10.1177/0146167200264010

Ito, T. A., & Urland, G. R. (2003). Race and gender on the brain: Electrocortical measures of attention to the race and gender of multiply categorizable individuals. *Journal of Personality and Social Psychology, 85*, 616–626. http://dx.doi.org/10.1037/0022-3514.85.4.616

Jost, J. T. (2006). The end of the end of ideology. *American Psychologist, 61*, 651–670. http://dx.doi.org/10.1037/0003-066X.61.7.651

Kang, J., & Lane, K. (2010). Seeing through color blindness: Implicit bias and the law. *UCLA Law Review, 58*, 465–520.

Kashy, D. A., & Kenny, D. A. (2000). The analysis of data from dyads and groups. In H. T. Reis & C. M. Judd (Eds.), *Handbook of research methods in social and personality psychology* (pp. 451–477). Cambridge, England: Cambridge University Press.

Kauff, M., Asbrock, F., Thörner, S., & Wagner, U. (2013). Side effects of multiculturalism: The interaction effect of a multicultural ideology and authoritarianism on prejudice and diversity beliefs. *Personality and Social Psychology Bulletin, 39*, 305–320. http://dx.doi.org/10.1177/0146167212473160

Major, B., & O'Brien, L. T. (2005). The social psychology of stigma. *Annual Review of Psychology, 56*, 393–421. http://dx.doi.org/10.1146/annurev.psych.56.091103.070137

Major, B., Spencer, S., Schmader, T., Wolfe, C., & Crocker, J. (1998). Coping with negative stereotypes about intellectual performance: The role of psychological disengagement. *Personality and Social Psychology Bulletin, 24*, 34–50. http://dx.doi.org/10.1177/0146167298241003

Markus, H. R., Steele, C. M., & Steele, D. M. (2000). Color blindness as a barrier to inclusion: Assimilation and nonimmigrant minorities. *Daedalus, 129*, 233–259.

Mendes, W. B., Blascovich, J., Lickel, B., & Hunter, S. (2002). Challenge and threat during social interactions with White and Black men. *Personality and Social Psychology Bulletin, 28,* 939–952. http://dx.doi.org/10.1177/014616720202800707

Mendes, W. B., & Koslov, K. (2013). Brittle smiles: Positive biases toward stigmatized and outgroup targets. *Journal of Experimental Psychology: General, 142,* 923–933. http://dx.doi.org/10.1037/a0029663

Morrison, K. R., Plaut, V. C., & Ybarra, O. (2010). Predicting whether multiculturalism positively or negatively influences White Americans' intergroup attitudes: The role of ethnic identification. *Personality and Social Psychology Bulletin, 36,* 1648–1661. http://dx.doi.org/10.1177/0146167210386118

Murphy, M. C., Richeson, J. A., Shelton, J. N., Rheinschmidt, M. L., & Bergsieker, H. B. (2013). Cognitive costs of contemporary prejudice. *Group Processes & Intergroup Relations, 16,* 560–571. http://dx.doi.org/10.1177/1368430212468170

Neville, H. A., Lilly, R. L., Duran, G., Lee, R. M., & Browne, L. (2000). Construction and initial validation of the color-blind racial attitudes scale (CoBRAS). *Journal of Counseling Psychology, 47,* 59–70. http://dx.doi.org/10.1037/0022-0167.47.1.59

Norton, M. I., Sommers, S. R., Apfelbaum, E. P., Pura, N., & Ariely, D. (2006). Color blindness and interracial interaction: Playing the political correctness game. *Psychological Science, 17,* 949–953. http://dx.doi.org/10.1111/j.1467-9280.2006.01810.x

Ortman, J. M., & Guarneri, C. E. (2009). *United States population projections: 2000 to 2050.* Washington, DC: U.S. Census Bureau.

Parents Involved in Community Schools v. Seattle School District No. 1, 551 U.S. 701 (2007).

Pearson, A. R., West, T. V., Dovidio, J. F., Powers, S. R., Buck, R., & Henning, R. (2008). The fragility of intergroup relations: Divergent effects of delayed audiovisual feedback in intergroup and intragroup interaction. *Psychological Science, 19,* 1272–1279. http://dx.doi.org/10.1111/j.1467-9280.2008.02236.x

Peery, D. (2011). Color-blind ideal in a race-conscious reality: The case for a new legal ideal for race relations. *Northwestern Journal of Law & Social Policy, 6,* 473–495.

Plant, E. A. (2004). Responses to interracial interactions over time. *Personality and Social Psychology Bulletin, 30,* 1458–1471. http://dx.doi.org/10.1177/0146167204264244

Plant, E. A., & Butz, D. A. (2006). The causes and consequences of an avoidance-focus for interracial interactions. *Personality and Social Psychology Bulletin, 32,* 833–846. http://dx.doi.org/10.1177/0146167206287182

Plant, E. A., & Devine, P. G. (1998). Internal and external motivation to respond without prejudice. *Journal of Personality and Social Psychology, 75,* 811–832. http://dx.doi.org/10.1037/0022-3514.75.3.811

Plaut, V. C. (2002). Cultural models of diversity in America: The psychology of difference and inclusion. In R. A. Shweder, M. Minow, & H. R. Markus, *Engaging cultural differences: The multicultural challenge in liberal democracies* (pp. 365–395). New York, NY: Russell Sage Foundation.

Plaut, V. C., Garnett, F. G., Buffardi, L. E., & Sanchez-Burks, J. (2011). "What about me?" Perceptions of exclusion and Whites' reactions to multiculturalism. *Journal of Personality and Social Psychology, 101,* 337–353. http://dx.doi.org/10.1037/a0022832

Pollock, M. (2004). Race bending: "Mixed" youth practicing strategic racialization in California. *Anthropology & Education Quarterly, 35,* 30–52. http://dx.doi.org/10.1525/aeq.2004.35.1.30

Reuters. (2013). *Many Americans have no friends of another race: Poll.* Retrieved from http://www.reuters.com/article/2013/08/08/us-usa-poll-race-idUSBRE97704320130808

Richeson, J. A., & Shelton, J. N. (2003). When prejudice does not pay: Effects of interracial contact on executive function. *Psychological Science, 14,* 287–290. http://dx.doi.org/10.1111/1467-9280.03437

Richeson, J. A., & Shelton, J. N. (2007). Negotiating interracial interactions costs, consequences, and possibilities. *Current Directions in Psychological Science, 16,* 316–320. http://dx.doi.org/10.1111/j.1467-8721.2007.00528.x

Richeson, J. A., Trawalter, S., & Shelton, J. N. (2005). African Americans' implicit racial attitudes and the depletion of executive function after interracial interactions. *Social Cognition, 23,* 336–352. http://dx.doi.org/10.1521/soco.2005.23.4.336

Ryan, C. S., Hunt, J. S., Weible, J. A., Peterson, C. R., & Casas, J. F. (2007). Multicultural and color-blind ideology, stereotypes, and ethnocentrism among Black and White Americans. *Group Processes & Intergroup Relations, 10,* 617–637.

Scheepers, D. (2009). Turning social identity threat into challenge: Status stability and cardiovascular reactivity during inter-group competition. *Journal of Experimental Social Psychology, 45,* 228–233. http://dx.doi.org/10.1016/j.jesp.2008.09.011

Schofield, J. W. (2007). The color-blind perspective in school: Causes and consequences. In J. A. Banks & C. A. McGee Banks (Eds.), *Multicultural education: Issues and perspectives* (6th ed., pp. 271–295). Hoboken, NJ: Wiley.

Shelton, J. N., West, T. V., & Trail, T. E. (2010). Concerns about appearing prejudiced: Implications for anxiety during daily interracial interactions. *Group Processes & Intergroup Relations, 13,* 329–344. http://dx.doi.org/10.1177/1368430209344869

Shook, N. J., & Fazio, R. H. (2008a). Interracial roommate relationships: An experimental field test of the contact hypothesis. *Psychological Science, 19,* 717–723. http://dx.doi.org/10.1111/j.1467-9280.2008.02147.x

Shook, N. J., & Fazio, R. H. (2008b). Roommate relationships: A comparison of interracial and same-race living situations. *Group Processes & Intergroup Relations, 11,* 425–437. http://dx.doi.org/10.1177/1368430208095398

Smith, H. J., & Tyler, T. R. (1996). Justice and power: When will justice concerns encourage the advantaged to support policies which redistribute economic resources and the disadvantaged to willingly obey the law? *European Journal of Social Psychology, 26,* 171–200. http://dx.doi.org/10.1002/(SICI)1099-0992(199603)26:2<171::AID-EJSP742>3.0.CO;2-8

Sommers, S. R., & Norton, M. I. (2008). Race and jury selection: Psychological perspectives on the peremptory challenge debate. *American Psychologist, 63,* 527–539. http://dx.doi.org/10.1037/0003-066X.63.6.527

Steele, C. M. (1997). A threat in the air. How stereotypes shape intellectual identity and performance. *American Psychologist, 52,* 613–629. http://dx.doi.org/10.1037/0003-066X.52.6.613

Steele, C. M., Spencer, S. J., & Aronson, J. (2002). Contending with group image: The psychology of stereotype and social identity threat. *Advances in Experimental Social Psychology, 34,* 379–440. http://dx.doi.org/10.1016/S0065-2601(02)80009-0

Thomas, D. A., & Ely, R. J. (1996). Making differences matter. *Harvard Business Review, 74,* 79–90.

Todd, A. R., & Galinsky, A. D. (2012). The reciprocal link between multiculturalism and perspective-taking: How ideological and self-regulatory approaches to managing diversity reinforce each other. *Journal of Experimental Social Psychology, 48,* 1394–1398. http://dx.doi.org/10.1016/j.jesp.2012.07.007

Toosi, N. R., Babbitt, L. G., Ambady, N., & Sommers, S. R. (2012). Dyadic interracial interactions: A meta-analysis. *Psychological Bulletin, 138,* 1–27. http://dx.doi.org/10.1037/a0025767

Trail, T. E., Shelton, J. N., & West, T. V. (2009). Interracial roommate relationships: Negotiating daily interactions. *Personality and Social Psychology Bulletin, 35,* 671–684. http://dx.doi.org/10.1177/0146167209332741

Trawalter, S., Richeson, J. A., & Shelton, J. N. (2009). Predicting behavior during interracial interactions: A stress and coping approach. *Personality and Social Psychology Review, 13,* 243–268. http://dx.doi.org/10.1177/1088868309345850

Vorauer, J. D., Gagnon, A., & Sasaki, S. J. (2009). Salient intergroup ideology and intergroup interaction. *Psychological Science, 20,* 838–845. http://dx.doi.org/10.1111/j.1467-9280.2009.02369.x

Vorauer, J. D., & Sasaki, S. J. (2010). In need of liberation or constraint? How intergroup attitudes moderate the behavioral implications of intergroup ideologies [for erratum, see http://dx.doi.org/10.1016/j.jesp.2014.09.008]. *Journal of Experimental Social Psychology, 46,* 133–138. http://dx.doi.org/10.1016/j.jesp.2009.08.013

West, T. V. (2011). Interpersonal perception in cross-group interactions: Challenges and potential solutions. *European Review of Social Psychology, 22,* 364–401. http://dx.doi.org/10.1080/10463283.2011.641328

West, T. V., Magee, J. C., Gordon, S. H., & Gullett, L. (2014). A little similarity goes a long way: The effects of peripheral but self-revealing similarities on improving and sustaining interracial relationships. *Journal of Personality and Social Psychology, 107,* 81–100. http://dx.doi.org/10.1037/a0036556

West, T. V., Shelton, J. N., & Trail, T. E. (2009). Relational anxiety in interracial interactions. *Psychological Science, 20,* 289–292. http://dx.doi.org/10.1111/j.1467-9280.2009.02289.x

Wolsko, C., Park, B., Judd, C. M., & Wittenbrink, B. (2000). Framing interethnic ideology: Effects of multicultural and color-blind perspectives on judgments of groups and individuals. *Journal of Personality and Social Psychology, 78,* 635–654. http://dx.doi.org/10.1037/0022-3514.78.4.635

U.S. Census Bureau. (2012). *State and county quick facts.* Retrieved from http://quickfacts.census.gov/qfd/states/00000.html

5

AN INTERNATIONAL PERSPECTIVE ON COLOR CONSCIOUSNESS: BRAZIL AND THE UNIVERSALIZATION OF ANTIRACIST COUNTER-PUBLICS

JONATHAN WARREN

On the eve of the centennial of the abolition of slavery in the United States, James Baldwin (1963) offered the following counsel to his nephew: "You can only be destroyed by believing that you really are what the white world calls a nigger. I tell you this because I love you, and please don't you ever forget it" (p. 18).

To follow such advice is not easy in the present, but it was even more challenging in the era of Jim Crow segregation in which anti-Black discourses emanated from almost every corner of White America. Baldwin, however, was no utopian. Black men and women could avoid such a fate because a vibrant Black *counterpublic* sphere existed—Nancy Fraser's (1990) word for the political space where "subordinated social groups invent and circulate counterdiscourses" and "formulate oppositional interpretations of their needs, identities and interests" (pp. 56–80). Over the centuries, Black churches, songs, schools, abolitionists, poets, journalists, activists, artists, educators, and essayists had

http://dx.doi.org/10.1037/14754-006
The Myth of Racial Color Blindness: Manifestations, Dynamics, and Impact, H. A. Neville, M. E. Gallardo, and D. W. Sue (Editors)

managed to forge a Black country against great odds (Singh, 2005). In this world, one heard a different story about nation, Blackness, and Whiteness. Here Blackness was celebrated rather than pathologized, Whites criticized and pitied, racism named and discussed, and American myths of fairness, individualism, exceptionalism, and freedom conditionalized, if not exploded.

Fifty years hence, it should be obvious to most that the liberation of the United States, and not just Black America, requires building on and universalizing the Black counterpublics that have allowed so many to escape self-destruction. Yet as the United States, or at least White America, has moved from essentialist racism (i.e., race as a marker of ontological or biological difference) toward racial color blindness (i.e., race as a marker of racism and thus something that should be overlooked), these counterpublics have been attacked rather than nurtured. This is largely because Black counterpublics practice color consciousness. For example, within these arenas, it is viewed as racist if one does not see race and the difference that it makes in people's lives. The racially color-blind code of conduct, in contrast, values avoiding or attempting to overlook race. Thus, from the vantage of racially color-blind America, these counterpublics should be reduced, if not eradicated, if racial progress is to be had. This built-in antipathy toward Black and other race-cognizant counterpublics is one of the central reasons critical race scholars have targeted racial color blindness for change. An understanding of race in Brazil, as I detail here, helps greatly to advance this project of undoing racial color blindness and building color consciousness in the United States.

THE BURDEN OF NOT BEING BLACK

A classic example of the attack on Black counterpublics in the era of racial color blindness is Signithia Fordham and John Ogbu's (1986) thesis of Black educational underachievement, or what they called the "burden of 'acting White.'" They argued that a primary reason that "caste-like minorities," both in the United States and elsewhere, tended to have poorer academic achievement was due to their counterpublics. Blacks and other marginalized racial groups putatively defined educational achievement in opposition to their racial identities and thus, according to Fordham and Ogbu, sabotaged themselves and their peers' educational performance (p. 177). In *The Journal of Blacks in Higher Education*, Cross and Slater (1995) put it this way: "Among young black men, in particular, studying hard and getting good grades are disparaged because these efforts are looked upon as 'acting white'" (p. 10). This thesis, based on a questionable interpretation of only 33 interviews, not only came to be widely accepted in the education literature but also among policymakers. For instance, Barack Obama (1994), as a state legislator, stated in an interview for National Public Radio that "many Black students think doing well in school is 'a White thing'" and this, he claimed, was one of the main reasons for Black underachievement in the United States.

If one assumes this is indeed a primary reason why Black children do not perform as well as White students, one straightforward policy response would be to attempt to harness these subjectivities by schooling Black children about the specifics of the ongoing, systemic efforts to ensure the miseducation of Black people and therefore, in this way, motivate them to study harder by demonstrating that, in fact, Black underachievement is very much a White thing. Yet such a course of action is never suggested. Instead, these theories are used to target Black counterpublics for elimination. Indeed, Fordham and Ogbu (1986) explicitly recommended that teachers encourage their Black students to detach themselves from Black counterpublics and think of themselves as nonracialized individuals (p. 192). True to the color-blind paradigm of race, they should detach and distance themselves from their race-based communities and work on identifying as nonracial individuals as a remedy to their subordination.

Brazil, much like the rest of Latin America, provides the opportunity to empirically test this thesis. Throughout the region, one encounters castelike minorities without a counterpublic. Consequently, most non-Whites have been found to covet rather than shun Whiteness (Hanchard, 1998; Twine, 1998; Warren & Twine, 2002). They aspire to Whiten themselves biologically, socially, and culturally. The following excerpt taken from an interview with Gabrielle (a 32-year-old Black maid and mother of three) is a common example of how Whiteness is hypervalued. "It's not that I felt better than Blacks, but I used to talk to my mother like this: 'Mother, when I get married I will marry a White man . . . because I don't want my children to be dark like me.' Then I used to say that, 'If I found a White man to marry, I would marry him so that my kids wouldn't be little darkies'" (Warren, 2001, p. 243).

To be clear, Black and other antiracist counterpublics exist in Brazil. But relative to the United States, they are fewer, more nascent, and less institutionalized. As a result, most people of color are not saddled with a concern with being associated with Whiteness, which the above quote helps to illustrate. However, contrary to what the "burden of acting White" boosters would predict, this has not translated into higher levels of educational achievement for caste-like minorities in Brazil. In fact, the educational gap between Blacks and Whites is far greater in Brazil than in the United States (Telles, 2004; Warren, 1997). The situation in Brazil has been described by many as "educational apartheid" because most Whites attend private schools while the vast majority of non-White students attend public schools, which have been neglected and sorely underfunded due to racist attitudes (Otis, 2013; Telles, 2004, p. 125). Some of the effects of this apartheid system have been mitigated at the higher education level by the implementation of affirmative action policies in the past decade. Yet Whites still continue to be 3 times more likely to attend college or university than Blacks ("Race in Brazil," 2012).

As if self-loathing were not enough, the relative absence of a counterpublic has resulted in the near universalization of the racial color blindness. There is a tendency among Brazilians of color to "refrain from discussions of racism even in the contexts of community and family" (Sheriff, 2001, p. 62; Twine, 1998). In her ethnography of a poor community in Rio de Janeiro, Robin Sheriff found that "very few informants . . . were able to recall hearing stories about the slavery era, although the grandparents and great-grandparents of a number of the older people I knew had been slaves" (Sheriff, 2001, p. 65). She continued,

> Most people told me . . . that their parents had talked about neither slavery nor racism when they were growing up. When I asked younger informants in their teens and twenties if their parents had ever discussed racism with them, they rarely elaborated, saying simply, 'No, they never talked about it' or 'They don't dwell on it.' (Sheriff, 2001, p. 66)

Such an absence of color consciousness in Black neighborhoods or families in the United States is rare and almost unimaginable. In these spheres, unlike what researchers have found among most African and indigenous-descent Brazilians, White privilege, race, and racism are frequently identified, analyzed, and critiqued.

Absent this space of withdrawal and group formation in Brazil, where social groups that are marginalized by race and class can create and disseminate alternative narratives and definitions of their needs, identities, and interests, it has proven extremely difficult to reduce racial inequalities and the symbolic forms of racism on which they hinge. Or, as Eugene Robinson (1999), a Latin American correspondent for the *The Washington Post* observed, the absence of a racial identity and concomitant counterpublic in Brazil has "left those at the bottom of the ladder without an identity to hold them together and push them forward, without a group. It [has] left them weaker, more helpless, more isolated. It [has] left them alone" (p. 266).

THE SUBJECTS OF HISTORY

A small but important subset of Brazilian educators and activists have long appreciated how debilitating the absence of such a counterpublic has been for the poor, the majority of whom are predominantly of color— the *povo* [people] as they are called in much of Brazil—not just in terms of education but also with regard to infant mortality (e.g., 37 per 1,000 for Whites versus 62 per 1,000 for non-Whites in 1997), homicide rates (non-Whites are 126% more likely to be killed by homicide in 2013), political representations (e.g., only two of the 81 senators are Black in 2013), and income (e.g., non-Whites have an income level half that of Whites in 2013; Bailey, 2009; "Desiqualdade Racial no Brasil e o Sistema das Cotas," 2013; Otis, 2013; Telles, 2004). Perhaps most famously, in *Pedagogy of the Oppressed*, Paulo Freire (2000) argued that the absence of a counterpublic among the poor in Brazil was what undergirded their marginalization. Freire believed that the *povo* would remain forever disempowered until they were able to purge the perceptions of themselves as subhuman and inferior. Thus, Freire worked on developing a methodology for eliminating this internalized racism and classism among the poor. He sought to turn the oppressed from objects, "those who are known and acted upon," to subjects, "those who know and act" (Freire, 2000, p. 20).

Freire focused his so-called pedagogy of the oppressed on literacy in part because literacy was required to be able to vote in the 1960s. Many of his disciples in Brazil and elsewhere have advanced his methodology but some-times through different means. For example, in the Jequitinhonha Valley in Brazil, a friar from the Netherlands, Johann van der Pole (aka Frei Chico), and a local artist of African and indigenous descent, Maria Lira Marques, focused on excavating, nurturing, and celebrating popular culture (Macklin & Warren, 2015). Rather than using Freire's approach—literacy campaigns as a tool for transforming subjectivities and advancing human security—they emphasized the culture of the people and most especially popular religion as a tool for "helping the people to value what they already have" (Warren, 2012, p. 135).

In interviews, Frei Chico told me that one of the first concrete steps taken in this direction began in the shower (Warren, 2012, p. 135). Because there are no ceilings in most homes in the Jequitinhonha Valley, sound car-ries readily from one room to the next. While bathing, Ms. Fila, the cook for the parochial house where the friar lived, would sing while carrying out her daily chores. Listening to them as he bathed, he was moved by their beauty. These songs inspired him to establish the Troubadours of the Valley, a choir that performed the songs of the people of the valley.

The members of the choir, encumbered as they were with a kind of internalized colonialism described by Frantz Fanon (2008) in North Africa, were initially reluctant to perform the songs of the *povo*. People's feelings of inferiority and inadequacy were reflected and intertwined with how they saw their own culture. According to Frei Chico, they would say, "Ah no, this is not beautiful, no, we are not going to sing this, no" (Warren, 2012, p. 135). Ms. Fila herself considered them *bobagem* ("foolishness"; Warren, 2012, p. 135).

The friar recalled that "they wanted to perform the songs that they heard on the radio. They were embarrassed and ashamed of their own culture. And when the choir eventually appeared on TV, the director of the bank and hospital," the descendants of the planter class, "reacted badly" (Warren, 2012, p. 135). They interpreted these shows as yet another way of signifying the Jequitinhonha Valley's lack of modernity, its backwardness. According to Frei Chico, there was the general mentality that "this culture didn't have any value" (Warren, 2012, p. 135). However, as this cultural movement grew, "the people," recalls the friar, "began to believe and have confidence in their culture and themselves" (Warren, 2012, p. 135). All observers of the region agree that this increase in the self-esteem of the people sparked a sociopolitical revolution that led to a substantial reduction in poverty, racism, and social inequalities (Warren, in press). The challenge, then, as is the case in the United States, is how to elaborate and scale up such counterpublics.

COMPARATIVE RACIAL FORMATIONS

The reasons for the meager antiracist counterpublics in Brazil have to do, of course, with many factors. One of them is the timing among working-class formations, slavery, and democracy. In the United States, White men who were not property owners achieved the right to vote before the abolition of slavery. Moreover, manufacturing expanded rapidly, especially in the Northeast, before abolition. As David Roediger (2007) pointed out in *The Wages of Whiteness*, this meant that Whiteness came to be a salient feature of the identities of the proletariat of European descent. Blue-collar work came to be associated with Whiteness—a racialization that labor encouraged for both symbolic and utilitarian reasons. Also political institutions—in particular, the Democratic Party—became complicit with nurturing White publics as a way to generate political support in opposition to the Republican Party.

In Brazil, the abolition of slavery took place before either industrialization or democratization. Slavery ended in 1888. Manufacturing began emerging in São Paulo in the 1910s, and suffrage was not extended to the nonelite until 1988. The end result was that a White proletariat—with a capital W—never emerged in Brazil. Consequently, the Brazilian racial order was not reinforced through White terrorism and aggressive intraclass racism. Most Blacks were kept out of manufacturing jobs (Andrews, 1991), and various pressure was applied to children not to partner with Blacks, but these forms of anti-Black racism were much less organized and institutionalized than in the United States. The bottom line was that poor people were less segregated and divided by race, which worked against the production of Black identified communities and counterpublics.

The distinction in slavery was another contributing factor to the different degrees and quality of Brazilian counterpublics. In the United States, the slave population was self-reproducing. In Brazil, as in the rest of Latin America, slaves were manumitted or worked to death and then replaced by the importation of new peoples from Africa. Among other things, this meant that ethnic distinctions were sharper and the language skills more diverse among Afro-Brazilians, which worked against the formation of race-based communitarian identities.

Another distinction was that enslaved people in Brazil worked in urban and rural areas and in various trades as well as in service jobs and the agricultural sector. In the United States, urban slaves existed, but the vast majority were rural, agricultural workers; this did not change much for free African American workers after abolition until the great migration during World War I. This occupational and regional homogeneity certainly also helped to facilitate cohesion, solidarity, and counterpublics in the United States.

Ironically, formal segregation in the United States—in which Black churches, schools, stores, neighborhoods, newspapers, and so on were fostered—was perhaps the most important variable responsible for creating vibrant Black counterpublics. Racial segregation had long existed in Brazil but in a much more de facto, less codified way than in the United States with its so-called "one-drop rule" and formalization of "separate but equal" by the U.S. Supreme Court through the *Plessy v. Ferguson* decision in 1896. Absent these Black institutions, and the Black professionals and intellectuals they supported, it should not be surprising that Black counterpublics did not emerge with nearly the same gusto in Brazil.

MESTIÇO NATIONALISM

Mestiço, or mixed-race nationalism, was another key variable working against the formation of a Black counterpublic in Brazil in the 20th century. In an attempt to challenge the tradition of Eurocentrism in Brazil (Skidmore, 1993), modernist Brazilian intellectuals of the 1920s and 1930s attempted to celebrate the culture of the common people instead of the elites and the Europeans that they aspired to emulate. The best-known figure of this movement was the sociologist Gilberto Freyre. A student of Franz Boas at Columbia University, Freyre "declared official Brazil a 'phony and ridiculous' Europhile version that 'hid' the real Brazil" (Vianna, 1999, p. 9). The real Brazil, in the opinion of Freyre and others, was the culture of the nonelite, mixed-race population who made up the vast majority of the country. As part of this project, academics, artists, and public intellectuals appreciated that the valorization of Brazilianness required an embrace, rather than negation, of Blackness. One of their first forays in this direction was the celebration of samba, the music created by those who lived in the poor, squatter communities of Rio de Janeiro. In a 1926 newspaper article titled "On the Valorization of Things Black," Freyre wrote:

> Yesterday, along with some friends . . . I spent an evening-that-almost-reached-morning listening to Pixinguinha, a mulato, playing some of his carnival music accompanied by Dong, another mulato, on the guitar and by a (really black) black fellow, Patricio, singing. . . . As we listened, [we] could feel the great Brazil that is growing half-hidden by [the mixed-race Brazilians who] try to appear European and North American. (as cited in Vianna, 1999, p. 9)

Freyre (1986) would go on to develop these ideas further in the canonical *The Master and the Slaves*. According to Vianna (1999),

> Freyre's great feat was to provide a positive theoretical color for mestiço culture, defining 'things Brazilian' as a combination—partly harmonious, partly conflictive—of African, Portuguese, and indigenous traits, the product of a historical encounter between "the big house and the slave quarters." (p. 43)

Thus, the *mestiço* was transformed from being a sign of Brazilian backwardness into something to be nurtured, the very guarantee of Brazil's distinctiveness among nations and the mark of its destiny.

The move to define racial mixing as a positive rather than a negative, as part of a broader strategy for embracing the ordinary Brazilian over the European, eventually took hold of official Brazil. In 1930, the professional and urban working classes, military, and manufacturing elite backed a revolution against the planter classes who had controlled Brazil for centuries. Searching for a way to distinguish and legitimate this regime, the *Estado Novo* ("New State"; 1930–1945), from the so-called First Republic (1889–1930), Getulio Vargas's administration adopted *mestiço* nationalism as state ideology. Consequently, many of the cultural products of the *povo*, which had been scorned by previous generations of elites and intellectuals, such as *feijoada* (a popular bean dish) and samba were embraced as the icons of nation. Perhaps most important, Brazilians adopted as their foundational narrative that they were a mixed-race people—a fact to take pride in and celebrate.

In Freyre's own texts, his celebration of the *mestiço* was still racist. Whites gave all the prized institutions such as democracy, markets, and Christianity; blacks contributed dance and music; and Indians, a few foods and some words to the Portuguese language (1986). This racist residue could have been rectified were it not for the fact that mixed-race nationalism became a tool for silencing a reckoning with racism. As Brazilians adopted the celebration of the *mestiço* as official orthodoxy, the corollary that took hold was that Brazil was a racial democracy. In the context of Nazi Germany and a Jim Crow United States, it is understandable why *mestiço* nationalism took on this meaning. Unfortunately, however, this interpretation created a silence around the question of race that resulted in halting most discussions of racism and with it discourses, identities, policies, institutions, and social movements that could have fostered greater racial equality. For to suggest that race mattered was to directly call into question and challenge the central myth of nation.

LEARNING RACIAL COLOR BLINDNESS AND CONSCIOUSNESS

Thus far, we have seen how Brazil can help one better appreciate the value of certain counterpublics that exist in the United States and why it would be a major mistake to attempt to eliminate them as part of a project to reduce or eliminate racial disparities. These are insights that have yet to be grasped by much of White America, and thus the study of race in Brazil offers a valuable heuristic tool when working with this population. Fortunately, however, these are not claims about which most U.S. antiracists (scholars, activists, and organizations working to reduce racial inequalities) need to be convinced. There is, in fact, an emerging consensus among critical race scholars that these counterpublics, or at least facets of them, should be expanded. Moreover, for reasons discussed earlier, there is broad agreement that the mainstream mode of race talk—namely, racial color blindness—needs to be superseded by color consciousness. For this task, too, a deeper understanding of race in Brazil is of great use.

Having grown up in White, rural Michigan in the 1960s and 1970s, I was accustomed to anti-Black and anti-Indian discourses as well as racially color-blind discourses in White institutions and cultural spaces, but not within communities of color. Blacks in lower Michigan and Chicago and indigenous peoples in Minnesota and Wisconsin—the principal communities of color with which I had contact—were race cognizant and held a very different vision of nation, Whiteness, and race. Thus, the absence of counterpublics among most African and indigenous descent Brazilians immediately captured my attention when I began conducting research on race in the state of Rio de Janeiro in 1992.

Despite the fact that everyone on TV was White; that all the local and national political and economic elite were White; that many physical spaces associated with status, such as private clubs and malls, were White only; and that crudely racist comments circulated widely (e.g., "Bananas are the favorite food of Blacks"), non-Whites, most of whom were the descendants of slaves, saw themselves and their world through the same lens that Whites did (Warren, 2001). This reality helped me to see an assumption that had previously been invisible. In the United States, I had presumed that people of color's competencies were largely a reflexive response to their racial location rather than something learned. Moreover, I chalked up White ineptitude and clumsiness in discussing race largely to the fact that they did not inhabit a racially subordinate position. In short, I had a social determinist understanding of racial consciousness.

In working with U.S. Whites, most of them political progressives, in classrooms and workshops in an attempt to build racial literacy, I have found that this assumption is widely shared (Warren, 2014, p. 111). This is a problem because it often lends itself to inaction or disengagement from the difficult and arduous task of building racial literacy. It can become an easy out, in my experience, for Whites unsettled by the challenges to their identities and social worlds that emerge as they become color conscious. If one assumes that one has to be "of color" to understand racism, then what is the point of studying racism? This belief can also render invisible the tremendous amount of labor and struggle that has gone and continues to go into the production of color-conscious counterpublics. Such knowledge is reduced to a mechanistic response to racism. Insight into the process of building racial literacy, a wisdom that could be gleaned from these communities, is not even considered, let alone consulted. Scrutiny is directed away from the true culprits: the families, schools, media, and communities, which are actively producing racial color blindness and its corollary, racial illiteracy (Warren, 2014, p. 111).

The supposition that oppression is the font of sociological wisdom can also result in the unhealthy tendency to exaggerate, distort, or even fabricate subaltern identities (Warren, 2014, p. 111). I, like others, have found that it is common for previously closeted, unknown, or forgotten ethnic/racial ancestries to be asserted as racially color-blind individuals become more racially cognizant. This can, of course, be salutary. For example, I have had some Asian American students begin to affirm their Asianness—something they may have minimized or hidden, due, in part, to the desire to "fit in" to White neighborhoods or social networks. The problem is not with the attempt to assert stigmatized ancestries but rather with the move to claim certain identities as a way of avoiding one's Whiteness, sidestepping one's deficits, or wanting to assert one's political allegiances because one presumes that one must be "of color" to be antiracist (see Kivel, 2002).

A related practice is the foregrounding of class, gender, and sexual discourses and identities. This too can be a positive development. It may indicate that students are appreciating how race is situated within a complex sociopolitical web and that they are considering, sometimes for the first time, the significance of other axes of power, such as sexuality. Yet more often than not, class, gender, and sexuality are raised to deflect attention away from race.

It is a way to suggest that race is really not as important as the tone or content of the course or workshop implies that it is.

The central point here is that a study of race in Brazil can help students, teachers, and scholars of race, as it once helped me, to see and problematize social determinism. This assumption—and the problems that come with it—can more easily be dislodged as one learns about race and the absence of counterpublics in Brazil. Familiarization with this empirical reality helps Whites and others to see more clearly how racial literacy is not the mechanistic by-product of racial marginalization, and therefore Whites, too, can become racially literate (Warren, 2014; Warren & Sue, 2011).

LIBERAL RACISM

It is common for critical race scholars to suggest that Whites balk at dealing with race because they do not wish to jeopardize or relinquish their relative group position and power. White investment in White privilege, it is argued, inhibits them from considering, let alone forging, counter-hegemonic racial understandings. For example, Zeus Leonardo (2005) wrote that "white subjects do not forge . . . counter-hegemonic racial understandings because their lives . . . depend on a certain development; that is, color-blind strategies that maintain their supremacy as a group" (p. 44). This could be read to suggest that White lives, meaning their identities and worldview, depend on their racial ignorance. However, given the influence of the rational choice assumption that human agency is driven by material gain or interests, such statements are usually interpreted as implying that White resistance to color consciousness is driven by a defense of their racial power and privilege. Whites are presumed to resist addressing and reflecting on race (i.e., becoming color conscious), let along challenging racist practices, because they materially benefit from the racial status quo.

It is dubious whether Whites have actually benefited from White supremacy given how racial politics were central to Nixon's silent majority, Reagan's neoliberalism, and Bush's electoral victory in 2000. The evidence is indisputable that this conservative project has had tremendously negative consequences for people of color *and Whites*: regressive taxation policy, investments in the military and prison system rather than education and transportation, unwise and costly wars, big business–biased policies and regulatory systems, poor or no health care, and the erosion of community and environmental destruction due to suburban sprawl anchored in White flight.

In my experience, the research on race in Brazil and throughout Latin America helps scholars and students of race to better grasp this important point about how racial frameworks and identities are not driven exclusively or even primarily by profit or material gain. As detailed earlier, communities of color have not constructed counter-hegemonic discourses in Brazil, even though it would clearly be in their socioeconomic interests to do so. Instead, a White supremacist consciousness—defined by racial color blindness, race evasiveness, and Whitening narratives—prevails. As is the case with U.S. Whites, the barriers to building color consciousness have to do with identities and worldviews rather than interests.

This is a significant insight, at least for antiracist pedagogues, because I have found that when I stopped assuming that White resistance was instrumental in origin, I became a more effective teacher. Working from the perspective that Whites were motivated primarily by their racial interests as Whites, I was not as concerned as I should have been with identifying the narratives and the social isolation that were impeding them from moving from racial color blindness to race cognizance, let alone developing ways to help Whites to renarrate their lives and cope with their ostracism from family and friends. Instead, I was focused on getting Whites to deal with their privilege, and then I would dismissively chalk up their resistance to this lesson as being motivated by a defense of this privilege (Warren, 2014).

The study of race in Brazil not only helps one to better see the fallacy of instrumentalist assumptions about racial color blindness but also proves a potent heuristic device for challenging the various cultural assumptions that impede the development of color consciousness and racial literacy. For example, one cornerstone of White identities in the United States is what bell hooks (1992) called the "myth of sameness." In teaching Whites, she found that they

> have a deep emotional investment in the myth of "sameness". . . . Often their rage erupts because they believe that all ways of looking that highlight difference subvert the liberal belief in a universal subjectivity (we are all just people) that they think will make racism disappear. (hooks, 1992, p. 167)

Thus, even when Whites appreciate that racism is a deep-seated problem in their communities and can reflect on it in fairly sophisticated ways, they often resist race-cognizant remedies. They do not readily appreciate, to quote Kimberle Crenshaw (1998), how "treating different things the same can generate as much inequality as treating the same things differently" (p. 285). Indeed, there is an inclination to consider unfair, if not racist, race-cognizant initiatives such as affirmative action or the establishment of Indian-only elementary schools.

This myth of sameness is rooted, as Ruth Frankenberg (1993) noted, in a liberal humanist assumption that "proposes an essential human sameness to which 'race' is added as a secondary characteristic" (p. 147). Humans are believed to be "composed of a core or essence to which other qualities," such as race, "are later added" (Frankenberg, 1993, p. 148). If human beings are ontological equivalents, then it follows that they should be dealt with the same regardless of race, class, gender, sexuality, and so on. Treating individuals differently based on nonessential social traits or locations such as race is judged improper. One of Frankenberg's interviewees, Irene Esterley, described her frustration looking for a teaching job in a school district that was at the time primarily recruiting teachers of color: "I resent it particularly because I feel that people should be considered for who they are as a human being and not as this, that, or the other—who you are, regardless of outside trappings—[there's an] inner person, shouting to get out" (Frankenberg, 1993, p. 149).

The belief that "we are all just people" also lends itself to postracial fantasies. Distinct from the race cognizant ideal in which subjects will one day be able to embrace their social, historical, cultural, and phenotypical distinctions and simultaneously enjoy the privileges of full citizenship, the liberal humanist vision for the future is one in which racial subjects no longer exist. This postracial dream feeds back into a racially color-blind sensibility. If the ultimate goal is racelessness, then the impulse is to regard as counterproductive social-cultural movements, which burnish racial and ethnic identities. They are believed to be animating identities that should be in decline as progress is made.

Here again, a familiarity with race in Brazil can be beneficial. One teaching approach that I often use to challenge the myth of sameness is to detail the Latin American experience with color-blind "antiracism." During much of the 20th century, Latin American governments, intellectuals, and publics attempted to undo racism via race-evasive approaches. Data on race were not kept. Citizens were encouraged to take on nonracial, universal identities such as those of nation, class, or modern cosmopolitans. The outcome was, as we have seen in the case of Brazil, disastrous. Counterpublics were stifled, and White supremacy became more entrenched (Warren & Sue, 2011). Thus, Latin America helps to teach how it is often through race—not by its negation or avoidance—that racial hierarchies are dismantled.

NEXT STEPS

The next phase of antiracism in the United States and Brazil will likely bump up against the epistemological limits of multiculturalism. To move closer toward full emancipation, cultures will have to be violated rather than respected. In the United States, the task is to expand on Black and other antiracist counterpublics that exist in the United States. This will inevitably entail upending White identities and worldviews to move a larger percentage of mainstream America from racial color blindness toward racial color consciousness.

Unfortunately, this is not a project that universities, funding entities, and public school systems in the United States are keen to support at present. In my experience, it is copacetic to seek and gain monies to enable White teachers to build color consciousness if done in the name of establishing rapport with Black students or out of respect for racial diversity. But administrators and publics, even in more progressive cities such as Seattle, do not want to hear that White students should be disabused of racial color blindness and schooled in race cognizance as part of a standard curriculum. This is politically beyond the pale at present (Warren, 2014).

This reality should not inhibit us from pushing forward in those arenas in which we have more influence and say: scholarship, workshops, and in the classroom. In my experience, U.S. antiracists doing good work in these spheres are largely unaware of the race scholarship in Brazil and elsewhere in the world. If nothing else, I hope that this chapter motivates some U.S. antiracists to explore and engage with this international scholarship by convincing them of how valuable this literature can be in helping to advance our theoretical understanding and developing effective teaching strategies for uprooting racial color blindness and building color consciousness in the United States.

REFERENCES

Andrews, G. R. (1991). *Blacks & Whites in São Paulo, Brazil, 1888–1988*. Madison: University of Wisconsin Press.

Baldwin, J. (1963). *The fire next time*. New York, NY: The Dial Press.

Bailey, S. R. (2009). *Legacies of race: Identities, attitudes, and politics in Brazil*. Stanford, CA: Stanford University Press.

Crenshaw, K. W. (1998). Color blindness, history, and the law. In W. Lubiano (Ed.), *The house that race built* (pp. 280–288). New York, NY: Vantage Books.

Cross, T., & Slater, R. B. (1995). Why, after 15 years of gains, are Black SAT scores now losing ground on White scores? *The Journal of Blacks in Higher Education, 9*, 10–11.

Desiqualdade racial no Brasil e o sistema das cotas [Racial inequality in Brazil and affirmative action]. (2013). *Imagohistoria* [Imagine history]. Retrieved from http://imagohistoria.blogspot.com/2013/06/desigualdade-racial-no-brasil-e-o.html

Fanon, F. (2008). *Black skin, White masks* (R. Philcox, Trans.; rev. ed.). New York, NY: Grove Press.

Fordham, S., & Ogbu, J. U. (1986). Black students' school success: Coping with the burden of "acting White." *The Urban Review, 18*, 176–206. http://dx.doi.org/10.1007/BF01112192

Frankenberg, R. (1993). *White women, race matters: The social construction of Whiteness*. Minneapolis: University of Minnesota Press.

Fraser, N. (1990). Re-thinking the public sphere: A contribution to the critique of actually existing democracy. *Social Text, 25/26*, 56–80. http://dx.doi.org/10.2307/466240

Freire, P. (2000). *Pedagogy of the oppressed, 30th anniversary edition*. (M. B. Ramos, Trans.). New York, NY: Bloomsbury Academic.

Freyre, G. (1986). *The masters and the slaves: A study in the development of Brazilian civilization*. Berkeley: University of California Press.

Hanchard, M. G. (1998). *Orpheus and power: The Movimento Negro of Rio de Janeiro and São Paulo, Brazil, 1945–1988*. Princeton, NJ: Princeton University Press.

hooks, b. (1992). *Black looks: Race and representation*. Boston, MA: South End Press.

Kivel, P. (2002). *Uprooting racism: How White people can work for racial justice*. Gabriola Island, Canada: New Society.

Leonardo, Z. (Ed.). (2005). *Critical pedagogy and race*. New York, NY: Blackwell.

Macklin, A., & Warren, J. W. (2015). *From the bottom up* [documentary film]. Motion picture submitted for production.

Obama, B. (1994, October 31). *All things considered*. Washington, DC: National Public Radio.

Otis, J. (2013, January 17). Brazil's "educational apartheid" cements inequality early in life. *Global Post*. Retrieved from http://www.globalpost.com/dispatch/news/regions/americas/brazil/130111/brazil-education-income-inequality

Plessy v. Ferguson, 163 U.S. 537 (1896).

Race in Brazil: Affirming a divide. (2012, January 28). *The Economist*. Retrieved from http://www.economist.com/node/21543494

Robinson, E. (1999). *Coal to cream: A Black man's journey beyond color to an affirmation of race*. New York, NY: Free Press.

Roediger, D. R. (2007). *The wages of Whiteness: Race and the making of the American working class*. New York, NY: Verso.

Sheriff, R. E. (2001). *Dreaming equality: Color, race, and racism in urban Brazil*. New Brunswick, NJ: Rutgers University Press.

Singh, N. P. (2005). *Black is a country: Race and the unfinished struggle for democracy*. Cambridge, MA: Harvard University Press.

Skidmore, T. E. (1993). *Black into White: Race and nationality in Brazilian thought*. Durham, NC: Duke University Press Books. http://dx.doi.org/10.1215/9780822381761

Telles, E. E. (2004). *Race in another America: The significance of skin color in Brazil*. Princeton, NJ: Princeton University Press.

Twine, F. W. (1998). *Racism in a racial democracy: The maintenance of White supremacy in Brazil*. New Brunswick, NJ: Rutgers University Press.

Vianna, H. (1999). *The mystery of Samba: Popular music and national identity in Brazil*. Chapel Hill: University of North Carolina Press.

Warren, J. W. (in press). *Cultures of development: Vietnam, Brazil, and the vanguard of prosperity*. New York, NY: Routledge.

Warren, J. W. (1997). O fardo de nao ser Negro: Uman analise comparativa do desempenho escolar de alunos Afro-Brasileiros e Afro-Norte-Americanos [The burden of not being Black: A comparative analysis of the educational performance of Afro-Brazilian and African American students]. *Estudos Afro-Asiaticos, 31*, 101–124.

Warren, J. W. (2001). *Racial revolutions: Antiracism and Indian resurgence in Brazil*. Durham, NC: Duke University Press. http://dx.doi.org/10.1215/9780822381303

Warren, J. W. (2012). "A little with God is a lot": Popular religion and human security in the land of the Brazilian colonels. In J. K. Wellman & C. B. Lombardi (Eds.), *Religion and human security: A global perspective* (pp. 130–149). New York, NY: Oxford University Press.

Warren, J. W. (2014). After color blindness: Teaching antiracism to White progressives in the U.S. In K. Haltinner (Ed.), *Teaching race and antiracism in contemporary America: Adding context to color blindness* (pp. 109–121). New York, NY: Springer. http://dx.doi.org/10.1007/978-94-007-7101-7_12

Warren, J. W., & Sue, C. S. (2011). Comparative racisms: What anti-racists can learn from Latin America. *Ethnicities, 11*, 32–58. http://dx.doi.org/10.1177/1468796810388699

Warren, J. W., & Twine, F. (2002). Critical race studies in Latin America: Recent advances, recurrent weaknesses. In D. T. Goldberg & J. Solomos (Eds.), *A companion to racial and ethnic studies* (pp. 538–560). Malden, MA: Blackwell.

6

TELLING ON RACISM: DEVELOPING A RACE-CONSCIOUS AGENDA

LEE ANNE BELL

Not everything that is faced can be changed, but nothing can be changed until it is faced.

—James Baldwin

Contemporary media commentary and popular discourse argue that the United States is now a "color-blind" society, evidenced by the election of our first Black president, and that we have entered a "postracial" age in which race no longer matters as a major issue of discrimination (Tesler & Sears, 2010). Color-blind discourse often goes further to assert that the problem now is those people who insist on bringing up race in situations where it does not belong (Foster, 2013; Kaplan, 2011; Wise, 2010). In 1978, U.S. Supreme Court Justice Harry Blackmun recognized that "to get beyond racism, we must first take account of race, there is no other way." In our current postracial age, Chief Justice John Roberts rationalized the elimination of race-conscious remedies for ongoing school segregation with the circular argument: "The way to stop discrimination on the basis of race is to stop discriminating on

http://dx.doi.org/10.1037/14754-007
The Myth of Racial Color Blindness: Manifestations, Dynamics, and Impact, H. A. Neville, M. E. Gallardo, and D. W. Sue (Editors)

the basis of race."[1] This is the color-blind position put simply: Ignore race, and racism will go away.

How can we ameliorate the material and social problems created by a society organized around racial hierarchy for almost three centuries[2] if we ignore race as a tool for understanding and addressing these consequences? Proponents of racial color blindness, like Justice Roberts, suggest that the solution is simply to ignore race, but in so doing, they overlook the cumulative and enduring ways in which race continues to shape life chances and opportunities unequally for people from different racialized groups (Massey, 2007). Adopting a color-blind stance only reinforces an unequal status quo, "feigning indifference to race while enforcing its practice" (Leonardo, 2013, p. 164). By leaving structural inequalities in place, racial color blindness has become the "new racism" (Bonilla-Silva & Forman, 2000).

In this chapter, I make the case for race consciousness as a more honest, effective, and hopeful alternative to racial color blindness. Only a race-conscious approach can show how the race construct developed historically, track both progress and retreat on racial issues over time, and explain the ways that race continues to shape status and opportunity today. The struggle to eliminate racism requires a conscious focus on how race operates, historically and in the present, to advantage Whites as a group and to disadvantage other racialized groups. Only clear-sightedness about the role race plays can provide the analytic tools necessary for developing successful strategies to dismantle racism. Furthermore, race consciousness not only provides better analytic tools, it also offers a more promising framework for envisioning a racially just future.

Both as an explanatory framework for making sense of racism and as grounds for imagining otherwise, racial color blindness fails. Color blindness offers an anemic explanation of current reality because it does not grapple with the inequities of structural racism and proposes a superficial remedy to institutionalized and entrenched patterns of inequality. Color blindness also falls short as an aspirational ideal, painting an impoverished image of what ought to be. As a framework for imagining inclusive community, it elides differences that should be embraced and celebrated in favor of an unmarked and exclusionary White racial norm.

Color blindness suggests a passive state, an immutable biological condition. Furthermore, it implies an innocence that excuses moral responsibility to

---

[1]Recently, Justice Sonia Sotomayor wrote in her dissent on the Court's ruling on affirmative action in Michigan (see Liptak, 2014), "The way to stop discrimination on the basis of race is to speak openly and candidly on the subject of race, and to apply the Constitution with eyes open to the unfortunate effects of centuries of racial discrimination." This is exactly the point made in this chapter.

[2]Depending on whether one counts from the time slaves were first brought to the colonies or from the beginning of the American state.

bear witness to and act against injustice. As such, racial color blindness operates as a form of "strategic ignorance" (Tuana & Sullivan, 2007) that enables the avoidance of the uncomfortable facts of racism. For Whites who espouse color blindness, it provides the "moral wiggle room" (Tuana & Sullivan, 2007) to escape confrontation with the possibility of one's own complicity in an unjust system. In the hands of cynical politicians and pundits, it becomes a tool for discrediting and silencing those who bring up race to challenge an unjust racial order (Haney-Lopez, 2014). We cannot will ourselves to unsee what we've already seen. Refusing to talk about powerful social realities does not make them go away but rather allows racial illiteracy, confusion, and misinformation to persist unchallenged. "Turning a blind eye" may be a more accurate term that at least acknowledges volition and responsibility.

In contrast, race consciousness is an active state, connoting awareness, responsibility, and action.[3] Synonyms for conscious are *awake, aware, mindful, informed,* and *intentional.* These are all aspects of race consciousness that I want to embrace and put in opposition to racial color blindness. Race consciousness signifies being awake to and mindful of the impact of policies and practices on different groups in our society. Race consciousness motivates a desire to become informed about how injustice occurs and to be intentional about seeking redress. Race consciousness not only counters fictions of racial color blindness by actively seeking to perceive, understand, and challenge racism but also paves the way for imagining what more just and inclusive community could look like. Diverse cultural, physical, and communal patterns would not be reduced to one normative ideal but rather recognized and affirmed as the bases for a yet to be imagined and realized multiracial democratic ideal.[4]

Some scholars worry that race consciousness has the potential to reinforce race as a biological construct, thus undermining efforts to eliminate racial hierarchy (Appiah & Gutmann, 1998). Others caution that race consciousness runs the danger of trapping people in categories that blunt complexity (Guinier & Torres, 2002). These are issues to be taken seriously. Appiah and Gutmann (1998) proposed *contingent color consciousness* to underscore the conditional use of race to understand its sociological and political effects while working against race essentialism. Similarly, Leonardo (2013) used *race ambivalence* to signal a way for race theory to be "aware of and reflective about its own conceptual apparatus" (p. 159). Guinier and Torres (2002) coined the

---

[3]Scholars use different terms for this idea: *race cognizance* (Frankenberg, 1993) or *color insight* (Wildman, 2006).

[4]The color-blind ideal references Martin Luther King's "I Have a Dream" speech for justification. However, King wanted a world where race would not be used to determine opportunity, not a world where racial diversity was eliminated.

term *political race* as a way to avoid both "the shoals of identity politics and the fantasies of colorblindness" (p. 9). Political race, they argued, "starts with race and all its complexity, and then builds cross-racial relationships through race and with race to issues of class and gender in order to make democracy real" (Guinier & Torres, 2002, p. 10). All seem to agree, however, that only through a race-conscious approach can we find ways to deconstruct race and dismantle racism.

Critical race scholars extend race consciousness to include attention to the ways in which race intersects with other aspects of identity such as gender, class, culture, language, and sexuality (Crenshaw, 1995; Hobbel & Chapman, 2009). We need a race consciousness, they argue, that attends to multiple forms of racialization and that acknowledges how this process intersects with gender, class, and other locations to affect various non-Black "minorities" in similar and different ways (Brayboy, 2005; Solorzano & Bernal, 2001; Teranishi, Behringer, Grey, & Parker, 2009). For example, many Latinas/Latinos and Asians consider language and immigration status to be as or more important than skin color for understanding the racism they experience (Leonardo, 2013). Likewise, gender and class may inflect in distinctive ways the diverse racialized experiences of women who are African American, Asian American, or Latina, immigrant or not, poor, working class or middle class (Delgado Bernal & Elenes, 2011; Wing, 2003). The specific historical trajectory of each group's experiences with racism is critical information.

Social justice requires eliminating race as an arbiter of life chances and opportunities by directly challenging racism and other forms of oppression (Adams, Bell, & Griffin, 2007). It does not mean erasing racial or cultural identities that are culturally and personally meaningful or reducing the experiences of diverse people and groups to a single normative standard.

> The goal of social justice is full and equal participation of all groups in a society that is mutually shaped to meet their needs. [It] includes a vision of society in which the distribution of resources is equitable and all members are physically and psychologically safe and secure. (Bell, 2007, p. 1)

THE STORIES WE TELL ABOUT RACE MATTER

I find the metaphor of story useful for deconstructing racial color blindness and promoting race consciousness because the stories we tell frame how we comprehend and explain our social world. In this sense, stories operate as historical, cultural, and ideological productions that explain the world as well as shape our imagination of what is possible and desirable. The stories we tell are both descriptive and prescriptive (Perry, 2011). In *Storytelling for Social Justice* (Bell, 2010), I outline four story types for looking at race and racism:

stock stories, concealed stories, resistance stories, and emerging/transforming stories. *Stock stories* rationalize and justify the status quo, thus preserving the particular interests, positions, and advantages of the dominant White racial group. In contrast, counterstories of racial privilege and disadvantage reveal the self-interested and partial nature of color-blind stock stories that parade as Truth. Such counterstories (*concealed, resistance,* and *emerging/transforming*) open up a much broader canvas for understanding social reality by drawing on marginalized stories from history to understand contemporary patterns and develop ways to resist them in the present.

The *stock story* of the American Dream, for example, is that anyone who works hard enough can make it in the United States, regardless of race, class, national origin, or other group status. This story presumes that the challenges of getting ahead are the same for all. This color-blind story resonates with liberal ideals of individualism, rationality, and universalism while foreclosing a critical examination of historical location, group position, and normative assumptions that turn out to be racially inflected. This story ignores the historically lived experiences of those who have been marginalized and fails to address the barriers they encounter to achieving the American Dream. By ignoring the structures that support racism, color-blind stock stories like the American Dream end up supporting the status quo and blocking change.

Concealed stories reveal patterns, invisible from a color-blind perspective, that illuminate how injustice is perpetuated. As race-conscious stories, they describe all the ways race matters to life chances and opportunities and articulate the diverse aspirations and experiences of marginalized peoples and communities. A race-conscious analysis of the American Dream, for example, unearths concealed stories about historically constructed barriers to socioeconomic mobility based on race and reveals the many ways these barriers, now normalized, continue to affect opportunity and outcomes in our society (Katznelson, 2005; Lipsitz, 2006; Massey & Denton, 1993; Oliver & Shapiro, 1997). Unearthing concealed stories in history, literature, and social science data provides a wealth of information for understanding how current patterns came to be. Patterns that are invisible from a color-blind perspective can be discerned once we apply race as an analytic lens.

A central aspiration of the American Dream is home ownership. Normative assumptions (stock stories) that the system is fair conceal the ways that race mediates access and opportunity. For example, home equity rises much faster for Whites than African Americans because of historical and contemporary patterns of redlining, discriminatory mortgage lending, lack of access to credit, and lower incomes. A recently published study revealed that the total wealth gap between White and African American families nearly tripled over the past 25 years (from $85,000 in 1984 to $236,500 in 2009; an increase of $152,000; Shapiro, Meschede, & Osoro, 2013). The housing collapse of 2007–2009 only exacerbated this problem (Rugh & Massey, 2010). Without an explicitly racial analysis of the wealth gap, we miss the concealed story of how communities of color have been historically and continue to be systematically targeted in racially specific ways.

Race-conscious *resistance stories* draw from historical and contemporary examples of resistance to racism, and other forms of discrimination to discern how people before us have challenged oppression and marginalization. Such accounts deepen the analysis of contemporary problems and provide inspiration and ideas for taking action in the present.

For example, although education is touted as a route to achieving the American Dream, ongoing and deepening residential and educational segregation prevents access to the kind of schooling that would make this possible. At a time when public commitment to integration is at a nadir (Orfield, 2009) and public schools are in danger of being taken over by corporate interests (Ravitch, 2013), we can look to the resistance stories of activists, lawyers, politicians, and community groups who fought for equitable education in the past as a basis for shaping strategy today. We learn from this history that African American educators and activists in both the Colonial era and post-Reconstruction viewed education as a means to full citizenship (Moss, 2009). In underresourced, segregated Black schools in the South, education was embraced as a source of liberation that should serve the interests not just of individuals but of the community as a whole (Anderson, 1988). Although African Americans welcomed working with White supporters, they worried about losing control of their collective goals for education. This turned out to be a prescient concern in the Jim Crow era as White philanthropists and politicians underwrote second-class, industrial education for Blacks (Anderson, 1988) and again in the post–*Brown v. Board of Education* (1954) era when Black educators lost jobs as Black schools were closed and Black children moved to hostile school environments that did not have their best interests at heart (Walker, 2013). Today, charter schools that ration access to high-quality schooling and often promote a rigid and rote curriculum for "other people's children" (Delpit, 1995, 2012) ultimately undermine the ideal of schooling as a path to the American Dream. As we formulate race-conscious responses to segregated and unequal schooling, we can learn from these early resisters about the dangers of "reform" strategies that do not include a collective vision for education that reflects these communities' interests and desires for their children and an ability to grapple with the tenacity of White supremacy in working against their desires (see, for example, a 2014 article on the resegregation of Tuscaloosa, Alabama, that illustrates precisely this problem; Hannah-Jones, 2014).

Emerging/transforming stories project the kind of world that would be possible if the diverse needs and interests of all the various groups in our society were the basis for organizing social and political life. Such stories are not the idealized, ahistorical imaginings of racial color blindness but rather are grounded in the collective knowledge of our past as essential to creating more just possibilities for the future. These stories are often the product of intergenerational, and multiracial, dialogue. For example, the Echoes of Brown project (Fine, Roberts, & Torre, 2004) brought together a racially diverse group of high school students, artists, academics, and elders from the Civil Rights movement to mark the 50th anniversary of the *Brown* decision by examining contemporary segregation through the lens of that history. Youth researched segregation and attitudes about race in their schools and challenged orthodoxies about the "achievement gap," arguing that the achievement gap individualizes the problem in students who fail to achieve. Rather, they asserted, the gap is an "opportunity gap," thus placing the problem on broader social failure to equally fund and resource good schools for all. They presented their findings through spoken word poetry and dance and, in the process, reimagined and created a collective response to racism in their schools and communities that built on what they learned from elders yet also created something new.[5]

DEVELOPING A RACE-CONSCIOUS AGENDA

Race-consciousness means to be awake, aware, mindful, informed and intentional about challenging racism and working toward racial justice. Counterstorytelling offers both an analytic tool and a method for generating alternatives to stock stories that invest in color-blind analysis and thus support an unjust status quo. In contrast, race-conscious diagnosis is premised on the belief that noticing rather than ignoring race will lead to fairer outcomes. A race-conscious analysis starts from the assumption that race is salient for understanding hierarchies of power and privilege that are normalized in *stock stories*. As an essential diagnostic tool for systemic critique, a race lens helps to "unmask apparently nonracial phenomena as precisely racial in nature" (Leonardo, 2013, p. 19). Race-conscious counterstories validate and draw on lessons from history and the hard-won knowledge in marginalized communities to develop a fuller understanding of how racism operates, how to survive with one's humanity intact, and how to generate new possibilities for organizing the social world. Using the story types as a heuristic device, we can develop guidelines for a race-conscious agenda.

---

[5]The Storytelling Project drew from this example to create a curriculum for challenging racism through storytelling and the arts (Bell, 2010). I thank the students who participated in the Race, Democracy, and Education Seminar, Spring 2014, for their careful reading and thoughtful comments on this chapter.

Recognize and Name Stock Stories

Research on race talk illustrates the tendency of many Whites and some people of color to use stock stories to minimize racism and justify the status quo (Bell, 2003, 2007; Bonilla-Silva & Dietrich, 2011; Bonilla-Silva, Lewis, & Embrick, 2004). Stock stories identified by researchers, such as "I don't see color, I just see people," usually operate precisely when race is the issue (see, e.g., Williams, 1998). Stock stories minimize racism in the present by overemphasizing progress and putting racism in the past, attributing it to "episodic malice" rather than categorical and cumulative factors (Haney-Lopez, 2010). Thus, it is important to notice when such stories are operating because only in noticing can one prepare to interrupt and challenge them. Explicitly teaching the storylines that have been identified in research is one useful way to make people aware of these stories and thus perturb their continued use. We can invite students and others with whom we work to point out and track stock stories that circulate in the media and public discourse. As "stock-story detectives," they become more conscious and critical of the stories they may themselves fall back on.

Embrace Concealed Stories of and From Those on the Margins as Critical Information

A race-conscious stance recognizes that social-historical location differentially shapes how diverse communities are affected by racism and the strategies and strengths they develop to resist; furthermore, racial and ethnic group membership is relevant to the ways individuals are treated and how they experience themselves in the world and is an important source of knowledge. Race-conscious stories enable a more complex understanding of social patterns and provide ways to imagine difference, rather than sameness, as a norm. For example, listening to stories from students and academics of color about their experiences provides insight into microaggressions, often invisible to White students and faculty, that undermine goals of diversity and inclusion (Gutierrez y Muhs, Nieman, Gonzalez, & Harris, 2012). These insights provide ways to understand and interrupt policies and practices that harm not only students and faculty of color but also the university's own ideals. Starting from race-conscious stories by people of color brings problems to the surface and generates solutions that make campuses more inclusive places for everyone.

Expose Invisible Norms of Whiteness

A race-conscious approach underscores that Whites are also a racialized group. Concealed stories about Whiteness flip the typical assumption that race is only about people of color and instead expose experiences and assumptions in the White community that reinforce and perpetuate White advantage. By puncturing the transparency of White advantage, concealed stories reveal the sociocultural and material conditions that enable it to endure (Flagg, 2005; Frankenberg, 1993; Wildman, 2006). Concealed stories "tell on" how Whites benefit from historically created advantages in housing, finance, and educational and social programs that accumulate and compound over time, without the need for any personal or deliberate steps to keep them going (Massey, 2007). Individual White people who become conscious of these advantages can tell on Whiteness in ways that expose and "denormalize" Whiteness to open spaces for critique and change.

Trace the Historical Roots of Current Problems

Race-conscious diagnosis recognizes discrimination and the broader context in which it occurs to develop systemic remedies that address cumulative advantages and disadvantages that have built up over time. Historical precedents help to explain both the ongoing patterns, as well as divergences and shifts, in policies and practices that maintain or disrupt racism. For example, precedents help to explain the disproportionate racialized incarceration rate in the United States, the highest in the world (Haney-Lopez, 2010). Today the United States comprises 5% of the world population but has 25% of the world's prisoners; the only country that comes close is Russia as a distant second (see National Association for the Advancement of Colored People, n.d.). The historical record of Black enslavement up to Emancipation, as well as debt peonage from post-Reconstruction to World War I (Blackmon, 2008), illustrates a long history of policies that have created and normalized racialized incarceration (Alexander, 2012). The drug war in the 1980s and differential sentencing guidelines built on and grossly expanded this system. The expansion of practices developed there have now bled into schooling (Gonzalez, 2012; Kim, Losen, & Hewitt, 2010), and other areas of social life where surveillance has become common practice, continually reinforced by media images that make these practices seem "normal" (Bissler & Conners, 2012). Understanding this historical trajectory offers a powerful lens for exposing and challenging these practices and their ongoing impacts in our society.

Expose Hidden Racial Outcomes in Purportedly Nonracial or Color-Blind Policies

Race-conscious diagnosis looks at the outcomes of policies, intentional or not, that have disparate effects. A focus on intent rather than outcome reinforces the idea that only conscious, deliberate action generates racism, thus obscuring how racism is sedimented in policies and practices that appear to be neutral. Shifting the focus to *outcomes* avoids getting mired down in second-guessing intentions and gets to the heart of the matter by identifying remedies that address the results of policies and practices that are harmful to people of color, whether intentional or not.

In a recent faculty search, for example, the committee conscientiously advertised in venues that reached out to scholars of color and redefined the subfield(s) to include areas that would be more likely to include diverse faculty. These efforts successfully yielded a diverse pool of candidates. Then the committee made what they assumed was a neutral decision: To narrow the list, they decided to weigh experience more heavily than other factors. With that single decision, they eliminated all of the candidates of color who, younger and newer to the field because of past exclusion, did not fit that supposedly neutral criterion. Without a race-conscious lens, this decision could be rationalized, as often happens, with: "We did our best to hire a person of color, but we just couldn't find the right candidates." The intent was to have a more inclusive search, but the outcome sustained the status quo once they lost sight of the unintended consequences of a "neutral" decision.

Draw Inspiration From Resisters in Other Eras and Contexts

Reading U.S. history through the lens of resistance movements and organized struggles for equality challenges the stock story that history is created by exceptional individuals acting alone. We see that joining with others to take action against injustice can create change. For example, Rosa Parks is typically presented as a tired seamstress who decided one day to refuse to give up her seat on a bus and started the Montgomery bus boycott. What we don't learn is that Mrs. Parks was in fact inspired by veteran organizers like Ella Baker and trained in the Highlander Folk School. She was part of an organized movement of people working together to challenge entrenched racism in Alabama (Collier-Thomas & Franklin, 2001; Theoharris, 2013). Sanitized versions of history strip away the stories of organized resistance that hold valuable tools and strategies for challenging racism in our own time.

Rehearse Interrupting Stock Stories Against Powerful Pressures to Stay Silent

Race-conscious responses can interrupt stock stories and expose their self-interested claims. "Hence, the task of progressive social analysts is to blow the whistle on color-blind racism" (Bonilla-Silva & Forman, 2000, p. 78). Rehearsal and role-playing is a useful way to prepare to speak up against powerful norms that silence disagreement and dissent. When increasing numbers of people begin to interrupt the repetition of stock stories, they puncture the taken for granted "Truth" of such stories and open up space for consideration of other ideas and analyses. For example, teachers can learn to first notice and then rehearse interrupting "deficit discourses" about African American and Latina/Latino children that circulate in their schools. In the safety of learning circles, they can practice formulating responses and get support and encouragement from their peers to build the skills and confidence needed to interrupt stock stories in their schools. Through group study, they can also bring forward concealed stories about their students' strengths, assets, resilience, and promise that talk back to stock stories of deficit.

Develop and Expect White Accountability for Interrupting Racism

Whites as a group share responsibility for unveiling and making a case against racism. "Doing nothing affirmative against racism is a default action contributing to its survival" (Leonardo, 2013, p. 17). We need to develop a "politics of accountability" based on the recognition that we are all complicit in the subordination of others; there is no neutral ground to which to retreat (hooks, 2012). We know from research on bullying and harassment that bystanders can do as much or more damage as perpetrators of racism by remaining silent, a silence that peers who are actively racist read as consensus (Watt & Larkin, 2010). White bystanders who may not themselves actively practice or profess racist policies are responsible for speaking up about policies and practices that perpetuate racial advantage and disadvantage. There is strong evidence that when White bystanders speak up about racism they can have a powerful impact on the perceptions and actions of their peers (Nelson, Dunn, & Paradies, 2011).

Build Solidarity Across Differences

The history of antiracism illustrates the power of coalitions among people from different racial and social groups as well as the lengths to which dominant groups will go to prevent or undermine such coalitions. We can take lessons from cross-race coalitions in other eras that were successful or fell apart as a way to resist divisive politics and build stronger coalitions today. For example, the original coalition between White suffragists and African Americans seeking the right to vote is first inspiring and then heartbreaking as we learn how the ruling White men and women pitted them against each other and broke down this coalition, giving Black men the right to vote but continuing to exclude women of all races. Guinier and Torres (2002) described successful cross-race coalitions and the conditions that enable them to work effectively. From such examples, we learn that successful organizing requires race consciousness and attending to both shared and distinctive goals to cocreate agendas that will sustain working together over time for the interests of all.

Highlight the Dangers to Democracy of Not Dealing With Racism

Like the miner's canary, "the distress of those who are racially marginalized is the first sign of a danger that threatens us all" (Guinier & Torres, 2002, p. 11). Contemporary stock stories of postracial color blindness rely on neoliberal ideas of privatization and personal culpability that erode notions of civic responsibility and the public good. Neoliberalism "privatizes blame" (Duggan, 2003) and makes it harder to expose systemic practices of inequality that work to the detriment of society as a whole. Haney-Lopez (2014) traced how politicians have used "dog-whistle politics" (the coded language of race) for the past three decades to tar liberal government as providing handouts to "undeserving" groups. He argued that this has led to the disparagement and underfunding of social programs that benefit everyone. Thus, working and middle-class White people, who benefit as much from health care and other reforms as people of color, frequently work against their own self-interests by refusing to support programs they have been convinced are for "undeserving" others. Note, for example, Southern states that have refused Medicare because politicians want to challenge the Affordable Health Care Act, cutting off access to large numbers of White constituents, as well as constituents of color, who desperately need these resources.

Promote Racial Literacy as an Essential Skill in a Diverse Democracy

Racial literacy, defined as "the ability to read, recast, and resolve racially stressful social interactions" (Stevenson, 2014, p. 27), is an essential skill in a diverse democracy. Rather than avoiding discussions about racism, racial literacy offers a way to make sense of often confusing situations and communications and to notice and resolve racial stress and conflict in interpersonal, cross-racial relationships. As well, racial literacy provides a powerful analytic tool for making sense of and challenging structural racism (Bell, 2010).

The benefits to students who are exposed to color-blind versus multicultural, antiracist (race-conscious) discourse are many. For example, exposure to information about race has been found to reduce prejudice, promote more complex thinking about social problems, develop understanding of the structural causes of inequality, and increase recognition of remedies that address the effects of past discrimination (Bonilla-Silva & Forman, 2000). Research on intergroup dialogues describes the positive benefits of explicit discussion about race (Gurin, Dey, Hurtado, & Gurin, 2002; Gurin, Nagda,

& Lopez, 2004; Lopez, Gurin, & Nagda, 1998). Among these benefits are increased awareness and understanding of racial (and other forms of) inequality and their structural causes, increased empathy and perspective taking, greater motivation to bridge differences and be actively engaged in influencing social policy to correct inequalities, and a greater sense of personal responsibility for taking action (Nagda, Gurin, Sorensen, & Zuniga, 2009). Those who learn to speak up and condemn racist beliefs and practices can have powerful prosocial effects on others and create social norms that are intolerant of racism (Nelson, Dunn, & Paradies, 2011). These are also shown to be skills of democratic citizenship (Levinson, 2012) that are crucial to addressing racism and other forms of discrimination in our society.

Create Diverse Counterstorytelling Communities to Support Learning, Visioning, and Action

Creating a community where discussion of race and racism is valued, where people from different social locations can come together to make sense of the factors that sustain racism and plan actions to interrupt it, provides a holding environment for analysis, critique, practice, and dreaming. Support is needed to go against powerful social norms that sustain racism and to embolden action. Together, people can create new stories that reimagine power relations and provide alternative ways of living democratically in diverse community (Bell, 2010).

CONCLUSION

We could say that Barack Obama's first election was based on the aspirational ideal of seeing diversity as our greatest asset (Haney-Lopez, 2014). The widespread excitement among people of all ages and from all racial groups about this history-making election created inspiring moments when large numbers of diverse Americans recognized and affirmed our "linked fates" (Guinier & Torres, 2002). We got a glimpse of what it might mean to imagine "difference without hierarchy: race without racism" (Li, 2011, p. 8). Although those moments seem far away today, they point to a clear desire for emerging/transforming stories that can move us toward that aspirational ideal. Such stories can only be created in communities that are committed to a clear-eyed understanding of the central role of racism in our history as a nation and a willingness to struggle for change over the long haul. Counterstorytelling communities act as incubators for the important work of imagining together and rehearsing the "more perfect union" outlined in our Constitution that is yet to be realized.

Antiracist work requires a balance of hope with critique. This challenging work requires an unflinching understanding of our racial past in all its ugly reality. We cannot overcome that reality without persistent committed struggle and recognition of the forces against change. In 2015, we celebrated the 90th anniversary of the birth of the great American writer James Baldwin; I draw again on his words to articulate the challenge:

> In great pain and terror, one begins to assess the history which has placed one where one is, and formed one's point of view. In great pain and terror, because, thereafter, one enters into battle with that historical creation, oneself, and attempts to recreate oneself according to a principle more humane and more liberating; one begins the attempt to achieve a level of personal maturity and freedom which robs history of its tyrannical power, and also changes history. (Baldwin, 1985, p. 410)

Race consciousness provides a way to work toward our ideals with no illusions about the persistence of racism and yet with hope that we can change ourselves and our history going forward if we generate the individual and social will necessary to understand and to finally atone and make reparations for the racial regime we have inherited.

REFERENCES

Adams, M., Bell, L. A., & Griffin, P. (Eds.). (2007). *Teaching for diversity and social justice: A sourcebook* (2nd ed.). New York, NY: Routledge.

Alexander, M. (2012). *The new Jim Crow: Mass incarceration in the age of colorblindness*. New York, NY: The New Press.

Anderson, J. (1988). *The education of Blacks in the South, 1860–1935*. Chapel Hill: University of North Carolina Press. http://dx.doi.org/10.5149/uncp/9780807842218

Appiah, K. A., & Gutmann, A. (1998). *Color conscious: The political morality of race*. Princeton, NJ: Princeton University Press.

Baldwin, J. (1985). White man's guilt. In *The price of the ticket: Collected nonfiction 1948–1985* (pp. 409–414). New York, NY: St. Martin's Press.

Bell, L. A. (2003). Telling tales: What stories can teach us about racism. *Race Ethnicity and Education, 6*, 3–28. http://dx.doi.org/10.1080/1361332032000044567

Bell, L. A. (2007). Theoretical foundations for social justice education. In M. Adams, L. A. Bell, & P. Griffin (Eds.), *Teaching for diversity and social justice* (2nd ed., pp. 1–15). New York, NY: Routledge.

Bell, L. A. (2010). *Storytelling for social justice: Connecting narrative and the arts in antiracist teaching*. New York, NY: Routledge.

Bissler, D. L., & Conners, J. L. (2012). Inequalities in CSI crime scene investigation: Stereotypes in the CSI investigators. In D. L. Bissler & J. L. Conners (Eds.), *The harms of crime media: Essays on the perpetuation of racism, sexism, and class stereotypes* (pp. 127–150). Jefferson, NC: McFarland.

Blackmon, D. A. (2008). *Slavery by another name: The re-enslavement of Black Americans from the Civil War to World War II*. New York, NY: Doubleday.

Bonilla-Silva, E., & Dietrich, D. (2011). The sweet enchantment of color-blind racism in Obamerica. *Annals of the American Academy of Political and Social Science, 634*, 190–206. http://dx.doi.org/10.1177/0002716210389702

Bonilla-Silva, E., & Forman, T. A. (2000). "I am not a racist but . . .": Mapping White college students' racial ideology in the USA. *Discourse & Society, 11*, 50–85. http://dx.doi.org/10.1177/0957926500011001003

Bonilla-Silva, E., Lewis, A., & Embrick, D. G. (2004). "I did not get that job because of a Black man . . .": The story lines and testimonies of color-blind racism. *Sociological Forum, 19*, 555–581.

Brayboy, B. M. J. (2005). Toward a tribal critical race theory in education. *The Urban Review, 37*, 425–446. http://dx.doi.org/10.1007/s11256-005-0018-y

Brown v. Board of Education, 347 U.S. 483 (1954).

Collier-Thomas, B., & Franklin, V. P. (2001). *Sisters in the struggle: African American women in the Civil Rights–Black Power movement*. New York: New York University Press.

Crenshaw, K. W. (1995). Mapping the margins: Intersectionality, identity politics, and violence against women of color. In K. Thomas (Ed.), *Critical race theory: The key writings that formed a movement* (pp. 357–383). New York, NY: The New Press.

Delgado Bernal, D., & Elenes, C. A. (2011). Chicana feminist theorizing: Methodologies, pedagogies, and practices. In R. R. Valencia, (Ed.) *Chicano school failure and success: Present, past, and future* (3rd ed., pp. 99–119). New York, NY: Routledge.

Delpit, L. (1995). *Other peoples' children: Cultural conflict in the classroom*. New York, NY: The New Press.

Delpit, L. (2012). "Multiplication is for White people": Raising expectations for other people's children. NY: The New Press.

Duggan, L. (2003). *The twilight of equality: Neoliberalism, cultural politics, and the attack on democracy*. Boston, MA: Beacon Press.

Fine, M., Roberts, R. A., & Torre, M. E. (2004). *Echoes of Brown: Youth documenting and performing the legacy of* Brown v. Board of Education [DVD/book]. New York, NY: Teachers College Press.

Flagg, B. J. (2005). Foreword: Whiteness as metaprivilege. *Washington University Journal of Law and Policy, 18*(1–2), 1–11.

Foster, J. D. (2013). *White race discourse: Preserving racial privilege in a post-racial society*. Boulder, CO: Lexington Books.

Frankenberg, R. (1993). *White women, race matters: The social construction of Whiteness*. Minneapolis: University of Minnesota Press.

Gonzalez, T. (2012). Keeping kids in schools: Restorative justice, punitive discipline, and the school to prison pipeline. *Journal of Law and Education, 41*, 281–335.

Guinier, L., & Torres, G. (2002). *The miner's canary: Enlisting race, resisting power, transforming democracy*. Cambridge, MA: Harvard University Press.

Gurin, P., Dey, E. L., Hurtado, S., & Gurin, G. (2002). Diversity and higher education: Theory and impact on educational outcomes. *Harvard Educational Review, 72*, 330–366.

Gurin, P., Nagda, B. A., & Lopez, G. E. (2004). The benefits of diversity in education for democratic citizenship. *Journal of Social Issues, 60*, 17–34. http://dx.doi.org/10.1111/j.0022-4537.2004.00097.x

Gutierrez y Muhs, G., Nieman, Y. F., Gonzalez, C., & Harris, A. P. (2012). *Presumed incompetent: The intersections of race and class for women in academia*. Boulder: University Press of Colorado.

Haney-Lopez, I. F. (2010). Post-racial racism, racial stratification and mass incarceration in the age of Obama. *California Law Review, 98*, 1023–1073.

Haney-Lopez, I. F. (2014). *Dog whistle politics: How coded racial appeals have reinvented racism and wrecked the middle class*. New York, NY: Oxford University Press.

Hannah-Jones, N. (2014, May). Segregation now . . . Sixty years after *Brown v. Board of Education*, the schools in Tuscaloosa, Alabama, show how separate and unequal education is coming back. *The Atlantic*. Retrieved from http://www.theatlantic.com/features/archive/2014/04/segregation-now/359813

Hobbel, N., & Chapman, T. K. (2009). Beyond the sole category of race: Using a CRT intersectional framework to map identity projects. *Journal of Curriculum Theorizing, 25*, 76–89.

hooks, b. (2012). *Writing beyond race: Living theory and practice*. New York, NY: Routledge.

Kaplan, R. (2011). *The myth of post-racial America: Searching for equality in the age of materialism*. Lanham, MD: Rowman & Littlefield.

Katznelson, I. (2005). *When affirmative action was White: An untold history of racial inequality in the twentieth century*. New York, NY: Norton.

Kim, C. Y., Losen, D., & Hewitt, D. T. (2010). *The school to prison pipeline: Structuring legal reform*. New York: New York University Press.

Leonardo, Z. (2013). *Race frameworks: A multidimensional theory of racism and education*. New York, NY: Teachers College Press.

Levinson, M. (2012). *No citizen left behind*. Cambridge, MA: Harvard University Press. http://dx.doi.org/10.4159/harvard.9780674065291

Li, S. (2011). *Signifying without specifying: Racial discourse in the age of Obama*. New Brunswick, NJ: Rutgers University Press.

Lipsitz, G. (2006). *The possessive investment in Whiteness: How White people profit from identity politics*. Philadelphia, PA: Temple University Press.

Liptak, A. (2014, April 22). Court backs Michigan on affirmative action case. *New York Times*. http://www.nytimes.com/2014/04/23/us/supreme-court-michigan-affirmative-action-ban.html

Lopez, G. E., Gurin, P., & Nagda, B. A. (1998). Education and understanding structural causes for group inequalities. *Political Psychology, 19*, 305–329. http://dx.doi.org/10.1111/0162-895X.00106

Massey, D. S. (2007). *Categorically unequal: The American stratification system*. New York, NY: Russell Sage Foundation.

Massey, D. S., & Denton, N. A. (1993). *American apartheid: Segregation and the making of the underclass*. Cambridge, MA: Harvard University Press.

Moss, H. (2009). *Schooling citizens: The struggle for African American education in antebellum America*. Chicago, IL: University of Chicago Press. http://dx.doi.org/10.7208/chicago/9780226542515.001.0001

Nagda, B. A., Gurin, P., Sorensen, N., & Zuniga, X. (2009). Evaluating intergroup dialogue: Engaging diversity for personal and social responsibility. *Diversity and Democracy, 12(1)*, 4–6.

National Association for the Advancement of Colored People. (n.d.). *Criminal justice fact sheet*. Retrieved from http://www.naacp.org/pages/criminal-justice-fact-sheet

Nelson, J. K., Dunn, K. M., & Paradies, Y. (2011). Bystander antiracism: A review of the literature. *Analyses of Social Issues and Public Policy, 11*, 263–284. http://dx.doi.org/10.1111/j.1530-2415.2011.01274.x

Oliver, M. L., & Shapiro, T. M. (1997). *Black wealth/White wealth: A new perspective on racial inequality*. New York, NY: Routledge.

Orfield, G. (2009). *Reviving the goal of an integrated society: A 21st century challenge*. Los Angeles, CA: The Civil Rights Project/Proyecto Derechos Civiles at UCLA.

Perry, I. (2011). *More beautiful and more terrible: The embrace and transcendence of racial inequality in the United States*. New York: New York University Press.

Ravitch, D. (2013). *Reign of error: The hoax of the privatization movement and the danger to America's public schools*. New York, NY: Knopf.

Rugh, J. S., & Massey, D. S. (2010). Racial segregation and the American foreclosure crisis. *American Sociological Review, 75*, 629–651. http://dx.doi.org/10.1177/0003122410380868

Shapiro, T., Meschede, T., & Osoro, S. (2013, February). *The roots of the widening racial wealth gap: Explaining the Black–White economic divide* [Research and Policy Brief]. Retrieved from Institute on Assets and Social Policy website: http://iasp.brandeis.edu/pdfs/Author/shapiro-thomas-m/racialwealthgapbrief.pdf

Solorzano, D., & Bernal, D. D. (2001). Examining transformational resistance through a critical race and latcrit theory framework: Chicana and Chicano students in an urban context. *Urban Education, 36*, 308–342. http://dx.doi.org/10.1177/0042085901363002

Stevenson, H. C. (2014). *Promoting racial literacy in schools: Differences that make a difference*. New York, NY: Teachers College Press.

Teranishi, R. T., Behringer, L. B., Grey, E. A., & Parker, T. L. (2009). Critical race theory and the research on Asian Americans and Pacific Islanders in higher education. *New Directions for Institutional Research, 142*, 57–68. http://dx.doi.org/10.1002/ir.296

Tesler, M., & Sears, D. O. (2010). *Obama's race: The 2008 election and the dream of a postracial America*. Chicago, IL: University of Chicago Press.

Theoharris, J. (2013). *The rebellious life of Mrs. Rosa Parks*. New York, NY: Beacon Press.

Tuana, N., & Sullivan, S. (2007). *Race and epistemologies of ignorance*. Albany: State University of New York Press.

Walker, V. S. (2013). Tolerated tokenism, or the injustice in justice: Black teacher associations and their forgotten struggle for educational justice, 1921–1954. *Equity & Excellence in Education, 46*, 64–80. http://dx.doi.org/10.1080/10665684.2012.751756

Watt, S. E., & Larkin, C. (2010). Prejudiced people perceive more community support for their views: The role of own, media, and peer attitudes in perceived consensus. *Journal of Applied Social Psychology, 40*, 710–731. http://dx.doi.org/10.1111/j.1559-1816.2010.00594.x

Wildman, S. M. (2006). The persistence of White privilege. *Journal of Law and Policy, 18*, 245–265.

Williams, P. J. (1998). *Seeing a color-blind future: The paradox of race*. New York, NY: Farrar, Straus & Giroux.

Wing, A. K. (Ed.). (2003). *Critical race feminism: A reader*. New York: New York University Press.

Wise, T. (2010). *Colorblind: The rise of postracial politics and the retreat from racial equality*. San Francisco, CA: City Lights.

II

CONTEXT AND COSTS

7

SEEING COLOR BLINDNESS: COLOR-BLIND RACIAL IDEOLOGY RESEARCH METHODS IN SOCIAL PSYCHOLOGY

MATTHEW C. JACKSON, VERA KATELYN WILDE, AND PHILLIP ATIBA GOFF

Reverend Martin Luther King, Jr., famously dreamed of an egalitarian world in which individuals' life chances depended on the "content of their character" and not the color of their skin (King, 2001, p. 95). Half a century later, Republican Texas governor and presidential hopeful Rick Perry refuted charges of racial bias as a factor in George Zimmerman's acquittal for murder after fatally shooting an unarmed Black teenager, Trayvon Martin, saying, "Our justice system is colorblind" (Millhiser, 2013). These sentiments both express color-blind racial ideology (CBRI), yet they express different conceptions of it. King's conceptualization of racial color blindness invited purposeful interventions to prevent life outcomes from being determined by a racial caste system. He articulated his dream at a rally to compel government intervention ensuring universal access to education, employment, and housing. In contrast, Perry suggested that color-blind procedures rather than color-blind outcomes are evidence of racial justice.

http://dx.doi.org/10.1037/14754-008

The Myth of Racial Color Blindness: Manifestations, Dynamics, and Impact, H. A. Neville, M. E. Gallardo, and D. W. Sue (Editors)

The difference between these conceptualizations of racial color blindness can be understood through the distinction between ideal and nonideal theories (Rawls, 1971). In the context of theories of social justice, King's nonideal racial color blindness operates under the assumption that members of society would not cooperate with the goal of achieving racial injustice and would require government intervention. By contrast, the logic of Perry's racial color blindness (an ideal conception assuming universal compliance) prescribes that the means to achieving racial color blindness must be color-blind themselves. These different conceptualizations of racial color blindness can engender very different reactions. Whereas King's "I Have a Dream" speech is widely lauded, the application of CBRI to procedures is often criticized. In procedural contexts, CBRI can be seen as legitimizing privilege and obscuring ongoing hostility toward racial equality (Haney-López, 2014; Sidanius & Pratto, 1999). Because "color blindness" in its various forms has become the dominant racial narrative in the United States (Harris & Lieberman, 2013), it is imperative to know how expressions of CBRI are received across various contexts, and why individuals endorse different forms of racial color blindness. Furthermore, because social psychology is principally concerned with how the attitudes and behaviors of one person or group influence the attitudes and behaviors of others, the field is peculiarly well-suited to address these questions. Consequently, understanding the research methods of the field is an important component of critiquing how we analyze the CBRI discourse and its influence on racial progress.

Although other areas of psychology also investigate CBRI, social psychology has a well-suited set of methods at its disposal for investigating the individual motivations and contextual factors during intergroup interactions on which CBRI can have an impact. As is the case broadly within social psychology research, laboratory experimental methods dominate the CBRI social psychology research literature, manipulating the individual endorsement of racially color-blind ideologies. By contrast, field studies are a less commonly used research method predominantly comparing fixed racially color-blind contexts against alternative racial ideologies. Resultant findings are mixed, providing novel contributions to our understanding of CBRI, yet leaving unsolved a number of empirical questions about the utility of CBRI, particularly about the boundary conditions of its effects. Specifically, when is CBRI beneficial to intergroup relations and when is it harmful? And which conception of CBRI is best for promoting positive intergroup contact across contexts? Future CBRI social psychology research aiming to further address these questions will benefit from mixed-method approaches.

This methods review proceeds as follows. First, we synthesize two groups of CBRI social psychology research methods (i.e., causes and consequences) and the findings they produce. The most popular method in experimental research examining the consequences of CBRI uses explicit priming to compare the effects of exposing participants to racially color-blind versus color-conscious (e.g., multicultural) narratives on cooperative efficiency and various measures of the racial climate (Apfelbaum, Pauker, Sommers, & Ambady, 2010; Apfelbaum, Sommers, & Norton, 2008; Goff, Steele, & Davies, 2008; Holoien & Shelton, 2012; Morrison, Plaut, & Ybarra, 2010; Richeson & Nussbaum, 2004; Richeson & Shelton, 2007; Todd & Galinsky, 2012; Vorauer, Gagnon, & Sasaki, 2009; Vorauer, Hunter, Main, & Roy, 2000; Vorauer, Main, & O'Connell, 1998; Wolsko, Park, & Judd, 2006; Wolsko, Park, Judd, & Wittenbrink, 2000). Field studies use a broader range of methods, including experimental and observational tools, but are more often correlational (e.g., Plaut, Thomas, & Goren, 2009). Conversely, research on the causes of CBRI uses measurements of the concern with appearing prejudiced and of antiegalitarianism to demonstrate that causes other than egalitarianism can motivate the endorsement CBRI (e.g., Goff et al., 2013; Knowles, Lowery, Hogan, & Chow, 2009).

Finally, we describe possible future advances in CBRI social psychology research methods by suggesting ways to disambiguate and extend previous CBRI findings. Specifically, the majority of CBRI research has been conducted in laboratories with participants who do not know one another. Conversely, social psychology as a whole is increasingly well-known across disciplines for researchers' ability to deploy multimethod research designs combining experimental laboratory studies with secondary data analyses from real-world institutional contexts such as schools, businesses, and hospitals. This type of strategy, long cited as best minimizing sources of potential error (e.g., Campbell & Fiske, 1959), is particularly well-suited to addressing enduring questions about how CBRI affects intergroup relations in actual workplaces, authentic interpersonal relationships, and other, more ecologically valid settings. Future multimethod research designs will enhance the ecological validity of findings and clarify the boundary conditions of where and when CBRI in various forms magnifies or ameliorates racial inequality.

WHITE COATS, COLOR-BLIND SUBJECTS: LABORATORY RESEARCH ON CBRI

Social psychologists have most extensively studied CBRI in laboratory experiments (as we have with most phenomena), and most of these experiments use one of two methods: supraliminal priming and a yes–no group task. *Priming studies* compare the effects of presenting color-blind versus color-conscious narratives as the contextual norm. *Yes–no group tasks* are behavioral measures of the collaborative efficiency of diverse groups of individuals when attempting to portray color blindness. Results show both positive and negative outcomes from CBRI but tend to suggest that CBRI negatively affects racial equity (e.g., Apfelbaum, Norton, & Sommers, 2012; Fryberg & Stephens, 2010; Knowles et al., 2009; Markus, Steele, & Steele, 2000; Peery, 2011; Rattan & Ambady, 2013; Rosenthal & Levy, 2010).

Priming Racial Color Blindness

Priming experiments have found that CBRI can have pernicious effects on intergroup interactions. For instance, Apfelbaum, Pauker, Sommers, and Ambady (2010) demonstrated that priming children with CBRI makes them less likely to recognize racial discrimination. These researchers asked elementary school children to read a story about a teacher who endorsed either a racially color-blind approach to promoting racial equality or a diversity-valuing approach. When the children subsequently read about a series of conflicts, those primed with CBRI were less likely to identify discrimination in both ambiguous and unambiguous discriminatory contexts. In other words, children exposed to CBRI are more likely to discount or normalize racial schoolyard bullying as typical misconduct rather than recognizing it as racial prejudice. In this sense, far from preventing or redressing racial prejudice, CBRI can actually render discrimination invisible to those most vulnerable to its effects.

Reflecting on this study provides insight into the strengths and weaknesses of the laboratory experimental method for probing latent racism. On the one hand, the ethical risks of exposing children to fictional discrimination in the form of written stimuli are smaller than the risks of exposing them to fully real discriminatory contexts during interpersonal interactions. On the other hand, replication of this laboratory experimental finding in something more closely approximating a field experimental context would strengthen its generalizability. Examining responses to fictional accounts of discrimination generates important evidence, but these conditions differ from field conditions where social cues could influence the recognition of actual discrimination.

Other laboratory experimental studies have supported the idea that priming CBRI affects more than just the conceptual understandings of intergroup interactions. Such priming also affects individuals' approach to the interactions themselves, often negatively, although findings on this point have been mixed. For example, individuals who read about the benefits of CBRI as opposed to multiculturalism subsequently demonstrate lower motivation to consider the perspectives of other racial groups (Todd & Galinsky, 2012). Similarly, White individuals primed with CBRI's benefits demonstrate more explicitly pro-White attitudes and more implicit racial bias against Blacks

(Richeson & Nussbaum, 2004). However, this finding contrasts with findings from a study using a similar paradigm priming CBRI versus multiculturalism (Wolsko et al., 2000). Wolsko and colleagues found that Whites primed with information about CBRI's benefits express fewer stereotypical beliefs about Blacks and more strongly endorse the belief that Blacks and Whites share core values. In similar research (Morrison et al., 2010; Wolsko et al., 2006), color-blind primes produced less positive evaluations of outgroups compared with multiculturalism primes. Under conditions of low conflict, then, CBRI can produce egalitarian gains, such as lower stereotype use. Yet it may also lower individuals' resolve to consider the perspectives of racial outgroups and elevate bias against those outgroups. In particular, under conditions of higher intergroup conflict, racially color-blind ideologies can have a different impact on the expression of racial bias.

Perhaps unsurprisingly, given that conflict can render cognitive processing more automatic as opposed to controlled (Fisk, Lee, & Rogers, 1991), conflict may increase the negative effects of CBRI versus multicultural ideology on racial bias. In a study in which students read about a fictional policy giving preferential treatment to minority students registering for scarce classes during a high-demand registration period, Whites espousing CBRI initially report lower bias than those holding a multicultural racial ideology immediately after being primed with high racial conflict (Correll, Park, & Smith, 2008). However, after a brief delay, this effect reversed, with racially color-blind Whites showing greater bias than their counterparts who espoused multicultural racial ideology. Correll et al. (2008) argued that in moments of conflict, individuals holding a CBRI may suppress negative attitudes in service of their ideals but continue holding the suppressed negative attitudes. This active suppression eventually depletes the cognitive resources used to suppress those latent attitudes in the first place. Thus, CBRI may increase the very prejudices it denies, particularly in conflict-riven contexts.

Again, however, we know that imagined conflict can be different from experienced conflict. Thus, supplementing the results from these laboratory experimental studies with more ecologically valid studies might resolve some of the inconsistencies and clarify the nuances found in previous research.

Just as its effects on attitudinal racial prejudice are mixed and sensitive to context, so too does CBRI cause mixed emotional and behavioral effects in interracial interactions. These consequences affect Whites and racial outgroup members in divergent ways. For example, Vorauer et al. (2009) found that priming racially color-blind (vs. multicultural) goals for participants anticipating interracial interactions causes White participants to worry more about the interaction going badly, leading to more negative affect. Conversely, priming Whites with a multicultural ideology causes less negative affect and more positive comments toward outgroup interaction partners. This pattern reverses for minorities. A color-blind prime *reduces* anxiety among minorities and improves how minorities expect to be treated when anticipating interracial interactions.

Yet highlighting again the importance of experimentation across methodological contexts, CBRI negatively affects intergroup interactions for minorities when actual interactions occur, perhaps because minority participants are exposed to their White partners' negative affect (Vorauer et al., 2009). Indeed, additional research shows that when primed with a CBRI before an interracial interaction, Whites exhibit more behavioral prejudice, leading ethnic minorities to find such interactions more challenging and cognitively depleting (Holoien & Shelton, 2012). Perhaps as a result, minority group members tend to view racially color-blind Whites as more prejudiced compared with those who are willing to discuss race (e.g., Apfelbaum, Sommers, et al., 2008) and can see CBRI in general as a set of ideologies that justify the unearned material benefits of dominant group membership (Bonilla-Silva, 2003). This disconnect between color-blind intentions and the perception of prejudice in color-blind contexts is ironic because, in practice, racial color blindness is an interactive social norm, such that Whites deploy and discontinue CBRI in response to others' behavior—and it also tends to backfire.

Individuals look to others to determine whether CBRI is an appropriate strategy (Norton, Sommers, Apfelbaum, Pura, & Ariely, 2006). Norton et al. (2006) recruited White participants for a study that was ostensibly on "communication and cognition." Participants were given a set of 32 photographs and told that their partner (a study confederate) held one of the 32 photos. Participants were tasked with quickly determining which one of the 32 photos their partner held by asking their partner the fewest possible yes–no questions to eliminate the other photographs. This task was designed to measure the efficiency with which diverse groups could work together to accomplish a common goal. The partner, who was either a Black or White confederate as determined by random assignment, modeled the task for participants by asking yes–no questions of the participant on a trial run of the identical task. Confederates mentioning race in this practice round predicted an increase in participants mentioning race, especially when the confederate was Black. These findings encouraged researchers to explore whether CBRI may be used strategically across contexts, instead of as a principled, constant belief.

Alleviating Concerns With Appearing Prejudiced Through CBRI

Evidence indicates that individuals do endorse CBRI strategically to avoid appearing prejudiced. How, after all, can a person who does not see race be racist? Such "strategic colorblindness" (Apfelbaum, Sommers, et al., 2008) helps Whites cope with the fear of being accused of racism and the anxiety of discussing the topic of race by avoiding race altogether (Apfelbaum, Sommers, et al., 2008; Goff et al., 2013; Richeson & Shelton, 2007; Vorauer et al., 1998, 2000).

In a subsequent yes–no task study, participants in interracial settings avoided asking questions related to race almost completely (mentioning race 10% of the time) unless the confederate partner had mentioned race previously, in which case participants mentioned race 88% of the time (Apfelbaum, Sommers, et al., 2008). Here, White participants who had expressed the most concern with appearing unbiased subsequently followed the racially colorblind norm set by a confederate most closely, particularly when this interaction partner was Black. Further research suggests that this behavior might stem from social desirability concerns: Children under age 10 (who are less attuned to social desirability) in the same experimental context asked about race to improve task efficiency, whereas older children mirrored the adult pattern (Apfelbaum, Pauker, Ambady, Sommers, & Norton, 2008).

Some people might be willing to accept the efficiency costs of CBRI to eliminate the concern with appearing prejudiced. However, CBRI can actually raise suspicions of prejudice in interracial interactions, and those suspicions have been empirically validated by hypothesis-blind raters' evaluations of interaction patterns. In one study, researchers videotaped one partner in a pair of actors playing participants engaging in the yes–no photo array task and asked Black study participants to evaluate those interactions (Apfelbaum, Sommers, et al., 2008). Although the interactions were designed to look natural, they were scripted for standardization purposes based on commentary in previous yes–no task interactions. One independent variable in the study's design was racial color blindness: In half of the videos, actors avoided talking about race. In the other half, actors mentioned race during the task. The other independent variable was perceived race of the actors playing study participants in the taped interactions, varying between two White partners and a White partner talking to an off-screen Black partner. Black participants assigned to the color-blind interracial conditions perceived greater prejudice in race-avoidant actors. Thus, strategic racial color blindness appears to be a bad strategy for both enhancing task efficiency during interracial interactions and minimizing the risk of being perceived as prejudiced. Despite the evidence that strategic color blindness may not be an effective strategy for enhancing intergroup relations, additional methodological techniques have found evidence of the strategic use of CBRI.

The yes–no group task method subset of CBRI laboratory experiments is stronger in terms of ecological validity than the priming and narrative method subset of these laboratory experiments. Studies that use paper and not people lose the richness of actual interpersonal interactions, although they gain clarity and strengthened internal validity by focusing strictly on a limited set of factors. Both main types of CBRI laboratory experiments have generated important and nuanced insights that provide the foundations on which future, multimethod research can build.

Beyond Priming and Yes–No Tasks

Most CBRI research in social psychology uses laboratory experiments and one of the priming and narrative or yes–no group task methods. Outside this fold, Goff and colleagues (2013) tested the motivations for strategic racial color blindness in less artificial interaction paradigms. Researchers coded student-run roundtable discussions about race to determine what motivated the strategic use of CBRI. Participants held 90-minute conversations on campus racial issues. Researchers then compared interracial conversations with conversations in all-White groups. Results suggest that White students used more strategic racial color blindness (e.g., "I don't like labeling people by their race") during interracial conversations. Ironically, in real-life conversations, being faced with racial difference made racial color blindness more salient for Whites. In addition, results show that students participating in interracial conversations expressed more concern both with being seen as prejudiced and for racial categorization's possible negative effects on racial minorities. Both the concern for being perceived as prejudiced and concern for harming outgroups, then, can motivate strategic racial color blindness.

A second study brought White students into the laboratory in an anticipated interaction paradigm, ostensibly to have a conversation with a Black student (Goff et al., 2013). Here, researchers manipulated students' concern with being seen as racist and perceptions of the harms that result from racial profiling of non-Whites and then measured the self-reported desire to use strategic racial color blindness before informing participants that the conversation would not actually take place. When White students were more concerned with appearing racist, they used strategic racial color blindness even when informed that racial categorization does not affect non-Whites. Together, these studies demonstrate that both egalitarian and self-presentational motives can lead individuals to employ CBRI.

In all, existing evidence strongly supports the idea that, far from enacting Reverend King's dream, CBRI actually represents a strategic error with respect to achieving the goal of racial equity in three distinct ways. First, CBRI decreases work efficiency in interracial contexts where race is relevant (Norton et al., 2006). This avoidance is interpersonal context–dependent: White study subjects waited for Black confederates (posing as subjects) to open the door to mentioning race and only then engaged in significant discussion of the subject (Apfelbaum, Sommers, et al., 2008). Letting Blacks set this conversational color-blindness norm might be perceived as a conflict avoidance strategy, albeit one with ironic interpersonal costs.

Second, avoiding race in interracial contexts lowers the quality of interracial interactions. Specifically, CBRI generated less friendly behavior on the part of Whites interacting with Blacks (e.g., less attempted eye contact) as judged by independent, hypothesis-blind coders (Norton et al., 2006). Consistent with this externally validated perception, strategic racial color blindness in contexts in which race is obviously relevant only increases Blacks' perception of White prejudice (Norton et al., 2006). These findings are particularly concerning because just as trust breeds trust, so, too, does mistrust breed mistrust, adversely affecting societal outcomes including national and regional patterns of crime, health, and economic development (Chandola, Marmot, & Siegrist, 2007; Lewis & Weigert, 1985; Nunn & Wantchekon, 2009; Pickett & Wilkinson, 2010; Schelling, 1980). Trust in interpersonal interactions helps society flourish, and CBRI seems to degrade the markers of that trust in some contexts.

Finally, CBRI can impair the recognition of overt racial discrimination. This effect is ironic with respect to one of CBRI's apparent motivations: aspirational racial color blindness stems from desire to attenuate racial inequality, yet evidence suggests it can impede recognition of that same inequality. Priming CBRI impairs individuals' ability to identify even unambiguous racial discrimination (Apfelbaum et al., 2010).

Overall, laboratory research shows that CBRI can produce inconsistent benefits and some decidedly negative attitudinal, affective, and behavioral consequences in interpersonal contexts. Laboratory experiments tend to show that people often feel positively toward the idea of racial color blindness and that, in practice, CBRI can dampen racial stereotyping. However, CBRI can also generate inefficient interactions, increase perceptions of bias, elevate expressions of ingroup favoritism, and lower recognition of bias. Further social psychology research addresses the impact of the endorsement of CBRI by organizations as opposed to individuals.

ORGANIZATIONS IN BLACK AND WHITE: CBRI OUTSIDE OF LABORATORY CONTEXTS

Experimental studies suggest that CBRI's established benefits extend to non-Whites and Whites in different ways in organizational as opposed to laboratory settings. Non-Whites tend to positively perceive companies that endorse a workplace culture of CBRI and whose recruitment materials show racially diverse employees (Jackson & Purdie-Vaughns, 2004; Purdie-Vaughns, Steele, Davies, Ditlmann, & Crosby, 2008; Purdie-Vaughns & Walton, 2011). That is, it is a combination of cues including CBRI and minority underrepresentation that together generate threats to identity and mistrust of White-dominated organizational settings among Blacks. Without the context of this representation, CBRI is not threatening per se to Blacks in organizational settings. Similarly, CBRI in the social context of dominance also has effects consistent with threat minimization. Highly racially identified Whites primed with CBRI as opposed to multiculturalism express lower social dominance orientation and prejudice (Morrison et al., 2010). Social dominance orientation's associations with group-based hierarchies suggest that lowering it in organizations in this way might advance equity by lessening not only racism but also other forms of prejudice such as homophobia, ethnocentrism, sexism, nationalism, classism, and regionalism (Sidanius & Pratto, 1999). In other words, Whites who strongly identify with being White are more likely to support egalitarian norms when they are exposed to CBRI. This group of findings is consistent with the idea that CBRI evokes shared core values across racial groups. CBRI thus has potential to decrease racial animosities and increase intergroup interactions by emphasizing what diverse racial group members share rather than how they differ, but this potential is context-dependent.

It is therefore unsurprising that methods examining CBRI's effects in different contexts produce different results. In correlational field studies, far from increasing Blacks' trust in organizations, CBRI is associated with non-Whites' perceptions of a hostile work climate. Specifically, White employees' endorsement of CBRI predicts non-White employees' perceptions that their organizational climate is racially biased (Plaut, Thomas, & Goren, 2009). This is consistent with experimental findings suggesting that Blacks sometimes experience Whites' performance or endorsement of CBRI as a form of prejudice. For example, prospective non-White employees' evaluations of a company's trustworthiness, and their own desire to work for it, decline when the company endorses CBRI and does not appear racially diverse (Purdie-Vaughns et al., 2008). Prospective non-White employees tend to perceive companies that endorse a culture of multiculturalism as more trustworthy relative to companies endorsing CBRI without respect to company diversity (Purdie-Vaughns et al., 2008).

Conversely, the alternative racial ideology of multiculturalism also has potential negative consequences for organizational climates. Specifically, multiculturalism can generate negative affect in Whites, leaving them feeling excluded or devalued (Plaut, Garnett, Buffardi, & Sanchez-Burks, 2011). This perception can drive more positive responses to CBRI relative to multiculturalism among Whites. For instance, in one series of studies, exposure to CBRI as opposed to multiculturalism decreased reported preferences for inequality and increased reported support for funding diversity-related organizations among White participants who were highly identified with their racial group (Morrison et al., 2010). Whites who were less identified with their racial group showed no differences after exposure to different racial ideologies. Morrison and colleagues suggested that CBRI's effects among highly racially identified Whites result from the multiculturalism prime threatening the core values of that subgroup of White subjects. In this context, CBRI appears less threatening than multicultural alternatives to highly racially identified Whites in ways that may affect socially and politically significant attitudes and behaviors. In other words, interventions that rely on multiculturalism to advance equity and minimize intergroup hostility may cause highly racially identified Whites to perceive more threat and generate more hostility toward members of the racial groups associated with that threat.

Unfortunately, racial minorities' experience of CBRI in organizations is not as positive. Plaut, Thomas, and Goren (2009) reported that White employees' endorsement of CBRI was associated with an increase in minority employees' perception that their organizational climate was racially biased. Thus, whereas multiculturalism can threaten highly racially identified Whites in organizational settings, CBRI can degrade minorities' perceptions of the organizational climate. This tension highlights an important area for future CBRI research on how to advance organizational equity by integrating the advantages of CBRI for Whites with the advantages of multiculturalism for minorities.

In all, relatively few field studies, and particularly field experiments, have assessed CBRI's effects in organizations. However, existing organizational research on CBRI has produced important insights. This research demonstrates that CBRI can lower non-Whites' institutional trust and generate suspicions of organizational bias. Conversely, diversity-related organizations that propound CBRI may receive more support from White evaluators. However, most CBRI research on organizations has occurred outside of everyday organizational contexts. Future experimental, observational, and multimethod studies about CBRI in organizations can best contribute to our growing cumulative knowledge about this important racial ideology by strengthening ecological validity through use of field settings.

CONCLUSION

Social psychology research on CBRI has mostly deployed experimental methods in laboratory settings. This research yields important insights into how individuals use strategic racial color blindness to avoid appearing racist. Yet research shows that, ironically, this strategy can degrade the very interracial interactions that Whites deploy CBRI to improve. Such consequences are heterogeneous. For instance, priming CBRI often leads to less stereotyping but can also generate greater expressions of prejudice (Morrison et al.,

2010; Richeson & Nussbaum, 2004). CBRI can also impair recognition of blatant racial bullying and discrimination (Apfelbaum et al., 2010). For racial minorities, CBRI can lower the quality of interracial interactions, as well as lower workplace trust and satisfaction (Apfelbaum, Sommers, et al., 2008; Holoien & Shelton, 2012; Plaut et al., 2009; Purdie-Vaughns et al., 2008). Fortunately, social psychology researchers have quantified these potential costs in large part by comparing CBRI with multiculturalism as an alternative racial ideology that sometimes offers its own potential advantages (Apfelbaum et al., 2010; Morrison et al., 2010; Purdie-Vaughns et al., 2008; Richeson & Nussbaum, 2004; Todd & Galinsky, 2012; Vorauer et al., 2009; Wolsko et al., 2000, 2006) but can also produce notable drawbacks (Plaut et al., 2011).

Overall, we celebrate the contributions that social psychology research has made to the scientific understanding of the dominant racial narrative in our society, which is CBRI. Laboratory experimental manipulations of CBRI have delineated different effects of color-blind versus color-conscious racial ideologies in otherwise identical contexts. Other experiments manipulated the racial composition of groups to determine when strategic racial color blindness is used in group interactions. Future such research can continue to broaden our understanding of both whether we should embrace CBRI as an aspirational orientation to racial equality in a perfect world (ideal theory) and what happens when real-world actors are focused on motivations beyond racial equality (nonideal theory). Ours is not a prescriptive argument about embracing the power of CBRI to benefit society—or fearing its potential to do harm—but rather a proscriptive argument to continue expanding and combining the methodological tools social psychologists deploy to address questions of when CBRI can positively affect intergroup relations and when other strategies work better to advance our shared egalitarian values. Specifically, longitudinal designs would provide an excellent supplement to research examining the impact of CBRI priming on interracial interactions and cooperative efficiency. Psychophysiological methods would enhance our ability to answer questions about the precise causal mechanisms of CBRI's effects on attitudes, emotions, and behaviors. Further exploring these effects with a diverse array of methods will continue to generate new and interesting insights enhancing our ability to understand where and when CBRI is most useful in advancing shared egalitarian norms.

Finally, moving away from the Black–White color binary will also help advance sharper conceptualization and richer diversity of methods in CBRI social psychology research. Most CBRI research operationalizes race in terms of Black and White. Social psychologists are aware that this binary does not fully capture the impact of CBRI in the rapidly diversifying racial context of contemporary America. Researchers tend to maximize statistical power and simplicity of narrative in our studies by simplifying this space, but that simplification generates its own forms of color blindness when it becomes a methodological norm, as is the case in CBRI research in social psychology. Appropriately enough, producing broader and deeper knowledge about the causes and consequences of CBRI thus requires more diverse experimentation with different ways of thinking about color—experimentation that the increasingly broad array of methods used to explore CBRI makes contemporary researchers better equipped than ever to undertake.

REFERENCES

Apfelbaum, E. P., Norton, M. I., & Sommers, S. R. (2012). Racial color blindness: Emergence, practice, and implications. *Current Directions in Psychological Science, 21*, 205–209. http://dx.doi.org/10.1177/0963721411434980

Apfelbaum, E. P., Pauker, K., Ambady, N., Sommers, S. R., & Norton, M. I. (2008). Learning (not) to talk about race: When older children underperform in social categorization. *Developmental Psychology, 44*, 1513–1518. http://dx.doi.org/10.1037/a0012835

Apfelbaum, E. P., Pauker, K., Sommers, S. R., & Ambady, N. (2010). In blind pursuit of racial equality? *Psychological Science, 21*, 1587–1592. http://dx.doi.org/10.1177/0956797610384741

Apfelbaum, E. P., Sommers, S. R., & Norton, M. I. (2008). Seeing race and seeming racist? Evaluating strategic color blindness in social interaction. *Journal of Personality and Social Psychology, 95*, 918–932. http://dx.doi.org/10.1037/a0011990

Bonilla-Silva, E. (2003). *Racism without racists*. Lanham, MD: Rowman & Littlefield.

Campbell, D. T., & Fiske, D. W. (1959). Convergent and discriminant validation by the multitrait–multimethod matrix. *Psychological Bulletin, 56*, 81–105. http://dx.doi.org/10.1037/h0046016

Chandola, T., Marmot, M., & Siegrist, J. (2007). Failed reciprocity in close social relationships and health: Findings from the Whitehall II study. *Journal of Psychosomatic Research, 63*, 403–411. http://dx.doi.org/10.1016/j.jpsychores.2007.07.012

Correll, J., Park, B., & Smith, J. A. (2008). Color-blind and multicultural prejudice reduction strategies in high-conflict situations. *Group Processes & Intergroup Relations, 11*, 471–491. http://dx.doi.org/10.1177/1368430208095401

Fisk, A. D., Lee, M. D., & Rogers, W. A. (1991). Recombination of automatic processing components: The effects of transfer, reversal, and conflict situations. *Human Factors, 33*, 267–280.

Fryberg, S. A., & Stephens, N. M. (2010). When the world is color blind, American Indians are invisible: A diversity science approach. *Psychological Inquiry, 21*, 115–119. http://dx.doi.org/10.1080/1047840X.2010.483847

Goff, P. A., Jackson, M. C., Nichols, A. H., & Di Leone, B. A. (2013). Anything but race: Avoiding racial discourse to avoid hurting you or me. *Psychology, 4*, 335–339.

Goff, P. A., Steele, C. M., & Davies, P. G. (2008). The space between us: Stereotype threat and distance in interracial contexts. *Journal of Personality and Social Psychology, 94,* 91–107. http://dx.doi.org/10.1037/0022-3514.94.1.91

Haney-López, I. (2014). *Dog whistle politics: How coded racial appeals have reinvented racism and wrecked the middle class.* New York, NY: Oxford University Press.

Harris, F. C., & Lieberman, R. C. (2013). *Beyond discrimination: Racial inequality in a postracist era.* New York, NY: Russell Sage.

Holoien, D. S., & Shelton, J. (2012). You deplete me: The cognitive costs of color blindness on ethnic minorities. *Journal of Experimental Social Psychology, 48,* 562–565. http://dx.doi.org/10.1016/j.jesp.2011.09.010

Jackson, M. C., & Purdie-Vaughns, V. (2004, August). *Is color blindness threatening? How social context shapes color-blind ideologies.* Paper presented at the American Psychological Association Annual Convention, Honolulu, HI.

King, M. L., Jr. (2001). *The words of Martin Luther King, Jr.* New York, NY: Newmarket Press.

Knowles, E. D., Lowery, B. S., Hogan, C. M., & Chow, R. M. (2009). On the malleability of ideology: Motivated construals of color blindness. *Journal of Personality and Social Psychology, 96,* 857–869. http://dx.doi.org/10.1037/a0013595

Lewis, J. D., & Weigert, A. (1985). Trust as a social reality. *Social Forces, 63,* 967–985. http://dx.doi.org/10.1093/sf/63.4.967

Markus, H. R., Steele, C. M., & Steele, D. M. (2000). Color blindness as a barrier to inclusion: Assimilation and nonimmigrant minorities. *Daedalus, 129,* 233–259.

Millhiser, I. (2013). Rick Perry reacts to Zimmerman verdict: "I think our justice system is color blind." Retrieved from *ThinkProgress.org* website: http://think progress.org/justice/2013/07/14/2297301/rick-perry-reacts-to-zimmerman-verdict-i-think-our-justice-system-is-color-blind

Morrison, K. R., Plaut, V. C., & Ybarra, O. (2010). Predicting whether multiculturalism positively or negatively influences White Americans' intergroup attitudes: The role of ethnic identification. *Personality and Social Psychology Bulletin, 36,* 1648–1661. http://dx.doi.org/10.1177/0146167210386118

Norton, M. I., Sommers, S. R., Apfelbaum, E. P., Pura, N., & Ariely, D. (2006). Color blindness and interracial interaction: Playing the political correctness game. *Psychological Science, 17,* 949–953. http://dx.doi.org/10.1111/j.1467-9280.2006.01810.x

Nunn, N., & Wantchekon, L. (2009). *The slave trade and the origins of mistrust in Africa* (NBER Working Paper 14783). Cambridge, MA: National Bureau of Economic Research.

Peery, D. (2011). The color-blind ideal in a race-conscious reality: The case for a new legal ideal for race relations. *Northwestern Journal of Law and Social Policy, 6,* 473–495.

Pickett, K., & Wilkinson, R. (2010). *The spirit level: Why greater equality makes societies stronger.* New York, NY: Bloomsbury.

Plaut, V. C., Garnett, F. G., Buffardi, L. E., & Sanchez-Burks, J. (2011). "What about me?" Perceptions of exclusion and Whites' reactions to multiculturalism. *Journal of Personality and Social Psychology, 101*, 337–353. http://dx.doi.org/10.1037/a0022832

Plaut, V. C., Thomas, K. M., & Goren, M. J. (2009). Is multiculturalism or color blindness better for minorities? *Psychological Science, 20*, 444–446. http://dx.doi.org/10.1111/j.1467-9280.2009.02318.x

Purdie-Vaughns, V., Steele, C. M., Davies, P. G., Ditlmann, R., & Crosby, J. R. (2008). Social identity contingencies: How diversity cues signal threat or safety for African Americans in mainstream institutions. *Journal of Personality and Social Psychology, 94*, 615–630. http://dx.doi.org/10.1037/0022-3514.94.4.615

Purdie-Vaughns, V., & Walton, G. M. (2011). Is multiculturalism bad for African Americans? Redefining inclusion through the lens of identity-safety. In L. R. Tropp & R. K. Mallett (Eds.), *Moving beyond prejudice reduction: Pathways to positive intergroup relations* (pp. 159–177). Washington, DC: American Psychological Association. http://dx.doi.org/10.1037/12319-008

Rattan, A., & Ambady, N. (2013). Diversity ideologies and intergroup relations: An examination of color blindness and multiculturalism. *European Journal of Social Psychology, 43*, 12–21. http://dx.doi.org/10.1002/ejsp.1892

Rawls, J. (1971). *A theory of justice*. Cambridge, MA: Harvard University Press.

Richeson, J. A., & Nussbaum, R. J. (2004). The impact of multiculturalism versus color blindness on racial bias. *Journal of Experimental Social Psychology, 40*, 417–423. http://dx.doi.org/10.1016/j.jesp.2003.09.002

Richeson, J. A., & Shelton, J. N. (2007). Negotiating interracial interactions: Costs, consequences, and possibilities. *Current Directions in Psychological Science, 16*, 316–320. http://dx.doi.org/10.1111/j.1467-8721.2007.00528.x

Rosenthal, L., & Levy, S. R. (2010). The color-blind, multicultural, and polycultural ideological approaches to improving intergroup attitudes and relations. *Social Issues and Policy Review, 4*, 215–246. http://dx.doi.org/10.1111/j.1751-2409.2010.01022.x

Schelling, T. C. (1980). *The strategy of conflict*. Cambridge, MA: Harvard University Press.

Sidanius, J., & Pratto, F. (1999). *Social dominance: An intergroup theory of social hierarchy and oppression*. New York, NY: Cambridge University Press.

Todd, A. R., & Galinsky, A. D. (2012). The reciprocal link between multiculturalism and perspective-taking: How ideological and self-regulatory approaches to managing diversity reinforce each other. *Journal of Experimental Social Psychology, 48*, 1394–1398. http://dx.doi.org/10.1016/j.jesp.2012.07.007

Vorauer, J. D., Gagnon, A., & Sasaki, S. J. (2009). Salient intergroup ideology and intergroup interaction. *Psychological Science, 20*, 838–845. http://dx.doi.org/10.1111/j.1467-9280.2009.02369.x

Vorauer, J. D., Hunter, A. J., Main, K. J., & Roy, S. A. (2000). Meta-stereotype activation: Evidence from indirect measures for specific evaluative concerns experienced by members of dominant groups in intergroup interaction. *Journal of Personality and Social Psychology, 78*, 690–707. http://dx.doi.org/10.1037/0022-3514.78.4.690

Vorauer, J. D., Main, K. J., & O'Connell, G. B. (1998). How do individuals expect to be viewed by members of lower status groups? Content and implications of metastereotypes. *Journal of Personality and Social Psychology, 75*, 917–937. http://dx.doi.org/10.1037/0022-3514.75.4.917

Wolsko, C., Park, B., & Judd, C. M. (2006). Considering the tower of Babel: Correlates of assimilation and multiculturalism among ethnic minority and majority groups in the United States. *Social Justice Research, 19*, 277–306. http://dx.doi.org/10.1007/s11211-006-0014-8

Wolsko, C., Park, B., Judd, C. M., & Wittenbrink, B. (2000). Framing interethnic ideology: Effects of multicultural and color-blind perspectives on judgments of groups and individuals. *Journal of Personality and Social Psychology, 78*, 635–654. http://dx.doi.org/10.1037/0022-3514.78.4.635

8

THE MEASUREMENT OF
COLOR-BLIND RACIAL IDEOLOGY

GERMINE AWAD AND KAREN MORAN JACKSON

The measurement of racial attitudes has evolved to reflect the zeitgeist of the times. In psychology, the study of racial attitudes started with the examination of explicit attitudes. Before avoiding racial topics was the norm, people openly expressed their views (usually negative) about ethnic minority groups. As it became less acceptable and distasteful to openly express negative, stereotypical, or hostile views toward ethnic minority groups, the expression of attitudes became more covert and harder to assess. The result of the shift from explicit to implicit expression of attitudes led scholars to develop more sophisticated ways to capture beliefs about racial groups. Some scholars developed methods that relied on reaction time and behavior, whereas others created self-report racial attitude measures that were less reactive, the purpose of which were harder to ascertain. When scales were developed that made it more difficult for participants to determine the purpose of self-report measures intended to gauge racial attitudes, it represented a shift in the literature from assessing old-fashioned racism to more modern forms of racial prejudice.

http://dx.doi.org/10.1037/14754-009
The Myth of Racial Color Blindness: Manifestations, Dynamics, and Impact, H. A. Neville, M. E. Gallardo, and D. W. Sue (Editors)

This chapter reviews instruments designed to measure aspects of color-blind racial ideology (CBRI). Both established instruments (i.e., those with both reliability and validity information) and less established measures are reviewed. The established instruments include the Color-Blind Racial Attitudes Scale (CoBRAS; Neville, Lilly, Duran, Lee, & Browne, 2000), the Mental Health Practitioner's Racial Socialization Practices: Color-Blind Ideology subscale (Brown, Blackmon, Schumacher, & Urbanski, 2013), the Teacher Cultural Belief Scale: Egalitarian subscale (Hachfeld, Hahn, Schroeder, Anders, Stanat, & Kunter, 2011), Multicultural–Color-Blind Scale: Color-Blind Ideology subscale (Ryan, Hunt, Weible, Peterson, & Casas, 2007), and the Intergroup Ideologies Measures: Color Blindness subscale (Rosenthal & Levy, 2012). A critique of the current instruments and future directions is also presented.

There are several measures designed to assess contemporary forms of prejudice. The Modern Racism Scale (MRS) was developed by McConahay (1986) to measure the construct of modern racism. *Modern racism* is the idea that racism is a thing of the past and ethnic minorities are pushing too hard and too fast in their fight for equal rights. Therefore, any gains made by ethnic minorities are considered undeserved because their tactics are perceived to be unfair (McConahay, 1986). This measure basically assesses the extent to which individuals are resentful toward ethnic minorities and issues related to ethnic minority rights. Similarly, *symbolic racism*, developed by Sears and Henry (2005), adds to this idea by assessing how racial resentment is coupled with traditional American values such as individualism and the Protestant work ethic. Over the years, these measures of prejudice have become more reactive and less sensitive in their assessment of prejudice (Fazio, Jackson, Dunton, & Williams, 1995; Neville et al., 2000). Because a more sensitive, contemporary, and ultramodern construct to assess racial prejudice was warranted, instruments measuring aspects of CBRI were created.

Neville, Awad, Brooks, Flores, and Bluemel (2013) outlined two dimensions of CBRI: color evasion and power evasion. *Color evasion* refers to the strategy of ignoring race as a means to emphasize similarity and reject racial superiority (Frankenberg, 1993). This strategy has the aspirational goal of reducing racism. *Power evasion* emphasizes the willful denial of power relationships designed to ignore racism and discrimination. Power evasion builds on the idea that everyone has the same chance to succeed, and therefore ethnic minorities who fail do so because of individual characteristics as opposed to external forces such as racism or discrimination (Frankenberg, 1993; Neville et al., 2013). A review of the PsycINFO database revealed 12 studies that introduced a measure of color-blind racial attitudes or ideology. Only five of the 12 scales consisted of more than one item, were used in more than one study, and had available reliability and validity information (see Table 8.1).

TABLE 8.1

Measures of Color-Blind Racial Ideology With Reliability and Validity Information From Initial Scale Construction Article

Scale	Dimension of CBRI assessed	Measurement scale	No. of items	Example item	Population	Reliability	Validity
CoBRAS (Neville et al., 2000)	Power evasion	6-point scale ranging from *strongly disagree* (1) to *strongly agree* (6).	20 total: Racial Privilege (7 items); Institutional Discrimination (7 items); Blatant Racial Issues (6 items); 14-item short form also available.	Racial Privilege subscale: "White people in the U.S. have certain advantages because of the color of their skin." Institutional Discrimination subscale: "Social policies, such as affirmative action, discriminate unfairly against White people." Blatant Racial Issues subscale: "Racial problems in the U.S. are rare, isolated situations."	1,171 White college students, community members, and ethnic minority students	$\alpha = .86–.91$ Gutman split-half reliability of .72 2-week test–retest reliability estimate of .68	Exploratory and confirmatory factor analysis performed. Estimates of convergent, discriminant, concurrent, and criterion validity available.
Multicultural-Color-Blind Scale: Color-Blind Ideology subscale (Ryan et al., 2007; revised in Ryan et al., 2010)	Color evasion	7-point scale ranging from *not likely to improve relations between groups* (1) to *likely to improve relations between groups* (7).	4	"Judging one another as individuals rather than members of an ethnic group."	248 Black and White community members and college students	$\alpha = .69$	Exploratory factor analysis performed. Estimates of convergent validity calculated.

(continues)

TABLE 8.1

Measures of Color-Blind Racial Ideology With Reliability and Validity Information From Initial Scale Construction Article (Continued)

Scale	Dimension of CBRI assessed	Measurement scale	No. of items	Example item	Population	Reliability	Validity
Teacher Cultural Belief Scale: Egalitarian subscale (Hachfeld et al., 2011)	Color evasion	6-point scale ranging from *strongly disagree* (1) to *strongly agree* (6).	4	"Schools should aim to foster and support the similarities between students from different cultural backgrounds."	773 German beginning teachers and teacher candidates	$\alpha = .78–.81$	Confirmatory factor analysis conducted. Factorial validity assessed in group comparison model of teachers with different diversity experiences.
Mental Health Practitioner's Racial Socialization Practices: Color-Blind Ideology subscale (Brown et al., 2013)	Power evasion	7-point scale ranging from *not likely* (1) to *very likely* (7).	4	"U.S. Society is fair toward Black people."	136 Black and White mental health practitioners	$\alpha = .81$	Subscale was created from one of five factors from a factor analysis of a larger 39-item scale on racial-socialization practices.
Intergroup Ideologies Measures: Color-Blindness subscale (Rosenthal & Levy, 2012)	Color evasion	7-point scale ranging from *strongly disagree* (1) to *strongly agree* (7).	5	"Ethnic and cultural group categories are not very important for understanding or making decisions about people."	Study 1: 694 majority White and Asian students; Study 2: 132 White and Black community members; Study 3: 101 White and Black community members	Study 1: $\alpha = .86$; Study 2: $\alpha = .76$; Study 3: no alpha for single item	Principal components factor analysis conducted.

Note. CoBRAS = Color-Blind Racial Attitudes Scale.

CoBRAS

The CoBRAS was designed to measure the construct of CBRI (Neville et al., 2000) and is the most widely used measure of color-blind racial attitudes. Many of the studies' samples that used the CoBRAS included White or a majority White population (e.g., Awad, Cokley, & Ravitch, 2005), whereas others have used the CoBRAS with African Americans (Barr & Neville, 2008; Coleman, Chapman, & Wang, 2013; Neville, Coleman, Falconer, & Holmes, 2005), Latinos (Kohatsu, Victoria, Lau, Flores, & Salazar, 2011), and Asian Americans (Chen, Lephuoc, Guzmán, Rude, & Dodd, 2006; Tawa, Suyemoto, & Roemer, 2012). Most of the studies were conducted using university or college students, but others have examined CBRI with counselors, practicing psychologists, and community service providers (e.g., Burkard & Knox, 2004; Chao, 2013; Johnson, Antle, & Barbee, 2009; Penn & Post, 2012), parents (Barr & Neville, 2008; Lee, Grotevant, Hellerstedt, Gunnar, et al., 2006), and working adults (Poteat & Spanierman, 2008). The CoBRAS has also been used to examine the effectiveness of interventions (Aldana, Rowley, Checkoway, & Richards-Schuster, 2012; Colvin-Burque, Zugazaga, & Davis-Maye, 2007; Kernahan & Davis, 2009; Soble, Spanierman, & Liao, 2011; Spanierman et al., 2008; Steinfeldt & Wong, 2010).

The CoBRAS was created to operationalize the cognitive aspects of the power-evasion dimension of CBRI. In the initial construction study, three interrelated subscales emerged in the exploratory factor analysis (Neville et al., 2000). The three subscales consist of (a) *Racial Privilege*, which assesses the extent to which individuals deny the existence of White privilege; (b) *Institutional Discrimination*, which measures awareness of institutional forms of discrimination; and (c) *Blatant Racial Issues*, which assess general unawareness to prevalent racial discrimination. In the 20-item version of the scale, Racial Privilege and Institutional Discrimination consist of seven items, and Blatant Racial Issues has six items. Example items include the following: "White people in the U.S. have certain advantages because of the color of their skin" (Racial Privilege subscale); "Social policies, such as affirmative action, discriminate unfairly against White people" (Institutional Discrimination subscale); and "Racial problems in the U.S. are rare, isolated situations" (Blatant Racial Issues subscale). This factor structure was validated by confirmatory factor analysis (CFA) in a subsequent study supporting three factors for the measure.

In addition, the CoBRAS demonstrated an acceptable split-half reliability estimate of .72 and Cronbach's alpha estimates of .70 to .86 in the initial validation sample. Concurrent validity was demonstrated for the CoBRAS via correlations with two just world belief scales indicating strong correlations ranging from .39 to .61. To establish discriminant validity, Neville and colleagues (2000) correlated the CoBRAS with the Marlowe–Crowne Social Desirability Scale and found no significant association between the two scales. Criterion-related validity was demonstrated by differences in CoBRAS scores based on racial group membership and gender. Test–retest reliability was .80 for the Racial Privilege and Institutional Discrimination subscales and .34 for the Blatant Racial Issues subscale. Overall, the original construction and validation study provided evidence that the CoBRAS is a robust, parsimonious, and valid measure of color-blind racial attitudes.

The CoBRAS remains the dominant measure of color-blind racial attitudes. However, the following scales demonstrate that the CoBRAS is not the exclusive measurement vehicle.

Often the choice of designing a separate scale appears to come from wanting a shorter measure than the 20-item CoBRAS or even the 14-item CoBRAS—short form. These shorter measures range from scales with sufficient reliability and validity information to scales made up of two items with little or no reliability and validity information.

Mental Health Practitioner's Racial Socialization Practices: Color-Blind Ideology Subscale

Brown and colleagues (2013) include a four-item color-blind subscale in a measure of the mental health practitioner's racial socialization practices. The authors created a 39-item survey for mental health professionals by incorporating existing scales on racial socialization and designing items based on the literature. The items were written to respond to the prompt: "Please indicate the likelihood that you have or would incorporate the following messages, similar statements, sentiments, or feelings in your therapeutic work with a client who self-identifies as African American or Black-U.S. born." The CBRI items derive from items found on the Teenager Experience of Racial Socialization Scale (TERS; Stevenson, Cameron, Herrero-Taylor, & Davis, 2002), a previously validated scale used with African American adolescents. Example items include "U.S. society is fair toward Black people," and "Whites do not have more opportunities." The original scale by Stevenson et al. was written to assess the racial socialization experiences of African American teenagers, including the importance and frequency of messages about cultural empowerment and familial experiences with racism. Although not directly addressing the issue of CBRI, the TERS does include items that more closely reflect the power-evasion aspect of color-blind racial attitudes because racial socialization of African American adolescents often includes attention to discrimination at both personal and societal levels.

Brown et al. (2013), however, were explicit that the goal of their study was not scale construction but rather to explore racial socialization patterns with mental health professionals. An exploratory factor analysis of the scale resulted in five coherent factors, all with sufficient coefficient reliabilities, including CBRI ($\alpha = .81$). Although the use of CBRI with clients was found to vary by clinician's race and client's age, no specific tests of validity were performed on the scale.

Teacher Cultural Belief Scale: Egalitarian Subscale

Hachfeld et al. (2011) created the Teacher Cultural Belief Scale to include both multicultural and egalitarian ideologies measured with a 6-point scale. The authors used the term *egalitarian*, a common term in the education and school literature; however, they explicitly acknowledged that their conceptualization is similar to the use of *color blind* from a color-evasion perspective in social psychology literature. The scale was developed on the basis of psychological research on intergroup contact, particularly the differences between egalitarian and multicultural viewpoints. For those with multicultural beliefs, differences between groups must be acknowledged, whereas those with egalitarian beliefs prefer to emphasize the commonalities between cultural groups. An example item from the egalitarian subscale is: "Children should learn that people of different cultural origins often have a lot in common."

The four egalitarian items, combined with four items to measure multiculturalism, were assessed in two studies. First, the scale was assessed with CFA using beginning teachers in Germany. The two-factor model showed a good fit to the data, with satisfactory factor loadings of all items, and an acceptable alpha of the egalitarian subscale of .78. The authors also conducted a multigroup CFA for measurement invariance with the same sample. They found that beginning teachers at both the start and end of their training period had similar means on the two subscales but that beginning teachers in vocational track schools endorsed both multicultural and egalitarian items higher than teachers in college track schools. The second study replicated the CFA from the first study with teaching and education students at a German university. The good fit of the two-factor structure, along with satisfactory factor loadings of all items, confirmed the structure that was found in the first study. The reliability alpha for this sample was .81. The second study also established concurrent validity for the scale by finding significant positive relations between egalitarianism and motivation to control prejudiced behavior and attitudes toward pluralism but found no relations as expected between egalitarianism and prejudices, acculturation, or authoritarianism.

Multicultural–Color-Blind Scale: Color-Blind Ideology Subscale

Ryan et al. (2007) also developed a scale to measure both multicultural and color-blind racial ideologies, based on research concerning intergroup relations, similar to the framework of Hachfeld et al. (2011). Ryan and colleagues created four items each to assess multicultural and color-blind racial ideologies on a 7-point scale in which multicultural items emphasize intergroup differences whereas color-blind items emphasize intergroup similarities. The question prompt asked individuals how likely the items were to improve group relations in the United States. An example item from the color-blind ideology subscale is: "Judging one another as individuals rather than members of an ethnic group." These items closely align with the color-evasion dimension of CBRI in which individuals attempt to minimize differences between groups as a tactic to reduce racism.

Ryan et al. (2007) conducted two studies using the scale to examine the relations among the ideologies, prejudice, and ethnocentrism. In the first study, the authors used principal components analysis to test a two-factor structure with adequate factor loadings of all items. Reported alphas were .78 for the multicultural subscale and .69 for the color-blind subscale using a majority White adult population. They also found that Black participants were less likely to endorse CBRI than White participants and more likely to endorse multicultural ideology. The second study, using Black and White college students, started with a CFA of the scale. The two-factor model fit the data significantly better than a one-factor model, indicating that the multicultural and color-blind subscales were distinct concepts. Similar mean difference scores between Black and White participants was also found in this sample, as in the first sample. For all participants, those with stronger multicultural beliefs compared with color-blind beliefs demonstrated less ethnocentrism.

One other study has included the four-item color-blind subscale designed by Ryan et al. (2007) and reported an alpha of .63 for White college students (Todd & Galinsky, 2012). A revised version of the measure, called the Multicultural–Color-Blind Scale, was reported in Ryan, Casas, and Thompson (2010), adding an additional item to assess both ideologies. This 10-item scale was used with White and Latino adult populations. Unfortunately, the authors did not report a Cronbach's alpha for this 10-item version.

Intergroup Ideologies Measures: Color-Blindness Subscale

Rosenthal and Levy (2012) also created their own measure of racial color blindness, although the main aim of their research was to verify polyculturalism as a distinct ideology from multiculturalism and color blindness. Their work derives from studies on intergroup relations within the same social psychology realm as Ryan et al. (2007) and Hachfeld et al. (2011). However, they supplemented the traditional multicultural–color-blind dichotomy with the ideology of polyculturalism, which recognizes differences between groups while acknowledging the nonstatic nature of culture and the interconnections between different races and cultural traditions. As with the other scales based on intergroup relations research, the color-blind subscale focuses exclusively on the color-evasion aspect of CBRI.

Rosenthal and Levy (2012) created a 15-item scale, with five items for each of the three ideologies. The five-item color-blind subscale includes items such as "Racial and ethnic group memberships do not matter very much to who we are." Items were measured with a 7-point Likert scale, and reported alphas for the color-blind subscale were .86 with a majority White and Asian American undergraduate sample and .76 with an adult sample. Using an undergraduate sample, the authors performed a principal components analysis and found a three-factor structure with satisfactory factor loadings of all items. With the undergraduate sample, the color-blind subscale showed a weak negative correlation with appreciation for diversity ($r = -.10$) but showed no correlations with social dominance orientation, right-wing authoritarianism, affirmative action, interest in diversity, comfort with differences, and willingness for intergroup contact. However, the multicultural and polycultural subscales were correlated with several of these variables, demonstrating some degree of conceptual differentiation.

OTHER MEASURES OF CBRI

There are additional measures of CBRI that have not been subjected to a rigorous construction or validation process. As a result, information about reliability and validity estimates as well as sample construction information was often unavailable. Many times, these scales aim to provide a short assessment of the construct. Most of these types of scales provide only reliability estimates and are typically used in only one study. For example, in an effort to use a shorter scale of CBRI, Plaut, Thomas, and Goren (2009) created a two-item measure of color-blind racial attitudes, informed from work by Wolsko, Park, and Judd (2006), within a larger survey study on the "diversity climate" of organizations. The two items, tapping into the dimension of color evasion in the workplace, were "Employees should downplay their racial and ethnic differences" and "The organization should encourage racial and ethnic minorities to adapt to mainstream ways." The scale had an alpha of .70 as measured by mainly White employees in a health care organization.

Similarly, a survey of households, the Portrait of American Life (PALS; Vargas, 2014), includes two items about CBRI based on the work of Bonilla-Silva

(2006). These two items are "One of the most effective ways to improve race relations in the United States is to stop talking about race" and "Government should do more to help minorities increase their standard of living." The first item addresses color evasion, whereas the second item addresses structural racism, which is more closely related to the power-evasion dimension of CBRI. Vargas (2014) used the PALS survey to examine the endorsement of CBRIs by people who identified as White but are perceived by others as non-White.

Another scale to operationalize the color-evasion perspective of CBRI is the Strategic Color-Blindness Scale (Goff, Jackson, Nichols, & Di Leone, 2013). This 11-item scale was measured on a 7-point Likert scale ranging from *strongly disagree* to *strongly agree*. An example item is "Seeing people in terms of race is a significant hindrance to racial harmony." The sample in this study consisted of 91 White undergraduate students. The Cronbach's alpha for the scale was .91. No validation information was reported for the measure.

Additional measures of racial color blindness can be found in Levin et al. (2012); Knowles, Lowery, Hogan, and Chow (2009); Morrison and Chung (2011); and Mazzocco, Cooper, and Flint (2012). These measures all operationalize the color-evasion perspective of CBRI and range from four to six items measured on 6- or 7-point scales. These studies generally provide only reliability estimates. Reliability coefficients were in the acceptable range from .77 to .88 depending on measure and samples. Of these, only the measure reported in Knowles et al. (2009) has been used in another published, peer-reviewed study. Sidanius et al. (2013) used three items from Knowles et al. (2009) to represent racial color blindness as a political ideology in a New Zealand postal survey of more than 4,000 individuals.

None of the scales described in this section were subjected to thorough scale construction and validation methodology. Specifically, items were not subjected to expert raters, tested on orthogonal samples, subjected to exploratory and CFA procedures, examined across time to provide test–retest statistics, or tested with other constructs to provide convergent validity estimates. It appears that many times, authors are creating a few color-blind racial attitude items to capture what they deem to be important for the purposes of their studies.

Critique and Future Directions

The differences in available instruments to assess CBRI may be a function of the aspect of CBRI measured (i.e., power evasion vs. color evasion) or disciplinary differences of scholars who study this construct within psychology. The majority of scales reviewed in this chapter operationalize the color-evasion aspect of CBRI with the exception of the CoBRAS (Neville et al., 2013) and the Mental Health Practitioner's Racial Socialization Practices:

Color-Blind Ideology subscale (Brown et al., 2013). Interestingly, the only measures that operationalize or include a power-evasion perspective were created by academics in counseling psychology, whereas almost all of the instruments that concentrate on color evasion were developed by social psychologists. There appears to be a disciplinary difference in the aspects of CBRI that scholars choose to study.

With the exception of a few of the five measures presented in Table 8.1, many instruments created to operationalize aspects of CBRI do not undergo a comprehensive scale construction process. The only type of reliability offered was internal consistency estimates using Cronbach's alpha. There were no estimates to gauge split-half or test–retest reliability. Most of the time, authors will only provide an estimate of internal consistency reliability using Cronbach's alpha. Estimates of validity were also lacking and were typically limited to an exploratory factor analysis, if conducted at all.

Methods of scale creation and use seem to reflect differences within sub-disciplines of psychology. Many of the studies that use quantitative measures of CBRI originate from counseling or social psychology. In counseling psychology, emphasis is placed on measurement and scale construction. Because many of the studies are correlational in nature, it becomes increasingly important that measures used adequately reflect the construct they are representing (Awad & Cokley, 2010). Therefore, it is imperative that measures undergo rigorous construction strategies. When they have not, scholars must justify their use.

On the other hand, in social psychological research, greater emphasis is placed on experimental methodology (see Chapter 7). Researchers typically randomly assign participants to conditions and then look for a causal relationship among variables. With the exception of personality and individual difference scholars, social psychological research tends to use scales to select participants (high or low on a construct), match participants for random assignment to conditions, or use scale items as a manipulation check. When scale scores are used as the outcome, it is common practice in social psychological research to create scales for the purposes of the current study. Therefore, scale construction and validation procedures are not emphasized or perceived as necessary because the causal relationship is deemed the most important in social psychology.

Often, authors are creating one- to three-item measures in an attempt to capture this complicated construct. There is a sense that some studies reinvent the wheel by creating measures without considering existing measures of CBRI. Thorough literature reviews need to be undertaken so that existing measures are used. Sometimes this issue can be ameliorated by simply venturing beyond one's subdiscipline of psychology. Limiting disciplinary myopia may increase the likelihood that scales from other subdisciplines will be considered.

Perhaps the primary reason scales that have undergone a more rigorous scale construction procedure are not used is their length. For example, one notable aspect about alternate scales to the CoBRAS is their length—only one includes more than six items. There appears to exist a need for a psychometrically validated short measure of color-blind racial attitudes. The length of the CoBRAS might preclude it from inclusion in studies with limited space or time constraints, and consequently researchers are creating scales that have not been validated to the same degree as CoBRAS. Beyond the CoBRAS, only the measures by Ryan et al. (2007), Hachfeld et al. (2011), Brown et al. (2013), and Rosenthal and Levy (2012) have undergone any type of factor analysis, and in all these cases, racial color blindness was a subscale of a larger measure (see Table 8.1). Because CoBRAS is the only measure of the power-evasion aspect of CBRI that has undergone a complete scale construction process, the authors would recommend its use when time and space allows. However, CoBRAS has not been psychometrically validated with diverse populations, and thus we would offer a caution to those using the scale with non-White, non-college-age populations. For researchers interested in the color-evasion aspect of CBRI, there is no comparable recommendation at this time, although the use of a scale that has some published reliability data is almost always preferable to a newly developed scale.

To advance the measurement of CBRI, future studies should validate the aforementioned measures on different populations to test whether the construct is robust and applicable to diverse samples. In addition, a comprehensive, rigorously constructed scale assessing the color-evasion perspective of CBRI is desperately needed. Some of the studies that use items assessing color-evasion aspects seem to be conceptually conflating similar constructs. For example, in one study egalitarianism and color-blind attitudes are presented as the same construct. Rigorous scale construction methods would greatly decrease issues of conceptual overlap. Given that time and space on surveys is limited, a shift toward creating short versions of scales seems warranted. However, the tension between creating a theoretically comprehensive scale and one that is short enough not to exhaust participants is not easily remediable. Scholars and researchers must continue to weigh the benefits and costs of using a comprehensive measure against using briefer forms that capture fewer elements of the construct.

REFERENCES

Aldana, A., Rowley, S. J., Checkoway, B., & Richards-Schuster, K. (2012). Raising ethnic–racial consciousness: The relationship between intergroup dialogues and adolescents' ethnic–racial identity and racism awareness. *Equity & Excellence in Education, 45*, 120–137. http://dx.doi.org/10.1080/10665684.2012.641863

Awad, G. H., & Cokley, K. O. (2010). Designing and interpreting quantitative research in multicultural counseling. In J. G. Ponterotto, J. Casas, L. A. Suzuki, & C. M. Alexander (Eds.), *Handbook of multicultural counseling* (3rd ed., pp. 385–396). Thousand Oaks, CA: Sage.

Awad, G. H., Cokley, K., & Ravitch, J. (2005). Attitudes toward affirmative action: A comparison of color-blind versus modern racist attitudes. *Journal of Applied Social Psychology, 35*, 1384–1399. http://dx.doi.org/10.1111/j.1559-1816.2005. tb02175.x

Barr, S. C., & Neville, H. A. (2008). Examination of the link between parental racial socialization messages and racial ideology among Black college students. *Journal of Black Psychology, 34*, 131–155. http://dx.doi.org/10.1177/0095798408314138

Bonilla-Silva, E. (2006). *Racism without racists.* Lanham, MD: Rowman & Littlefield.

Brown, D. L., Blackmon, S., Schumacher, K., & Urbanski, B. (2013). Exploring clinicians' attitudes toward the incorporation of racial socialization in psychotherapy. *Journal of Black Psychology, 39*, 507–531. http://dx.doi.org/10.1177/0095798412461806

Burkard, A. W., & Knox, S. (2004). Effect of therapist color blindness on empathy and attributions in cross-cultural counseling. *Journal of Counseling Psychology, 51*, 387–397. http://dx.doi.org/10.1037/0022-0167.51.4.387

Chao, R. (2013). Race/ethnicity and multicultural competence among school counselors: Multicultural training, racial/ethnic identity, and color-blind racial attitudes. *Journal of Counseling & Development, 91*, 140–151. http://dx.doi. org/10.1002/j.1556-6676.2013.00082.x

Chen, G. A., Lephuoc, P., Guzmán, M. R., Rude, S. S., & Dodd, B. G. (2006). Exploring Asian American racial identity. *Cultural Diversity and Ethnic Minority Psychology, 12*, 461–476. http://dx.doi.org/10.1037/1099-9809.12.3.461

Coleman, M., Chapman, S., & Wang, D. C. (2013). An examination of color-blind racism and race-related stress among African American undergraduate students. *Journal of Black Psychology, 39*, 486–504. http://dx.doi.org/10.1177/0095798412469226

Colvin-Burque, A., Zugazaga, C. B., & Davis-Maye, D. (2007). Can cultural competence be taught? Evaluating the impact of the SOAP model. *Journal of Social Work Education, 43*, 223–242. http://dx.doi.org/10.5175/JSWE.2007.200500528

Fazio, R. H., Jackson, J. R., Dunton, B. C., & Williams, C. J. (1995). Variability in automatic activation as an unobtrusive measure of racial attitudes: A bona fide pipeline? *Journal of Personality and Social Psychology, 69*, 1013–1027. http:// dx.doi.org/10.1037/0022-3514.69.6.1013

Frankenberg, R. (1993). *White women, race matters: The social construction of Whiteness.* Minneapolis: University of Minnesota Press.

Goff, P. A., Jackson, M. C., Nichols, A. H., & Di Leone, B. A. L. (2013). Anything but race: Avoiding racial discourse to avoid hurting you or me. *Psychology, 4*, 335–339.

Hachfeld, A., Hahn, A., Schroeder, S., Anders, Y., Stanat, P., & Kunter, M. (2011). Assessing teachers' multicultural and egalitarian beliefs: The Teacher Cultural Beliefs Scale. *Teaching and Teacher Education, 27*, 986–996. http://dx.doi.org/10.1016/j.tate.2011.04.006

Johnson, L. M., Antle, B. F., & Barbee, A. P. (2009). Addressing disproportionality and disparity in child welfare: Evaluation of an antiracism training for community service providers. *Children and Youth Services Review, 31*, 688–696. http://dx.doi.org/10.1016/j.childyouth.2009.01.004

Kernahan, C., & Davis, T. (2009). What are the long-term effects of learning about racism? *Teaching of Psychology, 37*, 41–45. http://dx.doi.org/10.1080/00986280903425748

Knowles, E. D., Lowery, B. S., Hogan, C. M., & Chow, R. M. (2009). On the malleability of ideology: Motivated construals of color blindness. *Journal of Personality and Social Psychology, 96*, 857–869. http://dx.doi.org/10.1037/a0013595

Kohatsu, E. L., Victoria, R., Lau, A., Flores, M., & Salazar, A. (2011). Analyzing anti-Asian prejudice from a racial identity and color-blind perspective. *Journal of Counseling & Development, 89*, 63–72. http://dx.doi.org/10.1002/j.1556-6678.2011.tb00061.x

Lee, R. M., Grotevant, H. D., Hellerstedt, W. L., Gunnar, M. R., & The Minnesota International Adoption Project Team. (2006). Cultural socialization in families with internationally adopted children. *Journal of Family Psychology, 20*, 571–580. http://dx.doi.org/10.1037/0893-3200.20.4.571

Levin, S., Matthews, M., Guimond, S., Sidanius, J., Pratto, F., Kteily, N., . . . Dover, T. (2012). Assimilation, multiculturalism, and color blindness: Mediated and moderated relationships between social dominance orientation and prejudice. *Journal of Experimental Social Psychology, 48*, 207–212. http://dx.doi.org/10.1016/j.jesp.2011.06.019

Mazzocco, P. J., Cooper, L. W., & Flint, M. (2012). Different shades of racial color blindness: The role of prejudice. *Group Processes & Intergroup Relations, 15*, 167–178. http://dx.doi.org/10.1177/1368430211424763

McConahay, J. B. (1986). Modern racism, ambivalence, and the Modern Racism Scale. In J. F. Dovidio & S. L. Gaertner (Eds.), *Prejudice, discrimination, and racism* (pp. 91–125). New York, NY: Academic Press.

Morrison, K., & Chung, A. H. (2011). "White" or "European American"? Self-identifying labels influence majority group members' interethnic attitudes. *Journal of Experimental Social Psychology, 47*, 165–170. http://dx.doi.org/10.1016/j.jesp.2010.07.019

Neville, H. A., Awad, G. H., Brooks, J. E., Flores, M. P., & Bluemel, J. (2013). Color-blind racial ideology: Theory, training, and measurement implications in psychology. *American Psychologist, 68*, 455–466. http://dx.doi.org/10.1037/a0033282

Neville, H. A., Coleman, M., Falconer, J., & Holmes, D. (2005). Color-blind racial ideology and psychological false consciousness among African Americans. *Journal of Black Psychology, 31*, 27–45. http://dx.doi.org/10.1177/0095798404268287

Neville, H. A., Lilly, R. L., Duran, G., Lee, R. M., & Browne, L. (2000). Construction and initial validation of the Color-Blind Racial Attitudes Scale (CoBRAS). *Journal of Counseling Psychology*, *47*, 59–70. http://dx.doi.org/10.1037/0022-0167.47.1.59

Penn, S. L., & Post, P. B. (2012). Investigating various dimensions of play therapists' self-reported multicultural counseling competence. *International Journal of Play Therapy*, *21*, 14–29. http://dx.doi.org/10.1037/a0026894

Plaut, V. C., Thomas, K. M., & Goren, M. J. (2009). Is multiculturalism or color blindness better for minorities? *Psychological Science*, *20*, 444–446. http://dx.doi.org/10.1111/j.1467-9280.2009.02318.x

Poteat, V., & Spanierman, L. B. (2008). Further validation of the Psychosocial Costs of Racism to Whites Scale among employed adults. *The Counseling Psychologist*, *36*, 871–894. http://dx.doi.org/10.1177/0011000007310002

Rosenthal, L., & Levy, S. R. (2012). The relation between polyculturalism and intergroup attitudes among racially and ethnically diverse adults. *Cultural Diversity and Ethnic Minority Psychology*, *18*, 1–16. http://dx.doi.org/10.1037/a0026490

Ryan, C. S., Casas, J. F., & Thompson, B. K. (2010). Interethnic ideology, intergroup perceptions, and cultural orientation. *Journal of Social Issues*, *66*, 29–44. http://dx.doi.org/10.1111/j.1540-4560.2009.01631.x

Ryan, C. S., Hunt, J. S., Weible, J. A., Peterson, C. R., & Casas, J. F. (2007). Multicultural and color-blind ideology, stereotypes, and ethnocentrism among Black and White Americans. *Group Processes & Intergroup Relations*, *10*, 617–637. http://dx.doi.org/10.1177/1368430207084105

Sears, D. O., & Henry, P. J. (2005). Over thirty years later: A contemporary look at symbolic racism. *Advances in Experimental Social Psychology*, *37*, 95–150. http://dx.doi.org/10.1016/S0065-2601(05)37002-X

Sidanius, J., Kteily, N., Sheehy-Skeffington, J., Ho, A. K., Sibley, C., & Duriez, B. (2013). You're inferior and not worth our concern: The interface between empathy and social dominance orientation. *Journal of Personality*, *81*, 313–323. http://dx.doi.org/10.1111/jopy.12008

Soble, J. R., Spanierman, L. B., & Liao, H. Y. (2011). Effects of a brief video intervention on White university students' racial attitudes. *Journal of Counseling Psychology*, *58*, 151–157. http://dx.doi.org/10.1037/a0021158

Spanierman, L. B., Oh, E., Poteat, V., Hund, A. R., McClair, V. L., Beer, A. M., & Clarke, A. M. (2008). White university students' responses to societal racism: A qualitative investigation. *The Counseling Psychologist*, *36*, 839–870. http://dx.doi.org/10.1177/0011000006295589

Steinfeldt, J. A., & Wong, Y. J. (2010). Multicultural training on American Indian issues: Testing the effectiveness of an intervention to change attitudes toward Native-themed mascots. *Cultural Diversity and Ethnic Minority Psychology*, *16*, 110–115. http://dx.doi.org/10.1037/a0018633

Stevenson, H., Cameron, R., Herrero-Taylor, T., & Davis, G. Y. (2002). Development of the Teenager Experience of Racial Socialization Scale: Correlates of race-related socialization frequency from the perspective of Black youth. *Journal of Black Psychology, 28,* 84–106. http://dx.doi.org/10.1177/0095798402028002002

Tawa, J., Suyemoto, K. L., & Roemer, L. (2012). Implications of perceived inter-personal and structural racism for Asian Americans' self-esteem. *Basic and Applied Social Psychology, 34,* 349–358. http://dx.doi.org/10.1080/01973533.2012.693425

Todd, A., & Galinsky, A. (2012). The reciprocal link between multiculturalism and perspective-taking: How ideological and self-regulatory approaches to manag-ing diversity reinforce each other. *Journal of Experimental Social Psychology, 48,* 1394–1398. http://dx.doi.org/10.1016/j.jesp.2012.07.007

Vargas, N. (2014). Off-White: Color-blind ideology at the margins of Whiteness. *Ethnic and Racial Studies, 37,* 2281–2302.

Wolsko, C., Park, B., & Judd, C. M. (2006). Considering the tower of Babel: Corre-lates of assimilation and multiculturalism among ethnic minority and majority groups in the United States. *Social Justice Research, 19,* 277–306. http://dx.doi.org/10.1007/s11211-006-0014-8

9

USING ETHNOGRAPHY AND INTERVIEWS TO STUDY COLOR-BLIND RACIAL IDEOLOGY

AMANDA E. LEWIS AND MARGARET ANN HAGERMAN

In an interview, a mother explains that she teaches her children that everyone is equal, that we are all the same. Proudly, she explains that she feels like she has been successful, that her kids are color blind. Later in the interview, she explains why she really would not want either of her (White) children to marry a Black person, although an Asian American would be okay. She explains all this while sitting on a couch in her house in an almost all-White suburb within a large multiracial metropolis. The demographics of the neighborhood school her children attend ensure that they are, at the very least, unlikely in the short term to even have an African American friend.

A teacher in a city school 10 miles away explains to his class that when we are cut, we all bleed red. Sounding much like the mother just described, he vigorously, even vehemently, proclaims to his class of Black, Latino, and White 10-year-olds that "Color. Does. Not. Matter." For an observer, his pronouncement sits in uneasy tension with the local realities in a school where

http://dx.doi.org/10.1037/14754-010
The Myth of Racial Color Blindness: Manifestations, Dynamics, and Impact, H. A. Neville, M. E. Gallardo, and D. W. Sue (Editors)

Black boys represent three quarters of the disciplinary referrals, even though they comprise less than 20% of the school population.

Rampant racial segregation in the city means that White, Black, and Latino students flow to school each day from quite different parts of town. White students walk to school each day from the surrounding middle-class neighborhood, while Black and Latino students are bused in from working-class communities several miles away. Captured through participant observation and interviewing during a single ethnographic study, these vignettes capture some of the contradictory realities of race in the United States today and raise a number of questions. How can one claim to be color blind but live in a segregated suburb? What does it mean to claim to be color blind or to convey to the children under your guidance that color does not matter even as it so clearly plays a part in shaping how their behavior in school is understood, the composition of the communities of which they are a part, and their parents' ideas about potentially appropriate life partners?

These vignettes present examples of what a growing body of empirical research on racial understandings and attitudes argues has emerged in the post-Civil Rights era as a central frame for making sense of racial issues—color-blind racial ideology (CBRI; Bonilla-Silva, 2013; Carr 1997; Forman, 2004; Lewis, Chesler, & Forman, 2000). Linked to the increasingly popular idea that the United States is "postrace," CBRI builds on the seemingly progressive Civil Rights era ideal of allowing people to be judged by the "content of their character, not the content of their skin" and declares this aspiration to be a reality—not "race should not shape people's life chances" but "we are color blind and race doesn't matter anymore." Although different authors have captured them using slightly varying language, the main tenets of CBRI include the following (Bonilla-Silva, 2013; Bonilla-Silva & Forman, 2000; Carr, 1997; Crenshaw, 1997; Forman 2004; Forman & Lewis 2006; Lewis 2003):

1. The claim that most people do not "see" or notice race anymore ("I am color blind"; "race doesn't matter to me"; "red, pink, yellow, blue—it's all the same").
2. The claim that racial parity has, for the most part, been achieved ("We are postrace"; "Anyone who is willing to work hard can make it today").
3. The assertion that any persisting patterns of racial inequality are the result of individual- or group-level shortcomings—shortcomings that are typically assumed to be cultural in nature ("If some people aren't successful these days, it is because they aren't motivated"; "Some groups struggle because they don't have the right family values").
4. The claim that because race does not matter anymore, there is no need for institutional remedies (such as affirmative action)

to redress racial inequalities and that any attempts to raise questions about race are problematic (e.g., "They are playing the race card"; "The real problem today is reverse racism").

Those writing about CBRI have identified it not merely as a way of making sense of racial matters but as an important ideological pillar in the maintenance of White supremacy because it protects a deeply unequal racial status quo by stigmatizing both personal claims of injustice and systematic attempts to mitigate inequality (Bonilla-Silva, 2013; Crenshaw, 1997; Gallagher, 2003). As Forman and Lewis (2006) put it, "In this context the outcomes of racial structures get naturalized as history is erased and we become a nation of atomized individuals all marching through our lives with our own skills, values, and abilities" (p. 178).

Scholars have used a wide variety of research methods to study the contours and content of new racial ideologies (Bobo, Kluegel, & Smith, 1997; Bonilla-Silva & Forman, 2000; Dovidio, 2001; Forman, 2001, 2004; Kinder & Sanders, 1996; Pettigrew & Meertens, 1995; Sears & Henry, 2003). Some of the earliest writing on CBRI or color-blind racism was, in fact, trying to explore some of the conflicting findings that had emerged in interview-based research as opposed to survey-based research on racial attitudes. Comparing college-student responses on surveys to those in interviews. Bonilla-Silva and Forman (2000) found that White respondents appeared far more prejudiced in the interviews when they had to talk about and explain their positions on racial issues than they did when responding to delimited survey items. However, they argued, this "prejudice" took a new form—a kind of "racetalk" or color-blind racism that allowed respondents to avoid appearing "racist" while still taking positions that opposed efforts to address persistent racial inequality. Thus, as they put it,

> Color-blind racism allows Whites to appear "not racist" ("I believe in equality"), preserve their privileged status ("Discrimination ended in the sixties!"), blame Blacks for their lower status ("If you guys just work hard!"), and criticize any institutional approach—such as affirmative action—that attempts to ameliorate racial inequality ("Reverse discrimination!"). (Bonilla-Silva & Forman, 2000, p. 78)

Other research followed, most of which, like Bonilla-Silva and Forman's (2000), set out to understand current racial attitudes and understandings and similarly found a pattern of explicit denial of the significance of race alongside evidence of its persistent meaning in respondents' lives. Like important work on laissez-faire racism, aversive racism, and symbolic racism, these efforts capture significant shifts in racial logic in the post-Civil Rights era in the United States (Bobo, Kluegel, & Smith, 1997; Dovidio, 2001; Sears & Henry, 2003).

One of the important insights or reminders of this overall body of work is that racial ideology is dynamic and that it is contested (Bonilla-Silva, 2001; Gramsci, 1971; Hall, 1990). That is, the content of racial logic has historically shifted as structural conditions have changed (e.g., from slavery to Jim Crow, from Jim Crow to the Civil Rights era), as have its forms, shifting from explicit and overt to more subtle and implicit. These shifts are to be expected because ideologies are, by their very nature, contested. They provide ways of making sense of the world, a common sense that helps us to understand our lives and also shapes action, but there is always more than one set of narratives at work at any moment. Some gain traction, or gain "hegemony," but such dominance is never total. The original articles on CBRI talked about it as a new variation on old themes—new but not unfamiliar, a new way of narrating racial inequality that spoke to a new context. Anyone setting out to study racial dynamics today will find color blindness operating alongside other racial ideologies. Competing racial logics identified in other research include diversity discourse (Bell & Hartmann, 2007), multiculturalism, and a more substantive antiracist or structural framing of racial issues (Hughey, 2012; O'Brien & Korgen, 2007; Warren, 2010) along with traditional old-fashioned Jim Crow racism (Hughey, 2012).

In this chapter, we discuss some of the strategies for studying these new racial dynamics. Specifically, we review some of the recent qualitative research on race that has identified CBRI as part of the dominant racial common sense in the contemporary United States. We outline ways of using ethnography and interviews to explore the racial landscape today and show how scholars using these methods have identified aspects of the substance and the mechanisms of CBRI. Much of this work has not focused on studying CBRI specifically but rather focused more broadly on trying to capture how people understand racial issues. If our goal is to capture how racial dynamics are unfolding in the present, then we do not set out to study any one set of racial narratives but instead try to understand how people today are making sense of race and how their ideas about race shape their action in the world. CBRI, then, has been a finding rather than a research objective. Ethnography and other forms of qualitative work have been particularly useful methods, however, for exploring CBRI as they allow for in-depth exploration of the current racial landscape with its many embedded contradictions and points of disjuncture.

For example, recent qualitative research (ranging from full long-term ethnographic work to interview studies to content analysis) that has identified ways that CBRI significantly shapes how race is lived today has included the following research aims:

- studying how race gets negotiated in everyday life in schools (Lewis, 2003),

- studying White racial socialization in upper-middle-class families (Hagerman, 2014a),
- studying experiences of those who were students in high schools desegregated in the first wave of desegregation in late 1960s (Forman & Lewis, 2006),
- studying how race is presented in role-playing video games through the creation of avatars (Dietrich, 2013),
- studying experiences of White middle-class girls growing up in suburbs of Long Island (Kenny, 2000),
- studying White youths participating in a local hip-hop scene (Rodriquez, 2006),
- interview study of how White adoptive parents rationalize choices about adoptee race (Sweeney, 2013), and
- studying the creation of a charter school in rural North Carolina (Urrieta, 2006).

These various studies began with broader research goals, but one contribution of each is to fill out and add detail to our understandings of how the logic of CBRI works in different contexts to shape social dynamics. Ethnographic research, and most but not all qualitative work more generally, is distinct from the abundance of recent survey and experimental work that, for the most part, is deductive in nature, using predetermined concepts and measures to test out, for example, the parameters of CBRI or to measure the conditions under which it gets expressed. Ethnographic work is more inductive in nature, seeking to understand how people make sense of the world and about the choices and actions they take in the context of their daily lives. Its goal, with regard to racial matters, is to understand how those under study function as racial actors in the world, even when they aren't necessarily talking about race specifically. This research strategy is particularly well suited to studying racial dynamics today because they have become more subtle and elusive.

ETHNOGRAPHIC METHODS IN CBRI

Broadly, as a method, *ethnography* allows for an exploration of how people "produce, perceive, and interpret their own and others' actions" (Emerson, 2001, p. 33). Through the integration of participant observation, formal and informal interviewing, and the collection of examples of material culture, ethnography enables scholars to study not only what people say—how they talk about and narrate the world—but how these ideas are formulated and how they are connected to social behavior. In this sense, ethnography involves both interviewing people and spending time with them in their everyday lives, watching them in action. Although it can be narrowly focused, ethnographic work also generally facilitates an examination of *shared* meaning-making processes among collectivities, within organizations, and throughout communities (as opposed to, for example, studying individual racial attitudes).

Ethnography is thus a particularly useful method for exploring how race is discussed and lived. For instance, scholars have found that White racial subjects experience and talk about race in ways that are often contradictory. Ethnographic work offers a way of accessing and understanding more deeply what these contradictions are and why they exist. As such, ethnography allows for a rich exploration of the potential disjunctures between what people say and what they do—disjunctures that often reveal important insights about how people understand race. As Lewis (2004) stated in her discussion of research on White racial subjects in particular: "Especially today when racial thinking and behavior remains pervasive but operates in much more covert ways, ethnographic work in white settings on the 'everydayness' of whiteness is essential"[1] (p. 637).

Although we do not delve into the logistics of conducting ethnographic work here (there are abundant methodological texts that provide such detail), we do offer examples from recent empirical studies that have identified color blindness in action to demonstrate how ethnography is a powerful tool for uncovering how people make sense of race in America today.

Although CBRI has been identified in a number of realms, in the examples in this section, we focus on studies of schools and families because they offer an opportunity not only to examine how racial dynamics unfold but also to witness what adults are trying to teach young people about how to make sense of their world. As the following examples illustrate, schools and families are institutions in which ideas about race are conveyed to children and where racial lines are constructed and negotiated. In each example, we briefly explain the overall goals and methods of the research and then describe some of the key findings.

Example 1: Negotiating Race in Everyday Life in Schools

Lewis (2003) drew on ethnographic data from research in three public elementary school communities (two urban and one suburban) in California to understand how schools were involved in the drawing and redrawing of racial lines. She explored these schools as settings where people acquire some version "of the rules of racial classification" and of their own racial identity

---

[1]Racially color-blind logic does not reside solely in the minds of White people. As this ideological perspective becomes hegemonic, it is adopted by members of other non-White racial groups as well. For instance, see Bonilla-Silva (2013).

(Omi & Winant, 1994, p. 60). Over the course of one academic year, she embedded herself in these three communities, spending upward of 35 hours a week in the schools (resulting in more than 1,500 pages of field notes) and conducted dozens of formal and informal interviews with school personnel, parents, and children. Broadly, she found that not only did the actual curriculum teach many racial lessons, but schools (and school personnel) served as a source of racial information, a location for interracial interaction, and a means of both affirming and challenging previous racial attitudes and understandings. Although the specific logic of race varied between communities, CBRI was prevalent and took many forms.

For example, in her exploration of Foresthills, a suburban school, Lewis (2003) found that almost all members of the school community denied the local salience of race. This took many forms, including, for instance, teachers referring to one of the few Black students as "playing the race card" when she claimed to have experienced racial harassment, parents reporting that they taught their children that "everyone was equal," as well as parents getting upset about state-mandated efforts to mark Black History Month ("We are all Americans!"). Although one might generally assume that it is a good thing that adults in the community wanted to assert that race did not matter, it is important to note that it functioned merely as an assertion—one that sat in uneasy contrast with seemingly pervasive group-level racial understandings that were deeply aware of color. Explicit color-blind race talk masked an underlying reality of racialized practices and understandings. For example, the Black student in question had been called the "n word" at school more than once, and other parents of children of color reported their children having to regularly navigate racialized remarks at lunchtime (e.g., "Oh, Catherine, since you're Mexican you can have free lunches" or "Where's your sombrero?"); Lewis herself observed racialized references to the Latino and Asian children students on the playground.

Clearly, it was not only children in the school community who saw color; despite their claims to the contrary, adults, too, operated with quite racialized or color-aware understandings. For example, at one moment in a conversation, a mother suggested that neither she nor the children in the community saw color, "which is good." Moments later, however, when asked how she would explain racism to her kids, she offered a quasi-cultural explanation of racial group difference and why she would not want to live in a Black neighborhood.

> *Amanda:* If one of the kids asked what racism was, how would you define it for them?
>
> *Mrs. Morning:* Um . . . I guess I would define it that, there's different cultures, and, with different races—um, like Chinese— they have their own culture and their own churches

that they go to, and their own food that they eat, and the same way with Black people. I mean they . . . like certain things, and when they go to their place of God or whatever, um, it seems to be more . . . when I drive around or whatever, you know you see all these Blacks coming out of a church, well that's where they go—I don't know what goes on in there and stuff, but it seems that certain—people seem to gravitate, and, and live in certain areas. I don't know why, but that's the way it, it seems. I mean personally, I don't think that we'd go looking in a neighborhood that was all Black. (Lewis, 2003, p. 23)

Another parent, a high school teacher, told Lewis that she tried to tell her children that "people are who they are, and you have to not make a judgment on what they look like or anything like that." She explained that she wouldn't even be able to tell me how many African American, Latino, or Asian students she had in her classes because she just didn't "notice" such things. Later in the conversation, however, she explained how she understood the differential success of the kids in her school with the following:

Do I think of those groups differently? . . . Yeah. I do. I think that the backgrounds, that a lot of the attitudes that those people have towards . . . how to be successful, are different. And I think that the Asian attitude, from parents who aren't far from being born in some place in Asia. Their attitudes towards success are that you work hard, and you keep working hard, and you keep working hard, that's the how you're successful. I don't find that attitude among Latinos or Blacks. (Lewis, 2003, p. 23)

White parents' claims that they did not see or notice race also sat in uneasy tension with their life choices, including living in an almost entirely White community within a multiracial metropolis.

Ethnographic work of this kind provides several advantages. First, it enables researchers to bring together a range of kinds of data—to ask people what they think, to watch what they do, to engage them over time. This kind of triangulation of multiple kinds of data from a single setting can greatly enhance one's ability to capture a fuller picture of racial dynamics—patterns observed in classrooms, on the playground, or in the neighborhood can be compared with data from informal and formal interviews or can be discussed with respondents in the field over time. Second, it also allows for building rapport. Discussions about racial issues, especially with White respondents who often hesitate to talk about race, can present challenges. As opposed to projects in which one is asking questions of a stranger, ethnography enables scholars to build trust with participants over time so that respondents feel more comfortable talking about difficult subjects.

Example 2: White Racial Socialization

Hagerman's (2014a) research on racial socialization of White middle-school children reveals the utility of ethnography in understanding how people form racial logic or common sense ideas about race. Hagerman embedded herself in a Midwestern city and conducted an in-depth ethnography of three communities. This effort included in-depth ethnographic interviews with 30 White families (including parents and children); systematic participant observations with these and other families in their homes and in the community; and a content analysis of local newspaper articles, websites, and parent blog posts. As a result of spending almost 2 years in the field with the families in her study as they went about their everyday lives, as well as working and living in the community (e.g., working as a coach and child-care provider in the community), Hagerman was able to document how the process of White racial socialization unfolds. One of the key findings of the research was that a number of families operate with a kind of racially color-blind logic that is communicated to children both implicitly and explicitly.[2] Through the triangulating of different kinds of data, facilitated in the ethnographic approach, Hagerman captured youth and adults deploying the explicit narratives of racial color blindness—denying the salience of race while simultaneously engaging in the world in numerous racialized ways.

For example, 12-year-old Edward Avery was quite chatty during an interview with Hagerman. He talked in great detail about his hobbies, his friends, and his family's recent vacation. However, when asked directly about racial matters, he became much more reticent, either avoiding answering or offering different versions of a short response: Race doesn't matter anymore. For instance, when asked if he talks about race at home, he replied, "Not really." When asked if his teachers discuss the topic at school, he said, "Mmm uhh. Nope." When asked if he thinks racial discrimination still happens in the United States, he stated, "The country has moved beyond it." And when asked what he thinks about the election of the first Black president in the United States, he responded that he didn't think it was a big deal because "the color of your skin doesn't matter. Everyone is the same." Yet observations of Edward in his everyday life revealed that race really does matter to this child, despite his claims to the contrary.

One example came up one afternoon as Hagerman drove Edward home from hockey practice. He asked her if they could stop on the way home at McDonald's for a milkshake, explaining that this was his usual routine with

---

[2]Importantly, reflecting our earlier point about the contested nature of ideology, some families operated with a quite distinct racial ideology that acknowledged and engaged with questions of privilege and structural racism.

his mother after hockey. As they approached the restaurant, Edward hesitated and reported to Hagerman, "This isn't where we usually go. We usually go to the one over by the mall." Hagerman responded that this was the closest McDonald's to their location and the easiest place to stop. As they waited in the drive-through line for his milkshake, seven Black children, both girls and boys, walked past the car into the McDonald's. The children appeared to be about the same age as Edward, perhaps in seventh or eighth grade, and were dressed similarly to him—wearing winter coats, jeans, and boots and carrying school backpacks. They were laughing and joking around. As Edward watched the kids walk past, he said nervously, "This neighborhood really isn't all that good, is it?" Hagerman replied, "What do you mean?" Edward said, "I dunno. It just seems like there are a lot of poor people around here. We don't usually stop here. My mom says it's dangerous" (Hagerman, 2014b, p. 109). Contrary to his claims in the interview context that "we are all the same," Edward clearly *saw* race and operated with stereotypes about different groups. The appearance of a group of Black youth prompted concern about his own safety and about the community writ large, despite the fact that the children were behaving in ways identical to how Edward behaved with his friends. Edward's observations indicated that he was thinking about and noticing race in his everyday world, despite not wanting to talk openly about it. The inconsistency in how he talked about race when asked directly (race doesn't matter; everyone's the same) and how he made sense of race in his everyday life (those Black kids look dangerous) maps onto the hegemonic racial ideological position of color blindness. This disjuncture demonstrates that these claims of racial color blindness are more rhetorical than realistic and shows how these claims mask the continuing importance of race. Without the multiple points of interaction made possible because of the ethnographic nature of this study, this particular insight would be difficult to observe.

Similarly, other children in the project generally tried to avoid talking about race explicitly in interviews. Hagerman (2010) included an exercise as part of the interview process that was initially intended to be an enjoyable and child-centered activity. In this exercise, children were presented with photographs of celebrities and asked to racially identify them, yet some of the kids in the study stated that they did not want to participate. For example, Lauren said the following:

Lauren: Um, well, I kinda feel like kind of like racist doing this.

Hagerman: Why do you feel racist?

Lauren: Because I'm just like, categorizing them by the color of their skin, and I don't think that's right. (Hagerman, 2014b, p. 117)

Lauren believed that merely racially identifying those in photographs was racist. She did not want to talk about race or use racial identifiers in referencing other people. However, in casual conversation with her sister while playing a board game a few hours later, they discussed how "all the black kids at school have pot on them" at the nearby public school that they do not attend because it is "too dangerous." They tell me, "Also the students just don't work as hard or care about school as much there" (Hagerman, 2014b, p. 114).

Similarly, in another interview, when 13-year-old Erica Schultz identified Kanye West as "Black," her 11-year-old sister Natalie yelled out in an accusatory fashion, "Racist!" When Hagerman asked Natalie why she believed this to be racist, she explained that it didn't matter what race people are because people are all the same. Later in the interview, though, while discussing different schools, Natalie explained, "In some schools, kids have lots of problems. Like in the city where there are lots of African Americans." She explained that these kids could have "something bad or hard in their life" and "a cold spirit" due to growing up in "bad surroundings" with other Black kids who "take drugs" and "steal stuff" and "have guns." "They probably follow in their footsteps. . . . Or if your family isn't very nice or [doesn't] care about you . . . I think that happens in city schools a lot. Like in Chicago or Milwaukee. But not here" (Hagerman, 2014b, p. 83). On the one hand, Natalie said that race didn't matter, yet on the other hand, she possessed a range of negative beliefs about Black children. Hagerman's research thus offers examples of how ethnography is a methodological tool that allows for a richer and deeper understanding of the complexity and contradictory nature of how White people make sense of race. This study (along with Lewis, 2003) also shows the advantages of comparing in-depth data collected from several communities. The similarities and differences in patterns in racial sense making across settings provides insights not ascertainable from focusing on a single setting.

INTERVIEW-BASED RESEARCH

Early in the work on CBRI, scholars advocated *interview-based research* as a way of improving on survey-based research. Arguing that survey researchers had consistently underestimated the extent of prejudice because of their reliance on delimited and often outdated questions, scholars suggested that this work was not capturing the new realities of race and that interviews offered the possibility of obtaining more ecologically valid data on the parameters of Whites' racial attitudes (Bonilla-Silva & Forman, 2000).[3] Compared with

---

[3]Since 2000, survey and experimental researchers have addressed many of these critiques by developing new items to test out the parameters and content of new forms of prejudice and racism.

ethnographic research, interview-based research has some drawbacks. For instance, interviews are often one-off conversations with strangers that do not facilitate the development of trust or rapport and may lead to more hesitation in responses. They also do not generally allow researchers to triangulate findings by checking what is reported in interviews with what subjects actually say and do in the context of their daily lives. On the other hand, interview-based projects do have some advantages—they are more delimited, less time- and resource intensive, and potentially allow for sampling a larger group of respondents. Like the early work of Bonilla-Silva and Forman (2000), interview-based studies have captured some of the important ways that participants deploy color-blind racial logic and allow researchers to engage participants about the contradictions of their thinking about race and racism.

Studying graduates of desegregated high schools in an interview-based study of middle-aged residents of a small Midwestern city who had all attended a desegregated high school in the late 1960s, Forman and Lewis (2006) found lots of evidence of color-blind racial logic and what they referred to as *racial apathy*. Respondents offered explicit claims that they were racially color blind but later in the same conversation expressed quite racialized or color-aware understandings. For example, when Janet, a retired UPS driver, talked about race relations today, she claimed to be color blind and believe in equality: "Bottom line, we're all human beings first off. The fact that your nationality comes from a different region that your skin is a different color doesn't matter. You got two arms, two legs, the same organs inside, what is the problem?" (p. 187). Soon after, however, Janet expressed a common narrative about Black cultural dysfunction when discussing her disgust for "slackers":

> more blacks seem to have less values. I'm not saying all, but those [Black students at the high school] had values were kind of shunned by the blacks because they weren't the norm. They wanted to go on with their education and had an aspiration of a vocation. And my only thought with that is that this stemmed from their home front. You know, like the old saying, "welfare breeds welfare." And you do see that, you see generation after generation. It's not just blacks on welfare, I'm not trying to imply that, but if they can get by, then that's good enough [for them]. (Forman & Lewis, 2006, p. 187)

In discussing her experience at the high school, Mary said it taught her to be more open. "You have to know someone, you can't just look at their skin. We should all be colorblind. Really" (Forman & Lewis, 2006, p. 187). In the same conversation, however, Mary explained that she was vehemently opposed to interracial unions, because "the children would suffer." She believes it is too hard for the offspring of such unions not knowing "where they belong." Similarly, Susan described herself as racially "open" and said she did not really think about or notice race. Yet when asked about the role of race in her life, she restated her position with a caveat: "I guess I must think about it some because I wouldn't want my kids to marry, you know, a black person" (p. 188).

These interviews reveal one of the important hallmarks of CBRI: Seemingly contradictory ideas can exist alongside each other without the speaker perceiving any inconsistency. By asking about race in different ways at different points in the interview process, including asking about both concrete experience and abstract beliefs and attitudes, this kind of interview process allows for exploring how subjects make meaning of a range of racial issues from their own identities to local issues to broad policy matters.

CONCLUSION

As the examples provided in this chapter illustrate, ethnography and interview-based research methods allow scholars to uncover both respondents' explicit and formal racial beliefs and what often lies beneath the surface of people's everyday thoughts and actions. In addition, these methods provide access to understanding how processes such as racial formation and racial socialization operate within important social institutions, such as schools and families. Given the often covert and subtle nature of racism in the United States today, ethnographic methods are particularly useful for exploring the ideologies that serve to reproduce the racial status quo.[4] Although other methods such as experimental studies or surveys offer insight into the prevalence or measurement of color-blind racial ideology, ethnographic work provides a window into racial meaning making and behavior in action that may otherwise go unnoticed. Bringing together data gathered from formal and informal interviews, observations, relevant site documents, and other examples of material culture allows the researcher to access the various dynamics, dimensions, and contradictions of the current racial landscape.

REFERENCES

Bell, J. M., & Hartmann, D. (2007). Diversity in everyday discourse: The cultural ambiguities and consequences of "happy talk." *American Sociological Review, 72,* 895–914. http://dx.doi.org/10.1177/000312240707200603

---

[4]Such work also has the potential to inform those living or working in the kinds of settings studied to gain insight into the dynamics that shape the experiences of those operating therein. For example, teachers trying to understand patterns of racial achievement of discipline may gain new insight into how their well-intentioned action to get beyond race might well lead them to ignore the way race continues to shape interactions and practices within their schools.

Bobo, L., Kluegel, J., & Smith, R. (1997). Laissez-faire racism: The crystallization of a kinder, gentler, anti-Black ideology. In S. A. Tuch & J. Martin (Eds.), *Racial attitudes in the 1990s: Continuity and change* (pp. 15–42). Westport, CT: Praeger.

Bonilla-Silva, E. (2001). *White supremacy and racism in the post-Civil Rights era*. Boulder, CO: Lynne Rienner.

Bonilla-Silva, E. (2013). *Racism without racists: Color-blind racism and the persistence of racial inequality in America* (4th ed.). Lanham, MD: Rowman and Littlefield.

Bonilla-Silva, E., & Forman, T. A. (2000). "I am not a racist but . . .": Mapping college students' racial ideology in the USA. *Discourse & Society, 11*, 50–85. http://dx.doi.org/10.1177/0957926500011001003

Carr, L. G. (1997). *"Colorblind" racism*. Thousand Oaks, CA: Sage.

Crenshaw, K. (1997). Color-blind dreams and racial nightmares: Reconfiguring racism in the post-Civil Rights era. In T. Morrison & C. B. Lacour (Eds.), *Birth of a nation'hood* (pp. 97–168). New York, NY: Pantheon Books.

Dietrich, D. (2013). Avatars of Whiteness: Racial expression in video game characters. *Sociological Inquiry, 83*, 82–105. http://dx.doi.org/10.1111/soin.12001

Dovidio, J. (2001). On the nature of contemporary prejudice. *Journal of Social Issues, 57*, 829–849. http://dx.doi.org/10.1111/0022-4537.00244

Emerson, R. M. (2001). *Contemporary field research: Perspectives and formulations*. Prospect Heights, IL: Waveland Press.

Forman, T. (2001). The social determinants of White youths' racial attitudes: Evidence from a national survey. *Sociological Studies of Children and Youth, 8*, 173–207. http://dx.doi.org/10.1016/S1537-4661(01)80009-X

Forman, T. A. (2004). Color-blind racism and racial indifference: The role of racial apathy in facilitating enduring inequalities. In M. Krysan & A. E. Lewis (Eds.), *The changing terrain of race and ethnicity* (pp. 43–66). New York, NY: Russell Sage.

Forman, T. A., & Lewis, A. E. (2006). Racial apathy and Hurricane Katrina: The social anatomy of prejudice in the post-Civil Rights era. *Du Bois Review, 3*, 175–202. http://dx.doi.org/10.1017/S1742058X06060127

Gallagher, C. (2003). Color-blind privilege. The social and political functions of erasing the color line in post-race America. *Race, Gender, & Class, 10*(4), 1–17.

Gramsci, A. (1971). *Selections from the prison notebooks*. New York, NY: International.

Hagerman, M. A. (2010). "I like being intervieeeeeeewed!": Kids' perspectives on participating in social research. *Sociological Studies of Children and Youth, 13*, 61–105. http://dx.doi.org/10.1108/S1537-4661(2010)0000013007

Hagerman, M. A. (2014a). White families and race: Color-blind and color-conscious approaches to White racial socialization. *Ethnic and Racial Studies, 37*, 2598–2614. http://dx.doi.org/10.1080/01419870.2013.848289

Hagerman, M. A. (2014b). *White kids and race: An ethnographic study of White racial socialization, privilege, and the (re)production of racial ideology in affluent families* (Doctoral dissertation). Department of Sociology, Emory University, Atlanta, GA.

Hall, S. (1990). The whites of their eyes: Racist ideologies and the media. In M. Alvarado & J. Thompson (Eds.), *The media reader* (pp. 18–22). London, England: British Film Institute.

Hughey, M. W. (2012). *White bound: Nationalists, antiracists, and the shared meanings of race*. Stanford, CA: Stanford University Press.

Kenny, L. D. (2000). *Daughters of suburbia: Growing up White, middle class, and female*. New Brunswick, NJ: Rutgers University Press.

Kinder, D. R., & Sanders, L. M. (1996). *Divided by color: Racial politics and democratic ideals* (pp. 92–127). Chicago, IL: University of Chicago Press.

Lewis, A. E. (2003). *Race in the schoolyard: Negotiating the color line in classrooms and communities*. New Brunswick, NJ: Rutgers University Press.

Lewis, A. E. (2004). What group? Studying Whites and Whiteness in the era of "color-blindness." *Sociological Theory, 22,* 623–646.

Lewis, A. E., Chesler, M., & Forman, T. (2000). The impact of "colorblind" ideologies on students of color: Intergroup relations at a predominantly White university. *Journal of Negro Education, 69,* 74–91.

O'Brien, E., & Korgen, K. O. (2007). It's the message, not the messenger. The declining significance of Black–White contact in a "colorblind" society. *Sociological Inquiry, 77,* 356–382. http://dx.doi.org/10.1111/j.1475-682X.2007.00197.x

Omi, M., & Winant, H. (1994). *Racial formation in the United States: From the 1960s to the 1990s*. New York, NY: Routledge.

Pettigrew, T., & Meertens, R. (1995). Subtle and blatant prejudice in Western Europe. *European Review of Social Psychology, 8,* 241–273. http://dx.doi.org/10.1080/14792779843000009

Rodriquez, J. (2006). Colorblind ideology and the cultural appropriation of hip-hop. *Journal of Contemporary Ethnography, 35,* 645–668. http://dx.doi.org/10.1177/0891241606286997

Sears, D. O., & Henry, P. J. (2003). The origins of symbolic racism. *Journal of Personality and Social Psychology, 85,* 259–275. http://dx.doi.org/10.1037/0022-3514.85.2.259

Sweeney, K. (2013). Race-conscious adoption choices, multiraciality, and color-blind racial ideology. *Family Relations: An Interdisciplinary Journal of Applied Family Studies, 62,* 42–57. http://dx.doi.org/10.1111/j.1741-3729.2012.00757.x

Urrieta, L., Jr. (2006). Community identity discourse and the heritage academy: Color-blind educational policy and White supremacy. *International Journal of Qualitative Studies in Education, 19,* 455–476. http://dx.doi.org/10.1080/09518390600773197

Warren, M. R. (2010). *Fire in the heart: How White activists embrace racial justice*. New York, NY: Oxford University Press.

III

MANIFESTATIONS OF COLOR-BLIND RACIAL IDEOLOGY

10

THE GOOD, THE BAD, AND THE UGLY: COLOR-BLIND RACIAL IDEOLOGY AND LACK OF EMPATHY

SHARON Y. TETTEGAH

It's hard work to understand people who are not like you and be able to empathize with those who have different experiences and different values than you. (Obama, 2004)

—Barack Obama

In a recent article, Neville, Awad, Brooks, Flores, and Bluemel (2013) presented a discussion of color-blind racial ideology (CBRI), its effect on society at large, and how damaging its effects can be on the perceptions, growth, and development of equality in society (see also the definition of color-blind racism by Bonilla-Silva, Chapter 1, this volume). Equal opportunity in the workforce, engagement in free speech, and basic human rights for all are included in equality in society. Equality should be associated with all aspects of success and failure in life regardless of skin color, racial, and cultural differences. Understanding the reasons equality is important can be directly linked to social justice, perspective taking, and empathy. In fact, most social scientists would agree that the ability to experience empathy for the plight of our fellow human beings is one of the most fundamental skills in the repertoire of human social behavior (Rameson, Morelli, & Lieberman, 2011).

http://dx.doi.org/10.1037/14754-011
The Myth of Racial Color Blindness: Manifestations, Dynamics, and Impact, H. A. Neville, M. E. Gallardo, and D. W. Sue (Editors)

As many societies, in the United States and beyond, are becoming increasingly diverse in terms of race, ethnicity, and culture, there has been growing interest in perceptions about race, culture, and empathy, sometimes described as *ethnocultural empathy* (Wang et al., 2003) or *intergroup empathy* (Howe, 2013). Ethnocultural empathy is an acquired moral emotion that develops across a lifespan involving feelings, thoughts, attitudes, and behaviors toward racial, cultural, or ethnic groups that are different from one's own racial, cultural, or ethnic group (Wang et al., 2003).

Intergroup empathy is also associated with CBRI; intergroup empathy affects interpersonal interactions and how empathic people are toward individuals and communities that differ from their own. Sometimes some racial groups (e.g., White racial groups) fail to understand or have empathic perspectives of other racial groups (e.g., Black racial groups). Failures in understanding racial or cultural perspectives other than one's own can have negative effects, resulting in what I consider to be an empathy bias. Bias, in general, has been defined as ignoring other category memberships and other personal attributes (Fiske, 2002, p. 123). An empathy bias involves a lack of compassion, perspective taking, concern, and understanding for an individual based on group membership or other personal characteristics and attributes. This lack of understanding often creates increased prejudice and negative stereotyping. One of our goals as humans should be perspective taking for other cultures, which includes an empathic understanding of differences.

Current work in popular culture has documented the importance of empathy in everyday lives, in part because of then-Senator Barack Obama's 2004 interview with Charlie Rose (cited at the start of this chapter) and his subsequent speeches that addressed the topic. Before Obama began to talk about empathy, it was discussed primarily in academic and literary circles. As president, Obama has passionately discussed why empathy is essential to human existence if we are to survive as a human race:

> If we hope to meet the moral test of our times . . . joblessness, homeless or any of the other issues [t]hen we need to talk more about the empathy deficit . . . the ability to put ourselves in someone else's shoes, to see the world through someone else's eyes. An empathy deficit, when we start thinking like this and choose to broaden the ambit of our concern and empathize with the plight of others, whether they are close friends or distant strangers it becomes harder not to act . . . not to help. . . . It is time for a sense of empathy to infuse our politics in America. It is time to stop making excuses for inaction and to start loving thy neighbor as thyself. (Obama, 2006)

How will we engage in empathic behaviors if we are steeped in negative associations and attributions of others who are racially different? We cannot and should not expect for everyone to be the same, but we should have the ability to see people and their behaviors from multiple perspectives and understand people who are racially different. The process of understanding differences while retaining an empathic understanding can be difficult. For example, in a recent Pew Report (Pew Research Center, 2013), 69% of Blacks compared with 30% of Whites believed that Blacks are not treated fairly in the criminal justice system (p. 12). In other words, 70% of Whites think that Blacks are treated fairly. In many cultures, we expect and appreciate differences in multifaceted ways of life (e.g., diversity of choices in the places we eat, clothing we wear, religions we embrace). We enjoy the diversity of those experiences in terms of interpersonal and intergroup preferences, yet many adopt a CBRI approach when it comes to opportunities that affect financial, educational, and economic outcomes. Strategically or not, individuals who espouse a CBRI wear a "virtual mask" when observing particular groups that are in distress. This virtual mask presents a false appearance to others; the individual appears to be color-blind when in fact, she or he is not. I think of this particular *masking phenomenon*—having empathy for some groups and not for others—as a strategic and preferential CBRI and therefore consider the process as an empathy bias.

In this chapter, I present competing and complementary definitions of empathy from psychology and neuroscience. I demonstrate through theoretical, empirical, and public commentary how groups or individuals lack empathy and adopt a preferential CBRI and empathy bias. *Preferential CBRI* is when an individual chooses to engage in racially color-blind behaviors in particular circumstances but not in others. It is similar to strategic CBRI, which I define later in the chapter. I also discuss empathy and an empathic disposition's connection to race in societies. I argue how empathy in everyday life presents different challenges for different groups. Finally, the chapter concludes, using a CBRI framework, with an examination of empathy or the lack of empathy and its effect on perceptions of race in a color-blind society.

EMPATHY DEFINED

Psychological Perspectives

Empathy has been defined as a "complex emotion with important attributes that involves affective and cognitive behaviors, such as caring and perspective taking in general populations and educational institutions" (Tettegah, 2007, p. 42). Defining empathy can be confusing and complex. For example, some scholars have viewed empathy as cognitive *or* affective (Feshbach & Roe, 1968; Mehrabian & Epstein, 1972), as cognitive *and* affective (Hoffman,

2000; Ickes, 1993), or as involving empathic dispositions (i.e., a tendency to behave or act in a particular way) that are multidimensional (Baron-Cohen, 2011; Davis, 1996). However, what is accepted by the majority of scholars in psychology and neuroscience is that empathy is a psychological state that describes our ability to accurately share emotions, manage control, and engage in perspective taking through observation of others and also by engaging in psychological inferences (Banissy, Kanai, Walsh, & Rees, 2012; Jackson, Meltzoff, & Decety, 2005).

Empathy as a moral emotion and its expression in everyday behavior are complex and involve multiple factors, including personal distress, altruism, and mirror neurons that are associated with all forms of life (for background related to personal distress and mirror neurons, see Iacoboni, 2008; Rizzolatti, Scandolara, Matelli, & Gentillucci, 1981a, 1981b). Hoffman (2000) argued that there are principally two dimensions of empathy, one cognitive and the other affective. He maintained that cognitive empathy involves two higher order cognitive models, mediated association and perspective taking. Mediated association involves associating one's own experience with that of the victim, whereas role or perspective taking involves imaging yourself in a victim's situation. Later in this chapter, I present how racial perspective taking can be more difficult and cognitively demanding for some groups compared with others. Racial perspective taking involves the process of an individual from one racial group taking on the perspective of an individual from another racial group (e.g., a White person taking the perspective of a Black person).

Davis's (1996) conceptualization of dispositional empathy is one of the more cited and adapted views of empathy in psychology, and it is flexible enough to consider the issue of racial perspective taking. Davis maintained that empathy is multidimensional and meditational depending on circumstances. He argued that empathy involves perspective or role taking, empathic concern, imagination (fantasy), and personal distress. "Depending on the situation that an individual encounters, and [the] behavior, the resulting perceptions by others could produce in the perceiver feelings of greater or lesser liking for an individual" (Davis, p. 178). In some cases, this would be true for those who maintain a high level of CBRI. That is, the individual is color blind in terms of race in some situations but has little or no empathy for those of another race in other situations, contradicting his or her previous claim of color blindness. In this case, people are inclusive in one situation in how they thinks but exclusive in another.

Pedersen, Crethar, and Carlson (2008) proposed the concept of *culturally inclusive empathy* and how it should apply to counseling and psychotherapy. Inclusive "empathy encompasses a process that involves moving from an individualistic conventional and western-based convergent definition of empathy to moving to contextual and cultural background relationships that engages the client in complementary ways" (Pedersen et al., 2008, pp. 42–43). It has been documented that cultural assumptions in psychotherapy provide misrepresentations of majority–minority cultural relationships (Sue & Sue, 1990). This misunderstanding can be attributed in part to a lack of empathy or resistance to having and exhibiting cultural empathy. By maintaining and engaging in an individualistic single-minded approach, the therapist is unable to provide an empathic understanding to clients from different racial groups.

Consider the notion of individualism versus collectivism. How does a person decide who is a member of the ingroup or outgroup of receiving or not receiving empathy? Many cultural psychologists have argued that some cultures socialize individuals to have more of a collective identity compared with those that focus more on individuality (Berry, Poortinga, & Pandey, 1997; Shweder, 1999). On the basis of the argument of collective versus individual cultures, how can it be that in many countries, individuals with darker complexions experience less empathic responses compared with other groups? What has caused less empathic concern and a reduction in morality in those who espouse a CBRI? Perhaps Baron-Cohen's (2011) explanation on empathy erosion can provide some insight on decreased empathy and empathic concern for individuals or groups who are perceived as outgroup members.

Similar to other definitions, Baron-Cohen (2011) defined empathy as "our ability to identify what someone else is thinking or feeling, and . . . to respond to his or her thoughts and feelings with an appropriate emotion" (p. 8). He also maintained that one of the reasons individuals may mistreat others is explained through the process of turning individuals into objects. This notion originated from philosopher Martin Buber as the (I–you) to (I–it) concepts. This process involves turning a person from a subject (I–you) to an object (I–it); therefore, the person (I) turns off his or her empathy for an individual (you) when the individual becomes an object (it). Objectification and stereotyping of Blacks can be observed throughout history. Blacks and other groups have been stereotyped as nonhuman (e.g., savage beasts, animalistic, depicting President Obama and the First Lady as apes). Baron-Cohen offered an explanation about the ability of humans to turn empathy on and off; he referred to this behavioral process as *empathy erosion*. By turning off empathy, individuals are only focused on their own interests and therefore reduce the other person(s) or racial group(s) to things or objects.

This process of erosion is similar to how an individual with a high level of CBRI responds to individuals from some racial groups. People who adopt a CBRI approach to race are in the I–it mode because this allows them not to engage differences in culture. However, this only serves to benefit the *I* when a person doesn't want to see another person as an individual or as an individual from another racial group. Legal battles, such as George Zimmerman's Florida murder trial for the death of Trayvon Martin, present a case in point regarding the ability to turn off empathy, particularly regarding race. During the innumerable discussions regarding Zimmerman's innocence or guilt, many White and Black Americans were divided. A large majority of White Americans argued that the killing was justified, whereas Black Americans maintained that Martin was a victim of racial profiling and discrimination. In this situation, some Whites would say that they "do not see race," yet in incidents in which racialized violence occurs, they fail to show empathy for the victims.

As a society, we have to ask ourselves what allows individuals who espouse a high level of CBRI to turn their racial color blindness on and off depending on the situation. What process allows some individuals to have empathy, suspending a single-minded approach and turning on a double-minded approach? Behaviors involving a lack of empathy and the single-minded approach are particularly evident among individuals who claim to not see race or avoid racial discourse (Goff, Jackson, Nichols, & Lewis Di Leone, 2013). For example, recent research examining racial discourse and strategic racial color blindness demonstrated that adopting a CBRI can lead to elevated racial prejudice (Goff et al., 2013). Could the problem of elevated prejudice be linked to current public discourse and feeling when White Americans enter into debates about the murder of innocent young men like Trayvon Martin and Michael Brown, an unarmed young man shot by a police officer in Ferguson, Missouri? In one situation (the case of Trayvon Martin), Whites avoided the appearance of racial bias by strategically denying race and suppressing racial prejudice, then when Whites have the opportunity to respond to other events involving African Americans (the case of Michael Brown), strategic CBRI results in diminished regulatory capacity and White rage (Apfelbaum, Sommers, & Norton, 2008). Whites become enraged, and their actual racial bias surfaces. Data from Pew Research Center (2014) polls indicate that 60% of Whites thought race was receiving too much emphasis in Trayvon Martin's murder case, compared with 13% of Blacks; in Michael Brown's case, the percentages were 47% of Whites compared with 18% of Blacks (p. 3). Perhaps studies in neuroscience can help to explain the process of empathy erosion and the lack of empathy involving race perceptions.

Neuroscience Perspectives

In social neuroscience, there has been much excitement about the activation of brain regions, visualized using functional magnetic resonance imaging (fMRI), when individuals observe others who are in pain (Gleichgerrcht & Decety, 2014; Singer et al., 2006). Within the past decade or so, neuroscientists have examined neurocorrelates of empathy from multiple perspectives that involve subcortical (primitive, affective, and automatic) and cortical (cognitive, strategic) areas of the brain. fMRI studies have demonstrated that empathy is multifaceted and that structural variations in brain regions supporting affect sharing and cognitive perspective taking act to facilitate self- and other-related empathic processes in different ways for different groups, depending on whether the individual perceives a group as a member of the ingroup or outgroup (Banissy et al., 2012; Cheon et al., 2011; Jackson et al., 2005).

Recent fMRI studies have found that White observers reacted with less empathy toward Black than toward White individuals (Forgiarini, Gallucci, & Maravita, 2011; Ofan, Rubin, & Amodio, 2011). Forgiarini et al. (2011) examined White observers' ($N = 90$) physiological reactions to Black, Asian, and White people shown in video clips. In the first experiment, skin conductance responses were measured while White observers viewed video of a male and female from each racial group being subjected to painful and neutral stimuli. Results indicated that empathy was expressed for all groups, but the empathic reactions toward Whites were significantly greater than the empathic reactions toward Blacks. Findings from the second experiment linked empathic racial bias with implicit racial bias. Empathic racial bias is associated with strong negative empathy bias for a person based on race (p. 2). The authors found a correlation between strong implicit racial bias and reduced empathy for Blacks. The results from this study did not support the ingroup empathy hypothesis because the empathic response toward Asians was not the same as for Blacks. Forgiarini et al. maintained that some racial groups may be perceived as less human that other groups, and this may account for the empathic racial bias toward Blacks.

Forgiarini et al. (2011) posited that a lack of empathy for the pain of other human beings might lead to violence, abuse, and deterioration of interpersonal and intergroup relationships. The limited empathic attitudes toward racial groups may be reflected in the almost automatic reactions people have in their interactions with others. We see examples of these behaviors in the news and social media daily, as in the shooting and murder of Michael Brown in Missouri. The shooting sparked increased racial tension between Black and White Americans. A 2014 headline read: "Ferguson Police Officer Was Doing His Job, Say Supporters"; the article noted that almost all of these supporters were White (Swaine, 2014). Swaine continues:

> While the crowds protesting in Ferguson have been predominantly African American, all but one of the demonstrators showing their support for Wilson were white. A stack of dark blue T-shirts, on sale for $7 and bearing a police-style badge stating: "Officer Darren Wilson—I stand by you," quickly sold out. (para. 9)

Could it be that Whites are automatically reacting to situations when they perceive Blacks as talking too much about race or "playing the race card"? Yet, when Blacks are not upfront about racial matters, Whites feel more comfortable with interactions between races and become strategically color blind.

The ability of Whites and other groups to see that Blacks and other underrepresented groups are different but still experience pain and suffering is key to improving human relations. More studies using physiological measures may help us understand the behavioral phenomenon of CBRI and empathy—in particular, the dehumanization of individuals from underrepresented groups and what are perceived as extreme outgroups (Forgiarini et al., 2011; Hein, Silani, Preuschoff, Batson, & Singer, 2010). In a recent book, *The Empathic Civilization*, Rifkin (2009) asserted that "a world without empathy is alien to the very notions of what a human being is, and that all human experiences are embodied" (pp. 142–145).

UNDERSTANDING THE GOOD, THE BAD, AND THE UGLY OF EMPATHY

This section focuses on the good, the bad, and the ugly of empathy and each element's relation to CBRI. The "good" are those who have a high level of empathy and empathic responses for everyone, regardless of race. The "bad" are those who have empathic responses toward no one (these individuals are usually defined as *psychopaths*). The "ugly" are those with preferential portrayals of empathy who are engaged in strategic color-blind racism that is hidden behind moral threads of consciousness. Individuals who adopt CBRI pretend that empathy is an equal-opportunity behavior; there is no need for moral emotional engagement because CBRI denies the existence of race, at least superficially. Yet, as described earlier, when it comes to justifying situations such as the murders of African American males and other events involving the pain and suffering of people of color, these individuals hide behind the mask of a CBRI to withhold feelings of rage toward Black populations.

An individual who claims the existence of racial equality hides behind the mask of CBRI while engaging in the silent stoning of those who are different. For example, consider that many Whites will claim there is racial equality, yet move to locations where there are few, if any, Black children in schools; when a Black family moves in next door, they may start to worry about the neighborhood going downhill; or when Whites seek a child to adopt, they look only for White children and avoid the adoption of Black children. *Silent stoning* is a process in which a person has a deep, perhaps unconscious, dislike for a person of color and in some ways juxtaposes

Whiteness onto the Black person because she or he does not want to see color; therefore, the person ignores or blames the victim when given an opportunity. This individual, one of the "ugly," has no empathy for some persons of color or racial groups and is thus similar to an individual with zero empathy (Baron-Cohen, 2011).

In relation to CBRI, the good, the bad, and the ugly can be captured using real-world multimedia and empirical studies. Multimedia exposes the public discourse that occurs when race is a factor. For example, recent studies using animated social simulations to examine teacher empathy toward students who are victimized within educational settings revealed less empathy toward a hypothetical Black child compared with a White child (Tettegah, 2007; Tettegah & Anderson, 2007). Specifically, the results indicated that when an African American female student was victimized, compared with a White female, the majority of the White educators expressed more empathy and empathic concern for the White student (Tettegah, 2007; Tettegah & Anderson, 2007).

EMPATHY, GROUP DIFFERENCES, AND PERCEPTIONS

Many among us might think that a CBRI perspective would mean higher empathic dispositions toward all groups. Yet quite often, racial color blindness does not extend to those who are different when the perceived racial outgroup is in pain and in need of empathy. That sameness applies only when people look the same, and looking the same varies depending on the behavior. For some reason, empathy has special qualities that ignore people of color when it comes to putting oneself in another's shoes; yet the same behavior often manifests itself as having a CBRI when it is associated with job opportunities and education. For example, a 2013 poll by the Pew Research Center (2013) asked: "How much more needs to be done in order to receive racial equality?" Seventy-nine percent of Blacks said a lot, compared with 44% of Whites (p. 9). Access to the Internet is another example. A Pew Report (Pew Research Center, 2010) involving job opportunities reported that African Americans and Latinos are more likely than White Americans to view a lack of broadband access as a major disadvantage. In other words, individuals who are White do not see broadband as an advantage. They see everyone as having the same job opportunities, perhaps because more White homes have broadband access (p. 14). Oddly enough, CBRI basically has the opposite affect: A CBRI supports the absence of empathy for individuals of color in one situation while maintaining the ideology of not seeing race when it is advantageous (Goff et al., 2013). This opposite affect relates back to what Obama called *empathy deficit* and also Anholt's notion of *cultural psychopaths*. In a 2014 Ted Talk, Anholt pointed out:

> Governments, just like the rest of us, are cultural psychopaths. [A psychopath is] a person who lacks the ability to empathize with other human beings. When they look around, they do not see other human beings with deep, rich three-dimensional personal lives and the same aims and ambitions. What they see is cardboard cutouts and it is very sad, lonely. . . . Yes, we are very good at empathy for people who kind of look like us, kind of walk, talk and eat, pray and wear like us, but when it comes to people who don't look, eat, pray and act like us, don't we have the tendency to also see them as cardboard cutouts, too? (Anholt, 2014)

Why do people claim that they do not see differences when it comes to certain racial matters, but they do see differences when it comes to empathy for another individual with perceived similar behaviors? This type of "racial empathy gap" was described in Silverstein's (2013) news article on the Zimmerman trial titled "I Don't Feel Your Pain." Silverstein mentioned findings from the neuropsychology and neuroscience literature documenting the racial empathy gap. This type of research shows that when it comes to the observation of individuals experiencing pain, participants have less empathy for Blacks in pain compared with Whites in pain (Avenanti, Sirigu, & Aglioti, 2010; Chiao & Mathur, 2010; Ito & Bartholow, 2009; Xu, Zuo, Wang, & Han, 2009).

Other media forms support the racial empathy gap. While conducting research, I found the online outlet KolorBlind. Its website tagline is: "The equality & acceptance of all races/ethnicities; the promotion of the Interracial/multiracial life through culture, fashion, language and food" (Kolorblindmag.com). I thought, what an interesting online magazine this is, focusing on acceptance. The exact goals of the site were unclear, however, as was the site's color-blind mission based on the articles I read. Despite the fact that the website claims to support color blindness, it points to examples of how discriminatory Whites and other groups can be toward Blacks; in this sense, it is not color blind. For example, one of the articles focused on interracial adoption ("Adopting mixed-race orphans," n.d.). The article noted that Black children were 3 times less likely to find new parents than White children. This discussion again demonstrates how there is less empathy for Black children compared with White children, both by Whites and other groups. The lack of empathy for Black children may be the result of having little contact with Black people, and therefore White adoptive parents have no need, or simply do not have the ability, to empathize with children who are different. Again, color blindness has a negative effect, and what is viewed as color blind in this situation can actually be viewed as hyper–color awareness (strategic color blindness; Goff et al., 2013).

With regard to empathy, strategic color blindness does not apply or help Black victims, despite comments from people with a CBRI (i.e., "We shouldn't even care if someone is black of white or pink or purple or whatever"; Goff et al., 2013, p. 336). If there is a lack of nonpreferential treatment and true CBRI, then what accounts for the preference of Whites to adopt children from all other racial groups at a higher rate than Black children? Individuals who have adopted a CBRI only care about racial equality when it works to their advantage; racial inequality exists even in the display of empathy toward Blacks. The problem of prejudice and discrimination based on racial inequality is institutional but also emotional and pervasive in many societies. In this sense, emotional inequality involves the expression of empathy for one racial group and reduced or lack of empathy for another racial group.

What is it going to take to get some groups in our society to step outside their world and walk in the shoes of the others? Anholt (2014) argued in his recent TED talk that human beings need to find ways to work together and stop making rules that only look inward. He made the case that if we are to advance as human beings, we need to replace our microscopic perspectives with a telescope lens that allows us to move beyond seeing every country as an island. Of course, this makes social life more complicated because, according to Hoffman (2000), evolutionary biology says that if we must choose whom to help, we will choose to help others to the extent that they share our genes; psychology says we will help others whom we care about and people who belong to our primary group. Such empathic bias is problematic in an increasingly global world where we must interact and depend on others who are different from us for our survival. We cannot ignore those differences, maintain a strategic CBRI approach, and refer to the "other" racial groups only when it is convenient. Individuals who have adopted a CBRI should move from this strategic, selective, and preferential approach to race and begin to recognize racial differences in socially just ways.

CONCLUSION

What do we need to do to improve our empathy quotient while recognizing individual differences? We should engage in more systematic studies in education, counseling psychology, social psychology, other humanities, social science, and STEM fields to determine empathic dispositions and empathy involving individuals and ingroup–outgroup memberships in communities and nations (Markowicz, 2009). If we as a nation are to recognize and engage in socially just ways, we should examine the very components of human behaviors that facilitate empathy, compassion, and social justice. We should continue to see and identify perceptual factors to be used as criteria for revealing empathic concern (Tettegah, 2007). Understanding these factors associated with behaviors involving empathy is important for the social survival of human beings. Although we cannot avoid and control corrosive emotions and such as anger, hatred, and discontent, we can focus more on positive emotions such as gratitude, hope, love, and compassion and begin to embrace differences.

Those claiming to be color blind are in complete denial because we are wired to see differences, but it is how we deal with and handle those differences that are important. As Baron-Cohen (2011) pointed out, we are wired to a have loyalty to our own social groups. The loyalty helps to protect us as members of our social group's identity through a collective and purposeful way. Less empathy by some groups for Black populations could perhaps be a way of punishing individuals from certain groups and displaying subtle hatred (i.e., silent stoning) of Blacks. Of course, social and mass media could also play a role in presenting negative images and representations involving antisocial behaviors to increase or reduce empathy bias toward people of color.

Empathy is complex, and there are many dimensions involved. It will be important for individuals to have more direct opportunities to strengthen their understanding of different cultural and racial groups and how such groups operate, while eliminating the need to engage in denial of differences. We have a direct opportunity to develop empathy by establishing relationships based on compassion and understanding, reducing segregation based on race, and making a commitment to convergence while maintaining individual racial and cultural differences (Turner, 1991).

One reason it is important to have empathy for outgroup members is that we are currently in a world where technology enables the intersection of many cultures. If we are to endure and prosper, it is necessary to empathize with those who are different—and not deny or distort those differences through a CBRI perspective. Research has shown that people empathize with and help others whom they believe share their preferences, attitudes, interests, life goals, and chronic concerns (Hoffman, 2000). There has been evidence demonstrating this to be true, and in the United States, this sense of "sameness" is situated in many ways along racial (skin color) lines. We should ask ourselves what psychological mechanism or process allows an individual within, for example, White racial groups to be less empathic or simply have no empathy for Blacks based on skin color? There are many factors, but some of them are group preferences, a history of prejudice against Blacks and other people of color, strategic CBRI, and dehumanization associated with internalized prior knowledge of a racial group within a specific society.

Frans de Waal (2009) wrote, "Greed is out, empathy is in" (p. ix). CBRI should be out, and part of the issue here is bringing the two concepts of CBRI and empathy together so that we can develop a clear discourse on the relationship between empathy and CBRI. Iacoboni (2008) noted that "when we see someone else suffering or in pain, neurons help us to read her or his facial expression and actually make us feel the suffering or pain of another . . . and this is the foundation of empathy" (p. 5). But if an individual relates to a CBRI, he or she will first reduce a person who is different to an object and then not see that an actual person is in pain. The individual who espouses a CBRI must first recognize and acknowledge differences among people and refuse to objectify human beings as nonhuman on the basis of skin color. We have opportunities to build powerful relationships through, by, and with technology; however, we must first recognize differences and see human beings who are different from us as subjects, not objects, to create an equal opportunity and socially just environment for our communities.

REFERENCES

Adopting mixed-race orphans. (n.d.). *KolorBlind Mag.* Retrieved from http://kolor blindmag.com/2013/02/08/mixed-race-orphans-placed-in-families-with-white-parents-are-deeply-affected-by-cultural-and-racial-differences

Anholt, S. (2014, June). *Which country does the most good?* TED Talks. http://www.ted.com/talks/simon_anholt_which_country_does_the_most_good_for_the_world

Apfelbaum, E. P., Sommers, S. R., & Norton, M. I. (2008). Seeing race and seeming racist? Evaluating strategic color blindness in social interaction. *Journal of Personality and Social Psychology, 95,* 918–932. http://dx.doi.org/10.1037/a0011990

Avenanti, A., Sirigu, A., & Aglioti, S. M. (2010). Racial bias reduces empathic sensorimotor resonance with other-race pain. *Current Biology, 20,* 1018–1022. http://dx.doi.org/10.1016/j.cub.2010.03.071

Banissy, M. J., Kanai, R., Walsh, V., & Rees, G. (2012). Inter-individual differences in empathy are reflected in human brain structure. *NeuroImage, 62,* 2034–2039. http://dx.doi.org/10.1016/j.neuroimage.2012.05.081

Baron-Cohen, S. (2011). *The science of evil: On empathy and the origins of cruelty.* New York, NY: Basic Books.

Berry, J. W., Poortinga, Y. H., & Pandey, J. (Eds.). (1997). *Handbook of cross-cultural psychology, Vol. 2. Basic processes and human development.* Boston, MA: Allyn Bacon.

Cheon, B. K., Im, D.-M., Harada, T., Kim, J.-S., Mathur, V. A., Scimeca, J. M., . . . Chiao, J. Y. (2011). Cultural influences on neural basis of intergroup empathy. *NeuroImage, 57,* 642–650. http://dx.doi.org/10.1016/j.neuroimage.2011.04.031

Chiao, J. Y., & Mathur, V. A. (2010). Intergroup empathy: How does race affect empathic neural responses. *Current Biology, 20,* R478–480.

Davis, M. H. (1996). *Empathy: A social psychological approach.* Boulder, CO: Westview Press.

de Waal, F. (2009). *The age of empathy: Nature's lessons for a kinder society*. New York, NY: Harmony Books.

Feshbach, N. D., & Roe, K. (1968). Empathy in six- and seven-year-olds. *Child Development, 39*, 133–145.

Fiske, S. T. (2002). What we know about bias and intergroup conflict, the problem of the century. *Current Directions in Psychological Science, 11,* 4, 123–128.

Forgiarini, M., Gallucci, M., & Maravita, A. (2011). Racism and empathy for pain on our skin. *Frontiers in Psychology, 2,* 108.

Gleichgerrcht, E., & Decety, J. (2014). The relationship between facets of empathy, pain perception, and compassion fatigue among physicians, *Frontiers in Behavioral Neuroscience, 8*(243), 1–9.

Goff, P. A., Jackson, M. C., Nichols, A. H., & Lewis Di Leon, B. A. (2013). Anything but race: Avoiding racial discourse to avoid hurting you or me. *Psychology, 4,* 335–339.

Hein, G., Silani, G., Preuschoff, K., Batson, C. D., & Singer, T. (2010). Neural responses to ingroup and outgroup members' suffering predict individual differences in costly helping. *Neuron, 68,* 149–160.

Hoffman, M. L. (2000). *Empathy and moral development: Implications for caring and justice*. Cambridge, England: Cambridge University Press.

Howe, D. (2013). *Empathy: What it is and why it matters*. New York, NY: Palgrave Macmillan.

Iacoboni, M. (2008). *Mirroring people*. New York, NY: Farrar, Strauss & Giroux.

Ickes, W. (1993). Empathic accuracy. *Journal of Personality, 61,* 587–610.

Ito, T. A., & Bartholow, B. D. (2009). The neurocorrelates of race. *Trends in Cognitive Sciences, 13,* 524–531.

Jackson, P. L., Meltzoff, A. N., & Decety, J. (2005). How do we perceive the pain of others? A window into the neural processes involved with empathy. *NeuroImage, 24,* 771–779.

Markowicz, J. A. (2009). *Intergroup contact experience in dialogues on race groups: Does empathy and informational identity style help explain prejudice reduction?* (Doctoral dissertation). Available from ProQuest Dissertations and Theses database. (UMI No. 3380965)

Mehrabian, A., & Epstein, N. (1972). A measure of emotional empathy. *Journal of Personality, 40,* 525–543.

Neville, H. A., Awad, G. H., Brooks, J. E., Flores, M. P., & Bluemel, J. (2013). Color-blind racial ideology. *American Psychologist, 68,* 455–466. http://dx.doi.org/10.1037/a0033282

Obama, B. (2004, November 23). An hour with Illinois Senator Barack Obama. In C. Rose (Producer) & Y. Vega (Executive Producer), *Charlie Rose* [season 11, episode 16]. New York, NY: Bloomberg Television Studios, PBS. Retrieved from http://theobamadiary.com/2011/04/18/the-charlie-rose-interviews-2

Obama, B. (2006, December 4). Speech delivered at the Kids In Distressed Situations (K.I.D.S.)/Fashion Delivers gala. Retrieved from https://www.youtube.com/watch?v=4md_A059JRc

Ofan, R. H., Rubin, N., & Amodio, D. M. (2011). Seeing race: 170 responses to race and their relation to automatic racial attitudes and controlled processing. *Journal of Cognitive Neuroscience, 23*, 3153–3161.

Pedersen, P. B., Crethar, H. C., & Carlson, J. (2008). *Inclusive cultural empathy: Making relationships central in counseling and psychotherapy.* Washington, DC: American Psychological Association.

Pew Research Center. (2010). Attitudes toward broadband and broadband investment. Retrieved from http://www.pewinternet.org/2010/08/11/attitudes-towards-broadband-and-broadband-investment

Pew Research Center. (2013). *King's dream remains an elusive goal; many Americans see racial disparities.* The Pew Research Center. Retrieved from http://www.pewsocialtrends.org/2013/08/22/kings-dream-remains-an-elusive-goal-many-americans-see-racial-disparities/4

Pew Research Center. (2014). *Stark racial divisions in reactions to Ferguson police shootings.* Retrieved from http://www.people-press.org/2014/08/18/stark-racial-divisions-in-reactions-to-ferguson-police-shooting/

Rameson, L. T., Morelli, S. A., & Lieberman, M. D. (2011). The neurocorrelates of empathy: Experience, automaticity, and prosocial behavior. *Journal of Cognitive Neuroscience, 24*, 235–245.

Rifkin, J. (2009). *The empathic civilization: The race to global consciousness in a world of crisis.* New York, NY: Tarcher/Penguin.

Rizzolatti, G., Scandolara, C., Matelli, M., & Gentilucci, M. (1981a). Afferent properties of periarcuate neurons in macaque monkeys: I. Somatosensory responses. *Behavioral Brain Research, 2*, 125–146.

Rizzolatti, G., Scandolara, C., Matelli, M. & Gentilucci, M. (1981b). Afferent properties of periarcuate neurons in macaque monkeys: II. Visual responses. *Behavioral Brain Research 2*, 147–163.

Shweder, R. A. (1999). Why cultural psychology? *Ethos, 27*, 62–73. http://dx.doi.org/10.1525/eth.1999.27.1.62

Silverstein, J. (2013, June 27). I don't feel your pain: A failure of empathy perpetuates racial disparities. *Slate.* Retrieved from http://www.slate.com/articles/health_and_science/science/2013/06/racial_empathy_gap_people_don_t_perceive_pain_in_other_races.html

Singer, T., Seymour, B., O'Doherty, J. P., Stephan, K. E., Dolan, R. J., & Firth, C. D. (2006). Empathic neural responses are modulated by the perceived fairness of others. *Nature, 439*, 466–469.

Sue, D. W., & Sue, S. (1990). *Counseling the culturally different* (2nd ed.). New York, NY: Wiley.

Swaine, J. (2014, August 17). Ferguson police officer was doing his job, say supporters. *The Guardian*. Retrieved from http://www.theguardian.com/world/2014/aug/18/ferguson-supporters-police-killed-teenager-protest

Tettegah, S. (2007). Pre-service teachers, victim empathy, and problem solving using animated narrative vignettes. *Technology, Instruction, Cognition and Learning, 5,* 41–68.

Tettegah, S., & Anderson, C. (2007). Preservice teachers' empathy and cognitions: Statistical analysis of text data by graphical models. *Contemporary Educational Psychology, 32,* 48–82.

Turner, J. C. (1991). *Social influence*. Buckingham, England: Open University Press.

Wang, Y., Davidson, M. M., Yakushiko, O. F., Savoy, H. B., Tan, T. A., & Bleier, J. K. (2003). The scale of ethnocultural empathy: Development, validations, and reliability. *Journal of Counseling Psychology, 50,* 221–234.

Xu, X., Zuo, X., Wang, X., & Han, S. (2009). Do you feel my pain? Racial group membership modulates empathic neural responses. *The Journal of Neuroscience, 29,* 8525–8529.

11

COLOR-BLIND RACIAL IDEOLOGY AND INTERNALIZED RACISM AMONG PEOPLE OF COLOR

SUZETTE L. SPEIGHT, AMBER A. HEWITT, AND HETHER R. COOK

This chapter examines the impact of people of color ascribing to color-blind racial ideology (CBRI). Although a widely propagated "racial project" (Omi & Winant, 1994), color blindness is infrequently associated with people of color. Instead, racial color blindness is thought of as a practice of the dominant society. Given the hegemony of CBRI and the racial inequality it supports, color blindness obviously influences the psyche of people of color. We examine racial color blindness first as a system justification theory. Second, we examine the research findings related to CBRI and people of color. Then we look at the link between racial color blindness and internalized racism with specific attention to the notion of covering. Finally, we suggest critical consciousness development as the corrective to the prevailing CBRI.

http://dx.doi.org/10.1037/14754-012

The Myth of Racial Color Blindness: Manifestations, Dynamics, and Impact, H. A. Neville, M. E. Gallardo, and D. W. Sue (Editors)

CBRI AND SYSTEM JUSTIFICATION THEORY

> Bureaucracy defends the status quo, long past the time when the quo has lost its status.
> —Dr. Laurence J. Peter, *Peter's Quotations: Ideas for Our Time*, 1977

System justification theory evolved to explain not only stereotypes, prejudice, and intergroup relations but also perceptions of the fairness and legitimacy of social arrangements and ideologies (Jost & van der Toorn, 2012). Initially, Jost and van der Toorn (2012) contended that architected stereotypes aimed at disenfranchised groups were promulgated to explain existing societal structures by groups positioned to benefit from preservation of the status quo; however, these architected stereotypes were eventually spread by the groups that are targets of these stereotypes as a way to explain and understand their own disenfranchised position as natural and just. System justification theories provide the rationale for the advantages and disadvantages that target and agent groups experience.

System justification is the "process by which existing social arrangements are legitimized, even at the expense of personal and group interest" (Jost & Banaji, 1994, p. 2). Ideologies such as CBRI and meritocracy are used to defend and bolster the status quo. System justification theory postulates that, to varying degrees, people are motivated (often unconsciously) to defend and bolster current economic, social, and political arrangements (Jost & van der Toorn, 2012). But why would people prefer to keep things the way they are?

> Sometimes people hold a core belief that is very strong. When they are presented with evidence that works against that belief, the new evidence cannot be accepted. It would create a feeling that is extremely uncomfortable, called cognitive dissonance. And because it is so important to protect the core belief, they will rationalize, ignore and even deny anything that doesn't fit in with the core belief. (Fanon, 1967, p. 194)

This quote from psychiatrist Frantz Fanon highlights the role of *cognitive dissonance*—the tension that results when attitudes and behaviors are not aligned—that compels people to reduce uncertainty and inconsistency. As applied to our social system, an individual has two options when confronted with racial injustice: First, if we recognize racial injustice, cognitive dissonance motivates us to act in a way that is consonant with our views. This means acting against racial injustice. However, acting against the system increases uncertainty and fear, leading to the popularity of the second option: aligning our beliefs to match our behavior. It is easier to continue in the status quo, which is certain, and align our thinking to reflect consistency. Motivation to maintain the current social order meets basic human needs for safety, certainty, justice, fairness, and predictability (Jost & Hunyady, 2005).

For members of privileged groups, justifying the system is directly correlated with self-esteem, ingroup favoritism, and long-term psychological well-being because it justifies the success of the advantaged person and their advantaged group (Jost & Thompson, 2000). But when those who are oppressed attempt to understand their low social status, it leads to conflicting motives to defend the system or to justify themselves and their group. Higher system justification tendencies in the disadvantaged have been found to be negatively correlated with self-esteem, ingroup favoritism, and long-term psychological well-being (Jost & Thompson, 2000). However, for both advantaged and disadvantaged groups, system justification serves a palliative function (Jost & Hunyady, 2005), meaning that in the short term, it appears to decrease distress. For example, in both groups, higher endorsement of system justification is related to more positive affect and less negative affect (Napier & Jost, 2008), reduced feelings of uncertainty, helplessness, cognitive dissonance, moral outrage, and other negative psychological experiences (Kay, Gaucher, Napier, Callan, & Laurin, 2008; Wakslak, Jost, Tyler, & Chen, 2007). Because system justification reduces moral outrage in low- and high-status groups, it is not surprising that endorsement of system justification motivation leads people to resist social change and to perceive social change as a threat to the status quo (Jost & van der Toorn, 2012).

CBRI can be endorsed by both Whites and people of color, serving a different purpose for each group. The adoption of CBRI prevents one from seeing the racial inequalities in contemporary society. The denial of the existence and experiences of racism is one of the central components of CBRI, and this system of beliefs is a schema through which individuals interpret information about race (Neville, Lilly, Duran, Lee, & Browne, 2000). CBRI is a distortion and minimization of racism. Consequently, for People of Color, internalizing the distorted messages about race, racism, and their group results in a state of false consciousness (Jost & Banaji, 1994).

False consciousness is a core tenet of system justification theory. It is defined as "the holding of false or inaccurate beliefs that are contrary to one's own social interest and which thereby contribute to the maintenance of the disadvantaged position of the self or the group" (Jost, 1995, p. 400). For instance, those disadvantaged by a particular public policy (e.g., lack of a living wage) may falsely believe that this policy is good for society as a whole, when, in fact, the lack of a federal living wage ensures maintenance of social stratification and even further increases economic and power disparities. Color-blind racial attitudes work against the individual and group interests of people of color to legitimize racism and protect group interest for Whites (Neville, Coleman, Falconer, & Holmes, 2005). Whites recruit racial color blindness for their benefit, to further solidify existing social hierarchies, and to legitimize systems of inequality (Knowles, Lowery, Hogan, & Chow, 2009).

RESEARCH ON CBRI AND PEOPLE OF COLOR

Everything that we see is a shadow cast by that which we do not see
—Reverend Martin Luther King, Jr., *The Measure of a Man*, 1958

Most of the empirical research on CBRI and its psychological correlates has been on European Americans, with a small amount of research conducted with African Americans (Neville, Coleman, Falconer, & Holmes, 2005; Neville, Lilly, Duran, Lee, & Browne, 2000). The initial validation on the Color-Blind Racial Attitudes Scale (CoBRAS; Neville et al., 2000) included a racially diverse, yet predominately White, sample. We know little about color-blind racial attitudes among other U.S. ethnic minorities, such as Asian Americans and Latina/Latino Americans. Some studies addressing CBRI have examined seemingly incidental populations of color (Chao, Wei, Good, & Flores, 2011; Worthington, Navarro, Loewy, & Hart, 2008). Other research appears to have been designed to incorporate comparison between racial groups. For instance, Oh, Choi, Neville, Anderson, and Landrum-Brown (2010) examined the relationship between affirmative action attitudes and racial color blindness in a study that included approximately 25% self-identified African American participants. The authors found that low racial color blindness was the best predictor of support for favorable affirmative action attitudes, race or ethnicity was the second best predictor (African Americans were higher in support), and beliefs about racism (i.e., racism is still a problem, not a problem, or has improved) was the third best predictor. The model combining CoBRAS and racism beliefs was a better predictor of affirmation action attitudes than race alone, and the combination of all three was the best predictor.

In a pre–post comparison design of White versus Black and Latino (combined into one group) college students, high racial color blindness in the fall predicted low engagement in formal campus diversity experiences, whereas high universal diverse orientation predicted high engagement in diversity experiences by Black and Latino participants (Spanierman, Neville, Liao, Hammer, & Wang, 2008). Students who attended more diversity events had lower color-blind attitudes and higher universal diverse orientation in the spring. These findings suggest that campus diversity experiences may have a positive influence on those who attend; however, one's racial ideology predicts whether these events are attended, and it is likely that students sought out those experiences that reinforced their preexisting ideologies.

Tynes and Markoe's (2010) mixed-methods study assessed the role of color-blind racial attitudes in participant reactions to social media pictures of racially themed parties (i.e., racial discrimination). In comparison with Whites, African Americans endorsed significantly fewer color-blind attitudes (although still endorsing moderate CBRI) and were less likely to be "not bothered or ambivalent" about the pictures than Whites. Higher CBRI in the entire sample did predict being "not bothered" by the discriminatory social media images. Some research has been designed exclusively to gain an understanding of the use of CBRI in African Americans. Coleman, Chapman, and Wang (2013) reported that African Americans endorse moderate levels of racial color blindness and that higher endorsement of color-blind racial beliefs predicted lower psychological well-being. However, higher color-blind racial beliefs also predicted lower levels of race-related stress. The authors emphasized that this result cannot be construed to mean "ignorance is bliss" but that CBRI may serve a protective function. One may also wonder whether CBRI is a way of coping in a racist world or whether it maintains social connectedness. Research by Barr and Neville (2008) revealed that African American students' reports of parental racial color blindness predicted their own racial color blindness and resulted in receipt of fewer protective messages about racial socialization. Exploring the ongoing impact of CBRI as a racialization socialization message via a longitudinal design would be a worthwhile investigation.

Neville et al. (2005) studied African Americans' CBRI and psychological false consciousness, the system justification beliefs that work against one's individual and group interest. Specifically, the relationship of CBRI to three of the six dimensions of psychological false consciousness was examined (i.e., victim blame, internalized oppression, and social dominance orientation). Findings demonstrated that African Americans who more strongly endorsed color-blind racial attitudes were also more likely to (a) internalize beliefs Whites hold that explain White superiority, (b) believe personal deficiencies are the reason some social groups experience economic and social problems, and (c) believe dominance of one group over another is natural and justifiable.

Thus, taken together, the scant research on CBRI and people of color suggests more questions than answers. Racial color blindness says that race does not and should not matter. For Whites, it provides a means to deny or evade the existence of their own White privilege (Neville et al., 2000) and to ignore the deleterious effects of racism. Yet race is not only salient, it is essential. What does it mean, then, to be a person of color who upholds color blindness and does not see, minimizes, or ignores race and racism? The system justification function of CBRI among people of color may reflect the internalization of White racism that maintains the psychological and structural oppression of people of color in U.S. society.

INTERNALIZED RACISM

I have freed thousands of slaves, but I could have freed thousands more if they had known they were slaves.
   —Commonly attributed to Harriet Tubman (Luker, 2008)

As has been discussed by many theorists, internalized oppression is a predictable consequence of any system of oppression. *Internalized racism* is the "individual inculcation of the racist stereotypes, images, values, ideologies perpetuated by the White dominant society about one's racial group, leading to feelings of self-doubt, disgust, and disrespect for one's self and/or ones race" (Pyke, 2010, p. 553). This internalization occurs when the subordinate group accepts as true the dominant society's view of them. People of color can end up believing the external characterization of themselves imposed on them by the oppressor. The dominant group denigrates, ignores, discounts, misrepresents, or eradicates the target group's culture, language, and history (Hardiman & Jackson, 1997). As Freire (1970/1999) described, "So often do they hear that they are good for nothing, know nothing and are incapable of learning anything—that they are sick, lazy, and unproductive—that in the end they become convinced of their own unfitness" (p. 45). According to Watts-Jones (2002), when people of color internalize racism, it is a degrading and alienating experience that reinforces their own sense of inferiority. Accommodating to the dominant society's prevailing racial ideology is to become, in Freire's view, "domesticated." Through its internalization, oppression becomes self-sustaining as it colonizes and recolonizes the subordinate group (Freire, 1970/1999).

Yet internalization of racism is a sociocultural phenomenon, not simply a psychological one. Tappan (2006) cautioned against minimizing the critical role of the dominant society in the internalization of racism by people of color. From a psychological perspective, it is tempting to locate the internalization of racism as an intrapsychic event, but psychological discourse must not obscure "the role that systemic, structural, institutionalized forces play in producing and reproducing both privilege and oppression" (Tappan, 2006, p. 2122). The oppressed peoples' internalization of racism is actually an (mal)adaptation to "what oppressors and systems of oppression *do to* the oppressed" (Pyke, 2010, p. 561, italics in original). Tappan suggested that we understand internalized racism as a consequence of the oppressed appropriating the dominant society's oppressive ideologies.

The internalization of dominant society's negative messages about one's group and an initial lack of salience of race are also found within most theories of racial and ethnic identity. For example, the Black racial identity development model (Cross, 1971, 1991) begins with the pre-encounter stage when the individual has absorbed the deleterious societal messages about his or her group. This absorption or internalization of negative societal messages is similar to the construct of internalized racism. In fact, Cokley (2002) found that pre-encounter racial identity attitudes as measured by the Cross Racial Identity Scale (Vandiver et al., 2000) were positively related to internalized racism (e.g., beliefs in the mental and genetic deficiencies and the sexual prowess of Blacks). Bailey, Chung, Williams, Singh, and Terrell (2011) reported a similar finding demonstrating that internalized racial oppression significantly correlated with items on the Pre-Encounter subscale of the Racial Identity Attitude Scale—B (Helms & Parham, 1996), which measures anti-Black attitudes and negative stereotypes about Blacks. Although these racial identity models do not use the term *color blindness*, the minimization of race and racism they describe is reminiscent of CBRI attitudes.

In a similar vein, Goffman (1963) discussed the notion of *covering*, a process in which the person with a stigma "makes a great effort to keep the stigma from looming large" (p. 102). Covering is different from passing in that passing involves the visibility of the stigmatizing characteristic and covering involves the obtrusiveness of the stigma. Covering removes attention from the stigmatized identity through minimizing the identity. By downplaying the devalued aspect of one's identity, the stigmatized person hopes that the devalued identity will be neither noticed nor judged. Covering is an attempt to fit into the norms of the dominant society by minimizing indicators of one's difference. The performance of covering requires stigma consciousness, the awareness that some aspect of the self is stereotyped and devalued by the larger society (Pinel, 1999). Covering is a means of coping with society's expectations by adjusting oneself to better conform to the dominant norms.

Yoshino (2006) explored this societal pressure to conform by recounting many instances of a subtle form of discrimination aimed at those who do not fit into to the dominant social norms. For instance, an American Airlines employee, Renee Rogers, was fired for wearing cornrows to work, which was against the company's grooming policy. In 1981, a federal court rejected Rogers's appeal finding that "because hairstyle, unlike skin color, was a mutable characteristic, discrimination on the basis of grooming was not discrimination on the basis of race" (Yoshino, 2006, p. 2). Thus, the court distinguished between being a member of a legally protected group and the behaviors associated with that group. Consequently, African Americans could not be fired for their race but could be fired for their culturally based hairstyles. Yoshino saw this as reinforcement of societal demands for assimilation. The message is that one can be different from the mainstream but just not "too different."

In fact, the societal pressure to conform emerged recently when the parents of Tiana Parker, a 7-year-old African American girl, removed her from Deborah Brown Community School in Tulsa, Oklahoma, after being told that her dreadlocks were not presentable. According to the charter school's dress code, faddish hairstyles such as dreadlocks, afros, or mohawks, are deemed unacceptable (Klein, 2013). Interestingly, this school is located within an underresourced, urban, African American community where the vast majority of the school's children are African American and all of the school's board of directors and administrators are African American, according to the school's website. This incident sparked a lively debate within the beauty magazine *Essence* about hair in the workplace. Lisa Reddock (2014), an African American female partner in a law firm in Los Angeles, argued:

> A Black woman's hair choice can limit her mobility, depending on how progressive her work environment may be. . . . You develop a sense of what makes people feel more comfortable in corporate America. The reason many of us straighten our hair is to take hair out of the equation. Folks in the boardroom can actually hear what we're saying instead of being distracted by our hair. . . . When you get to corporate America, you most likely will choose to go with what may be considered mainstream, and let's face it, straight hair is just nonthreatening. (p. 49)

Reddock's position is a strategy for managing her racial identity by downplaying her natural "Black" (i.e., coarse, curly, nappy) hair by chemically straightening it to appear more mainstream and therefore more acceptable. By covering or deemphasizing one aspect of her Blackness, Reddock's hope is that her coworkers will focus on her other qualities—her credentials and skills—and take her seriously as a professional. Applying Goffman's (1963) conceptualization, Reddock is endeavoring to minimize the obtrusiveness of her stigma (i.e., Black-ness) as an adaptation to a potentially oppressive environment. Minimizing one's Black-ness—or Latino-ness or Asian-ness—to avoid or lessen the negative judgment of the dominant society suggests that one has internalized the dominant society's view of the stigmatized identity to some degree. There are important unanswered empirical questions here: To what extent does covering reflect internalized oppression, and what is the psychic toll of covering or adjusting one's self to fit into dominant society's norms?

Minimizing race is a hallmark of CBRI. Color blindness "whitewashes" away difference, which may serve to decrease conflict and increase comfort for those invested in maintaining the status quo. Yet diminishing race could be problematic for people of color. Racial identity provides a collective sense of self, history, connection, and belonging for many people of color. The minimization of race for a person of color threatens to negate a key aspect of self. Fanon (1967) attempted to capture this tension by imagining a situation in which the kindly masters decided to free their slaves. When the former slave and the former master encounter one another, the White master claims that there is no difference between the two of them. The formerly oppressed African American man, in contrast, profoundly understands the importance of the racial difference between them. Ironically, the fact of the difference and the meaning assigned to the racial "otherness" of the former enslaved were integral to the system of racial oppression. Race was the marker used to differentiate and dole out advantages and disadvantages. The system of oppression was based on the notions of White supremacy and Black inferiority. As Akbar (1984) explained, "the very condition of the African's slavery was done on the basis of skin color. . . . The African's black skin was considered as evidence for his cursed state to serve as a slave" (pp. 35–36).

CBRI's invitation to disregard one's race appears as an empty promise in our racialized society. There is a denigration of "otherness" inherent in CBRI. Through CBRI, people of color are encouraged to "become like us and we will accept you into our group. But they never are" (Pyke, 2010, p. 557). Color blindness for a person of color presents a cruel illusion, a promise of acceptance wrapped up in the very negation of ones' racial identity. Thus, CBRI represents a potentially dangerous situation for people of color's sense of self and agency.

CRITICAL CONSCIOUSNESS

I am not the slave of the Slavery that dehumanized my ancestors.
—Frantz Fanon, *Black Skin, White Masks*, 1967 (p. 230)

The consequences of CBRI and internalized oppression can be buffered by the development of critical consciousness and subsequent psychological liberation. People of color's sense of self and agency are directly addressed by what Freire (1970/1999) called *consceintizaco* (i.e., critical consciousness), which highlights the importance of self-determination and its role in resisting oppression. Critical consciousness came to the forefront with Brazilian philosopher and educator Freire's (1970/1999) seminal work *Pedagogy of the Oppressed*, a text based largely on his experience in political exile. Freire's *consceintizaco* is a mechanism through which individuals who are oppressed can liberate themselves (and their oppressor) from oppression. Watts, Diemer, and Voight's (2011) theoretical formulation of social political development, based largely on the work of Freire, consists of three components: critical reflection, political efficacy, and participation in civic or political action. According to Watts et al. (2011), critical reflection must occur before any type of action can occur. This critical reflection involves an understanding of inequity on a systemic level. Political efficacy is described as the belief in one's ability to effect change, individually or collectively, on a social and political level. The third component, civic or political action, involves taking individual or collective action to change institutional and societal policies that are unjust. Critical consciousness involves both reflection and action, or what Freire called *praxis*. Freire posited that both critical reflection and action are necessary for transformation of the individual and the society.

Sociopolitical development (SPD) describes the process of growth in an individual's "knowledge, analytical skills, emotional faculties, and capacity for action in political and social systems" (Watts, Griffith, & Abdul-Adil, 1999, p. 185). A key feature of SPD theory is for the individual who is oppressed to take action against the system that perpetuates such oppression. SPD theory arose initially on the basis of the earlier writings on oppression by Freire (1970/1999) and Serrano-Garcia and Lopez-Sanchez (1992). The theory was then expanded on the basis of interviews with young Black activists (Watts, Williams, & Jagers, 2003) and a group-based intervention for Black boys called the Young Warriors program (Watts, Abdul-Adil, & Pratt, 2002). The authors delineated a five-stage model of SPD in which each stage corresponds with the individual's level of awareness of societal inequities or and the frequency of behavior to challenge the status quo. In the first stage, the Acritical Stage, asymmetry of resources is stated to be outside of conscious awareness and the individual believes in a "just world." In the next, the Adaptive Stage, asymmetry is acknowledged; however, the status quo seems unchangeable. In the Pre-Critical Stage, the individual becomes even more aware of asymmetry and inequality and begins to question the previous accommodation strategies he or she used to deal with injustice. In the Critical Stage, the individual desires to learn more about oppression and liberation and through this process may begin to take action to end oppression. The fifth stage, Liberation, is marked by "liberation behavior," in which individuals become change agents for social justice. SPD attempts to describe the developmental process of acquiring the critical thinking skills necessary for subsequent action in political and social systems. Similarly, on the basis of qualitative interviews with African American youth, Isom (2002) captured a four-step process of critical awareness: seeing it, naming it, resisting it, and transforming it. In other words, being able to recognize oppression when it occurs, correctly labeling the experience, externalizing blame or responsibility, and finally taking action to end oppression. This critical awareness serves as an antidote against the poisonous effects of internalized oppression.

The beliefs endorsed in the beginning stages of sociopolitical and critical consciousness development are similar to those endorsed under the framework of CBRI. For example, the color-blind racial framework includes beliefs in a "just world" and is characterized by a lack of awareness of social inequities. Just as oppression is both a process and an outcome, so is critical consciousness. The development of critical consciousness is a psychological process, involving both affective and cognitive components, which results in an individual's ability to perceive oppression and, most important, to take action against oppression.

Given the deleterious effects of a racial ideology that works against one's individual and group interests and serves to maintain the status quo and the legitimacy of racism and oppression, how does one liberate oneself from such a state? The development of critical consciousness can serve as a buffer against internalized oppression and aid in the transformation of self from a false sense of consciousness to a critical consciousness (Quintana & Segura-Herrera, 2003). It can be argued that the development of critical consciousness and a sociopolitical perspective among people of color would reduce color-blind racial attitudes. An individual aware of asymmetry of resources in society and racial inequity with a sense of agency to change unjust political and institutional polices cannot uphold a CBRI. The promotion of critical consciousness for people of color not only facilitates self-liberation but, ultimately, also liberates oppressors from the cycle of oppression (Freire, 1970/1999). Critical consciousness interrupts the entire system of oppression. By disrupting the entire system, the oppressors are freed from their internalized domination mentality and its resultant unjust use of power and are able to critically examine their role in the oppressive system. This liberation from the internalized oppression leads to the collective and concerted action, which frees both the oppressor and the oppressed. The psychology of liberation involves resistance to and rejection of the psychological processes that maintain the oppressive system. Thus, true liberation is both an internal and an external process, involving psychological, political, and social components.

Psychologists and social scientists, generally, should critique systems to elucidate their pathologies and ultimately to facilitate the elimination of social inequalities and the promotion of social justice. Remedial and preventative interventions, educational programs, and community partnerships that challenge the status quo are all needed to grow critical consciousness among people of color. Specifically, Jost and van der Toorn (2012) called for social scientists to speak directly to the ways that "resistance to change and political acquiescence can be transformed into an open, restless, critical, constructive search for forms of social organization that are better, truer, freer, more sustainable and just" (p. 338). Furthermore, researchers should examine the psychological dynamics that both sustain and resist oppressive ideologies. Critical psychologists Prilleltensky and Nelson (2002) asserted that science should advance knowledge that aids in creating social change to benefit marginalized groups. Thus, psychologists can and should play a key role in challenging the status quo and those system-justifying ideologies (like CBRI) that support social inequalities.

Upholding the status quo through color-blind racial beliefs is anathema to equity and will neither promote nor sustain justice. Because CBRI is potentially toxic to the well-being of people of color, only a critical awareness and analysis of the social environment will provide an opportunity to contest and transform the status quo. Critical consciousness of race and racism must replace color blindness to ensure the self-development and self-determination of people of color.

REFERENCES

Akbar, N. (1984). *Chains and images of psychological slavery*. Jersey City, NJ: New Mind Productions.

Bailey, T. K., Chung, Y. B., Williams, W. S., Singh, A. A., & Terrell, H. K. (2011). Development and validation of the Internalized Racial Oppression Scale for Black individuals. *Journal of Counseling Psychology*, 58, 481–493. http://dx.doi.org/10.1037/a0023585

Barr, S. C., & Neville, H. A. (2008). Examination of the link between parental racial socialization messages and racial ideology among Black college students. *Journal of Black Psychology*, 34, 131–155. http://dx.doi.org/10.1177/0095798408314138

Chao, R. C. L., Wei, M., Good, G. E., & Flores, L. Y. (2011). Race/ethnicity, color-blind racial attitudes, and multicultural counseling competence: The moderating effects of multicultural counseling training. *Journal of Counseling Psychology*, 58, 72–82. http://dx.doi.org/10.1037/a0022091

Cokley, K. O. (2002). Testing Cross's revised racial identity model: An examination of the relationship between racial identity and internalized racialism. *Journal of Counseling Psychology*, 49, 476–483. http://dx.doi.org/10.1037/0022-0167.49.4.476

Coleman, M. N., Chapman, S., & Wang, D. C. (2013). An examination of color-blind racism and race-related stress among African American undergraduate students. *Journal of Black Psychology*, 39, 486–504. http://dx.doi.org/10.1177/0095798412469226

Cross, W. E., Jr. (1971). The Negro-to-Black conversion experience. *Black World*, 20, 13–27.

Cross, W. E., Jr. (1991). *Shades of black: Diversity in African-American identity*. Philadelphia, PA: Temple University Press.

Fanon, F. (1967). *Black skin, White masks*. New York, NY: Grove Press.

Freire, P. (1999). *Pedagogy of the oppressed*. New York, NY: Continuum. (Original work published 1970)

Goffman, E. (1963). *Stigma: Notes of the management of spoiled identity*. Englewood Cliff, NJ: Prentice-Hall.

Hardiman, R., & Jackson, B. W. (1997). Conceptual foundations for social justice courses. In M. Adams, L. A. Bell, & P. Griffin (Eds.), *Teaching for diversity and social justice: A sourcebook* (pp. 6–29). New York, NY: Routledge.

Helms, J. E., & Parham, T. A. (1996). The Racial Identity Attitude Scale. In R. L. Jones (Ed.), *Handbook of tests and measurements for Black populations* (Vol. 2, pp. 167–174). Hampton, VA: Cobb & Henry.

Isom, D. A. (2002). *"Me, I got a lot of parts." Tainted by, struggling against, striving for racialized gender identity constructs in African American children* (Doctoral dissertation). Available from ProQuest Dissertations and Theses database (UMI No. 3085085).

Jost, J. T. (1995). Negative illusions: Conceptual clarification and psychological evidence concerning false consciousness. *Political Psychology, 16,* 397–424. http://dx.doi.org/10.2307/3791837

Jost, J. T., & Banaji, M. R. (1994). The role of stereotyping in system-justification and the production of false consciousness. *British Journal of Social Psychology, 33,* 1–27. http://dx.doi.org/10.1111/j.2044-8309.1994.tb01008.x

Jost, J. T., & Hunyady, O. (2005). Antecedents and consequences of system-justifying ideologies. *Current Directions in Psychological Science, 14,* 260–265. http://dx.doi.org/10.1111/j.0963-7214.2005.00377.x

Jost, J. T., & Thompson, E. P. (2000). Group-based dominance and opposition to equality as independent predictors of self-esteem, ethnocentrism, and social policy attitudes among African Americans and European Americans. *Journal of Experimental Social Psychology, 36,* 209–232. http://dx.doi.org/10.1006/jesp.1999.1403

Jost, J. T., & van der Toorn, J. (2012). System justification theory. In P. A. M. Van Lange, A. W. Kruglanski, & E. T. Higgins (Eds.). *The handbook of theories of social psychology* (Vol. 2, pp. 313–342). Thousand Oaks, CA: Sage.

Kay, A. C., Gaucher, D., Napier, J. L., Callan, M. J., & Laurin, K. (2008). God and the government: Testing a compensatory control mechanism for the support of external systems. *Journal of Personality and Social Psychology, 95,* 18–35. http://dx.doi.org/10.1037/0022-3514.95.1.18

Klein, R. (2013). Tiana Parker, 7, switches schools after being forbidden from wearing dreads. *The Huffington Post*. Retrieved from http://www.huffington post.com/2013/09/05/tiana-parker-dreads_n_3873868.html

Knowles, E. D., Lowery, B. S., Hogan, C. M., & Chow, R. M. (2009). On the malleability of ideology: Motivated construals of color blindness. *Journal of Personality and Social Psychology, 96,* 857–869. http://dx.doi.org/10.1037/a0013595

Luker, R. E. (2008, February 13). Pimpin' out Harriet Tubman [Web log post]. Retrieved from http://historynewsnetwork.org/blog/47301

Napier, J. L., & Jost, J. T. (2008). Why are conservatives happier than liberals? *Psychological Science, 19*, 565–572. http://dx.doi.org/10.1111/j.1467-9280.2008.02124.x

Neville, H. A., Coleman, M. N., Falconer, J. W., & Holmes, D. (2005). Color-blind racial ideology and psychological false consciousness among African Americans. *Journal of Black Psychology, 31*, 27–45. http://dx.doi.org/10.1177/0095798404268287

Neville, H. A., Lilly, R. L., Duran, G., Lee, R. M., & Browne, L. (2000). Construction and initial validation of the Color-Blind Racial Attitudes Scale (CoBRAS). *Journal of Counseling Psychology, 47*, 59–70. http://dx.doi.org/10.1037/0022-0167.47.1.59

Oh, E., Choi, C. C., Neville, H. A., Anderson, C. J., & Landrum-Brown, J. (2010). Beliefs about affirmative action: A test of the group self-interest and racism beliefs models. *Journal of Diversity in Higher Education, 3*, 163–176. http://dx.doi.org/10.1037/a0019799

Omi, M., & Winant, H. (1994). *Racial formulation in the United States* (2nd ed.). New York, NY: Routledge.

Pinel, E. C. (1999). Stigma consciousness: The psychological legacy of social stereotypes. *Journal of Personality and Social Psychology, 76*, 114–128. http://dx.doi.org/10.1037/0022-3514.76.1.114

Prilleltensky, I., & Nelson, G. (2002). *Doing psychology critically: Making a difference in diverse settings*. New York, NY: Palgrave Macmillan.

Pyke, K. D. (2010). What is internalized racial oppression and why don't we study it? Acknowledging racism's hidden injuries. *Sociological Perspectives, 53*, 551–572. http://dx.doi.org/10.1525/sop.2010.53.4.551

Quintana, S. M., & Segura-Herrera, T. A. (2003). Developmental transformations of self and identity in the context of oppression. *Self and Identity, 2*, 269–285. http://dx.doi.org/10.1080/714050248

Reddock, A. (2014, January). The great hair dilemma. *Essence, 44*(9), 48–49.

Serrano-Garcia, I., & Lopez-Sanchez, G. (1992, August). *Asymmetry and oppression: Prerequisites of power relationships*. Presented at the annual convention of the American Psychological Association, Washington, DC.

Spanierman, L. B., Neville, H. A., Liao, H. Y., Hammer, J. H., & Wang, Y. F. (2008). Participation in formal and informal campus diversity experiences: Effects on students' racial democratic beliefs. *Journal of Diversity in Higher Education, 1*, 108–125. http://dx.doi.org/10.1037/1938-8926.1.2.108

Tappan, M. B. (2006). Reframing internalized oppression and internalized domination: From the psychological to the sociocultural. *Teachers College Record, 108*, 2115–2144.

Tynes, B. M., & Markoe, S. L. (2010). The role of color-blind racial attitudes in reactions to racial discrimination on social network sites. *Journal of Diversity in Higher Education, 3*, 1–13. http://dx.doi.org/10.1037/a0018683

Vandiver, B. J., Cross, W. E., Jr., Fhagen-Smith, P. E., Worrell, F. C., Swim, J., & Caldwell, L. (2000). *The Cross Racial Identity Scale*. Unpublished manuscript.

Wakslak, C. J., Jost, J. T., Tyler, T. R., & Chen, E. S. (2007). Moral outrage mediates the dampening effect of system justification on support for redistributive social policies. *Psychological Science, 18*, 267–274. http://dx.doi.org/10.1111/j.1467-9280.2007.01887.x

Watts, R. J., Abdul-Adil, J. K., & Pratt, T. (2002). Enhancing critical consciousness in young African American men: A psychoeducational approach. *Psychology of Men & Masculinity, 3*, 41–50. http://dx.doi.org/10.1037/1524-9220.3.1.41

Watts, R. J., Diemer, M. A., & Voight, A. M. (2011). Critical consciousness: Current status and future directions. *New Directions for Child and Adolescent Development, 134*, 43–57. http://dx.doi.org/10.1002/cd.310

Watts, R. J., Griffith, D. M., & Abdul-Adil, J. (1999). Sociopolitical development as an antidote for oppression—theory and action. *American Journal of Community Psychology, 27*, 255–271. http://dx.doi.org/10.1023/A:1022839818873

Watts, R. J., Williams, N. C., & Jagers, R. J. (2003). Sociopolitical development. *American Journal of Community Psychology, 31*, 185–194. http://dx.doi.org/10.1023/A:1023091024140

Watts-Jones, D. (2002). Healing internalized racism: The role of a within-group sanctuary among people of African descent. *Family Process, 41*, 591–601. http://dx.doi.org/10.1111/j.1545-5300.2002.00591.x

Worthington, R. L., Navarro, R. L., Loewy, M., & Hart, J. (2008). Color-blind racial attitudes, social dominance orientation, racial-ethnic group membership and college students' perceptions of campus climate. *Journal of Diversity in Higher Education, 1*, 8–19. http://dx.doi.org/10.1037/1938-8926.1.1.8

Yoshino, K. (2006). The pressure to cover. *New York Times Magazine*. Retrieved from http://www.nytimes.com/2006/01/15/magazine/15gays.html?pagewanted=all&_r=0

12

COLOR-BLIND RACIAL IDEOLOGY IN K–12 SCHOOLS

SHERI A. CASTRO-ATWATER

I took my kids out of that school because of the principal. They were called the "n-word," and when they told the principal, she said "oh, that's just a word, they didn't mean anything by it and words won't hurt you." But it isn't just a word, words have meaning.
— Statement from an African American man living in a midsized southern city (Meece & Wingate, 2009–2010, p. 37)

In an ideal world, students are treated fairly regardless of race, ethnicity, and social position. Unfortunately, the education system in the United States is far from achieving this ideal; it continues to support espoused ideologies, structures, and policies that contribute to racial inequality. African American and Hispanic children were 3 times as likely to be poor as non-Hispanic White children in 2012; in 2010, 39% of homeless families with children were African American (Child Trends Databank, 2012a). In recent years, high school dropout rates for African American students in the United States have been twice as high as those for White students and nearly 3 times higher for Hispanic than White students (Child Trends Databank, 2012b).

Racial inequality is often produced by adopting a color-blind racial ideology (CBRI) in which race-based decision making is seen as antithetical to the goal of an ideal, "color-blind" world. CBRI has been defined as the "new racism," the covert methods of which are "subtle, institutional, and

http://dx.doi.org/10.1037/14754-013
The Myth of Racial Color Blindness: Manifestations, Dynamics, and Impact, H. A. Neville, M. E. Gallardo, and D. W. Sue (Editors)

apparently non-racial" (Bonilla-Silva, 2009, p. 3). Even without deliberate malice or forethought on the part of those in power within the educational system, "treating others all the same because we *are* all the same" (one of the main tenets of CBRI) is often the attitude adopted by educators who believe strongly that by simply ignoring racial group membership or skin color, all resulting decisions and practices will be fair.

As Meece and Wingate (2009–2010) stated, the school principal in the example that opened this chapter may have had a well-intentioned goal of instilling the victimized children with a "bounce-back, resilient attitude"; however, she neglected to take an active teaching opportunity to discuss with all of the children how racial slurs demean the value and dignity of people of color and are unacceptable at her school. This "passive" espousal of CBRI is not uncommon; it is frequently documented as an ideology used by teachers, administrators, and others in the K–12 educational system (Boutte, Lopez-Robertson, & Powers-Costello, 2011; Han, 2009; Lewis, 2001; Marx, 2002; Schofield, 1982, 1986; Ullucci & Battey, 2011; Wynne, 1999).

This chapter demonstrates that although CBRI has historically been marketed as a positive—skin color should not matter; therefore, ignoring it will eradicate racial problems—it actually leads to a misrepresentation of reality in ways that allow and even encourage discrimination against students of color in K–12 education, and it contributes to a shared, communal ignorance that permits those in power to ignore the realities of racism.

The chapter first reviews current research that explores the notion of CBRI and its impact on teachers and students in K–12 public schools. Evidence from research is presented to show how skin color and race affect teachers' unconscious biases and their expectations of students, which can, in turn, hinder student success. The detrimental effect of CBRI in schools on both student outcomes and teacher effectiveness is then discussed, including how educators' use of CBRI can hinder the progression of students' critical thinking skills, have an impact on their feelings of validity and trust, and affect their cognitive growth. Finally, strategies to address these concerns are discussed. What educational policies, practices, and curriculum changes must be created to counteract the documented negative effects of CBRI in K–12?

DEFINING CBRI

According to P. Williams (1997), the notion of color blindness

> constitutes an ideological confusion at best, and denial at its very worst. . . . Much is overlooked in the move to undo that which clearly

and unfortunately matters just by labeling it that which "makes no difference." This dismissiveness, however unintentional, leaves [people of color] pulled between the clarity of their own experience and the often alienating terms in which they must seek social acceptance. (p. 7)

Neville, Awad, Brooks, Flores, and Bluemel (2013) defined CBRI as being characterized by the interrelated domains of *color evasion* (i.e., denial of racial differences by emphasizing sameness) and *power evasion* (i.e., denial of racism by emphasizing equal opportunities). CBRI in schools can include both domains and can be seen when educators engage in a denial of (a) race (e.g., "we are all the same"), (b) blatant racial issues (i.e., racial discrimination based on skin color), (c) institutional racism (e.g., cumulative polices, practices, and norms that disadvantage students of color), and (d) White privilege (e.g., superior access and opportunities based on skin color advantage). Furthermore, Ullucci and Battey (2011) contended that the foundation of CBRI lies in the interconnected U.S. historical ideas of merit (hard work will objectively earn one's rewards, regardless of historical constructs) and individualism (personal characteristics, rather than group membership, are the sole determinant in one's life outcomes), both of which fail to accept that life rewards, such as upward socioeconomic mobility, are historically connected to racial group membership and social class. The authors further noted that "Whiteness" is the third foundational idea on which CBRI is based. The idea of equating "White" with "normal" encourages a monolithic racial worldview in which other racial worldviews are judged as "less than" or "different."

The denial that race matters, or that racial inequality and institutional racism exist, means that K–12 educators who adopt a CBRI perspective do not acknowledge the structures, policies, and racial beliefs that unfairly discriminate against students of color. As Ullucci and Battey (2011) stated when referring to the frequent statements affirming color blindness among their teacher education students, "Why do students need a course on race and education if they have decided race plays *no role in education?*" (p. 1196, italics in original).

CBRI must first be recognized as being problematic before it can be reversed (Boutte et al., 2011). In today's racially stratified U.S. educational system, color blindness masks important aspects of the identity, history, and daily struggles of a student of color. As the current chapter examines, ignoring the realities of racism and the impact of CBRI allows educators to use this ideology without addressing the negative student outcomes (in student achievement, motivation, and social cognitive skills, to name a few) that result.

EFFECT OF SKIN COLOR ON TEACHERS' EXPECTATIONS AND RESULTING STUDENT ACHIEVEMENT

Biases in Teacher Expectations

Rosenthal and Jacobson's 1966 study on teacher expectations revealed that the unintentional expectations teachers bring to classroom situations wield significant influence on students. In this classic study on the "Pygmalion effect," children were administered a nonverbal test of intelligence masked as a test that would predict intellectual growth. After teachers were told to expect surprising gains in intellectual achievement among a few randomly "chosen" children over the next several months, these identified children showed significantly greater intellectual gains than did other children at the end of the school year.

Research shows that teachers often hold cultural biases that can spark racialized, or cultural *Pygmalion effects*, in the classroom as well. Masten, Plata, Wenglar, and Thedford (1999) asked elementary school teachers to rate 86 White and 63 Hispanic fifth-grade students on elements of learning, motivation, creativity, and leadership. Findings showed that ratings varied considerably on the basis of the students' ethnic status and acculturation level: White students were rated higher on these positive attributes than their Hispanic peers, and highly acculturated Hispanic students received higher ratings than their low-acculturated Hispanic peers. Wynne (1999) found similar results in teachers working with African American, low-income children. In a study focusing on an effort to create better learning environments for African American children, researchers who attempted to implement the reform effort observed that teachers (mostly White) often unconsciously operated from a framework of low expectations for African American student success.

Many teachers continue to hold racial biases, expectations, and preferences of which they are often unaware (Blaisdell, 2005; Boutte et al., 2011; Wynne, 1999). It can be assumed that teaching, like most helping professions, tends to attract caring and egalitarian personalities. Why, then, does research continue to show that teachers' differences in student expectations, however inadvertent or unintentional, are affected by a student's skin color, race, or ethnicity?

Marx (2002) explored this question by examining the altruistic incentives of nine White, female preservice teachers who tutored Hispanic English-language learners during a semester course. Using observations, journal entries, and detailed interviews with the teachers on their teaching aspirations, the children they tutored, and their own racial identity, the study revealed that all participants were influenced by their own sense of White identity, which influenced their beliefs about the children of color they tutored. Although the participants were devoted to children and were generous with their time and efforts, the teachers shared a vision of the children's Hispanic culture as a "deficit" to their success. This deficit affected teachers' contact with and beliefs about their Hispanic students in the forms of antipathy, resentment, and low academic expectations. Rather than focusing more on the children's academic needs, the teachers in the study consistently focused on an effort to interfere with what they believed were the students' parental, emotional, and social disadvantages. Although all teacher participants described themselves as nonprejudiced, the study clearly revealed their cultural biases.

Thus, despite good intentions, teachers often inadvertently bring to the classroom unconscious biases or conscious beliefs that certain cultural practices are "deficits" that hinder individual growth, both of which result in low student expectations of success. Immersed in deficit theories, teachers may view their own students of color as burdens rather than assets in the classroom; these negative thoughts then infect the teaching and learning that occurs (Milner, 2012; Ullucci & Battey, 2011). In what ways does such thinking affect students?

Student Achievement

Teachers' biased expectations—often based on unconscious or unintentional racial assumptions—can have a very real effect on student achievement. McKown and Weinstein (2002) examined the relationship between elementary teachers' expectations of students at the beginning of the year and subsequent year-end achievement among 561 children in first, third, and fifth grades. After controlling for previous achievement and class membership, they found that student ethnicity (e.g., African American ancestry) moderated expectancy effects, particularly in reading achievement. Thus, students from stigmatized ethnic groups were found to be more susceptible to teacher underestimates of ability than their nonstigmatized peers.

In a subsequent study, McKown and Weinstein (2003) examined the consequences of children's awareness of stereotypes ("stereotype consciousness") on resulting academic achievement. Two hundred and two ethnically diverse children ages 6 to 10 years participated in the study; children from academically stigmatized ethnic groups (e.g., African Americans and Latinos) were, at all ages, more cognizant of broadly held ethnic stereotypes than children from academically nonstigmatized ethnic groups (e.g., Whites and Asians). The researchers then examined the effects of "stereotype threat" (i.e., feelings of anxiety when students have the potential to confirm a negative stereotype about their ethnic group; see Steele & Aronson, 1995) among children from the stigmatized ethnic groups by examining the results of their performance and effort on challenging cognitive measures. On one of two challenging cognitive tasks and on self-reported effort, testing conditions did indeed lead to stereotype threat effects.

Whether CBRI is a consciously promoted philosophy or "hidden" within the attitudes and practices of school staff, teachers' avoidance of racial differences can lead to discrimination, favoritism, or classroom conflict. Teachers may believe that by ignoring a students' racial group membership, they are treating their students "all the same" and that discussing racial differences would only create uncomfortable moments; however, as we see in the sections that follow, avoiding discussions of racial inequalities can affect students' conceptual development of the topic in a negative way.

HOW CBRI AFFECTS STUDENTS' THINKING

Elementary school teachers act as primary adult models in student lives, influencing not only their academic achievement but also their social and emotional competence, self-confidence, and excitement about learning (National Scientific Council on the Developing Child, 2004). Given the enormous impact teachers have, it behooves us to examine more explicitly how their adherence to CBRI may affect their students' thinking about racial concepts.

Teachers who adopt CBRI are likely to avoid racial questions or comments from students because they are "uncomfortable" or "sensitive" and because they believe in emphasizing "sameness" over difference. However, teachers who dismiss students' questions or comments about race, fearing that they will introduce prejudice into the child's life or assuming that differences do not matter, thwart the child's ability to engage in constructive discourse and to develop critical thinking on the subject (Castro-Atwater, 2008). Moreover, these effects may be profoundly different for White children and children of color; for White children, this avoidance may emphasize that racial differences are negative and are not "fit" for discussion or analysis; it can also lend credence to the belief that being "White" is equated with "normal" and that anything different is thus "less than" (Ullucci & Battey, 2011) and may also reinforce the notion that racial discrimination is "a thing of the past" because it is not acknowledged or discussed.

For children of color, this lack of acknowledgment of racial differences from teachers and students may also dismiss or trivialize the discrimination that they regularly encounter, causing them to question whether their "reality" of discrimination is even accurate (Han, 2009; Lewis, 2001; Marx & Larson, 2012; Schofield, 1986). As Bouknight (2010) stated, one important aspect of perceptions of a positive school climate among students of color is the ability to talk with school staff about personal issues or concerns. Thus, a continual trivialization of differences may lead children of color to be silent on issues of discrimination because they perceive a lack of support at school. They may begin to question themselves and their own experiences, wondering if racial discrimination is "only in their head" or even whether they themselves were the cause of such differential treatment or whether they "deserved" it. Finally, educators' reliance on CBRI can also lead to an erosion of the self-worth of students of color or to feelings of "self-blame," as their experiences of racial inequality and treatment are devalued (P. Williams, 1997).

Adherence to CBRI also greatly influences how educators develop curricula: If race problems are a thing of the past and "no longer important," then they should not be given any special attention or discussion within the history or social studies curriculum. As a result, students learn a "color-blind" version of history without a necessary focus on the unique accomplishments and contributions of people of color or the cruel realities of oppression that were sanctioned by certain racial groups over others.

This lack of reporting multiple perspectives and identities affects the historical perspective that students come away with. As Richeson and Nussbaum (2004) noted, ignorance of the accomplishments of people of color has been found to predict negative racial attitudes. This suggests that a CBRI-inspired curriculum may negatively affect the development of racial attitudes of students in schools. Simply by failing to call attention to noteworthy successes, examples, and struggles of people of color, CBRI curriculum can lead students to conclude that there are no such examples or that there are not important contributions from people of color (see also, Blum, 2002). As Milner (2012) noted, when teachers do not include curriculum content related to a certain racial/ethnic group, "students are actually learning something about [the excluded group] through the absence of the content in the curriculum" (p. 869).

From a curriculum perspective, then, it becomes imperative for teachers to reject CBRI by encouraging discussions about racial identity, historical and present-day inequalities, and the accomplishments of people of color within a curriculum because this can provide a safe forum for both White children and children of color to gain assistance in their reasoning on these issues and stimulate critical thinking and discussion about race. As Milner (2012) stated, what material teachers cover, how much time they spend on aspects of the curriculum, and whether curricular materials are appropriate and accurate representations of people of color's experiences are all essential in developing a "race-conscious" curriculum (Milner, 2012, p. 869). Roberts, Bell, and Murphy (2008) analyzed how students used one such curriculum "to grapple with their own racialized experiences and to question and talk back to the broader society" (p. 335), allowing them to wrestle with the contradictions of race within in a contemporary color-blind context.

However, implementing a race- or color-conscious curriculum may be daunting because of the fear, uncertainty, or discomfort of many teachers. Milner (2012) stated, "Sadly, teachers can sometimes design curriculum and instructional practices which are grounded in a 'White norm' (Foster, 1999) that students of color simply have to accept . . . because they may not have the power to counter what is emphasized" (p. 871). For this reason, Lin, Lake, and Rice (2008) argued that the reflection of cultural values and the dismantling of a CBRI, both of which are crucial to easing such discomfort, should begin in teacher preparation programs with an *antibias framework* (see the section Exposure to Cultural Pedagogy in this chapter for further discussion on color-conscious teacher education). The anti-bias framework has also been developed for use as a color-conscious curriculum tool for K–12 (for standards and learning outcomes K–12 teachers can use to develop a color-conscious curriculum, see The Anti-Bias Framework section in this chapter; *Teaching Tolerance*, 2014). For teachers currently in practice who wish to "lose the color-blind mind," Milner (2012, p. 873) suggested beginning with a series of self-reflections questions that he has found useful in his own practice in challenging the CBRI thinking of teachers.

DOCUMENTING CBRI IN K–12 SCHOOLS

A number of studies have documented the existence and effects of CBRI in schools (Blaisdell, 2005; Han, 2009; Schofield, 1982, 1986; Lewis, 2001). One of the first, and most comprehensive, studies to examine CBRI was Schofield's (1982) multiyear ethnographic study of a desegregated 1,200-student middle school in the northeastern United States. The school opened as a desegregated institution with a roughly 50:50 Black:White student ratio; the majority of students came from elementary schools that were highly segregated. Data showed that the color-blind perspective was widely held by the school community. Teachers not only consistently denied that they noticed children's race, both to researchers and among themselves, they also believed students did not notice the race of their peers; interviews with students revealed the opposite. Schofield also found that race was a taboo topic: Words such as *Black* and *White* were rarely used, and when they were used, were viewed as racial epithets. Although the school went to great lengths to prepare the physical campus for desegregation, and teachers believed they treated all students equally, over time clear "color" stereotypes emerged among the school community: White was synonymous with "success," and Black was associated with academic weakness (Cose, 1997; Schofield, 1982, 1986). Schofield concluded that CBRI was relied on so heavily within the school because it served several functions, including (a) reducing the potential for overt racial conflict, (b) minimizing discomfort or embarrassment among teachers and students, and (c) increasing teachers' freedom to make what appeared to be "non–race-based" decisions.

Despite these alleged advantages, CBRI caused several setbacks within the school environment. First, school personnel's failure to acknowledge cultural differences influenced the different ways White and Black students functioned and succeeded in school and caused a number of misinterpretations and misunderstandings of student behavior, often resulting in increased discipline action toward Black students. Second, teachers' color blindness enabled them to believe that implementing course materials that reflected this new diversity was irrelevant because race "does not matter"; consequently, Black students were unable to see themselves as validated in the curriculum.

More recently, in a yearlong ethnographic study of a predominantly White, middle-class suburban school, Lewis (2001) examined the racial discourse of teachers, parents, and administrators and found similar evidence of a CBRI among the school community. Interestingly, unlike Schofield's earlier study within the context of desegregation, Lewis purposely chose a predominantly White, middle-class school community to examine the impact of Whites' lack of contact with members of other races on their multicultural attitudes and school practices. Similar to Schofield's findings, although school community members consistently denied the salience of race and advocated a color-blind racial paradigm, Lewis documented an underlying reality of "racialized practices and color-conscious understandings" (p. 781) that directly affected the school's few racial minority students and indirectly supported White students' views of the inferiority of their non-White peers. With the exception of parents of biracial students, who discussed race as being very relevant to their lives, race was perceived as a nonissue. Yet rather than truly believing "everyone is the same," data revealed that many White adults in the community had distinct ideas and biases regarding people of color.

Lewis (2001) also documented evidence of what Ullucci and Battey (2011), Pappas (1996), and others have referred to as the "invisible" culture of Whiteness—the belief among White Americans that they have no unique, identifiable culture and view the world through a monolithic, rather than a pluralistic, lens. Studies on "Whiteness" ultimately seek to educate White Americans that they "are so accustomed to being part of a privileged majority that they do not see themselves as part of a race" (Fears, 2003, p. A12). The invisible cultural assumptions of Whiteness and the dynamics of White privilege are seen as ultimate barriers toward social justice (see Rodriguez & Villaverde, 2000, for a detailed review). Neville et al. (2013) considered "White privilege" to be a primary tenet of CBRI. Moreover, empirical research indicates that White students often do not recognize the dynamics of White privilege intuitively and must be taught about its phenomena and effects explicitly (Choi, 2008; Meece & Wingate, 2009–2010; K. Williams & Okintunde, 2000).

Reliance on CBRI has been shown to occur at all levels of K–12. Han (2009) explored the multicultural beliefs of 95 kindergarten teachers through surveys and randomly selected follow-up interviews and recorded rich narrative that revealed a reliance on CBRI when teaching. Indeed, the teachers interviewed often justified their use of CBRI through the "young age" or simple curriculum of the kindergarten child, whose worlds could not possibly be affected by race or skin color; in one participant's words, "Everything is wonderful when you're 5" (p. 90). Given what we know about when racial awareness and attitudes begin to take cognitive shape in the young child, one could argue that this is exactly the age at which teachers should use a clear, color-conscious paradigm when discussing racial and cultural differences with students.

Similarly, ethnographic interviews with White secondary school teachers have also revealed a reliance on CBRI in either overt beliefs, in practice, or both, often in complex ways. For example, Blaisdell (2005) and Castro-Atwater (2008) found that the use of CBRI among White teachers interviewed was rarely straightforward; even when denying their reliance on color blindness, teachers often relied on it in practice (e.g., stating that students of color should be given extra attention to overcome stereotypes but not following through in the classroom). Blaisdell (2005) noted that one difficulty in addressing CBRI in the schools is that it is often entangled with, and operates alongside, ideas of color-conscious beliefs or practices. He noted that "teachers are often colorblind and color conscious at the same time" (p. 35).

Given this difficulty, is it possible for researchers to identify a school where the adoption of CBRI has led to negative student outcomes and help educators make a "shift" to color-conscious practices? Marx and Larson (2012) set out to answer this question by using a narrative critical race theory approach in a predominately White school where CBRI had led to the marginalization of Latino(a) students and their exclusion from the "mainstream" curriculum. Following several recommendations from researchers who approached the high school's racial inequalities from a critical race theory perspective, administrators were able to recognize the adherence to CBRI in their school, understand its flaws in addressing ethnic disparity, and ultimately put into practice specific color-conscious policies and practices that incorporated the strengths and struggles of the Latino(a) experience at the school.

We can see that teachers often rely on CBRI because of its seeming advantages: When there is fear of conflict or of appearing prejudiced, the "race does not matter" approach offers a paradigm of easy escapism to avoid dealing with the reality of racial inequities. However, CBRI is often not as straightforward as it seems; teachers may use CBRI in practice but deny that it is part of their belief system, making interventions to alter CBRI complex. Finally, teachers have been found to rely on CBRI both in their dealings with students and in their classroom and curriculum decisions. This ideology appears to be influenced by a number of interrelated variables, including teachers' cultural worldview (monolithic-ethnocentric vs. pluralistic–ethnorelative), the amount and type of prior exposure they have had to cultural pedagogy, their racial identity (or lack of one), and their perception of the school climate as open to racial awareness and color-conscious practices. The next section examines the current research and informed practice within each of these interrelated variables; it also reminds us of the challenge and complexity inherent in adopting a color-conscious curriculum and the resistance that preservice teachers may bring in creating this fundamental shift in ideology from CBRI to color consciousness.

TEACHER VARIABLES INFLUENCING COLOR-CONSCIOUS IDEOLOGY

Although a review of current research identifies a number of factors that may affect teachers' ability to engage in racial discourse and apply color-conscious classroom practices, four distinct variables repeatedly emerge as particularly influential in teachers' willingness and practice of open racial discourse: (a) a teacher's cultural worldview (including adherence to an ethnocentric, color-blind worldview versus an ethnorelative perspective), (b) racial/ethnic group membership (e.g., as "White" or a person of color), (c) the perceived level of support for race discussions and color-conscious practices within the school (Bonilla-Silva, 2009; Boutte et al., 2011; Han, 2009; Marx & Larson, 2012; Meece & Wingate, 2009–2010), and (d) exposure to cultural pedagogy (e.g., critical race theory, antibias, or color-conscious curriculum) in teacher education programs. These interrelated variables often interact in a dynamic way to affect teachers' classroom practices.

Teachers' Cultural Worldview

On the basis of observations and interactions with individuals as they learned to become more competent intercultural communicators, Bennett and Bennett (2004) published a developmental framework that is useful in understanding how teachers may confront and respond to cultural differences. Bennett and Bennett's developmental model of intercultural sensitivity

(DMIS) is composed of six stages that describe the increasingly sophisticated cognitive skills individuals acquire as they are confronted with individual cultural differences in others. The first three stages come from an "ethnocentric" perspective: Individuals interpret events, actions, and behaviors from their own cultural viewpoint. This *monocultural* ethnocentrism (or *monolithic* from Ullucci and Battey's, 2011, work) functions as a method of avoiding cultural differences by *denying* their existence (Stage 1), using *defenses* against them (Stage 2), or *minimizing* their importance (Stage 3; Van Hook, 2000, p. 69). Notably, the ethnocentric perspective (particularly the Stage 3 minimization worldview) relies on the major tenet of CBRI: ignoring or avoiding differences in the belief that race does not matter.

According to the DMIS, as one's intercultural sensitivity increases, an individual's worldview becomes more *ethnorelative*: One's own culture is experienced within the context of other cultures (Ullucci and Battey, 2011, referred to this as a *pluralistic* worldview). Shifting conceptual thinking to an ethnorelative perspective involves the three stages of *acceptance of* the existence and importance of cultural differences (Stage 4), *adaptation* of one's perspective to consider other cultural perspectives (Stage 5), and *integration* of the importance of racial and cultural differences into one's own identity (Stage 6; Bennett & Bennett, 2004; Van Hook, 2000).

To avoid reliance on a color-blind, ethnocentric worldview, teachers must reach the ethnorelative stages in which differences are accepted and integrated into their own conception of reality. The DMIS can thus serve as a useful tool for analysis in understanding and classifying teachers' main cultural perspectives, as well as a tool for teachers' own self-reflection and growth as they progress through the DMIS stages.

Racial/Ethnic Group Membership

Teachers' racial/ethnic group membership can be a fundamental force in creating a "cultural lens" through which they view and interact with the world. One's racial/ethnic group membership provides a set of prescribed values, norms, and social behaviors—a framework in which people view themselves, members of other races, society, and their future (Gibbs & Huang, 1998). Educational research informs us that the invisible "White" culture can profoundly affect both beliefs and behavior of White and non-White individuals with respect to diversity, racism, and racial/cultural exploration (Boutte et al., 2011; Pappas, 1996; Rodriguez & Villaverde, 2000). To add to this complexity, many White preservice teachers have been found to be at the minimization stage where they deny having a culture (Choi, 2008; Meece & Wingate, 2009–2010). Moreover, teachers who identify themselves within the majority "White" culture often hold different beliefs about how to discuss race and whether it is important or effective to do so in their classrooms (Han, 2009). Conversely, teachers of color may be more hesitant about adopting CBRI, an ideology that reportedly denies the experience and heritage of students of color because of their own unique experiences as former students of color (Choi, 2008). As Bennett and Bennett's (2004) DMIS's integration stage reveals, teachers of the nondominant culture likely experience their cultural identity in relation to other cultures and may be adept at recognizing—and thus responding to—cultural differences and at viewing the world through a pluralistic lens. These teachers are often less apt to espouse and use CBRI when their professional and personal experiences have consistently taught them that racial differences matter (Choi, 2008; Kohli, 2012).

Perception of a Supportive, Color-Conscious School Climate

The school community in which teachers are employed can have an impact on their philosophy of how and when to discuss issues of race. According to the U.S. Department of Education, Office for Civil Rights (1999), establishing a school climate that respects individual differences and promotes appreciation of cultural diversity can affects teachers' and students' efforts to eliminate racial and sexual harassment. Effective school programs therefore "endeavor to provide students with a curriculum, teaching methods, and school activities that discourage stereotypes and respond to the concerns of students of different races and cultural backgrounds" (U.S. Department of Education, Office for Civil Rights, 1999, p. 8). School climate has been positively associated with students' academic achievement, school success, self-esteem and the teacher–student relationship. For example, Bouknight (2010) examined high school teachers' level of adherence to color-blind or color-consciousness ("race awareness") racial ideology and their perceptions of school climate. They found a significant relationship between positive views of school climate and level of increased racial awareness.

The school climate is formed not only by individual teachers but also by the decisions and ideological practices of school administrators. Teachers employed in schools where administrative efforts are made to create a color-conscious, spoken affirmation of racial disparities have been found to be more likely to engage students in racial discourse and to move toward more color-conscious practices (Marx & Larson, 2012). Why? Diverse school settings with such a climate tend to send the message to teachers that it is acceptable to encourage color-conscious understandings and discuss racial inequalities, which can in turn lead to a feeling of freedom in talking openly about previously taboo subjects (Marx & Larson, 2012).

Exposure to Cultural Pedagogy

Cultural pedagogy in teacher training programs has become an increasingly mandated component of preservice and in-service teacher education over the past 30 years. This concept is referred to in the research under a number of labels, for example, "tourist" multicultural education (Banks, 2009), antibias curriculum (Derman-Sparks & Edwards, 2010), critical race theory (Blaisdell, 2005; Choi, 2008), and color-conscious training. In his comprehensive review of teacher education programs, Zeichner (1993) delineated a set of 10 key elements related to cultural pedagogy curricula that exist, in varying degrees, within such programs (see Zeichner, 1993, p. 24). Zeichner's elements and a review of research on existing training programs (Banks, 2009; Cochran-Smith, 1995; Cooney & Akintunde, 1999) allow us to delineate two main paradigms of diversity training: (a) *cultural knowledge* training, which emphasizes learning about differences in culture/cultural learning styles, versus (b) *color-conscious* training, which enables teachers to create a fundamental shift in their conceptual thinking about racism, their own racial attitudes and identity, and the effects of skin color and institutional discrimination on the opportunities of non-White students.

Although cultural knowledge training can provide helpful information on the relationship between language and culture, and knowledge of various cultural learning styles of students of color, this model does not emphasize teachers' reflection on their own racial biases or identity, nor does it strive to shift teachers' conceptual thinking about racism or institutional discrimination—both of which have been found to be critical first steps in combating CBRI (Boutte et al., 2011; Choi, 2008; Meece & Wingate, 2009–2010). Subsequently, such an approach may inevitably enable teachers' reliance on CBRI to go unchallenged.

Conversely, color-conscious training takes considerably more time and may be more sociopolitically focused. The focus of color-conscious training (also known as *antibias* or *sensitivity* training; see Derman-Sparks & Edwards, 2010; Milner, 2012; it also often incorporates critical race theory; see Blaisdell, 2005; Choi, 2008) is to enable teachers to examine the world through a more ethnorelative cultural world view (Bennett & Bennett, 2004) and shift their conceptual thinking about racism, their own racial attitudes and identity, and the effects of institutional discrimination on the opportunities of students of color. Such training encourages teachers to recognize what research has shown to be the negative effects of racialized practices on students of color. If approached with ample opportunity for teachers to be self-reflective, color-conscious training can go beyond the "cultural knowledge" training paradigm and avoid merely perpetuating existing stereotypes. It can also help teachers confront their own biases and prepare them for how to deal with race and racism directly in the classroom.

COLOR-CONSCIOUS APPROACHES IN TEACHER EDUCATION

A number of teacher educators have documented programs and interventions designed to move preservice teachers toward color-conscious ideology and to disassemble their previously held beliefs and reliance on CBRI, including the use of antibias training, critical race theory, and color-conscious practices (Blaisdell, 2005; Choi, 2008; Derman-Sparks & Edwards, 2010; Kohli, 2012; Meece & Wingate, 2009–2010; Schniedewind, 2005; Ullucci & Battey, 2011).

Schniedewind (2005) examined the impact of color-conscious training on the practices of five teachers who participated in a long-term professional development program in diversity education and documented their reflections on their own emergent consciousness of race, racism, and Whiteness. She found that teachers often provided revealing narratives, reflecting common themes that later emerged as color-conscious practices (e.g., supporting students of color, educating about stereotyping, addressing White privilege, challenging institutional racism).

Ullucci and Battey (2011) provided a comprehensive review of color-conscious interventions that they have found to be successful in their own teacher education practice. After listing desirable student outcomes of color-conscious teacher education, they list specific interventions that address each outcome that they have used successfully (including article and course readings, videos, course exercises, critical race biographies, and field placement activities). Similarly, Choi (2008) described how her own remarkable transformation from an educator who was ill prepared to confront the frequent espousal of CBRI among her preservice students to one who was willing to adopt a successful critical race theory narrative has helped her combat the classroom discourse that espouses CBRI as an acceptable response to racial issues.

Recently, the infusion of color-conscious training into teacher preparation programs has allowed ample time and opportunity to shift teachers' racial ideology and help them to recognize their own "invisible" Whiteness, confront their own racial biases, and grasp the effect of systemic and institutional racism (Boutte et al., 2011). Research on the effectiveness of such a color-conscious paradigm suggests that it can have an impact on teachers' attitudes, decrease adherence to CBRI, and help teachers understand and confront social inequality and White privilege in their own practices (Blaisdell,

2005; Choi, 2008; Derman-Sparks & Edwards, 2010; Meece & Wingate, 2009–2010).

CONCLUSION

The use of CBRI in K–12 schools allows for denial and lack of attention to the documented racial inequalities that exist in the educational system; indeed, CBRI has been called "the new, gentler form of racism" (Bonilla-Silva, 2009). Studies to date on CBRI have helped delineate the ways it serves the needs of teachers to the detriment of themselves and their students. Despite recent interest in documenting CBRI in the schools, however, questions remain. Empirical measurement of teachers' color-blind racial attitudes, especially in environments where teachers work daily with diverse students, should be further explored, as should the impact of personal and situational variables (e.g., teachers' racial group membership, diversity training, perceived school climate) to understand how these factors contribute to the adoption of CBRI or color-conscious ideology.

To eradicate the negative outcomes of CBRI, educators must acknowledge the existence of racial inequalities and be open to learning about CBRI's consequences. Once armed with a shared acknowledgment of the negative outcomes of CBRI and an informed understanding of how CBRI contributes to these outcomes, educators can begin to embrace the adoption of viable alternative ideologies.

REFERENCES

Banks, J. A. (2009). *Multiethnic education: Theory and practice* (7th ed.). Boston, MA: Allyn & Bacon.

Bennett, J. M., & Bennett, M. J. (2004). Developing intercultural sensitivity: An integrative approach to global and domestic diversity. In D. Landis, J. M. Bennett, & M. J. Bennett (Eds.), *Handbook of intercultural training* (3rd ed., pp. 147–165). Thousand Oaks, CA: Sage.

Blaisdell, B. (2005). Seeing every student as a 10: Using critical race theory to engage White teachers' color blindness. *International Journal of Educational Policy, Research, and Practice: Reconceptualizing Childhood Studies, 1*(6), 31–50.

Blum, L. (2002). *I am not a racist, but . . . The moral quandary of race.* Ithaca, NY: Cornell University Press.

Bonilla-Silva, E. (2009). *Racism without racists: Color-blind racism and the persistence of racial inequality in America* (3rd ed.). Lanham, MD: Rowman & Littlefield.

Bouknight, T. (2010). School climate and racial awareness: An exploratory analysis. *Dissertation Abstracts International Section A: Humanities and Social Sciences, 70(7-A)*, p. 2382.

Boutte, G. S., Lopez-Robertson, J., & Powers-Costello, E. (2011). Moving beyond color blindness in early childhood classrooms. *Early Childhood Education Journal, 39*, 335–342. http://dx.doi.org/10.1007/s10643-011-0457-x

Castro-Atwater, S. (2008). "Did they say what I think they said?" A multicultural response framework to address racial comments in the classroom. *Journal of Education and Human Development, 2*(1). Retrieved from http://www.scientific journals.org/journals2008/articles/1324.pdf

Child Trends Databank. (2012a). *Children in poverty.* Retrieved from http://www.childtrends.org/?indicators=children-in-poverty

Child Trends Databank. (2012b). *High school dropout rates.* Retrieved from http://www.childtrends.org/?indicators=high-school-dropout-rates

Choi, J. (2008, Summer–Fall). Unlearning color-blind ideologies in education class. *Educational Foundations*, 53–71.

Cochran-Smith, M. (1995). Color blindness and basket making are not the answers: Confronting the dilemmas of race, culture, and language diversity in teacher education. *American Educational Research Journal, 32*, 493–522. http://dx.doi.org/10.3102/00028312032003493

Cooney, M., & Akintunde, O. (1999). Confronting White privilege and the "color blind" paradigm in a teacher education program. *Multicultural Education, 7*(2), 9–14.

Cose, E. (1997). *Color blind: Seeing beyond race in a race-obsessed world.* New York, NY: HarperCollins.

Derman-Sparks, L., & Edwards, J. (2010). *Anti-bias education for young children and ourselves.* National Association for the Education of Young Children. Retrieved from http://www.naeyc.org/store/files/store/TOC/254.pdf

Fears, D. (2003, June 20). "Whiteness studies" stir interest and ire. *The Washington Post*, pp. A1, A12.

Foster, M. (1999). Race, class, and gender in education research: Surveying the political terrain. *Educational Policy, 13*, 77–85.

Gibbs, J., & Huang, L. N. (1998). *Children of color: Psychological interventions with culturally diverse youth.* San Francisco, CA: Jossey-Bass.

Han, S. (2009). Sociocultural influence on children's social competence: A close look at kindergarten teachers' beliefs. *Journal of Research in Childhood Education, 24*, 80–96. http://dx.doi.org/10.1080/02568540903439425

Kohli, R. (2012). Breaking the cycle of racism in the classroom: Critical race reflections from future teachers of color. In S. Hughes & T. R. Berry (Eds.), *The evolving significance of race: Living, learning, and teaching* (pp. 85–98). New York, NY: Lang.

Lewis, A. (2001). There is no "race" in the schoolyard: Color-blind ideology in an (almost) all-White school. *American Educational Research Journal, 38,* 781–811. http://dx.doi.org/10.3102/00028312038004781

Lin, M., Lake, V., & Rice, D. (2008). Teaching anti-bias curriculum in teacher preparation programs: What and how? *Teacher Education Quarterly, 35,* 187–200.

Marx, S. (2002, April). *Entanglements of altruism, Whiteness, and deficit thinking.* Paper presented at the Annual Meeting of the American Educational Research Association, New Orleans, LA.

Marx, S., & Larson, L. (2012). Taking off the color-blind glasses: Recognizing and supporting Latina/o students in a predominantly White school. *Educational Administration Quarterly, 48,* 259–303. http://dx.doi.org/10.1177/0013161X11421923

Masten, W., Plata, M., Wenglar, K., & Thedford, J. (1999). Acculturation and teacher ratings of Hispanic and Anglo-American students. *Roeper Review: A Journal on Gifted Education, 22,* 64–65. http://dx.doi.org/10.1080/02783199909554001

McKown, C., & Weinstein, R. (2002). Modeling the role of child ethnicity and gender in children's differential response to teacher expectations. *Journal of Applied Social Psychology, 32,* 159–184. http://dx.doi.org/10.1111/j.1559-1816.2002.tb01425.x

McKown, C., & Weinstein, R. S. (2003). The development and consequences of stereotype consciousness in middle childhood. *Child Development, 74,* 498–515. http://dx.doi.org/10.1111/1467-8624.7402012

Meece, D., & Wingate, K. (2009–2010). Providing early childhood teachers with opportunities to understand diversity and the achievement gap. *Journal of the Southeastern Regional Association of Teacher Educators, 19*(1), 36–43.

Milner, H. R. (2012). Losing the color-blind mind in the urban classroom. *Urban Education, 47,* 868–875. http://dx.doi.org/10.1177/0042085912458709

National Scientific Council on the Developing Child. (2004). *Young children develop in an environment of relationships* (Working Paper No. 1). Retrieved from http://developingchild.harvard.edu/resources/reports_and_working_papers/working_papers/wp1/

Neville, H. A., Awad, G. H., Brooks, J. E., Flores, M. P., & Bluemel, J. (2013). Color-blind racial ideology: Theory, training, and measurement implications in psychology. *American Psychologist, 68,* 455–466. http://dx.doi.org/10.1037/a0033282

Pappas, G. (1996). *Unveiling White privilege.* Denver, CO: Latin American Research and Service Agency. (ERIC Document Reproduction Service No. ED395085)

Richeson, J. A., & Nussbaum, R. J. (2004). The impact of multiculturalism versus color blindness on racial bias. *Journal of Experimental Social Psychology, 40,* 417–423. http://dx.doi.org/10.1016/j.jesp.2003.09.002

Roberts, R., Bell, L., & Murphy, B. (2008). Flipping the script: Analyzing youth talk about race and racism. *Anthropology & Education Quarterly, 39,* 334–354. http://dx.doi.org/10.1111/j.1548-1492.2008.00025.x

Rodriguez, N., & Villaverde, L. (Eds.). (2000). Dismantling White privilege: Pedagogy, politics, and Whiteness. *Counterpoints: Studies in the Postmodern Theory of Education* (Vol. 73). New York, NY: Lang.

Rosenthal, R., & Jacobson, L. (1966). Teachers' expectancies: Determinants of pupils' IQ gains. *Psychological Reports, 19*, 115–118. http://dx.doi.org/10.2466/pr0.1966.19.1.115

Schniedewind, N. (2005). "There ain't no White people here!": The transforming impact of teachers' racial consciousness on students and schools. *Equity & Excellence in Education, 38*, 280–289. http://dx.doi.org/10.1080/10665680500299668

Schofield, J. W. (1982). *Black and White in school: Trust tension or tolerance?* New York, NY: Praeger.

Schofield, J. W. (1986). Causes and consequences of the color-blind perspective. In S. Gaertner & J. Dovidio (Eds.), *Prejudice, discrimination, and racism: Theory and practice* (pp. 231–253). New York, NY: Academic Press.

Steele, C. M., & Aronson, J. (1995). Stereotype threat and the intellectual test performance of African Americans. *Journal of Personality and Social Psychology, 69*, 797–811. http://dx.doi.org/10.1037/0022-3514.69.5.797

Teaching Tolerance. (2014). *Introducing the tolerance anti-bias framework*. Retrieved from http://www.tolerance.org/sites/default/files/general/Anti%20bias%20framework%20pamphlet.pdf

Ullucci, K., & Battey, D. (2011). Exposing color blindness/grounding color consciousness: Challenges for teacher education. *Urban Education, 46*, 1195–1225. http://dx.doi.org/10.1177/0042085911413150

U.S. Department of Education, Office for Civil Rights. (1999, January). *Protecting students from harassment and hate crime: A guide for schools*. Retrieved from http://www.ed.gov/offices/OCR/archives/Harassment/harass_intro.html

Van Hook, C. (2000, November). Preparing teachers for the diverse classroom: A developmental model of intercultural sensitivity. In *Issues in Early Childhood Education: Curriculum, Teacher Education, & Dissemination of Information* (pp. 67–71). Proceedings of the Lillian Katz Symposium, Champaign, IL.

Williams, K., & Okintunde, O. (2000). Colorless, tasteless, and odorless? College students' perceptions of their racial and ethnic identities. *Journal of Early Education and Family Review, 8*(2), 22–31.

Williams, P. (1997). *Seeing a color-blind future: The paradox of race*. New York, NY: The Noonday Press.

Wynne, J. (1999, April). *The elephant in the living room: Racism in school reform*. Paper presented at the Annual Meeting of the American Educational Research Association, Montreal, Quebec, Canada.

Zeichner, K. (1993). *Educating teachers for cultural diversity* (NCRTL Special Report). East Lansing: Michigan State University, National Center for Research on Teacher Learning.

13

RAISING AWARENESS AND REDUCING COLOR-BLIND RACIAL IDEOLOGY IN HIGHER EDUCATION

CYNDI KERNAHAN

In November 2013, Professor Shannon Gibney, an instructor of English and of African diaspora studies, was reprimanded as a result of teaching about structural and institutional racism. The discussion she was leading as part of a mass communications course was apparently upsetting to three White male students. After a back and forth with the students, professor Gibney invited them to file a harassment complaint if they felt it necessary. Two of the students did file that complaint, and Professor Gibney says that she was later told that she had created a "hostile work environment" by the vice president for academic affairs (Watson, 2013). Although her reprimand was eventually rescinded, it is not the first time Professor Gibney has been investigated or reprimanded for discussing race and racism (Gibney, 2013). Gibney's story is compelling for many reasons, and it illustrates the challenge that higher education faces when it comes to raising awareness about racism and challenging the ideology of racial color blindness.

http://dx.doi.org/10.1037/14754-014

The Myth of Racial Color Blindness: Manifestations, Dynamics, and Impact, H. A. Neville, M. E. Gallardo, and D. W. Sue (Editors)

Although students of color have made strides in recent years, Whites are still overrepresented on college campuses and are the racial group least likely to have had interethnic contact before beginning college (Sidanius, Levn, van Laar, & Sears, 2008). At the same time, demographic changes are building a nation that will look very different in the future. According to the U.S. Census Bureau (2012), the White population is projected to begin declining while the growth among other racial groups is expected to grow more rapidly, leading to a "minority-majority" country by 2043. As a result, many colleges and universities in the United States explicitly tout a commitment to increasing the diversity of their campuses and to helping their students learn to effectively navigate an increasingly diverse society.

But what strategies work best? Professor Gibney, according to her own statements, was trying to bridge the gaps in her students understanding, gaps that likely resulted from racial segregation and *color-blind racial ideology* (CBRI), a set of beliefs resting on the core notion that race is no longer relevant in American life (Neville, Lilly, Duran, Lee, & Browne, 2000). As a result, experiences of racial discrimination and racial stress are minimized, and institutional and cultural racism is denied or unexamined. These beliefs clearly trumped Professor Gibney's ability to communicate how race structurally and institutionally influences us all. The students involved described feeling "vilified" and "singled out" and argued that Gibney herself was being "racist" (Kingcade, 2013). In remarking that the professor should not focus on race in her teaching, the students seemed to believe that merely discussing race or racism is, in and of itself, the problem. Furthermore, the students seemed to feel that ignoring race as a cause of oppression is the correct way to address any problems associated with race.

This way of thinking, of course, is not exclusive to college students (Apfelbaum, Norton, & Sommers, 2012), and echoes of the problems Professor Gibney faced can certainly be found in other educational settings. Most notably, Arizona banned the teaching of ethnic studies in all public schools (K–12) in 2010. Interestingly, one of the tenets of the law is that courses cannot be taught in a way that "promotes resentment toward a race or class of people" (Galvin, 2015) presumably in an attempt to prevent students, especially White students, from feeling "vilified" or bad about themselves. Given the treatment of Dr. Gibney and the experiences of those in Arizona, it seems clear that CBRI presents a unique challenge for those of us whose focus is on teaching students, especially White students, about race and racism.

According to Sidanius et al. (2008), most students experience a "liberalizing" effect on their racial attitudes during the college years. This liberalization occurs across racial groups but is relatively small in size, and the authors describe their findings as illustrating more stability than change in terms of attitudes: "continuity, not radical change, is closer to the norm through college" (Sidanius et al., 2008, p. 318). As noted, however, many colleges and universities set explicit goals with respect to improving students' racial attitudes and, presumably, their ability to work and live in an increasingly diverse society. One way colleges and universities go about this work is through diversity courses. As noted by Bowman (2010), a slight majority of U.S. colleges require at least one diversity course as part of the standard curriculum, and a recent meta-analysis (Denson, 2009) suggests that these courses have modestly positive effects for most students. Although there are other, cocurricular diversity experiences available on most college campuses (McCauley, Wright, & Harris, 2000), this chapter focuses primarily on the curricular strategy. What are the primary effects of diversity courses for students, and what are the ways in which the gaps in understanding between students (especially White students) and professors can be successfully bridged? Can these courses help students move beyond a CBRI? In reviewing the work to date, it is clear that raising awareness is not just a matter of teaching the right content. It's also a matter of connecting students to the real, lived experiences of others and helping them to voice their own experiences. Only through such connections can real understandings emerge.

THE EFFECTS OF DIVERSITY COURSES

To begin, we need to know how diversity courses influence students' racial attitudes, particularly in this age of CBRI. To do so, several researchers have used the Color Blind Racial Attitudes Scale (CoBRAS; Neville et al., 2000), a scale that can be broken into subscales to assess awareness of White privilege, awareness of institutional discrimination, and awareness of the pervasiveness of racial discrimination. Kernahan and Davis (2007, 2010) were able to show that a course on the psychology of prejudice and racism significantly improved awareness over the course of a semester (and in comparison with a control course) and that the increased awareness levels were stable for up to a year after the course ended. Similarly, Case (2007) showed an increase in awareness of racism over a semester for those taking a course on the psychology of gender and race, and Probst (2003) found increased awareness for those in a workplace diversity course. Finally, Cole, Case, Rios, and Curtin (2011) examined first-year students from across several diversity courses and compared them with those taking an introductory psychology course. Those in the diversity courses were more aware of White privilege and racism at the end of the semester regardless of the specific course they were taking.

Other work has shown similar results but with different racial attitude measures. Both Pettijohn and Walzer (2009) and Hogan and Mallott (2005) were able to show reductions in racist attitudes (Modern Racism Scale; McConahay, 1986), although some of these findings were relatively short-lived, diminishing once the course was finished. In an early study, Henderson-King and Kaleta (2000) surveyed a large number of students at the University of Michigan who had taken a course on race and ethnicity, which had been selected among four designated diversity courses. They then, over the course of a semester, compared this group with to another group of randomly chosen students who had not taken such a course. Using a variety of quantitative measures, including beliefs about racism and sexism and feeling thermometer scales (designed to assess feelings toward a variety of social groups ranging from gender to race to student athletes), the researchers found that the race and ethnicity courses did not necessarily improve student attitudes so much as they prevented declines. That is, those who had taken the diversity classes remained the same in terms of their racial attitudes and endorsement of stereotypes, whereas those who had not taken such courses showed higher levels of stereotyped attitudes over time (one semester) and more racist and sexist attitudes. Finally, Rudman, Ashmore, and Gary (2001) examined students enrolled in a prejudice and conflict seminar. The results of two iterations of this study showed that explicit and implicit racism as well as stereotyped attitudes were reduced for those in the prejudice course (compared pre- and postcourse and compared with a control course). Furthermore, both cognitive and affective factors correlated with changes in student attitudes.

THE LEARNING PROCESS

Taken together, these studies, along with others on racial identity development (Lawrence, 1997; Lawrence & Bunche, 1996; Tatum, 1992, 1994) and those examining modules or pieces of introductory courses (Boatright-Horowitz, 2005; Boatright-Horowitz, Marraccini, & Harps-Logan, 2012), point overwhelmingly to the same conclusion: Teaching about race and racism can increase awareness of privilege and discrimination and, in some cases, reduce bias and stereotypes. Indeed, it seems possible that such coursework is likely the main driver of any liberalizing effect of a college education (Sidanius et al., 2008). The question that is not as clearly answered, however, is how best to reach that awareness. That is, what aspects of these courses are most helpful to student learning and to reducing the default CBRI of many (especially White) students? One possibility is that learning about race and racism will increase critical thinking skills. The evidence for this, however, is somewhat mixed. Pascarella, Palmer, Moye, and Pierson (2001) did indeed find that diversity experiences in college were related to increases in critical thinking (using standardized, objective measures), but Bowman (2009), using the same critical thinking measure, did not replicate these gains in a larger study of first-year students from across 19 universities and colleges. Bowman did find increases in need for cognition (e.g., the tendency to engage in and enjoy thinking) for those students who had taken at least one diversity course in their first year, but this finding was limited to White students. Additionally, Bowman (2009) reported that whereas other studies have sometimes shown gains for critical thinking as a result of diversity courses, these results are not consistent and seem unlikely to persist over time.

Setting aside this type of improvement, another way to think about the effects of diversity courses might be to look more deeply at the classes them-selves and what happens to students as they learn. A number of instructor-scholars have documented the ways in which students resist learning about race and racism (M. Adams, Bell, & Griffin, 1997; Case, 2013; Fallon, 2006; Goldsmith, 2006; Tatum 1992, 1994). In experiences similar to that of Shannon Gibney, many of us (myself included) have been challenged in our teaching and have experienced fierce resistance on the part of our students. Moving away from a CBRI and toward a more complex understanding of ideas such as White privilege, race as a social construction, and institutional racism can lead to anger, guilt, shame, and denial on the part of many students. Although scholars have offered excellent advice for how to deal with these obstacles (e.g., M. Adams et al., 1997; Case, 2013), other work has closely examined the learning processes of students to provide even more guidance and evidence-based strategies.

The default position of color blindness is quite evident to many instruc-tors. For example, Modica (2012) conducted an analysis of her course website postings and found that most White students had not discussed race or racism with their families (only one of 37 had), many had little understanding of the history of race relations in the United States, and most stated explicitly that color blindness was the appropriate strategy for dealing with race. This contrasted with the experiences of students of color who were much more likely to have discussed race and racism within their families. In keeping with their beliefs about color blindness, most students—including some students of color—believed racism to be an individual rather than an institutional phenomena and something reflected through isolated or individual acts as opposed to a result of larger policies or structures. Although her students did report changing some of these beliefs as a result of the coursework, Modica did not specifically examine their learning processes or the extent of potential student change after taking the course in detail.

In trying to better understand how students move from this default position to one of more complexity and understanding, both Goldsmith (2006) and Fallon (2006) used the structures of their own disciplines to ana-lyze their students' learning. Goldsmith, a sociologist, developed and tested a method known as *writing answers to learn*. As part of this comprehensive study, Goldsmith analyzed students' writing, including journal entries and assignments. She also gave pre- and posttests to assess learning as well as a follow-up test occurring 10 months after the class ended. She identified four distinct ideologies that students used during the course that seemed to drive their misconceptions about racism (blaming the victim, justifying inequality, naturalizing inequality, and, of course, racial color blindness). The use of these ideologies decreased over time, however, and the follow-up test showed an increase in the use of sociological ideas and understanding. Within the humanities, Fallon was also able to illustrate student progression over time. Using several assigned writings, Fallon developed the *taxonomy of diversity learning outcomes, behaviors, and attitudes*. The first stages that she identified clearly represent a denial of racism and the espousal of a CBRI (*Antagonistic* and *Naïve*). But as students learned, she documented new levels of awareness, labeling them: *Coming Into Awareness, Accepting/Connecting/Embracing* and finally *Striving for Complexity* (Fallon, 2006, p. 414). She also described a nuance and three-dimensionality among her students that led her to ask: "Why, then, did some students whose presentations demonstrated an understanding of the complexity of diversity issues 'fall back' into more simplified or positions? And were these apparently 'simplified' or 'reductionist' positions as simple as they might seem?" (Fallon, 2006, p. 412). Her analysis revealed that her students' learning was not linear but instead appeared to fluctuate, moving "up" in the taxonomy and then sometimes slipping back into earlier, more simplistic understandings that were "more comfortably aligned with, or less challenging to, [their] value system and experiences" (Fallon, 2006, p. 413). She called this kind of learning "metastable." Earlier researchers also noted this sort of "forward/back" progression in terms of learning and development (e.g., Lawrence, 1997; Tatum 1992, 1994).

STRATEGIES FOR INCREASING LEARNING AND AWARENESS

The work just described clearly illustrates that diversity courses can improve attitudes and increase awareness, but what sorts of strategies work best? To better understand how their students were learning and how they might learn best, Nagda, Kim, and Truelove (2004) collected data from four cohorts of undergraduate social work students, all taking a required course on cultural diversity and justice. The course involved both "enlightenment" or content-based elements, such as lectures and readings, as well as an "encounter" element, involving intergroup dialogue. This distinction between the enlightenment and encounter elements of a course might also be thought of as the distinction between the cognitive or information-based elements of the course compared with the emotional or affective-based elements of the course. Although most of the work in this area does not make such a distinction (see Rudman et al., 2001, for an exception), Nagda et al. focused their research on these elements to help better describe how students learn and how they might learn best.

Providing their students with lectures and readings (enlightenment) as well as structured intergroup dialogues (encounter), Nagda and colleagues (2004) then assessed how important each of these course components was to the students as well as how involved they had been with each element during the course of the class. Although CBRI was not measured, the authors did ask the students how important they felt it was to engage in intergroup learning ("mutual and reciprocal learning" about race), to take antiprejudice actions, how confident they felt in taking antiprejudice actions, and how much they would monitor their own prejudice. Overall, the results showed that the course had a positive influence on students, increasing their willingness to promote diversity and to engage in intergroup learning as well as their confidence in doing so. Each element of the course, enlightenment and encounter, had positive effects for the students and each was independently and significantly related to the outcomes. However, the students, especially by the students of color, rated the encounter element as more important. The authors concluded,

> While lectures and readings provide students with the tools to understand issues of difference on an intellectual level, face-to-face encounters and the sharing of personal experiences enable students to actualize and directly apply their content-based learning. Students who may have previously felt uncertain about why a comment or action intuitively felt wrong now have the tools to explain why it was prejudicial or oppressive as well as the confidence to interrupt negative actions. (Nagda et al., 2004, p. 210)

The findings of Nagda et al. (2004) provide us with an important tool for raising awareness and improving outcomes: that of students speaking about their experiences and hearing the experiences of others. In an echo of these ideas, McIntosh (2012), reflecting back on over 20 years of teaching about privilege, noted the importance of having people talk about and share their experiences, both of unearned privilege and disadvantage. She argued that it is one of the key ways to teach about these issues while diminishing "blame, shame, guilt, or anger" (McIntosh, 2012, p. 202).

One more investigation of teaching provides further evidence for this idea via a different mechanism. In an in-depth, qualitative and quantitative analysis of the question "How do they learn," Chick, Karis, and Kernahan (2009) investigated four diversity courses. In addition to pre- and posttests of CBRI (using the CoBRAS; Neville et al., 2000), students were asked to write about what they felt helped them learn. They answered a series of short-answer questions at two points during the semester. In answering one of the prompts ("What helped you make sense of your learning?"), many students noted that both class discussion and reading their classmates' reflections were critical. They specifically cited, over and over, hearing and reading the experiences of other students who were learning the same content and reflecting on a variety of real-life examples and struggles. Through these insights, students described being able to empathize with and understand different perspectives and to have their own responses validated and normalized. Indeed, analysis of the CoBRAS scores showed that those in the discussion-based courses showed gains in awareness, whereas those in the lecture-based course did not show any change from pre- to postcourse. Although all of these courses were taught on predominantly White campuses (all in Wisconsin) and involved mostly White students, the ability to share examples and to discuss and hear the experiences of others proved important to learning.

Aside from the hearing and sharing of experiences, another key to their learning from the students' own descriptions were the use of narrative within course content. When asked which particular aspects of each course was helpful to their learning, most discussed specific course readings or video presentations that allowed them to sample the experiences of people dealing with racism and oppression. For example, the use of slave narratives, stories about the immigrant experience, and personal stories illustrating the impact of institutional racism (e.g., in housing, wealth, health care) were all cited by students as important and as having helped them better understand such new and complex topics. These findings mesh nicely with recent research illustrating the power of narrative, especially literature, in helping people to take the perspective of others. Kidd and Castano (2013) showed specifically that reading literary fiction, compared with popular fiction or non-fiction, improved performance on tests of affective theory of mind—that is, the ability to detect and understand the emotions of others. Djikic, Oatley, and Moldoveanu (2013) showed that reading short stories, compared with reading nonfiction essays, led to less of a need for cognitive closure, a decreased need for order, and a decreased discomfort with ambiguity on the part of the participants. These studies follow others that show similar effects, and Djikic et al. speculated that perhaps the reading of fiction allowed one to take the perspective of another person without "feel[ing] the need to defend one's own perspective" (p. 153). In other words, when we take the perspective of another as a result of reading their story, our own defensiveness or anxiety is less likely to get in the way. Because we are reading, we are simulating their experiences rather than trying to understand them through the prism of our own. One can imagine, then, how narrative might indeed make it easier to learn about things such as racial privilege and institutional and cultural racism, topics that so easily inspire threat and resistance.

LEARNING OUTSIDE THE CLASSROOM

In attempting to help students move past simplistic notions of color blindness and presumed racial equality, it is clear that certain strategies work best. Importantly, work from outside the classroom supports these notions. Pettigrew, Tropp, Wagner, and Christ's (2011) meta-analysis of more than 500 studies found that the more contact one has with an outgroup, the less prejudice one is likely to feel. The findings are especially robust for those in the majority group, and the outcomes of contact often include increased empathy, decreased outgroup anxiety, and increased trust, among others. These effects seem to be mediated more by affective factors such as increased empathy and decreased anxiety than cognitive factors such as knowledge. As Pettigrew et al. stated, "positive contact enhances empathy for the outgroup and adoption of the outgroup's perspective. One begins to sense how outgroup members *feel and view the world*" (p. 277, emphasis added).

Other research, specifically examining the experiences of college students, bears out these findings. Martin, Trego, and Nakayama (2010), for example, found that students who reported more friendships outside their race had more complex definitions of race. Those with fewer friends outside their own race were the most likely to define race solely by skin color. In an exhaustive, 6-year study of students at the University of California, Los Angeles, Sidanius et al. (2008) showed that across a variety of forms of contact (friendship, roommate relationships, dating relationships), students' racial attitudes became more positive as a result of that contact. Similar to the findings of Pettigrew et al. (2011), these changes were especially strong for White students paired with students of color, and these effects seemed to generalize to other racial groups. That is, a White student paired with a Hispanic roommate felt more positively toward African Americans as well other Hispanics. The only exception to these findings involved students paired with Asian American roommates. In those cases, prejudice increased on the part of the student. Nevertheless, the general findings seem to indicate the importance of contact on college campuses, particularly for White students (although the effects were seen for students of color as well). Sidanius et al. argued that these effects are likely a result of the low levels of cross-race contact that most students, especially Whites, report before attending college. Thus, befriending, dating, or living with someone of another race likely allows that student to experience the world through the eyes of someone different, something that their previous experiences have not made possible.

Although contact appears to be a positive experience for many students, and one that allows them to gain new perspectives, universities should be mindful of the unique stresses such contact creates for students of color. Trail, Shelton, and West (2009) examined the daily interactions and feelings of students paired with same-race or cross-race roommates over several weeks at the beginning an academic year. In doing so, they found that mixed-race pairs experienced declining positive emotions and intimacy compared with same-race pairs. Interestingly, these changes seemed to be driven primarily by the White students, resulting in a cycle that became less positive over time. Specifically, the White roommate's intimacy-building behaviors decreased, precipitating a decrease in the positive emotions of the African American or Latino roommate (there were no reported differences between these groups). The authors speculated that perhaps it just takes time for these living arrangements to yield positive effects. People may need time to get past the initial awkwardness and difficulty of an interracial relationship before they can begin to see the perspective of the other person and experience a shift in attitude (see also Putnam, 2007, for more evidence on a larger scale).

CONCLUSION AND FUTURE QUESTIONS

As colleges and universities attempt to live up to their mission and vision statements regarding diversity, it seems clear that the keys to success involve a curriculum that allows students to learn more about other groups as well as ample opportunities for meaningful contact across racial groups. Denson and Chang (2009) found that increased cross-racial interaction and an increased number of students taking diversity courses resulted in higher levels of general academic skills and greater racial engagement among all the students on campus, even those engaging in the activities less. The authors argue that these behaviors create a normative context that is more positive with respect to diversity and that this norm then positively affects all students regardless of their own individual contact and classroom experiences. Not surprisingly, the more positively campuses engage with diversity, the better students' attitudes are likely to be. As shown in this chapter, a deeper analysis of why these methods (curriculum and contact) may work suggests the importance of truly hearing and understanding the experiences and perspectives of others. Yet although the evidence for this idea is compelling (e.g., Chick et al., 2009; McIntosh, 2012), more work clearly needs to be done to help universities and instructors.

First, the classroom environment should be investigated further. Using the methods of the scholarship of teaching and learning (Bishop-Clark & Dietz-Uhler, 2012) and applying them to diversity courses, instructors can rigorously examine student learning and pull apart the pieces of instruction that are most important. One fruitful avenue of research could be the "encounter" (dialogue) and "enlighten" (content) pieces examined by Nagda et al. (2004). As noted, both parts of the course were related to student learning, but the students deemed the encounter piece more important. Future work could examine each of these pieces to understand them better and to understand how each leads to learning. For example, affective learning seems to be a key mediator for reducing prejudice (Pettigrew et al., 2011), so perhaps research should focus on how encounter experiences help to generate emotional responses and increase learning and awareness. Is it about reducing anxiety for students or increasing trust? Also, what sorts of encounter experiences are necessary? Many of us teach in relatively homogeneous environments where intergroup dialogue is less likely. Would narrative experiences create the same kinds of learning as earlier research might suggest (Chick et al., 2009), or is intergroup contact and dialogue across racial groups the best teacher?

Content choices present another interesting avenue for research. G. Adams, Edkins, Lacka, Pickett, and Cheryan (2008) presented compelling evidence that the "standard" portrayal of racism is unlikely to increase awareness of systemic racism (thereby leaving CBRI intact). By standard, the authors mean racism discussed and taught as individual prejudice (common in psychology classes especially) rather than a focus on larger institutional forces. Across two studies, they show how this standard portrayal led to no increases in students' understanding of racism as systemic or to support for policy changes that might ameliorate racism (compared with a control condition). In another condition, participants were taught about both individual and institutional forms of racism and were much more likely to endorse the idea that racism is systemic and that policy changes are necessary. Clearly our content choices matter, and further study of content could help instructors best choose their materials.

While teaching about the systemic nature of racism is essential to reducing color blindness and increasing learning, it is certainly not easy. As many instructors are aware (e.g., Case, 2013) and as research has shown (Unzueta & Lowery, 2008), raising awareness of institutional racism and White privilege tends to be threatening, particularly for Whites. Many instructors have thus focused on the ways in which to make the classroom "safe" for students, but less work has identified what that means exactly. As noted earlier, McIntosh (2012) argued that the ability of students to share their experiences and to hear from others is essential to learning (and to their ability to accept White privilege), and the findings of Chick et al. (2009) certainly suggest the importance of this, but future work might better clarify how these experiences reduce threat and can best be facilitated.

Finally, universities and colleges have to create a stronger environment for doing this difficult teaching work. It is not enough to encourage the development of diversity courses without also providing ample faculty development and faculty support. Centers for teaching and learning and other administrative bodies can provide workshops and training specifically geared toward teaching about racism (or other difficult topics) and rooted in the evidence-based strategies described in this chapter. If everyone on campus is committed to truly understanding these issues and avoiding racial color blindness, instructors and students alike should feel supported and safe.

REFERENCES

Adams, G., Edkins, V., Lacka, D., Pickett, K. M., & Cheryan, S. (2008). Teaching about racism: Implications of the standard portrayal. *Basic and Applied Social Psychology, 30*, 349–361. http://dx.doi.org/10.1080/01973530802502309

Adams, M., Bell, L. A., & Griffin, P. (1997). *Teaching for diversity and social justice* (2nd ed.). New York, NY: CRC Press.

Apfelbaum, E. P., Norton, M. I., & Sommers, S. R. (2012). Racial color blindness: Emergence, practice, and implications. *Current Directions in Psychological Science, 21*, 205–209. http://dx.doi.org/10.1177/0963721411434980

Bishop-Clark, C., & Dietz-Uhler, B. (2012). *Engaging in the scholarship of teaching and learning: A guide to the process, and how to develop a project from start to finish.* Sterling, VA: Stylus.

Boatright-Horowitz, S. L. (2005). Teaching antiracism in a large introductory psychology course: A course module and its evaluation. *Journal of Black Studies, 36*, 34–51. http://dx.doi.org/10.1177/0021934704266508

Boatright-Horowitz, S. L., Marraccini, M., & Harps-Logan, Y. (2012). Teaching antiracism: College students' emotional and cognitive reactions to learning about White privilege. *Journal of Black Studies, 43*, 893–911. http://dx.doi.org/10.1177/0021934712463235

Bowman, N. A. (2009). College diversity courses and cognitive development among students from privileged and marginalized groups. *Journal of Diversity in Higher Education, 2*, 182–194. http://dx.doi.org/10.1037/a0016639

Bowman, N. A. (2010). Disequilibrium and resolution: The nonlinear effects of diversity courses on well-being and orientations toward diversity. *Review of Higher Education: Journal of the Association for the Study of Higher Education, 33*, 543–568. http://dx.doi.org/10.1353/rhe.0.0172

Case, K. A. (2007). Raising White privilege awareness and reducing racial privilege: Assessing diversity course effectiveness. *Teaching of Psychology, 34*, 231–235. http://dx.doi.org/10.1080/00986280701700250

Case, K. A. (Ed.). (2013). *Deconstructing privilege: Teaching and learning as allies in the classroom.* New York, NY: Routledge.

Chick, N. L., Karis, T., & Kernahan, C. (2009). Learning from their own learning: How metacognitive and meta-affective reflections enhance learning in race-related courses. *International Journal for the Scholarship of Teaching and Learning, 3*, 1–26.

Cole, E. R., Case, K. A., Rios, D., & Curtin, N. (2011). Understanding what students bring to the classroom: Moderators of the effects of diversity courses on student attitudes. *Cultural Diversity and Ethnic Minority Psychology, 17*, 397–405. http://dx.doi.org/10.1037/a0025433

Denson, N. (2009). Do curricular and cocurricular diversity activities influence racial bias? *Review of Educational Research, 79*, 805–838. http://dx.doi.org/10.3102/0034654309331551

Denson, N., & Chang, M. J. (2009). Racial diversity matters: The impact of diversity-related student engagement and institutional context. *American Educational Research Journal, 46*, 322–353. http://dx.doi.org/10.3102/0002831208323278

Djikic, M., Oatley, K., & Moldoveanu, M. C. (2013). Opening the closed mind: The effect of exposure to literature on the need for closure. *Creativity Research Journal, 25*, 149–154. http://dx.doi.org/10.1080/10400419.2013.783735

Fallon, D. (2006). "Lucky to live in Maine": Examining student responses to diversity issues. *Teaching English in the Two-Year College, 33*, 410–420.

Galvin, A. (2015, January 12). Arizona ban on ethnic studies goes before appeals court. *Arizona Central.* Retrieved from http://www.azcentral.com/story/news/arizona/politics/2015/01/12/arizona-ethnic-studies-ban-court-hearing/21636929

Gibney, S. (2013, November 30). Teaching while Black and Blue. *Gawker.* Retrieved from http://gawker.com/teaching-while-black-and-blue-1473659925

Goldsmith, P. A. (2006). Learning to understand inequality and diversity: Getting students past ideologies. *Teaching Sociology, 34*, 263–277. http://dx.doi.org/10.1177/0092055X0603400305

Henderson-King, D., & Kaleta, A. (2000). Learning about social diversity: The undergraduate experience and intergroup tolerance. *The Journal of Higher Education, 71*, 142–164. http://dx.doi.org/10.2307/2649246

Hogan, D. E., & Mallott, M. (2005). Changing racial prejudice through diversity education. *Journal of College Student Development, 46*, 115–125. http://dx.doi.org/10.1353/csd.2005.0015

Kernahan, C., & Davis, T. (2007). Changing perspective: How learning about racism influences student awareness and emotion. *Teaching of Psychology, 34*, 49–52. http://dx.doi.org/10.1080/00986280709336651

Kernahan, C., & Davis, T. (2010). What are the long-term effects of learning about racism? *Teaching of Psychology, 37*, 41–45. http://dx.doi.org/10.1080/00986280903425748

Kidd, D. C., & Castano, E. (2013). Reading literary fiction improves theory of mind. *Science, 18*, 377–380. http://dx.doi.org/10.1126/science.1239918

Kingcade, T. (2013, December 9). Professor claims racial discrimination, but former student remembers incident differently. *Huffington Post*. Retrieved from http://www.huffingtonpost.com/2013/12/09/mctc-racism_n_4394555.html

Lawrence, S. M. (1997). Beyond race awareness: White racial identity and multicultural teaching. *Journal of Teacher Education, 48*, 108–117. http://dx.doi.org/10.1177/0022487197048002004

Lawrence, S. M., & Bunche, T. (1996). Feeling and dealing: Teaching White students about racial privilege. *Teaching and Teacher Education, 12*, 531–542. http://dx.doi.org/10.1016/0742-051X(95)00054-N

Martin, J. N., Trego, A. B., & Nakayama, T. K. (2010). College students' racial attitudes and friendship diversity. *Howard Journal of Communications, 21*, 97–118. http://dx.doi.org/10.1080/10646171003727367

McCauley, C., Wright, M., & Harris, M. E. (2000). Diversity workshops on campus: A survey of current practice at U.S. colleges and universities. *College Student Journal, 34*, 100–115.

McConahay, J. B. (1986). Modern racism, ambivalence, and the Modern Racism Scale. In J. F. Dovidio & S. L. Gaertner (Eds.), *Prejudice, discrimination, and racism* (pp. 91–125). San Diego, CA: Academic Press.

McIntosh, P. (2012). Reflections and future directions for privilege studies. *Journal of Social Issues, 68*, 194–206. http://dx.doi.org/10.1111/j.1540-4560.2011.01744.x

Modica, M. (2012). Constructions of race among religiously conservative college students. *Multicultural Perspectives, 14*, 38–43. http://dx.doi.org/10.1080/15210960.2012.646850

Nagda, B. A., Kim, C., & Truelove, Y. (2004). Learning about difference, learning with others, learning to transgress. *Journal of Social Issues, 60*, 195–214. http://dx.doi.org/10.1111/j.0022-4537.2004.00106.x

Neville, H. A., Lilly, R. L., Duran, G., Lee, R. M., & Browne, L. (2000). Construction and initial validation of the Color-Blind Racial Attitudes Scale (CoBRAS). *Journal of Counseling Psychology, 47*, 59–70. http://dx.doi.org/10.1037/0022-0167.47.1.59

Pascarella, E. T., Palmer, B., Moye, M., & Pierson, C. T. (2001). Do diversity experiences influence the development of critical thinking? *Journal of College Student Development, 42*, 257–271.

Pettigrew, T. F., Tropp, L. R., Wagner, U., & Christ, O. (2011). Recent advances in intergroup contact theory. *International Journal of Intercultural Relations, 35*, 271–280. http://dx.doi.org/10.1016/j.ijintrel.2011.03.001

Pettijohn, T. F., II, & Walzer, A. S. (2009). Reducing racism, sexism, and homophobia in college students by completing a psychology of prejudice course. *College Student Journal, 42*, 459–468.

Probst, T. M. (2003). Changing attitudes over time: Assessing the effectiveness of a workplace diversity course. *Teaching of Psychology, 30*, 236–239. http://dx.doi.org/10.1207/S15328023TOP3003_09

Putnam, R. D. (2007). E pluribus unum: Diversity and community in the twenty-first century. The 2006 Johan Skytte Prize lecture. *Scandinavian Political Studies*, *30*, 137–174. http://dx.doi.org/10.1111/j.1467-9477.2007.00176.x

Rudman, L. A., Ashmore, R. D., & Gary, M. L. (2001). "Unlearning" automatic biases: The malleability of implicit prejudice and stereotypes. *Journal of Personality and Social Psychology*, *81*, 856–868. http://dx.doi.org/10.1037/0022-3514.81.5.856

Sidanius, J., Levin, S., Van Laar, C., & Sears, D. O. (2008). *The diversity challenge: Social identity and intergroup relations on the college campus*. New York, NY: Russell Sage Foundation.

Tatum, B. D. (1992). Talking about race, learning about racism: The application of racial identity development theory in the classroom. *Harvard Educational Review*, *62*, 1–24.

Tatum, B. D. (1994). Teaching White students about racism: The search for White allies and the restoration of hope. *Teachers College Record*, *95*, 462–476.

Trail, T. E., Shelton, J. N., & West, T. V. (2009). Interracial roommate relationships: Negotiating daily interactions. *Personality and Social Psychology Bulletin*, *35*, 671–684. http://dx.doi.org/10.1177/0146167209332741

Unzueta, M. M., & Lowery, B. S. (2008). Defining racism safely: The role of self-image maintenance on White Americans' conceptions of racism. *Journal of Experimental Social Psychology*, *44*, 1491–1497. http://dx.doi.org/10.1016/j.jesp.2008.07.011

U.S. Census Bureau. (2012, Dec 12). *U.S. Census Bureau projections show a slower growing, older, more diverse nation a half century from now*. Retrieved from https://www.census.gov/newsroom/releases/archives/population/cb12-243.html

Watson, J. (2013, December 16). *Minneapolis community college professor denounced for structural racism teachings*. Retrieved from http://diverseeducation.com/article/59525/

14

THE IMPACT OF COLOR-BLIND RACIAL IDEOLOGY ON MAINTAINING RACIAL DISPARITIES IN ORGANIZATIONS

CARYN J. BLOCK

The dominant diversity philosophy espoused in most U.S. organizations is characterized by racial color blindness (Stevens, Plaut, & Sanchez-Burks, 2008), stressing the existence of equal opportunities for all due to adherence to meritocratic principles. This form of color-blind racial ideology (CBRI) influences both White employees and employees of color in ways that contribute to and maintain persistent disparities in workplace outcomes.

In this chapter, I take a social constructionist view and contend that structural relations in a setting give meaning to racial group membership (DiTomaso, 2010; Thomas & Alderfer, 1989). Thus, I begin with an examination of existing racial disparities in the workplace in the United States to understand the context in which a CBRI is espoused. I then discuss the impact of both types of CBRI as identified by Neville, Awad, Brooks, Flores, and Bluemel (2013), beliefs about power distribution in the system (*power evasion*) and beliefs about individual differences (*color evasion*), on employees'

http://dx.doi.org/10.1037/14754-015
The Myth of Racial Color Blindness: Manifestations, Dynamics, and Impact, H. A. Neville, M. E. Gallardo, and D. W. Sue (Editors)

understanding of the reasons for the existing racial disparities in the workplace and how each of these manifestations of CBRI contributes to and maintains these disparities. Given the existing racial disparities in workplace outcomes, a color-blind approach to race will lead to the inference that these disparities are not due to either institutional racism or individual racism and therefore can only be due to individual differences in ability and motivation across racial groups. Seeing disparities as a function of traits of different racial groups creates the conditions that are necessary to invoke stereotype threat in employees of color, which is another systemic threat within which they must navigate their careers. I discuss ways to counter the negative effects of CBRI in organizational settings by cultivating an awareness of diversity dynamics.

EXISTENCE OF RACIAL DISPARITIES IN THE WORKPLACE

As the American workforce continues to grow increasingly diverse, overcoming discrimination and embracing diversity in the workplace have become important stated goals for many organizations. Yet despite widespread Equal Employment Opportunity initiatives and efforts to combat discrimination, racial inequalities continue to persist in U.S. organizations. These racial inequalities are apparent at every step of an individual's participation in the labor force, including entering the job market, the type of job an individual is assigned, career advancement, and the associated wages that accompany each of these decisions (Roberson & Block, 2001; Spalter-Roth & Lowenthal, 2005).

Disparities in Entering the Workforce

African Americans are almost twice as likely to be unemployed than Whites, and this has been shown to be the case consistently over time, regardless of economic conditions, as has the employment gap between Whites and Hispanics (Spalter-Roth & Lowenthal, 2005). The U.S. unemployment rate was 8.9% in 2011, but the unemployment rates for African Americans (15.9%), American Indians/Alaska Natives (14.6%), people of two or more races (13.6%), Native Hawaiians/other Pacific Islanders (11.8%), and Hispanics (11.5%) were far higher, and the unemployment rates for Whites (7.2%) and Asians (7.0%) were lower (U.S. Department of Labor, Bureau of Labor Statistics, 2012). Thus, it seems that entering or reentering the labor force may prove more or less difficult depending on racial group membership.

Not surprisingly, race has been shown to be a key factor influencing hiring decisions, with Whites consistently faring better than African Americans (Pager & Shepherd, 2008). Field-based audit studies have demonstrated that, compared with their equally qualified White counterparts, African Americans encounter obstacles entering the labor market, receiving fewer interview call-backs (Bertrand & Mullainathan, 2004) and fewer job offers after an interview (Bendick, Jackson, & Reinoso, 1994). In a controlled field experiment, equivalent resumes with African American- or White-sounding names were sent to more than 1,300 job postings in newspapers (Bertrand & Mullainathan, 2004). Resumes with White-sounding names were called back for interviews 50% more often than equivalent resumes with African American-sounding names, and this was true across occupation, employer size, and industry. In fact, it was found that having a White-sounding name attached to a resume yielded as many more callbacks as 8 years of experience. In trying to understand the reasons behind their striking results in the interview callback study, Bertrand and Mullainathan (2004) concluded that employers may be using racial group membership as a heuristic in reading resumes.

Furthermore, an audit study demonstrated that if African Americans do receive interview callbacks, their chances of receiving a job offer are still lower. Bendick et al. (1994) found that Black applicants who did receive an interview were offered a job 11.3% of the time, whereas their equally qualified White counterparts who received an interview were offered a job 46.9% of the time. The implication of these studies is that employers are using racial group membership as a factor in making employment decisions, and thus, these decisions are not color-blind but instead color-based.

Disparities in Treatment in Organizations

Once in the labor force, obstacles continue, with African Americans receiving lower performance appraisals from their supervisors (Sackett & DuBois, 1991), holding jobs of lower complexity and authority (Mueller, Parcel, & Tanaka, 1989; Smith, 2002), receiving lower wages (Bendick et al., 1994; U.S. Department of Labor, Bureau of Labor Statistics, 2013) and receiving fewer promotions (Baldi & McBrier, 1997; Greenhaus & Parasuraman, 1993; Pager, 2007), all of which potentially contribute to the disparity in job outcomes across racial groups. One study based on data from a nationally representative sample found that African Americans were only 50% as likely as their equally qualified White counterparts to have been promoted (Baldi & McBrier, 1997). This racial difference in promotion rates was found to persist while controlling for education, work experience, and firm composition.

Thus, it is not surprising that in 2012, the highest status occupations (managerial, professional, and related occupations) reflected these disparities, with 39% of Whites and 49% of Asians holding these positions, compared with 30% of Blacks and 21% of Hispanics. Conversely, there are greater percentages of both Blacks (47%) and Hispanics (58%) in lower status occupations (service, construction, and transportation) than Whites (39%) and

Asians (31%; U.S. Department of Labor, Bureau of Labor Statistics, 2013). This occupational segregation results in persistent wage gaps, with Blacks and Hispanics earning considerably less in median weekly earnings ($568 and $621, respectively) than their White and Asian counterparts ($792 and $920, respectively). However, these differences in earnings cannot be accounted for by occupational segregation alone. In 2010, Asian men and White men working in higher status positions (management, professional, and related professions) earned considerably more in median weekly earnings ($1,408 and $1,273, respectively) than their Hispanic or Black counterparts ($1,002 and $957, respectively) in their same occupational group (Bureau of Labor Statistics, 2010).

Although Asians do not appear to be experiencing the same disparities in earnings as Blacks and Hispanics and, in fact, Asians' earnings are higher than those of Whites, there is evidence that Asians face disparities in terms of the qualifications that are required to achieve this level of earnings. Asians have higher educational levels than all other racial groups (U.S. Census Bureau, 2012). Asians are more likely to enroll in first-tier universities and are more likely to receive postgraduate degrees (Kim & Sakamoto, 2010). However, despite these educational achievements, Asians still do not achieve salary parity with their equally qualified White counterparts. In a recent study using the 2003 National Survey of College Graduates, it was found that Asian men were paid significantly less than equally qualified White men (Kim & Sakamoto, 2010). Thus, compared with Whites, Asians are required to make a higher investment in their education to achieve the same level of earnings and have more difficulty translating their educational achievement into gains in income, resulting in a lower return on investment for education (Hirschman & Snipp, 2001).

Racial group membership has also been found to be a key factor in influencing layoff decisions. Analyzing 3 years of personnel data from a financial firm, Elvira and Zatick (2002) found that racial group membership significantly influenced layoff decisions, such that Whites were laid off less than all non-Whites, controlling for occupation, job level, and business unit membership. Asians were laid off less than Black and Hispanic employees.

Disparities in Senior Leadership Positions

Who gets promoted to the most senior positions is also influenced by racial group membership. African Americans, Hispanics, and Asian Americans are severely underrepresented in senior leadership positions in U.S. organizations. Corporate boards of Fortune 500 companies continue to be dominated by Whites, who represent 90.3% of corporate board memberships, with African Americans representing only 4.6%, Hispanics 3.0%, and Asian Americans, despite their success in other job outcomes, representing only 2.1% of corporate board members (Alliance for Board Diversity, 2011). A similar picture emerges when examining the representation of CEOs in Fortune 500 companies. In 2015, 95% of Fortune 500 CEOs were White, 1% were African American, 2% were Hispanic, and only 2% were Asian (DiversityInc, 2015). Thus, at the most senior levels in organizations, the largest racial disparities exist, with Whites overrepresented and members of other racial groups underrepresented in the positions that are imbued with the most power. It is noteworthy that although Asian Americans have been successful in obtaining managerial and professional positions, they have not been able to translate these gains in occupational status to greater representation in senior leadership positions.

In summary, race continues to be a key factor in the decisions that employers make about who to interview, who to offer a job to, who to promote, and who to layoff contributing to the racial disparity in job outcomes. As concluded by the American Sociological Association in their report on racial differences in the labor force, "the labor market is neither race neutral nor color-blind despite laws that prohibit deliberate discrimination" (Spalter-Roth & Lowenthal, 2005, p. 9). Racial disparities in job outcomes persist throughout the course of an individual's career trajectory. It is within this context that we now turn to understanding the impact of diversity philosophies that espouse racial color blindness as a value.

MAKING SENSE OF RACIAL DISPARITIES IN THE WORKPLACE

How do members of organizations understand these persistent racial disparities, despite legislation and diversity initiatives that are designed to prohibit discrimination? In making sense of these persistent racial disparities in job performance and outcomes, Roberson and Block (2001) highlighted different frameworks that have historically predominated this discussion in the research literature. Three of these frameworks for understanding racial disparities in performance and outcomes are discussed here (see Figure 14.1). The first framework locates the primary causes of these differential workplace outcomes in the *internal traits* of members of various racial groups. There is an extensive literature that focuses on stable person-based factors, such as ability and motivation, as the cause of the racial disparities in outcomes in the workplace (Gottfredson, 1986; Hartigan & Wigdor, 1989). This framework is based on the assumption that cognitive ability and motivation are predictive of job performance (Schmidt, Ones, & Hunter, 1992) and that there are differences in cognitive ability and motivation across racial groups (Campbell, 1996; Graham, 1994), which accounts for the persistent racial disparities that exist in the workforce.

Figure 14.1. Frameworks for understanding racial disparities in performance and outcomes in the workplace.

The second framework that has been frequently used in the research literature to understand racial disparities in workplace outcomes focuses on *bias and discrimination* of organizational decision makers. This model locates the reason for disparities in organizational decision makers' stereotypes and biased behavior toward members of different racial groups. There has been a great deal of research demonstrating that racial stereotypes of decision makers influence their perceptions of employees, resulting in more positive evaluations of Whites than members of other racial groups (Chen & DiTomaso, 1996; Sy et al., 2010). In fact, research has demonstrated that the prototypical leader is considered to be White (Rosette, Leonardelli, & Phillips, 2008) and that Whites are seen as having more characteristics in common with successful managers than other racial groups (Block, Aumann, & Chelin, 2012; Chung-Herrera & Lankau, 2005; Tomkiewicz, Brenner, & Adeyemi-Bello, 1998).

Both the internal trait and the bias and discrimination frameworks locate the cause of the racial disparities in the workplace within individuals— either employees (internal trait) or organizational decision makers (bias/ discrimination), ignoring the context in which these racial disparities are occurring. The third framework focuses on features of the workplace context and locates the cause of racial disparities in the situation as opposed to the individual. This research examines the *sociocultural organizational context* in which these racial disparities in outcomes occur as a critical contributing factor. An important factor in the organizational context is the structural relations across racial groups. Structural relations are defined as differences in power, status, and numbers (DiTomaso, 2010). The structural relations among racial groups in organizations provide information that employees use in making sense of the meaning diversity has in the workplace (Thomas & Alderfer, 1989). The structure of who is in power provides employees with answers to the following questions about the meaning of their racial group membership at work. In this organization, what meaning does my racial group membership hold for me and for others? Will my identity as an employee be threatened or privileged because of my racial group membership? Will I be allowed to perform up to capacity without being stereotyped on the basis of my racial group membership?

Given the existing racial disparities in the workplace, the structural relations in organizations provide a very different context for employees who are White than employees of color. The organizational context for Whites is one in which they are similar to those in positions of senior leadership, whereas for people of color, this is not the case. This sociocultural organizational context results in fewer networking opportunities, more distant relationships with senior leaders, and less access to informal information about politics in the workplace for people of color, all of which are critical for climbing the organizational ladder (Ibarra, 1995; Mehra, Kilduff, & Brass, 1998). Simultaneously, this sociocultural organizational context unfairly advantages Whites who have far greater access to this critical information. DiTomaso (2013) interviewed 250 Whites about their job history and discovered that 99% of her sample found 70% of their jobs through information obtained via their social networks. Thus, the sociocultural context results in "unequal opportunity" for members of different racial groups throughout the course of individuals' careers (DiTomaso, 2013). In sum, according to the sociocultural organizational model, racial disparities in the workplace are not a function of differential traits of employees or bias of managers but instead of the different systemic inequalities that differentially advantage members of different racial groups.

IMPACT OF CBRI ON MAKING SENSE OF RACIAL DISPARITIES IN THE WORKPLACE

CBRI is likely to enhance certain explanations for these disparities and inhibit or entirely eliminate other explanations. CBRI, as conceptualized by Neville et al. (2013), can be enacted by beliefs about the systems in which individuals function (power evasion) or beliefs about individuals (color evasion). How does a color-blind approach to diversity influence how individuals will make meaning of these racial disparities in the workplace? What is the implicit message sent about these existing racial disparities if an organization claims to be racially color blind as part of their diversity philosophy?

Power and Privilege Evasion

The dimension of CBRI known as *power evasion* is characterized by the belief that systems treat individuals similarly regardless of their racial group membership. It is characterized by the denial of institutional differences in how individuals are treated, and the emphasis is placed on seeing institutions as fair and color-blind. Another way to think about the power-evasion dimension is that it is also about privilege evasion (Neville et al., 2013). When individuals see systems as fair, institutional racism and their own privilege can be denied. When people do not see institutional racism, they do not see the way the system unfairly advantages them. The opposite perspective to power evasion, as noted by Neville et al. (2013), is *color consciousness*, which is characterized by an understanding of institutional differences in how members of various racial groups are treated. However, it may be useful to think of the opposite perspective as *power and privilege awareness*. The opposite of being blind to the forces that power and privilege exert on outcomes experienced by different racial groups in institutional contexts, is to be aware of how forces of power and privilege operate to shape outcomes.

How does power blindness influence individuals understanding of the racial disparities that exist in the workplace? If individuals are blind to power dynamics in the workplace, viewing the organization as based on a meritocracy, then the organizational systems that result in existing racial disparities are seen to be fair and not to differ for members of various racial groups. Thus, power blindness results in the denial of the sociocultural organizational context as a factor in accounting for the existing racial disparities in organizations. In making sense of existing racial disparities in the workplace, contextual factors, represented in the sociocultural organizational model, are eliminated as possible explanations for the existing disparities. Thus, not seeing disparities as resulting from systems that differentially advantage and disadvantage members of different racial groups means that we must focus on individuals (either employees of color or organizational decision makers) as the cause of these disparities.

Color and Bias Evasion

The other dimension of CBRI discussed by Neville et al. (2013) is *color evasion*, which is characterized by the belief that all individuals are the same regardless of racial group membership. It is characterized by the denial of racial group differences and the emphasis on universal similarities. However, when individuals do not see color or race, then individual racism is also denied. Thus, *not seeing race* and *not seeing racism* are two sides of the same coin, so that color evasion is really about bias evasion. When people say, "I don't see race," what they likely mean is, "I don't see racism." Race is about what "I see" and not what others experience. The opposite perspective of color evasion, as identified by Neville et al. (2013), is multiculturalism, acknowledging racial differences among individuals. However, if color evasion is also about evading bias, it may be useful to think of the opposite perspective as *bias awareness*. The opposite of being blind to the impact that bias or racism can have on outcomes experienced by different racial groups is being aware of the role that bias can play.

When making sense of existing racial disparities in the workplace, being "bias or color blind" will eliminate bias and discrimination of organizational decision makers as a potential factor in accounting for existing racial disparities in the workplace. If individuals do not see organizational decision makers as biased or do not acknowledge the impact of stereotyping on important organizational decisions, then de facto, the only factor that can account for the existing racial disparities in the workforce is differences in individual traits and abilities across racial groups. Therefore, being "bias blind" means that you *do see race* of individual employees as the critical factor in explaining these differential outcomes, because you *don't see racism* of organizational decision makers.

In sum, when an organization's diversity philosophy is color-blind due to both bias evasion and power evasion, the only explanation for racial disparities we are left with is individual traits of employees. Because the system is seen as equitable (power evasion) and organizational decision makers are not seen as biased (bias evasion), the only explanation to make sense of these disparities is that they are due to differences in the internal traits of racial group members. Thus, the only place to locate the cause of these persistent racial disparities is in the individual traits (or deficits) of people of color. When color blindness is the espoused diversity philosophy, deficits in individual employees of color are seen as the only possible source of racial disparities.

IMPACT OF CBRI ON MAINTAINING EXISTING RACIAL DISPARITIES: CREATING THE CONDITIONS FOR STEREOTYPE THREAT

What does it mean for employees of color to navigate their careers in organizational contexts in which their lack of representation is seen to be due to their deficits in ability and motivation? How do individuals navigate their careers in environments that are infused with unspoken, negative stereotypes about their group's propensity to succeed? Attributing differential workplace outcomes to individual differences in ability and motivation of different racial groups sets the stage for the experience of stereotype threat. Stereotype threat is the environmental threat that is present when there is a belief that a negative stereotype about your group's ability to perform may be operating (Steele, Spencer, & Aronson, 2002). Thus, the belief that the underrepresentation of members of different social identity groups is due to individual characteristics of members of these social identity groups is in and of itself a form of stereotype threat.

Hundreds of studies have demonstrated the negative impact that working under the threat of a stereotype about one's group has on performance. Stereotype threat has been shown to negatively affect African American and Hispanic students on standardized cognitive ability tests, women MBA students on negotiation tasks, and White men's athletic performance (see Steele et al., 2002, for a review). Thus, stereotype threat can be experienced by anyone working in a situation in which there is a negative stereotype about their group's performance and potential. Moreover, the negative effects of stereotype threat on performance have been found regardless of whether the individual believes the stereotype and regardless of the accuracy of the stereotype.

Stereotype threat is induced when an individual must work under conditions in which there is a fear of being treated and judged according to a negative stereotype about one's group. Because stereotype threat is context dependent, the context in which the task is being performed must bring to light the relevance of the stereotype. One factor that has been shown to reinforce the stereotype that an individual's group is not able to perform in a given context is a lack of members of this identity group working in the context. Research has demonstrated that working in a situation where an individual is in the demographic minority is a factor that leads to the experience of stereotype threat (Sekaquaptewa, Waldman, & Thompson, 2007). In a field study, Black managers who were the only member of their racial group in their work unit experienced greater levels of stereotype threat than those who worked with other Black managers (Roberson, Deitch, Brief, & Block, 2003). Another contextual factor that signals that a stereotype is being applied in a given context is the organization's cultural centeredness (Steele et al., 2002). Cultural centeredness of a setting refers to the extent to which a particular social identity is seen as normative (e.g., "central") for effective functioning in that setting. This is signaled through the diversity (or lack of diversity) of those in positions of power and whether in a given setting there is variance in the type of intellectual and leadership styles of those who are authorized. Stereotype threat is more likely to be experienced in a setting that is culturally centered for employees who do not share the favored social identity. Thus, being in the demographic minority in a culturally centered organization is likely to lead to the experience of stereotype threat. Unfortunately, this is likely to be a common experience for many people of color in the workplace (Roberson & Kulik, 2007). These conditions that lead to stereotype threat are further exacerbated by a CBRI in which racial disparities in the workplace are attributed, by default, to deficits in internal traits of people of color because bias and discrimination of White organizational decision makers, and the differing sociocultural organizational contexts for members of different racial groups, are ignored.

Stereotype threat can be considered a chronic condition within which individuals must manage their careers (Block, Koch, Liberman, Merriweather, & Roberson, 2011; Kalokerinos, von Hippel, & Zacher, 2014). In the workplace, stereotype threat has been shown to not only affect performance but also to lead to more negative job attitudes (Roberson et al., 2003; von Hippel, Issa, Ma, & Stokes, 2011), increased turnover intentions (von Hippel et al., 2011), greater discounting of feedback (Roberson et al., 2003) and more time spent indirectly monitoring one's own performance (Roberson et al., 2003). Thus, stereotype threat is something that employees of color must contend with over the course of their careers. This threat is made more salient in color-blind organizations because only internal traits could be responsible for structural disparities.

COUNTERING CBRI IN ORGANIZATIONAL SETTINGS: CULTIVATING AN AWARENESS OF DIVERSITY DYNAMICS

Unfortunately, the dominant diversity philosophy that is espoused in most U.S. organizations is characterized by color blindness stressing equal opportunities due to adherence to meritocratic principles (Stevens, Plaut, & Sanchez-Burks, 2008). According to DiTomaso (2010), holding a color-blind diversity philosophy can function as "a political resource for groups who are privileged in terms of power, status, and/or numbers, as has happened in the post-civil rights period" (p. 103). This color-blind racial ideology leads individuals to interpret racial disparities in the workplace as due to individual characteristics of employees rather than other factors, such as biased decision makers and structural inequalities in the workplace. Thus, color blindness in the workplace is about being unaware of diversity dynamics that exist. Ignored are the environmental factors that give rise to the meaning of diversity in a given context. Ignored are the effects of stereotyping and bias that impact important personnel decisions. So CBRI does not reduce prejudice or stereotyping; in fact, it creates the perfect conditions for White people to remain unaware of how diversity dynamics operate in contexts of power imbalances and for people of color to experience stereotype threat.

Although espoused as an alternative to a CBRI, multiculturalism is not likely to be an effective philosophy for improving existing racial disparities in the workplace either. In organizational settings, a multicultural philosophy focuses on valuing employees' cultural differences (Stevens et al., 2008). This philosophy is enacted through diversity awareness events that highlight the value of different cultures (e.g., Black history month) and the creation of affinity groups, mentoring programs, and other programs that focus on people of color (Purdie-Vaughns & Walton, 2011). These types of programs may add value and acknowledge diversity, but they are usually silent as to the systems that create and maintain these disparities. A multicultural diversity philosophy targets diversity as something that individuals have, rather than something that is given meaning by the system. Multiculturalism focuses primarily on seeing differences at the individual level but does nothing to counter the systemic issues that result in these disparities. In fact, White employees can endorse multiculturalism, seeing and valuing differences across racial groups, and still benefit from the privileges that are associated with being White in the workplace (DiTomaso, 2010). Thus, many Whites may believe themselves to be outside of this issue and absent of blame because they are multicultural but fail to see the way they benefit from these structural relations on a daily basis at work.

Multicultural practices in organizations may also have ill-intended effects for employees of color. Within-racial group differences are ignored, resulting in greater stereotyping by Whites and a much less complex understanding or the meaning of racial group membership. A multicultural diversity philosophy that focuses on seeing differences across racial groups has the unintended effect of leading to the assumption that all individuals in a given racial group are homogenous. Individuals with intersectional identities become invisible (Purdie-Vaughns & Walton, 2011). Also ignored are within-racial group differences in how individuals of color contend with stereotype threat. Block et al. (2011) discussed three response patterns that individuals may have when contending with stereotype threat over the course of their careers: *fending off the stereotype*—demonstrating that the stereotype is not self-relevant; *discouraged by the stereotype*—distancing oneself from the stereotype threatening context; and *resilient to the stereotype*—redirecting their energy to taking care of themselves and other members of their social identity group in a stereotype-threatening context. Thus, an individual who is fending off the stereotype may respond to stereotype threat by overefforting, making internal attributions for failure to achieve one's goals, and attempting to distance oneself from the devalued identity. An individual who is discouraged by the stereotype may disengage and withdraw from the workplace, distancing oneself from the threatening context and making external attributions for failure to achieve one's goals. An individual who is resilient to the stereotype may respond by challenging the negative stereotypes, via pointing out positive distinctiveness of one's group, promoting collective action, and redefining the criteria for success. A multicultural diversity philosophy that focuses on highlighting cultural differences between racial groups is likely to obscure critical differences within racial groups of how employees are responding to stereotype threat. This results in diversity practices that may well do more harm than good. For example, an affinity group that is designed to bring together employees of color may be appreciated by individuals who are discouraged by the stereotype while alienating individuals who are fending off the stereotype. Thus, both color-blind and multicultural practices in organizational settings create the conditions to enhance stereotyping of people of color and allow for the maintenance of systems that differentially advantage and disadvantage employees.

To improve racial disparities in the workplace, we need to cultivate awareness of diversity dynamics in organizations. We need to cultivate *bias awareness* about the role that stereotyping and discrimination by organizational decision makers plays in the career outcomes experienced by people of color. We need to cultivate *power and privilege awareness* about the systemic inequities that result from a sociocultural organizational context that differentially advantages and disadvantages members' of different racial groups. Finally, we need to cultivate *an awareness of how these diversity dynamics are differentially experienced by people of color* so that White individuals have a more complex understanding of the experience of race as something that varies not only between racial groups but also within racial groups. In support of the importance of awareness of diversity dynamics, Liberman, Block, and Koch (2011) found that White people were only seen as effective in diversity roles when they understood the dynamics of institutional racism. Roberson and Kulik (2007) pointed out the benefits for people of color of having managers who are able to discuss the influence of racial stereotypes in the workplace. For executives of color, having an early career mentor who could discuss racial dynamics in the workplace was predictive of later career success (Thomas, 2001).

As long as racial disparities continue to persist in the workplace, these disparities will provide the context for employees to understand the meaning of racial group membership in these settings. To break the cycle of persistent disparities across racial groups in the workplace, we must increase the literacy of organizational members about the diversity dynamics that contribute to these existing disparities. Without this understanding, white organizational members will continue to attribute these disparities to deficits in employees of color, leading to stereotype threat, another barrier that must be navigated. If we continue to remain unaware of diversity dynamics in the workplace and focus on diversity as something that individuals do (or do not) have, we are at risk of seeing individuals as the cause of these disparities, perpetuating these existing inequalities. Whether individuals are color-blind (and do not see race) or multicultural (and see race in terms of individual differences) does not change this troubling reality. Diversity dynamics characterize a system, not an individual. Awareness of these dynamics is critical to breaking this cycle.

REFERENCES

Alliance for Board Diversity. (2011). Missing pieces: Women and minorities on Fortune 500 Boards. *2010 Alliance for Board Diversity Census*. Retrieved from http://theabd.org/2012_ABD%20Missing_Pieces_Final_8_15_13.pdf

Baldi, S., & McBrier, D. B. (1997). Do the determinants of promotion differ for Blacks and Whites? Evidence from the U.S. labor market. *Work and Occupations, 24*, 478–497. http://dx.doi.org/10.1177/0730888497024004005

Bendick, M., Jackson, C. W., & Reinoso, V. A. (1994). Measuring employment discrimination through controlled experiments. *The Review of Black Political Economy, 23*, 25–48. http://dx.doi.org/10.1007/BF02895739

Bertrand, M., & Mullainathan, S. (2004). Are Emily and Greg more employable than Lakisha and Jamal? A field-experiment on labor market discrimination. *The American Economic Review, 94*, 991–1013. http://dx.doi.org/10.1257/0002828042002561

Block, C. J., Aumann, K., & Chelin, A. (2012). Assessing stereotypes of Black and White managers: A diagnostic ratio approach. *Journal of Applied Social Psychology, 42*(Suppl. 1), E128–E149. http://dx.doi.org/10.1111/j.1559-1816.2012.01014.x

Block, C. J., Koch, S. M., Liberman, B. E., Merriweather, T. J., & Roberson, L. (2011). Contending with stereotype threat at work: A model of long-term responses. *The Counseling Psychologist, 39*, 570–600. http://dx.doi.org/10.1177/0011000010382459

Bureau of Labor Statistics. (2010). *The editor's desk: Earnings and employment by occupation, race, ethnicity, and sex*. U.S. Department of Labor. Retrieved from http://www.bls.gov/opub/ted/2011/ted_20110914.htm

Campbell, J. P. (1996). Group differences and personnel decisions: Validity, fairness, and affirmative action. *Journal of Vocational Behavior, 49*, 122–158. http://dx.doi.org/10.1006/jvbe.1996.0038

Chen, C. C., & DiTomaso, N. (1996). Performance appraisal and demographic diversity: Issues regarding appraisals, appraisers, and appraising. In E. E. Kossek & S. A. Lobel (Eds.), *Managing diversity: Human resource strategies for transforming the workplace* (pp. 137–163). Oxford, England: Blackwell.

Chung-Herrera, B. G., & Lankau, M. J. (2005). Are we there yet? An assessment of fit between stereotypes of minority managers and the successful-manager prototype. *Journal of Applied Social Psychology, 35*, 2029–2056. http://dx.doi.org/10.1111/j.1559-1816.2005.tb02208.x

DiTomaso, N. (2010). A sociocultural framework on diversity requires structure as well as culture and social psychology. *Psychological Inquiry, 21*, 100–107. http://dx.doi.org/10.1080/1047840X.2010.483570

DiTomaso, N. (2013). *The American non-dilemma: Racial inequality without racism*. New York, NY: Russell Sage Foundation.

DiversityInc (2015, January 29). McDonald's CEO to retire; Black Fortune 500 CEOs decline by 33% in past year. Retrieved from http://www.diversityinc.com/leadership/mcdonalds-ceo-retire-black-fortune-500-ceos-decline-33-past-year/

Elvira, M. M., & Zatick, C. D. (2002). Who's displaced first? The role of race in layoff decisions. *Industrial Relations, 41*, 329–361.

Gottfredson, L. (1986). Societal consequences of the *g* factor in employment. *Journal of Vocational Behavior, 29*, 379–410. http://dx.doi.org/10.1016/0001-8791(86)90015-1

Graham, S. (1994). Motivation in African Americans. *Review of Educational Research, 64*, 55–117. http://dx.doi.org/10.3102/00346543064001055

Greenhaus, J. H., & Parasuraman, S. (1993). Job performance attributions and career advancement prospects: An examination of gender and race effects. *Organizational Behavior and Human Decision Processes, 55*, 273–297. http://dx.doi.org/10.1006/obhd.1993.1034

Hartigan, J. A., & Wigdor, A. K. (Eds.). (1989). *Fairness in employment testing: Validity generalization, minority issues, and the General Aptitude Test Battery*. Washington, DC: National Academy Press. http://dx.doi.org/10.1126/science.2740906

Hirschman, C., & Snipp, M. (2001). The state of the American dream: Race and ethnic socioeconomic inequality in the United States, 1970–1990. In D. B. Grusky (Ed.), *Social stratification* (pp. 623–642). Boulder, CO: Westview.

Ibarra, H. (1995). Race, opportunity, and diversity of social circles in managerial networks. *Academy of Management Journal, 38*, 673–703. http://dx.doi.org/10.2307/256742

Kalokerinos, E. K., von Hippel, C., & Zacher, H. (2014). Is stereotype threat a useful construct for organizational psychology research and practice? *Industrial and Organizational Psychology: Perspectives on Science and Practice, 7*, 381–402. http://dx.doi.org/10.1111/iops.12167

Kim, C., & Sakamoto, A. (2010). Have Asian American men achieved labor market parity with White men? *American Sociological Review, 75*, 934–957. http://dx.doi.org/10.1177/0003122410388501

Liberman, B. E., Block, C. J., & Koch, S. M. (2011). Diversity trainer preconceptions: The effects of trainer race and gender on perceptions of diversity trainer effectiveness. *Basic and Applied Social Psychology, 33*, 279–293. http://dx.doi.org/10.1080/01973533.2011.589327

Mehra, A., Kilduff, M., & Brass, D. J. (1998). At the margins: A distinctiveness approach to the social identity and social networks of underrepresented groups. *Academy of Management Journal, 41*, 441–452. http://dx.doi.org/10.2307/257083

Mueller, C. W., Parcel, T. L., & Tanaka, K. (1989). Particularism in authority outcomes of Black and White supervisors. *Social Science Research, 18*, 1–20. http://dx.doi.org/10.1016/0049-089X(89)90001-X

Neville, H. A., Awad, G. H., Brooks, J. E., Flores, M. P., & Bluemel, J. (2013). Color-blind racial ideology: Theory, training, and measurement implications in psychology. *American Psychologist, 68,* 455–466. http://dx.doi.org/10.1037/a0033282

Pager, D. (2007). The use of field experiments for studies of employment discrimination: Contributions, critiques, and directions for the future. *Annals of the American Academy of Political and Social Science, 609,* 104–133. http://dx.doi.org/10.1177/0002716206294796

Pager, D., & Shepherd, H. (2008). The sociology of discrimination: Racial discrimination in employment, housing, credit, and consumer markets. *Annual Review of Sociology, 34,* 181–209. http://dx.doi.org/10.1146/annurev.soc.33.040406.131740

Purdie-Vaughns, V., & Walton, G. (2011). Is multiculturalism bad for Black Americans? In R. Mallett & L. Tropp (Eds.), *Beyond prejudice reduction: Pathways to positive intergroup relations* (pp. 159–177). Washington, DC: American Psychological Association. http://dx.doi.org/10.1037/12319-008

Roberson, L., & Block, C. J. (2001). Explaining racioethnic group differences in performance and related outcomes: A review of theoretical perspectives. In B. Staw & R. Sutton (Eds.), *Research in organizational behavior* (pp. 247–326). Greenwich, CT: JAI Press.

Roberson, L., Deitch, E., Brief, A. P., & Block, C. J. (2003). Stereotype threat and feedback seeking in the workplace. *Journal of Vocational Behavior, 62,* 176–188. http://dx.doi.org/10.1016/S0001-8791(02)00056-8

Roberson, L., & Kulik, C. T. (2007). Stereotype threat at work. *The Academy of Management Perspectives, 21,* 24–40. http://dx.doi.org/10.5465/AMP.2007.25356510

Rosette, A. S., Leonardelli, G. J., & Phillips, K. W. (2008). The White standard: Racial bias in leader categorization. *Journal of Applied Psychology, 93,* 758–777. http://dx.doi.org/10.1037/0021-9010.93.4.758

Sackett, P. R., & DuBois, C. L. Z. (1991). Rater–ratee race effects on performance evaluation: Challenging meta-analytic conclusions. *Journal of Applied Psychology, 76,* 873–877. http://dx.doi.org/10.1037/0021-9010.76.6.873

Schmidt, F. L., Ones, D. S., & Hunter, J. E. (1992). Personnel selection. *Annual Review of Psychology, 43,* 627–670. http://dx.doi.org/10.1146/annurev.ps.43.020192.003211

Sekaquaptewa, D., Waldman, A., & Thompson, M. (2007). Solo status and self-construal: Being distinctive influences racial self-construal and performance apprehension in African American women. *Cultural Diversity and Ethnic Minority Psychology, 13,* 321–327. http://dx.doi.org/10.1037/1099-9809.13.4.321

Smith, R. A. (2002). Race, gender, and authority in the workplace: Theory and research. *Annual Review of Sociology, 28,* 509–542. http://dx.doi.org/10.1146/annurev.soc.28.110601.141048

Spalter-Roth, R., & Lowenthal, T. (2005). *Race, ethnicity, and the American labor market: What's at work?* (American Sociological Association Series on How Race and Ethnicity Matter). Retrieved from http://www.asanet.org/images/research/docs/pdf/RaceEthnicity_LaborMarket.pdf

Steele, C. M., Spencer, S. J., & Aronson, J. (2002). Contending with group image: The psychology of stereotype and social identity threat. *Advances in Experimental Social Psychology, 34*, 379–440.

Stevens, F. G., Plaut, V. C., & Sanchez-Burks, J. (2008). Unlocking the benefits of diversity: All-inclusive multiculturalism and positive organizational change. *Journal of Applied Behavioral Science, 44*, 116–133. http://dx.doi.org/10.1177/0021886308314460

Sy, T., Shore, L. M., Strauss, J., Shore, T. H., Tram, S., Whiteley, P., & Ikeda-Muromachi, K. (2010). Leadership perceptions as a function of race-occupation fit: The case of Asian Americans. *Journal of Applied Psychology, 95*, 902–919. http://dx.doi.org/10.1037/a0019501

Thomas, D. A. (2001). The truth about mentoring minorities. Race matters. *Harvard Business Review, 79*(4), 98–107, 168.

Thomas, D. A., & Alderfer, C. P. (1989). The influence of race on career dynamics: Theory and research on minority career experiences. In M. B. Arthur, D. T. Hall, & B. S. Lawrence (Eds.), *Handbook of career theory* (pp. 133–158). Cambridge, MA: Cambridge University Press. http://dx.doi.org/10.1017/CBO9780511625459.009

Tomkiewicz, J., Brenner, O. C., & Adeyemi-Bello, T. (1998). The impact of perceptions and stereotypes on the managerial mobility of African Americans. *The Journal of Social Psychology, 138*, 88–92. http://dx.doi.org/10.1080/00224549809600356

U.S. Census Bureau. (2012). *Educational attainment in the United States: 2012*. Retrieved from http://www.census.gov/population/www/socdemo/educ-attn.html

U.S. Department of Labor, Bureau of Labor Statistics. (2012, September 5). Racial and ethnic characteristics of the U.S. labor force, 2011. *The Economics Daily*. Retrieved from http://www.bls.gov/opub/ted/2012/ted_20120905.htm

U.S. Department of Labor, Bureau of Labor Statistics. (2013, December 31). Forty-nine percent of employed Asians in management, professional, and related occupations, 2012. *The Economics Daily*. Retrieved from http://www.bls.gov/opub/ted/2013/ted_20131231.htm

von Hippel, C., Issa, M., Ma, R., & Stokes, A. (2011). Stereotype threat: Antecedents and consequences for working women. *European Journal of Social Psychology, 41*, 151–161.

15

IDENTITY MANAGEMENT STRATEGIES IN WORKPLACES WITH COLOR-BLIND DIVERSITY POLICIES

MARGARET SHIH AND MAIA J YOUNG

Allowing employees equal access and opportunities and leveling the playing field for individuals from different backgrounds can be a concern for many organizations. Whether organizational leaders are focused on creating a meritocratic work environment because they think it is morally right or whether they are avoiding negative consequences of unfairness such as lower employee motivation (e.g., Lawler & O'Gara, 1967), increased organizational distrust (Colquitt, Conlon, Wesson, Porter, & Ng, 2001), and backlash in the form of theft and litigation (Greenberg, 1990), many leaders will adopt formal diversity policies to guide decisions in hiring, retention, promotion, and compensation.

Diversity policies differ in the extent to which they acknowledge group differences. Color-blind racial policies emphasize an overarching organizational identity and ignore differences in race, culture, and ethnicity (Stevens,

http://dx.doi.org/10.1037/14754-016

The Myth of Racial Color Blindness: Manifestations, Dynamics, and Impact, H. A. Neville, M. E. Gallardo, and D. W. Sue (Editors)

Plaut, & Sanchez-Burks, 2008). An organization might adopt color-blind racial policies based on an ideology that either denies that racial differences exist (*color evasion*) or, relatedly, denies that racial inequality exists (*power evasion*; Neville, Awad, Brooks, Flores, & Bluemel, 2013). Scholars have also used the terms *gender-blind* and *sex-blind* to refer to the analogous concept of blindness with regard to gender, and we draw on the research in this area as well. We recognize that there are significant differences between gender and race, but there are also some shared experiences stemming from being a member of a disadvantaged group. We focus on these shared experiences. Thus, we use the term *color-blind organization* to refer to one that attempts not to recognize any differences in identity such as gender, culture, age, or disability.

Multicultural policies, in contrast, acknowledge and celebrate group differences as valuable assets and encourage individuals to learn about and accept differences among groups (Gutiérrez & Unzueta, 2010). Multicultural initiatives include activities such as having mentoring groups, seminars, fairs, and workshops for underrepresented minorities (Stevens et al., 2008). Because multicultural policies approach diversity from a different lens—one that acknowledges differences among groups and the potential for differential treatment—multicultural organizations face a different set of challenges than do color-blind organizations.

Organizations adopting a color-blind approach to race hope to eliminate bias by ignoring group differences and treating all members of the organization the same. That is, they attempt to judge all members by the same standard. What these organizations often fail to recognize, however, is that organizational standards for desirable and rewarded behavior are often based on dominant group norms and that these norms set the standards for employee actions, perceptions, and judgments.

Women and minorities may be implicitly or explicitly expected to assimilate to these norms to advance in the organization. For instance, networking is crucial for career advancement (Wolff & Moser, 2009). However, traditional networking behaviors may be based on dominant group (i.e., White male) norms. Female employees may be expected to adopt behaviors that may not come naturally to women, such as bonding over "beers and sports." Similarly, minority employees may be expected to drop their cultural customs and learn American norms of politeness, such as friendly hugs or boastful self-promotion, which may create some discomfort. Because women and minorities are expected to assimilate, the playing field is not equal for all individuals in racially color-blind workplaces.

Color-blind organizations also fail to recognize that not only are these expected behaviors based on dominant group norms but evaluation standards are as well. Research has found that individuals who fit a prototype (e.g., business leader) are evaluated more favorably for the same behaviors and outcomes than those who do not fit the prototype. For instance, leadership categorization theory finds that people who possess prototypical characteristics of a leader are appraised more favorably than individuals who do not possess prototypical characteristics of a leader (Lord & Maher, 1991). "Being White" is considered a prototypical characteristic of business leaders, and White leaders are evaluated more favorably than racial minority leaders for the same behaviors and outcomes (Rosette, Leonardelli, & Phillips, 2008). Similarly, people are more likely to think of a man than a woman when they think of a successful leader (Schein, 1973). This tendency to think of men as being more prototypical leaders may be due to the stereotype of men as agentic and mastery-oriented versus interpersonal and communally oriented (Abele, 2003). In fact, the same behavior that is status-enhancing for men, such as showing disapproval and anger, is status-diminishing for women (Brescoll & Uhlmann, 2008). Thus, women and minorities who do not fit the prototype based on dominant group norms in the workplace may find themselves at a disadvantage when being evaluated. Moreover, these biases in judgment occur automatically, outside of awareness or intention, making them difficult to identify and correct.

Not only are biased judgments difficult to identify, but biased behaviors are as well. Harmful behaviors such as microaggressions (Sue, 2010) are often enacted through subtle behaviors and are ambiguous in their intent to harm (Hebl, Foster, Mannix, & Dovidio, 2002). *Microaggressions* are "brief and commonplace daily verbal, behavioral or environmental indignities, whether intentional or unintentional, that communicate hostile, derogatory or negative racial slights and insults" (Sue et al., 2007, p. 271) targeting a person or group. Examples of microaggression may be mistaking a person of color for a service worker, implying that people of color are servants (Sue et al., 2007). The subtlety of these behaviors makes it difficult to identify definitively whether this treatment is the result of prejudice based on group membership (Crocker & Major, 1989).

Color-blind approaches fail to correct for subtle, unintentional, and automatic biases that harm members of disadvantaged groups. In fact, research has found that greater racial bias is associated with color-blind approaches than multicultural approaches (Richeson & Nussbaum, 2004). Moreover, minority members distrust a color-blind approach to race because they perceive them to be exclusionary (Purdie-Vaughns, Steele, Davies, Ditlmann, & Crosby, 2008). In this chapter, we (a) explore the challenges of addressing discrimination in racially color-blind workplaces, (b) discuss the identity management strategies that minorities can use to help cope with discrimination, and (c) identify the challenges, benefits, and costs associated with using identity management strategies.

CHALLENGES IN ADDRESSING DISCRIMINATION IN COLOR-BLIND WORKPLACES

Color-blind racial policies are meant to eliminate discrimination, but they do not (Neville et al., 2013). Ironically, these policies actually make it harder for the person suffering from biased treatment to discuss it with employers. These policies create an erroneous narrative in which employers can tell themselves that by treating everybody the same way, they have eliminated bias in their organization. This narrative makes it difficult for minority employees to bring attention to actual experiences of discrimination and to get the employer to recognize that bias exists in the organization.

There are several reasons minority employees may have a more difficult time in color-blind organizations than in multicultural organizations in getting their concerns addressed. First, individuals who bring attention to disparate treatment or outcomes based on group identity find that their claims are often met with denial. Organizational leaders might reason that if race is not recognized, then it is not possible for anybody be treated differently because of his or her race. A common line in response to a claim of racism might be, "I don't see race. Therefore, how can I treat you differently because of your race?" This denial places an additional burden on the employee. Rather than simply discussing discrimination, he or she must first educate the organization about the nature of prejudice and how these subtle processes disadvantage women and employees of color.

Second, by denying group identities, the color-blind racial policies also hinder constructive discussion about politically sensitive issues such as race or gender (American Psychological Association, Presidential Task Force on Preventing Discrimination and Promoting Diversity, 2012). For instance, when confronted with issues surrounding race, many White Americans adopt a color-blind approach in which they do not acknowledge race because they perceive that race is a taboo topic (Apfelbaum, Sommers, & Norton, 2008). Scholars attribute the reluctance to discuss politically controversial issues such as racism among White Americans to anxiety about appearing prejudiced (Apfelbaum et al., 2008; Sue, Rivera, Capodilupo, Lin, & Torino, 2010) and discomfort at the potential of learning about one's own implicit biases and guilt at learning how people of color have been treated in the United States (Sue et al., 2007).

By discouraging deep discussion about social identity issues and discouraging employees from bringing up experiences of bias, color-blind policies contribute to the perpetuation of the illusion that prejudice does not exist within the organization. One of the consequences of this illusion is that organizations adopting color-blind policies neglect their legal responsibility to address discrimination and unjustly shift the burden on targets to navigate and manage their experiences.

By discussing coping strategies that minority employees may adopt, we do not mean to imply that the burden of dealing with prejudice should rest on the shoulders of the targets. There are many things that color-blind workplaces can do to improve the environment for minority employees. If organizations are open to the possibility that discrimination exists, they can implement measures such as establishing safe channels of communication for individuals to report bias and educating managers and human resource professionals about the nature of prejudice.

IDENTITY MANAGEMENT STRATEGIES

To cope with disparate treatment, minority employees can use identity management strategies in the workplace. Individuals can manage their identities by changing (a) their identification with a particular group (i.e., identity switching) or (b) the stereotypes associated with the identities (i.e., identity redefinition; Shih, Young, & Bucher, 2013). Identity switching changes the emphasis among an individual's multiple social identities while keeping the stereotypes associated with those identities constant. Identity redefinition keeps the identity constant but attempts to change the stereotypes.

Identity Switching

One type of identity management that individuals may use to mitigate many negative consequences of prejudiced treatment is to switch among their different social identities. In identity switching, individuals place different emphases on their various distinct identities, depending on how beneficial each identity is in a particular situation (Pittinsky, Shih, & Ambady, 1999). Identity switching consists of two component processes: *deemphasizing a negatively valued identity* and *emphasizing or replacing a negative identity with a positively regarded identity*.

Deemphasizing a Negatively Valued Identity

To switch one's identity, one must first deemphasize a negatively valued target identity. Minority employees can deemphasize a disadvantageous identity by using different methods, including concealing the identity, using "disidentifiers" (i.e., identity cues), and keeping the identity in the background (i.e., discretion). For instance, gay men conceal their sexual orientation by not talking about their personal lives at work when they feel that revealing their sexual orientation could expose them to unfair treatment there (Clair, Beatty, & MacLean, 2005).

Recategorizing With a Positively Valued Identity

The second component process in the identity switching strategy, identity recategorization, is to replace the negatively valued identity with a more positively valued one. For instance, an Asian female scientist might emphasize her Asian identity by choosing to highlight her last name an e-mail username because the Asian identity is stereotypically associated with mathematic and scientific aptitude (Shih, Pittinsky, & Ambady, 1999; Shih, Pittinsky, & Trahan, 2006). An African American Harvard student might emphasize his racial identity in a basketball game because the African American identity is stereotypically associated with being athletic, whereas the Harvard identity is not.

Identity Regeneration

Redefining the target identity is a second identity management strategy target individuals can use. Individuals can redefine their identities through two processes: (a) *stereotype reassociation* (i.e., changing the stereotypes associated with an identity) and (b) *stereotype regeneration* (i.e., changing the meaning of the stereotypes associated with the identity).

In *stereotype reassociation*, individuals may disassociate their identities from negative stereotypes and strengthen their association with positive stereotypes. Older workers may counteract ageism by emphasizing positive traits associated with older workers such as loyalty and having more experience (Berger, 2009). African American students might emphasize their intelligence and resilience.

In *stereotype regeneration*, individuals might also redefine the traits or behaviors associated with a negatively stereotyped identity. For instance, funeral directors can redefine their identity from being someone who does dirty or taboo work (Ashforth, Kreiner, Clark, & Fugate, 2007) by thinking of themselves as specialists who help people deal with grief rather than individuals who profit from others' losses (Thompson, 1991).

The ability for a person to implement these two types of strategies and the effectiveness of these two strategies for minority employees may depend on the diversity policies adopted in the organization.

IDENTITY MANAGEMENT STRATEGIES IN COLOR-BLIND ORGANIZATIONS

Organizations that take a color-blind approach to race focus on an overarching shared identity, such as emphasizing the organizational identity, a task identity, or a superordinate identity (e.g., being a human being) over other group identities (Stevens et al., 2008). As a consequence, characteristics closely associated with individual group identities (e.g., different cultural norms or languages spoken) are deemphasized. In other words, color-blind organizations externally define an identity for their members (e.g., "you are all human beings," "you are all members of our organization") and discourage recognition of different social identities among their members. The goal of this approach is to treat all individuals equally (Plaut, 2002).

However, by forcing an identity on and deemphasizing differences among their members, organizations adopting a color-blind approach make it difficult for targets to negotiate among their different social identities. Because different identities are not recognized, employees in workplaces using a color-blind approach may find it difficult, if not impossible, to implement identity switching strategy.

Some might argue that identity switching might be more likely to occur in color-blind workplaces because they highlight cues that are already associated with the advantaged identity. However, by adopting a color-blind racial policy, the organization is forcing the individual to deemphasize his or her individual identities and to highlight his or her overarching shared identity, and thus such behavior is not self-initiated by the individual. This forced identification makes it difficult for the individual to switch to other beneficial identities that may not be shared. Because cues associated with unshared identities are not recognized and are even discouraged, the individual may not derive any benefits from highlighting unshared identities. As a consequence, minority employees in color-blind organizations may need to rely more heavily on identity redefinition strategies.

Color-blind organizations may be more receptive to identity redefinition strategies than multicultural organizations. Researchers have found that while stereotypical minority members are viewed more positively in multicultural contexts, counterstereotypical minority members are viewed positively in color-blind contexts (Gutiérrez & Unzueta, 2010). Thus, organizations adopting color-blind racial policies may be more receptive to counterstereotypical minority members because it reinforces their implicit belief that group differences are irrelevant and do not reflect any important aspects of a person.

At the same time, minority employees may also be constrained in how they use identity regeneration strategies in color-blind workplaces. Social identities are not explicitly recognized, and thus employees cannot try to redefine their identities through blatant, explicit arguments (e.g., boldly declaring a stereotype to be false). Explicitly calling attention to social identities that are not shared may not be well received. Thus, only implicit methods used to redefine disadvantaged identities (e.g., subtle use of identity cues) may be effective.

In addition, the frequency and intensity of identity regeneration efforts cannot be too high. Individuals, who highlight unshared identities too much, even through subtle cues, may find that their attempts can backfire. Highlighting unshared identities more than shared ones might alienate coworkers and lead them to question targets' commitment and identification to the organization. However, engaging in identity regeneration efforts with too little intensity would make these efforts ineffective.

BENEFITS

There are several benefits to the individual and the organization in using identity management strategies. The use of identity management strategies can help individuals control how they experience discrimination in the organization.

Protecting Self-Esteem

One set of benefits for the individual is that identity regeneration can help to protect his or her self-esteem from the identity threats. According to self-affirmation theory, after receiving negative feedback, people can protect their self-esteem by downplaying their failures and emphasizing their successes in other domains (Steele, 1988). Redefining an identity by downplaying negative stereotypes and emphasizing positive one can also help highly identified target individuals to protect their self-esteem.

Raising Esteem for the Identity Group

Redefining the identity can also help raise esteem for the identity group in the eyes of others in the organization. By redefining the negatively viewed group in terms of its advantages and skills, the highly identified individual both downplays the negative aspects of the group and alerts others to the strengths of the group. This can lead to better psychological outcomes (Steele, 1988).

Improving Performance Outcomes

Redefining an identity could also potentially help performance outcomes for the target. Research has found that changing the stereotypes associated with an identity could improve performance on negotiation tasks. Kray, Galinsky, and Thompson (2002) found that women are generally not stereotyped to be strong negotiators and underperform on negotiation tasks relative to men. However, when the stereotype associated with women and negotiation was changed and women were taught to think of women as skilled negotiators, they would outperform men on negotiation tasks. Thus, changing the negative stereotypes to positive stereotypes can have positive performance outcomes.

Increasing Comfort in Intergroup Interactions

The use of identity management strategies may also provide some benefits to individuals in terms of guiding and increasing comfort levels in interpersonal interactions. Identity cues may provide interaction partners with clues as to which script they can use when interacting with somebody from another group. For instance, research on interracial interactions find that White participants often feel discomfort in interacting with Black interaction partners. Some of this discomfort comes from not knowing how to behave and the potential of unintentionally appearing prejudiced or offending their partner. However, research has found that providing White participants with behavioral scripts to guide them in the interracial interaction reduced anxiety in such interactions (Avery, Richeson, Hebl, & Ambady, 2009).

Reducing anxiety in intergroup interactions can also benefit performance. Research on intergroup interactions has found that White individuals interacting with Black partners monitor their behaviors to appear unprejudiced (Vorauer & Kumhyr, 2001). This monitoring in turn depletes mental resources and lowers performance on cognitive tasks (Richeson & Shelton, 2007).

However, it is important to note that the use of identity management strategies can only smooth out interactions that occur at the superficial level. Because color-blind racial policies hinder substantive discussions about group identity issues, identity management strategies cannot improve deeper and more meaningful relationships and interactions.

COSTS

Although there are benefits to using identity management strategies, there are also several costs to the individual for using these strategies. Thus, minority individuals need to make trade-offs when they use identity management strategies. Following are some of those potential costs.

Backlash Effects

Although counterstereotypical targets are liked more than stereotypical targets in color-blind racial contexts (Gutiérrez & Unzueta, 2010), this difference may depend on whether the stereotypes are descriptive or prescriptive. *Descriptive* stereotypes describe how members "are" (e.g., African Americans are athletic), and *prescriptive* stereotypes describe how members of a group "should be" (e.g., women should be warm and nurturing). Disconfirming descriptive stereotypes may lead to greater liking, but disconfirming prescriptive stereotypes may lead to lower liking (i.e., backlash effects). Thus, an employee engaging in identity redefinition efforts by emphasizing that she possesses counterstereotypical traits may suffer backlash from being a counterstereotypical group member (Phelan & Rudman, 2010).

Missing Important Feedback

Another negative consequence of identity redefinition is that it may allow targets to ignore important information. By constantly deemphasizing negative information and focusing on positive information, individuals face the danger of missing important feedback.

Double Bind

Another potential pitfall associated with using identity regeneration is the double bind. Employees who are able to redefine the disadvantaged identity at the individual level and replace stereotypes associated with incompetence with more competent stereotypes may be penalized in other dimensions, such as warmth. Professional women who are highly successful need to behave in assertive, agentic, and self-promotional ways to be able to succeed. However, although these women may be perceived as more competent, they also pay a penalty for this perception in terms of being perceived as less likeable (Rudman & Glick, 2001).

Alienation From the Group

There may be long-term harmful consequences associated with identity redefinition. One potential consequence of consistent efforts to redefine one's social identity group is disidentification with the group. As individuals try to redefine the negative stereotypes associated with their identities, they may choose to avoid activities or locations that are stereotype consistent. This avoidance may also deprive targets of the positive effects related to social identification, such as access to social support networks. Losing access to social support networks would deprive the individual of important resources such as emotional support.

Costs to the Organization

Organizations may also bear some costs when employees use identity management strategies. When employees try to redefine their unshared distinct social identities to more closely resemble shared identities, one of the most obvious costs to organizations is the loss of diversity in perspectives, and such diversity is key to avoidance of decision-making biases that lead to suboptimal decision processes and outcomes in organizations, such as groupthink or the overconfidence bias.

CONCLUSION

Although companies may adopt color-blind approaches to race to eliminate discrimination, doing so can, ironically, make life harder for employees who belong to minority groups. Minority employees can use two types of identity management strategies to manage discrimination: identity switching and identity regeneration. However, the use of these strategies comes with costs, which must be weighed against the benefits.

REFERENCES

Abele, A. E. (2003). The dynamics of masculine-agentic and feminine-communal traits: Findings from a prospective study. *Journal of Personality and Social Psychology*, 85, 768–776. http://dx.doi.org/10.1037/0022-3514.85.4.768

American Psychological Association, Presidential Task Force on Preventing Discrimination and Promoting Diversity. (2012). *Dual pathways to a better America: Preventing discrimination and promoting diversity*. Washington, DC: American Psychological Association.

Apfelbaum, E. P., Sommers, S. R., & Norton, M. I. (2008). Seeing race and seeming racist? Evaluating strategic color blindness in social interaction. *Journal of Personality and Social Psychology*, 95, 918–932. http://dx.doi.org/10.1037/a0011990

Ashforth, B. E., Kreiner, G. E., Clark, M. A., & Fugate, M. (2007). Normalizing dirty work: Managerial tactics for countering occupational taint. *Academy of Management Journal*, 50, 149–174. http://dx.doi.org/10.5465/AMJ.2007.24162092

Avery, D. R., Richeson, J. A., Hebl, M. R., & Ambady, N. (2009). It does not have to be uncomfortable: The role of behavioral scripts in Black–White interracial interactions. *Journal of Applied Psychology*, 94, 1382–1393. http://dx.doi.org/10.1037/a0016208

Berger, E. D. (2009). Managing age discrimination: An examination of the techniques used when seeking employment. *The Gerontologist*, 49, 317–332. http://dx.doi.org/10.1093/geront/gnp031

Brescoll, V. L., & Uhlmann, E. L. (2008). Can an angry woman get ahead? Status conferral, gender, and expression of emotion in the workplace. *Psychological Science*, 19, 268–275. http://dx.doi.org/10.1111/j.1467-9280.2008.02079.x

Clair, J. A., Beatty, J. E., & MacLean, T. L. (2005). Out of sight but not out of mind: Managing invisible social identities in the workplace. *The Academy of Management Review, 30,* 78–95. http://dx.doi.org/10.5465/AMR.2005.15281431

Colquitt, J. A., Conlon, D. E., Wesson, M. J., Porter, C. O. L. H., & Ng, K. Y. (2001). Justice at the millennium: A meta-analytic review of 25 years of organizational justice research. *Journal of Applied Psychology, 86,* 425–445. http://dx.doi.org/10.1037/0021-9010.86.3.425

Crocker, J., & Major, B. (1989). Social stigma and self-esteem: The self-protective properties of stigma. *Psychological Review, 96,* 608–630. http://dx.doi.org/10.1037/0033-295X.96.4.608

Greenberg, J. (1990). Employee theft as a reaction to underpayment inequity: The hidden cost of pay cuts. *Journal of Applied Psychology, 75,* 561–568. http://dx.doi.org/10.1037/0021-9010.75.5.561

Gutiérrez, A. S., & Unzueta, M. M. (2010). The effect of interethnic ideologies on the likability of stereotypic vs. counterstereotypic minority targets. *Journal of Experimental Social Psychology, 46,* 775–784. http://dx.doi.org/10.1016/j.jesp.2010.03.010

Hebl, M. R., Foster, J. B., Mannix, L. M., & Dovidio, J. F. (2002). Formal and interpersonal discrimination: A field study of bias toward homosexual applicants. *Personality and Social Psychology Bulletin, 28,* 815–825. http://dx.doi.org/10.1177/0146167202289010

Kray, L. J., Galinsky, A. D., & Thompson, L. (2002). Reversing the gender gap in negotiations: An exploration of stereotype regeneration. *Organizational Behavior and Human Decision Processes, 87,* 386–410. http://dx.doi.org/10.1006/obhd.2001.2979

Lawler, E. E., III, & O'Gara, P. W. (1967). Effects of inequity produced by underpayment on work output, work quality, and attitudes toward the work. *Journal of Applied Psychology, 51,* 403–410. http://dx.doi.org/10.1037/h0025096

Lord, R. G., & Maher, K. J. (1991). Cognitive theory in industrial and organizational psychology. In M. D. Dunnette, L. M. Hough, & H. C. Triandis (Eds.), *Handbook of industrial and organizational psychology* (Vol. 2, pp. 1–62). Sunnyvale, CA: Consulting Psychologists Press.

Neville, H. A., Awad, G. H., Brooks, J. E., Flores, M. P., & Bluemel, J. (2013). Color-blind racial ideology: Theory, training, and measurement implications in psychology. *American Psychologist, 68,* 455–466. http://dx.doi.org/10.1037/a0033282

Phelan, J. E., & Rudman, L. A. (2010). Reactions to ethnic deviance: The role of backlash in racial stereotype maintenance. *Journal of Personality and Social Psychology, 99,* 265–281. http://dx.doi.org/10.1037/a0018304

Pittinsky, T. L., Shih, M., & Ambady, N. (1999). Identity adaptiveness and affect across one's multiple identities. *Journal of Social Issues, 55,* 503–518. http://dx.doi.org/10.1111/0022-4537.00130

Plaut, V. C. (2002). Cultural models of diversity in America: The psychology of difference and inclusion. In R. A. Shweder, M. Minow, & H. R. Markus (Eds.), *Engaging cultural differences: The multicultural challenge in liberal democracies* (pp. 365–395). New York, NY: Russell Sage Foundation.

Purdie-Vaughns, V., Steele, C. M., Davies, P. G., Ditlmann, R., & Crosby, J. R. (2008). Social identity contingencies: How diversity cues signal threat or safety for African Americans in mainstream institutions. *Journal of Personality and Social Psychology, 94,* 615–630. http://dx.doi.org/10.1037/0022-3514.94.4.615

Richeson, J. A., & Nussbaum, R. J. (2004). The impact of multiculturalism versus color blindness on racial bias. *Journal of Experimental Social Psychology, 40,* 417–423. http://dx.doi.org/10.1016/j.jesp.2003.09.002

Richeson, J. A., & Shelton, J. N. (2007). Negotiating interracial interactions: Costs, consequences, and possibilities. *Current Directions in Psychological Science, 16,* 316–320. http://dx.doi.org/10.1111/j.1467-8721.2007.00528.x

Rosette, A. S., Leonardelli, G. J., & Phillips, K. W. (2008). The White standard: Racial bias in leader categorization. *Journal of Applied Psychology, 93,* 758–777. http://dx.doi.org/10.1037/0021-9010.93.4.758

Rudman, L. A., & Glick, P. (2001). Prescriptive gender stereotypes and backlash toward agentic women. *Journal of Social Issues, 57,* 743–762. http://dx.doi.org/10.1111/0022-4537.00239

Schein, V. E. (1973). The relationship between sex role stereotypes and requisite management characteristics. *Journal of Applied Psychology, 57,* 95–100. http://dx.doi.org/10.1037/h0037128

Shih, M., Pittinsky, T. L., & Ambady, N. (1999). Stereotype susceptibility: Identity salience and shifts in quantitative performance. *Psychological Science, 10,* 80–83. http://dx.doi.org/10.1111/1467-9280.00111

Shih, M., Pittinsky, T. L., & Trahan, A. (2006). Domain-specific effects of stereotypes on performance. *Self and Identity, 5,* 1–14. http://dx.doi.org/10.1080/15298860500338534

Shih, M., Young, M., & Bucher, A. (2013). Working to reduce the effects of discrimination: Identity management strategies in organizations. *American Psychologist, 68,* 145–157. http://dx.doi.org/10.1037/a0032250

Steele, P. D. (1988). Employee assistance programs in context: An application of the constructive broker role. *Journal of Applied Behavioral Science, 24,* 365–382.

Stevens, F. G., Plaut, V. C., & Sanchez-Burks, J. (2008). Unlocking the benefits of diversity: All-inclusive multiculturalism and positive organizational change. *Journal of Applied Behavioral Science, 44,* 116–133. http://dx.doi.org/10.1177/0021886308314460

Sue, D. W. (2010). *Microaggressions in everyday life: Race, gender, and sexual orientation.* Hoboken, NJ: Wiley.

Sue, D. W., Capodilupo, C. M., Torino, G. C., Bucceri, J. M., Holder, A. M., Nadal, K. L., & Esquilin, M. (2007). Racial microaggressions in everyday life: Implications for clinical practice. *American Psychologist, 62,* 271–286. http://dx.doi.org/10.1037/0003-066X.62.4.271

Sue, D. W., Rivera, D. P., Capodilupo, C. M., Lin, A. I., & Torino, G. C. (2010). Racial dialogues and White trainee fears: Implications for education and training. *Cultural Diversity and Ethnic Minority Psychology, 16,* 206–214. http://dx.doi.org/10.1037/a0016112

Thompson, W. E. (1991). Handling the stigma of handling the dead: Morticians and funeral directors. *Deviant Behavior, 12,* 403–429. http://dx.doi.org/10.1080/01639625.1991.9967888

Vorauer, J. D., & Kumhyr, S. M. (2001). Is this about you or me? Self- versus other-directed judgments and feelings in response to intergroup interaction. *Personality and Social Psychology Bulletin, 27,* 706–719. http://dx.doi.org/10.1177/0146167201276006

Wolff, H. G., & Moser, K. (2009). Effects of networking on career success: A longitudinal study. *Journal of Applied Psychology, 94,* 196–206. http://dx.doi.org/10.1037/a0013350

16

RACIAL COLOR BLINDNESS AND BLACK–WHITE HEALTH CARE DISPARITIES

LOUIS A. PENNER AND JOHN F. DOVIDIO

The major question addressed in this chapter is whether racial color blindness, which refers to denying, minimizing, or attempting to ignore racial differences, can result in disparities in health care. Our core thesis is that racial color blindness can negatively affect the quality of health care received by Black, relative to White, patients by affecting the quality of medical interactions between Black patients and non-Black[1] physicians. We restrict our focus to Black–White disparities in health care in the United States because

The authors gratefully acknowledge the following sources of support for the research reported in and the writing of this chapter. The first author received support from a Eunice Kennedy Shriver National Institute of Child Health and Human Development Award (1R21HD050445001A1), a Society for Psychological Study of Social Issues Sages Award, and a National Cancer Institute Program Award (1U54CA153606-01) to T. Albrecht and R. Chapman. The second author received support from National Institutes of Health awards RO1HL 0856331-0182 and 1R01DA029888-01.

[1]Although most of the physicians who treat Black patients self-identify as White, a substantial minority self-identify their heritage as from a Latin, Middle Eastern, or Asian country. Therefore, we use the term *non-Black physicians*. All three groups show similar levels of anti-Black racial bias (Sabin, Nosek, Greenwald, & Rivara, 2009).

http://dx.doi.org/10.1037/14754-017
The Myth of Racial Color Blindness: Manifestations, Dynamics, and Impact, H. A. Neville, M. E. Gallardo, and D. W. Sue (Editors)

most of the empirical work on this topic has been concentrated in the U.S. and has primarily examined this particular form of racial bias. Although there are unique elements to different forms of racial or ethnic bias, they share many basic dynamics of intergroup bias. Thus, our arguments about the causes of health and health care disparities may generally apply to other racial/ethnic minorities in the U.S. and in many other countries around the world, where there are also well-documented racial and ethnic health and health care disparities (see Penner, Hagiwara, et al., 2013).

In this chapter, we first discuss the disparities between the general health of Blacks and Whites in the United States and between the quality of medical care each group receives. We then consider how patients' and physicians' racial attitudes influence critical aspects of the health care Black patients receive. Next, because there is limited evidence specifically about how racial color blindness shapes racially discordant medical encounters, we draw on the general research literature about how attempting to be color blind affects interracial interactions. This review focuses on color blindness as a general strategy used in interracial interactions rather than as an individual difference in racial ideology that exists more or less independently of the social context (see Neville, Awad, Brooks, Flores, & Bluemel, 2013). Finally, we use the findings from the research literature to suggest how attempts of physicians to be color blind can influence, and potentially adversely affect, health care for Black patients. We conclude by discussing implications for reducing health care disparities.

BLACK–WHITE DISPARITIES IN HEALTH AND HEALTH CARE

In the United States, Whites are healthier than Blacks (National Center for Health Statistics [NCHS], 2014; Smedley, Stith, & Nelson, 2003). Table 16.1 presents racial disparities in mortality rates in the United States in 2010 (the most recent year for which data available). As the table shows, Blacks have higher mortality rates than Whites. Mortality rates from the three leading causes of disease-related deaths are 15% to 27% higher for Blacks than for Whites. These kinds of disparities contribute to the average life expectancy for Blacks (75.1 years) being less than that for Whites (78.9 years), and Blacks being much more likely than Whites to experience a premature death (NCHS, 2014). Consistent with these findings, the percentage of Blacks who report that their health is only poor or fair (14.9%) is about 1.7 times as great as the percentage among Whites (8.8%; NCHS, 2014). The mortality statistics become more troubling when placed in a historical context. Not surprisingly, mortality rates among both Blacks and Whites have declined dramatically over the past half-century. However, the disparity in Black–White mortality rates has essentially remained the same over the past 60 years. In 1950,

TABLE 16.1
Racial Health Disparities in Mortality and Their Causes

Mortality rate	Blacks (n)	Whites (n)	Mortality ratio
Overall[a]	898.2	741.8	1:21
Infant[b]	4.1	1.7	2:41
For three most frequent causes of disease-related deaths[a]			
Heart disease	224.9	176.9	1:27
Coronary artery disease	131.2	113.5	1:15
Cancer	203.8	172.4	1:18

Note. Adapted from *Health, United States, 2013: With special feature on prescription drugs*, by National Center for Health Statistics, 2014, Hyattsville, MD: U.S. Government Printing Office. In the public domain.
[a]Annual rate/100,000 people. [b]Annual rate/1,000 live births.

the age-adjusted death rate per 100,000 people among Blacks was 1.22 times greater than the death rate among Whites; in 2010, the ratio was 1.21 times greater. Among men, the disparity in mortality rates has actually increased over this time period. Although health clearly improves for both Blacks and Whites as socioeconomic status (SES) increases, health disparities remain even at high income levels.

Obviously, part of the reason for racial mortality disparities is differences in the incidence or frequency of certain diseases. However, for many diseases, disparities in mortality rates are substantially greater than the differences in incidence rates. In the case of cancer, for example, Black women are about 10% to 12% less likely to develop breast cancer than White women, but they are about 35% more likely to die from this disease (National Cancer Institute, 2008).

Blacks and Whites may differ in their health for a variety of reasons. Members of different population groups potentially may differ in their susceptibility to some diseases and conditions because of genetic and related biological factors that vary across groups with different genetic heritages (e.g., Salami, Etukakpan, & Olapade-Olaopa, 2007). However, these differences may also occur as a consequence of social, political, or economic processes that produce different levels of exposure to environmental toxins or to social stressors (e.g., greater stress among Blacks due to the experience of discrimination; Penner & Hagiwara, 2014). In this chapter, we focus on a third social–political–economic cause of differences in the health of Blacks and Whites: systematic differences in the quality of health care members of each group typically receive—that is, health care disparities.

Black–White disparities in health care are typically the largest of any racial/ethnic health disparities (Penner, Hagiwara, et al., 2013; Smedley et al., 2003). The Agency for Healthcare Research and Quality (2012) provided a rough estimate of the extent to which Black patients experience health care disparities relative to White patients. Of the 191 measures of quality of care the agency looked at, Blacks received lower quality health care than Whites on 43% and better care on only 18%.

Racial disparities in health care range from quality of annual examinations to treatments for life-threatening diseases, and these effects are usually present even after controlling for patient differences in patient SES, access to insurance, and medically relevant variables (e.g., severity of disease, presence of other complicating diseases; Smedley et al., 2003). In a retrospective study that examined more than one million clinical visits for children with symptoms of various infections (e.g., ear or respiratory infections), Gerber, Prasad, et al. (2013) found that when pediatricians diagnosed an infection in a child, they were significantly less likely to give standard antibiotics to Black children than White children. A review of almost 800,000 hospital discharge records found that Blacks with peripheral arterial disease were 77% more likely than Whites to have the affected limb amputated (Durrazzo, Frencher, & Gusberg, 2013). A study of more than 15,000 patients seeking emergency treatment for chest pain found that Black patients were significantly less likely than White patients to receive pain medications and appropriate testing for causes (Venkat, Hoekstra, et al., 2003). There is also substantial evidence that, as a group, Black patients receive less aggressive and less appropriate treatments for most cancers than do White patients (Penner, Eggly, et al., 2012). For example, using national archival data, Griggs and associates (Griggs, Culakova, et al., 2007; Griggs, Sorbero, et al., 2003) found that Black women being treated for breast cancer were much more likely than White women with the same disease to receive chemotherapy that was (a) below the recommended dosages to effectively treat the disease and (b) deviated from standard recommended chemotherapy drugs. In summary, racial health care disparities are pervasive: They exist in the treatments of most medical problems in most treatment settings.

Our consideration of possible causes of these treatment disparities focuses on what transpires during and after racially discordant medical interactions. We adopt this approach because we believe that these interactions play a critical role in treatment disparities. Guided by the conclusions of the 2003 report of the Institute of Medicine on inequalities in health care (Smedley et al., 2003) and our own research on interracial interactions, we argue that racial attitudes among Black patients and their physicians play important roles in these interactions and, thus, health care disparities.

CONTEMPORARY RACIAL ATTITUDES

Blatant forms of racial prejudice and discrimination have substantially declined over the past 50 years in the United States. However, new and subtle forms of racism continue to have a significant negative impact on the economic, physical, and mental well-being of Black Americans, as well as that of other racial/ethnic minority groups. As Bonilla-Silva and Dietrich (2011) observed, "today, discrimination is mostly subtle, apparently non-racialized, and institutional" (p. 191).

Implicit prejudice plays a central role in subtle forms of bias. In contrast to *explicit* processes, which are conscious and deliberative expressions, *implicit* processes involve a lack of awareness and intention. Implicit biases arise through overlearned associations (Kawakami, Dovidio, Moll, Hermsen, & Russin, 2000), which may be rooted in early childhood socialization, repeated personal experience, widespread media exposure, or cultural representations of some target group. Thus, whereas explicit prejudice reflects people's conscious endorsement of negative beliefs, implicit biases often involve the internalization of negative cultural associations. Whereas people who are more highly educated or are higher in SES exhibit relatively low levels of explicit prejudice, implicit biases are automatically activated for a majority of Americans, regardless of age, SES, and political orientation (Blair et al., 2013; Kuppens & Spears, 2014). In particular, physicians display significant implicit racial bias, commonly at a level comparable to the general White population (Sabin, Nosek, Greenwald, & Rivara, 2009).

Self-reports of explicit bias and implicit measures of prejudice and stereotyping are usually only weakly correlated. Moreover, for most non-Black Americans, explicit and implicit racial biases are dissociated in a particular way: Although the majority of non-Black Americans today consider themselves to be egalitarian and relatively free of explicit racial bias, they still exhibit high levels of implicit racial bias. Put differently, explicit and implicit biases likely have common origins, but they are two distinct and unique psychological phenomena. This dissociation between positive explicit feelings and beliefs and negative implicit feelings and beliefs concerning Blacks is particularly relevant to understanding the nature and outcomes of interactions between non-Black physicians and Black patients. Specifically, implicit racial biases typically operate unconsciously to influence behavior (Dovidio & Gaertner, 2004).

PHYSICIANS' AND PATIENTS' RACIAL ATTITUDES AND MEDICAL CARE

For the majority of Black patients, their medical encounters involve a non-Black physician, most commonly a White physician. In this section, we consider the influence of physician and patient attitudes—independently and jointly—on the dynamics of racially discordant medical interactions.

Physicians' Attitudes

It is our contention that physician racial attitudes do contribute to health care disparities, but this process occurs primarily at the implicit level. To be sure, explicit racial bias exists among some physicians, but its direct impact on the treatment of Black patients is greatly reduced if not eliminated by strong personal and professional norms to provide the same high quality of care to all patients, irrespective of their race or ethnicity.

The strong condemnation of racial bias in the medical profession and in society in general helps make non-Black physicians aware of their explicit feelings about Blacks. Physicians actively attempt to control how these feelings are expressed in racially discordant medical interactions. They closely monitor certain behaviors and attempt to regulate them and are likely to be strongly motivated not to appear racially biased when interacting with a Black patient (Dovidio & LaFrance, 2013). Indeed, physicians often state that because of their sensitivity to racial bias, they tend to give higher quality care to Black than to White patients in their practice (Sabin, Rivara, & Greenwald, 2008).

As already noted, considerable archival data demonstrate that Blacks receive lower quality health care than Whites, and there is experimental and quasi-experimental evidence that patients' race affects physicians' perceptions and treatment decisions (e.g., Bogart, Catz, Kelly, & Benotsch, 2001). However, we are not aware of any experimental research showing that the level of non-Black physicians' explicit racial bias directly predicts lower quality care for a Black than a White patient. Thus, motivations to be egalitarian and unbiased in the quality of care they provide appear to successfully limit the influence of physicians' personal explicit bias on the medical care they provide.

Despite the fact that non-Black physicians may be able to inhibit the direct influence of their conscious racial biases on treatment, biases may still operate subtly and indirectly. One way this occurs is that disparate medical treatment is justified on the basis of other seemingly nonracial factors. For example, Calabrese, Earnshaw, Underhill, Hansen, and Dovidio (2014) studied physicians' willingness to provide protective or prophylactic antiretroviral drugs to Blacks and Whites who were at risk for HIV. They found that physician racial attitudes did not directly predict differential willingness to prescribe antiretroviral drugs to Blacks and Whites. However, more racially biased physicians perceived that Blacks would engage in greater sexual risk behavior if they received the drug. Concerns about increased sexual risk behavior, in turn, predicted less willingness to prescribe the drugs to Blacks than to Whites.

In addition, as noted earlier, there is evidence that, on average, there may be relatively high levels of implicit racial bias among non-Black physicians (Sabin et al., 2009). This implicit bias affects their perceptions of Black patients, their treatment decisions, and their interactions with Black patients. For example, non-Black physicians harbor implicit stereotypes of Blacks as less compliant, less trustworthy patients, and more likely than Whites to engage in risky behaviors (D. Moskowitz et al., 2011; Sabin et al., 2008). These implicit stereotypes predict biases in prescribing medications and treatments to Black patients in ways that produce lower quality of care for Black than for White patients (Sabin & Greenwald, 2012).

Because implicit biases often operate unconsciously and physicians are able to inhibit the effects of explicit bias in their medical care, physicians are likely unaware of the existence of implicit bias and may, in fact, be resistant to recognizing its effects. An example of this is one physician's reaction to the conclusion of the Institute of Medicine (Smedley et al., 2003) that subtle forms of physician racial bias played a significant role in health care disparities: "It is doubtful that hidden forms of discrimination are prevalent in a profession whose professional norms are set so strongly against it" (Epstein, 2005, p. 26). In 2002, the vast majority of doctors asserted that the medical community was indeed color blind, at least in terms of the quality of care it provided: Specifically, 69% of physicians surveyed said that health care system "rarely" or "never" treated patients unfairly because of their racial or ethnic background (Institute for Ethics, 2005). Nevertheless, there is now ample evidence of racial bias among health care professionals and its effects on health care "even in the absence of the practitioners' intent or awareness" (G. B. Moskowitz, Stone, & Childs, 2012, p. 996).

Although physicians may be unaware of how implicit bias affects the medical care they provide to Black patients, our own and others' work suggests that physicians' implicit bias does influence how their patients see them. The core premise of this work is that physician implicit bias is manifested in subtle verbal, nonverbal, and paraverbal behaviors that affect the quality of communication (Dovidio & LaFrance, 2013), and consequently interpersonal perceptions, in racially discordant medical interactions. Black patients detect these physician behaviors associated with implicit racial bias and react negatively (Blair et al., 2013; Cooper et al., 2012; Penner, Hagiwara, et al., 2013). Blair et al. (2013), for example, measured implicit racial bias among physicians who saw Black patients and then asked these patients to rate their physician on patient centeredness, which is the perception that a physician is respectful of and responsive to the patient's preferences, needs, and values (Stewart et al., 2000). The Black patients viewed more implicitly racially biased physicians as being lower in patient centeredness. Other studies have replicated Blair et al.'s findings and further found that Black patients perceived physicians higher in implicit bias as less trustworthy and expressed less satisfaction in their medical interaction with them (Cooper et al., 2012; Penner et al., 2010).

In addition, Black patients in medical encounters may be particularly attuned to the discrepancy between a physician's explicit egalitarian beliefs and implicit bias. As noted earlier, non-Black physicians generally express strong egalitarian beliefs and appear to consciously regulate their overt actions in interracial medical encounters. Penner et al. (2010) investigated the joint effects of physician implicit and explicit bias of non-Black physicians' on Black patients' perceptions of their medical encounter. The only evidence of any impact of physician explicit bias was in their own perceptions of the patients. In general, physicians higher in explicit prejudice reported that they felt less like part of a "team" while working with their Black patients. Physician explicit bias had no effect on patient perceptions of them. In contrast, physicians' implicit bias had a systematic effect on patients' perceptions of them. Overall, Black patients saw physicians who were higher in implicit bias as less warm, less friendly, and not as patient centered. However, Black patients had the strongest negative reactions to physicians who had relatively strong implicit biases but who explicitly professed egalitarian attitudes.

Patients' Attitudes

Black patients typically enter medical interactions, particularly racially discordant ones, with relatively low levels of trust (Dovidio et al., 2008). Moreover, there is substantial evidence that Black patients' level of trust and other race-related attitudes affect what happens during and after racially discordant medical interactions. Our own work has focused on Black patients' perceptions of personal past discrimination and their race-based suspicion of the medical system (see Hagiwara et al., 2013; Penner et al., 2009; Penner, Hagiwara, et al., 2013). This suspicion represents the belief that Blacks as a group will be treated poorly by the health care system and may even experience harm because of their race (Thompson, Valdimarsdottir, Winkel, Jandorf, & Redd, 2004).

Importantly, the past discrimination reported by Black patients is not necessarily just discrimination related to medical care. Penner et al. (2009) found that Black patients who reported experiencing relatively high levels of past discrimination in general felt less close to the physician they had just seen and expressed significantly less satisfaction with their medical interactions. Black patients who perceived high levels of discrimination generally were also less likely to adhere to their physician's recommendations 4 weeks after the visit, and this lower adherence was associated with poorer health status 16 weeks after the visit (Hagiwara et al., 2013; see also Casagrande, Gary, LaVeist, Gaskin, & Cooper, 2007). One consequence of perceiving high levels of discrimination generally is that Black patients are more active (e.g., ask for more details, ask more questions) and talk more in their medical encounters (Hagiwara et al., 2013), which may reflect attempts to control the interaction and avoid being the target of discrimination in this setting (Penner, Hagiwara, et al., 2013).

Recently, Penner (2014) examined how Black patients' suspicion affects their reactions to oncological interactions. His analyses show that high suspicious patients see the interactions as less patient centered and, as a result, are less likely to accept treatment recommendations. Other researchers have found that low levels of trust and high levels of perceived discrimination among Black patients are associated with a lower likelihood of getting appropriate preventive services, such as cancer screenings (Carpenter et al., 2009) and adhering to treatment regimens (Saha, Jacobs, Moore, & Beach, 2010).

Physician and Patient Attitudes

Although most of the research on physician and patient racial attitudes on medical care has focused on one perspective or the other, quality of care depends upon the relationship between physicians and patients. The amount of research is limited, but it does suggest an important reciprocal role of physician and patient attitudes in producing health care disparities. Penner (2014), for example, found an indirect link between oncologists' implicit bias and Black patients' perceptions of the treatments that the oncologists recommended. Specifically, oncologists who were more implicitly racially biased were perceived by Black patients to be less patient centered. These perceptions that the oncologist was less patient centered, in turn, led patients to believe that the treatment would be more difficult to complete and the side effects would be more serious. Perhaps as a consequence, Black patients had less confidence in the physician's treatment recommendations.

In summary, physician bias (particularly implicit bias) and patient attitudes both contribute to racial disparities in health care. Moreover, physician and patient biases may combine in dynamic ways to produce lower quality care for Black patients, even though neither the physician nor the patient intended this outcome. For instance, Black patients generally perceive physicians who are higher in implicit racial bias, even when they have positive explicit racial attitudes, as less warm and friendly (Penner, Hagiwara, et al., 2013) and have less trust and confidence in them (Blair et al., 2013; Cooper et al., 2012). Less patient satisfaction, perceived patient centeredness, and trust and confidence in one's physician, in turn, predict less adherence to the physicians' recommendations (Penner, Gaertner, et al., 2013) and weakens patients' interest in pursuing further care (Bogart, Wagner, Galvan, & Banks, 2010; Dovidio et al., 2008; Hagiwara et al., 2013), diminishing the effectiveness of the health care. As a result, the physicians' behaviors, driven by their implicit bias, and the Black patients' responses to these behaviors combine to reduce the effectiveness of their health care interactions in ways counter to their consciously intended goal. We note, however, that the research on physician implicit bias has focused on more proximal outcomes rather than on actual long-term effects on health. As far as we are aware, no one has yet shown a direct or indirect link between physician implicit bias and more tangible health care outcomes, such as Black patients' long-term health and health behavior or control of some chronic disease.

RACIAL COLOR BLINDNESS: IDEOLOGY AND STRATEGY

We now examine color blindness in the context of the kind of medical interactions that most Black patients have: racially discordant ones, in which the physician is non-Black. It is estimated that in the United States, at least 80% of Black patients have racially discordant medical interactions (LaVeist, Nuru-Jeter, & Jones, 2003). As already mentioned, racial color blindness has been studied as both a strategy and an ideology. The former conceptualization concerns an interpersonal strategy that many people may adopt in racially discordant interactions to avoid the impression that they are racially biased by behaving as if they do not notice or are unaware of the other person's race (Apfelbaum, Norton, & Sommers, 2012). The latter conceptualization views racial color blindness as a modern kind of racist ideology (Neville et al., 2013). People who strongly hold a color-blind racial ideology endorse the status quo with regard to the relative political and economic power of racial majorities and minorities and justify this position primarily on the basis of two kinds of beliefs: (a) race is no longer an important factor in professional and personal relationships and (b) racial discrimination is a thing of the past (Neville et al., 2013).

We certainly acknowledge the importance of this ideology in understanding many aspects of race relations, including health disparities. For example, endorsing a color-blind racial ideology might cause individuals to oppose programs to improve access to medical care for disadvantaged minority group members, or perhaps even deny personal requests for help in obtaining medical services. However, in this chapter, we focus on color blindness as a possible strategy used by physicians to guide their medical interactions with Black patients. We do this for two primary reasons. First, we believe that many non-Black physicians who would not endorse a color-blind racial ideology often use a color-blind strategy when interacting with their Black patients. Second, in the terms we have just used, a color-blind racial ideology is an explicit racial attitude. We reiterate the fact that the available research evidence suggests that it is physicians' implicit racial attitudes that have an influence on racially discordant medical interactions. That is, non-Black physicians appear highly motivated to suppress and control any general racial bias of which they are aware (e.g., a color-blind racial ideology) when they interact directly with a Black patient, and, as a consequence, they do seem to be able to inhibit the most direct and blatant effects of any explicit attitudes in patient care. Thus, we emphasize the more implicit and subtle causes and consequences of color-blind strategies in medical interracial interactions.

Racially discordant medical interactions, like all interracial interactions, are shaped jointly by the interpretations and responses of members of both majority and minority groups. Thus, a non-Black physician's attempts to be color blind will almost certainly produce a series of reciprocal effects. Perhaps the most important of these effects would be Black patients' perceptions of the physician in domains that may be related to health outcomes, such as perceived patient centeredness and trust. There is good reason to believe such perceptions would be negatively affected when a physician adopts a color-blind strategy.

We first consider the impact of adopting a color-blind strategy on the thoughts and actions of nonminority participants in an interracial interaction. Most of the studies discussed in what follows involve social interactions between Whites and Blacks, but we believe their findings can be extrapolated to other racially discordant interactions. Race is an automatically activated social category in the United States. Thus, attempts to be color-blind require cognitive effort to suppress the recognition of race, which can negatively affect the quality and outcomes of interracial interactions, often without awareness of the negative impact on the Black partners in the interaction. Furthermore, when Whites attempt to be color blind, they tend to be self-focused and more oriented toward monitoring their own performance than toward learning about the particular needs and concerns of the Black person with whom they are interacting.

Concerns about how well one is "performing" and how one is perceived by other people in interracial interactions may impair the ability of people (in particular, less explicitly prejudiced individuals) to engage in intimacy-building behaviors. For example, Vorauer, Gagnon, and Sasaki (2009) found that when participants in interracial interactions adopted a color-blind orientation, they were less positive, supportive, and other-oriented than when they adopted a multicultural orientation that acknowledged differences between them and the Black participants in the interaction. According to Vorauer et al. (2009), attempting to be color blind led people in these exchanges to avoid topics that would bring to light meaningful differences between them. Instead, they displayed a cautious preventive focus, in which one is primarily concerned with avoiding negative outcomes rather than achieving positive ones (i.e., a promotion focus). By contrast, a multicultural perspective involves the appreciation of differences and of common connections, and encourages a promotion-oriented focus. In the context of a racially discordant medical interaction, physicians who adopt a color-blind strategy may be less patient centered.

Attempts to be color blind may also affect the observable manifestations of implicit bias among physicians. Despite egalitarian explicit racial attitudes, automatically activated implicit biases influence people's behaviors, particularly behaviors that are more spontaneous and more difficult to control, such as nonverbal behavior. Whites' implicit prejudice is manifested in behaviors that reflect both anxiety (rate of blinking) and dislike (gaze aversion; Dovidio & LaFrance, 2013). Also, McConnell and Leibold (2001) found that Whites' implicit racial attitudes (but not their explicit racial attitudes) tended to correlate with leaning away from their partner and adopting further seating distances during interracial interactions; they also talked more, hesitated more, and made more speech errors. In medical settings, both Cooper et al. (2012) and Hagiwara et al. (2013) found that physicians higher in implicit bias talked more in their medical interactions with Black patients. More recently, Hagiwara et al. (2014) reported that non-Black physicians higher in implicit bias also use more anxiety-related words (e.g., worried, afraid, nervous) when they interacted with their Black patients. It seems reasonable to propose that the cognitive effort expended to appear color blind may deplete the cognitive monitoring and control resources that might ordinarily be used to inhibit these kinds of manifestations of implicit bias.

Finally, attempts to be color blind may be especially challenging for physicians because they run counter to their medical training, which often emphasizes differences among population groups in the incidence and biology of certain diseases. The challenge of having contradictory orientations—being color blind socially versus considering the person's ethnicity or race in making a diagnosis—may further increase cognitive demands placed on a non-Black physician in a racially discordant interaction. From this perspective, physicians' attempts to be racially color blind could contribute to health care disparities in two ways. First, it could impair the quality of the medical interaction. Second, it can produce poorer treatment decisions if a physician does not take actual relevant racial information into account. Attempts to be color blind may lead physicians to ignore the very real role of minority patient experiences and attitudes when they interact with them. Ignoring patients' past social experiences and present circumstances associated with their race (or ethnicity) may produce treatment recommendations that are inappropriate.

These effects of physicians' attempts to be racially color blind may be exacerbated by Blacks' reactions to color-blind strategies in interracial interactions. Blacks are suspicious of Whites who adopt a color-blind racial perspective. They often conclude that a White person who avoids acknowledging race is racist, regardless of what their actual motivations were (Apfelbaum et al., 2012). Moreover, because Blacks anticipate rejection in interracial interactions and are vigilant for and sensitive to signs of racial bias (Richeson & Shelton, 2005), they tend to interpret cues of anxiety, such as speech disfluencies and averted gaze, which physicians are likely to exhibit because of the cognitive demand when attempting to be color blind, as cues of dislike and racial bias when displayed by Whites (Dovidio & LaFrance, 2013). In general, interracial interactions are less smooth and effective when Whites have to expend greater effort to suppress negative feelings and beliefs and monitor their own behavior to appear nonprejudiced and color blind (e.g., Vorauer & Sasaki, 2009). Blacks weigh Whites' nonverbal behavior heavily in forming impressions of Whites, and thus nonverbal cues, which may reflect anxiety, arouse suspicion and discomfort among Blacks and impair the development of social rapport (Pearson et al., 2008). These negative attributions are particularly likely in medical contexts in which Blacks are primed to mistrust their physicians and may occur more often among Black patients higher in suspicion about how the health care system treats members of their group (Thompson et al., 2004).

CONCLUSION

In general, despite compelling data that show racial disparities in health and health care, there is little evidence that physicians' personal, explicit racial prejudice biases them in ways that directly lead to lower quality of care for Black patients. Physicians are generally low in explicit bias and appear to be effective at inhibiting the impact of any conscious racial bias on their medical decisions or overt behaviors in interactions with Black patients. However, implicit bias primarily operates independently of explicit bias and, irrespective of their level of explicit bias, most physicians show relatively high levels of implicit anti-Black bias. The expression of implicit bias is difficult to control and may significantly affect medical experiences and outcomes for Black patients. Physicians' attempts at conscious control and regulation of their behaviors in racially discordant medical interactions are likely to be awkward and sometimes counterproductive, actually exacerbating the existing intergroup biases and distrust that non-Black physicians and their Black patients bring to racially discordant medical interactions.

There is little question that there is a strong and widespread personal and professional commitment among physicians to make the outcomes of medical interactions color blind—that is, to provide care that is equivalently effective across patients of different races. Nevertheless, the social psychological and medical literature reveals that efforts to be color blind in racially discordant interactions will most likely not serve this goal. Race is an automatically activated social category in the United States generally, and medical training emphasizes differences in base rates among members of different population groups in prevalence of diseases and conditions, which makes a patient's perceived race especially salient in medical encounters. Physicians have significant levels of implicit prejudice, and attempts to deny or suppress the effects of this bias require an expenditure of conscious effort. In the medical context, the added demand of attempting to suppress implicit bias through racial color blindness may interfere with the level of thinking and analysis physicians require to make accurate diagnoses and offer optimal treatment recommendations. To the extent that these physicians devote more attention to avoiding negative outcomes of racially discordant medical interactions (e.g., appearing prejudiced) than achieving positive ones, they will dedicate more effort to monitoring their own behavior and, consequently, be less attentive and responsive to the behaviors and needs of their patient.

Blacks, who are often suspicious of medicine as an institution and have generally higher levels of mistrust, are sensitive to subtle cues of bias, such as nonverbal signals, and are apparently quite accurate in their detection of implicit bias in non-Blacks in both social and medical interactions. In addition, Blacks interpret the avoidance of race when it is relevant to the interaction as racial bias, and thus may be particularly mistrustful of physicians who do not appropriately acknowledge their race in this context. Black patients who have less trust in their physician are less likely to subsequently adhere to the physician's medical recommendations.

The literature review and analysis we present in this chapter reveals the challenges unintentional racial biases present to providing high-quality health care in racially discordant medical encounters. One possible solution would be to apply interventions to reduce or eliminate implicit biases among physicians. However, implicit biases are overlearned associations that cannot be readily unlearned. Alternatively, it may be possible to recognize race in physician–patient interactions, but in circumstances in which the impact of race-related attitudes is reduced and concerns about appearing biased become less relevant. Although racial categories may be automatically activated, people can categorize others in multiple ways. Thus, race can remain salient in medical interactions, but it can be placed in the context of a more relevant and important other identity. Research on the common ingroup identity model (Gaertner & Dovidio, 2012) demonstrates that it is possible for people to acknowledge a difference on one dimension (e.g., race), but in the context of a larger shared (superordinate) identity. When people of different racial/ethnic groups share a sense of this "dual identity," they are more attentive to the needs of others, more self-disclosing, and more oriented toward learning from the other person than being concerned about their own "performance."

It may be possible for physicians and patients to see themselves as members of the "same team," sharing a common goal with each having something to contribute to achieving that goal. This superordinate group perspective, which allows recognition of race, should produce a promotion orientation rather than the prevention orientation elicited by racial color blindness. Penner, Gaertner, et al. (2013) used this intervention with Black patients being seen by non-Black physicians at a primary care clinic. Compared with a standard-of-care control condition, patients who were induced to feel a common identity and team goal (successful resolution of their medical problem) had more successful interactions. Patients in the common identity condition reported more trust of their physician than did patients in the control condition 4 weeks after the interaction. This greater trust led to greater subsequent adherence to physician treatment recommendations. Note that the immediate goal of the common identity model is not to change deeply held racial attitudes but rather to make those less salient than the common goal that physicians and patients share.

In conclusion, race plays a significant and systematic role in the health of Black Americans and the quality of health care they receive. Although physicians show a high level of conscious commitment to providing care in an unbiased way, they harbor unconscious biases that affect the nature of their interactions with Black patients and how they are perceived by these patients. Physicians' attempts to be color blind may actually exacerbate racial mistrust and impair the quality of medical interactions with Black patients. Understanding the psychology of medical interactions can thus guide interventions that include the recognition of race in ways that improve, rather than interfere with, the development of productive physician–patient interactions and ultimately reduce racial disparities in health care and health.

REFERENCES

Agency for Healthcare Research and Quality. (2012). *National healthcare disparities report*. Hyattsville, MD: U.S. Government Printing Office.

Apfelbaum, E. P., Norton, M. I., & Sommers, S. R. (2012). Racial color blindness: Emergence, practice, and implications. *Current Directions in Psychological Science*, 21, 205–209. http://dx.doi.org/10.1177/0963721411434980

Blair, I. V., Steiner, J. F., Fairclough, D. L., Hanratty, R., Price, D. W., Hirsh, H. K., . . . Havranek, E. P. (2013). Clinicians' implicit ethnic/racial bias and perceptions of care among Black and Latino patients. *Annals of Family Medicine*, 11, 43–52. http://dx.doi.org/10.1370/afm.1442

Bogart, L. M., Catz, S. L., Kelly, J. A., & Benotsch, E. G. (2001). Factors influencing physicians' judgments of adherence and treatment decisions for patients with HIV disease. *Medical Decision Making*, 21, 28–36. http://dx.doi.org/10.1177/0272989X0102100104

Bogart, L. M., Wagner, G., Galvan, F. H., & Banks, D. (2010). Conspiracy beliefs about HIV are related to antiretroviral treatment nonadherence among African American men with HIV. *Journal of Acquired Immune Deficiency Syndromes*, 53, 648–655.

Bonilla-Silva, E., & Dietrich, D. (2011). The sweet enchantment of color-blind racism in Obamerica. *Annals of the American Academy of Political and Social Science, 634,* 190–206. http://dx.doi.org/10.1177/0002716210389702

Calabrese, S. K., Earnshaw, V. A., Underhill, K., Hansen, N. B., & Dovidio, J. F. (2014). The impact of patient race on clinical decisions related to prescribing HIV pre-exposure prophylaxis (PrEP): Assumptions about sexual risk compensation and implications for access. *AIDS and Behavior, 18,* 226–240. http://dx.doi.org/10.1007/s10461-013-0675-x

Carpenter, W. R., Godley, P. A., Clark, J. A., Talcott, J. A., Finnegan, T., Mishel, M., . . . Mohler, J. L. (2009). Racial differences in trust and regular source of patient care and the implications for prostate cancer screening use. *Cancer, 115,* 5048–5059. http://dx.doi.org/10.1002/cncr.24539

Casagrande, S. S., Gary, T. L., LaVeist, T. A., Gaskin, D. J., & Cooper, L. A. (2007). Perceived discrimination and adherence to medical care in a racially integrated community. *Journal of General Internal Medicine, 22,* 389–395. http://dx.doi.org/10.1007/s11606-006-0057-4

Cooper, L. A., Roter, D. L., Carson, K. A., Beach, M. C., Sabin, J. A., Greenwald, A. G., & Inui, T. S. (2012). The associations of clinicians' implicit attitudes about race with medical visit communication and patient ratings of interpersonal care. *American Journal of Public Health, 102,* 979–987. http://dx.doi.org/10.2105/AJPH.2011.300558

Dovidio, J. F., & Gaertner, S. L. (2004). Aversive racism. In M. P. Zanna (Ed.), *Advances in experimental social psychology* (Vol. 36, pp. 1–51). San Diego, CA: Academic Press.

Dovidio, J. F., & LaFrance, M. (2013). Race, ethnicity, and nonverbal behavior. In J. A. Hall & M. Knapp (Eds.), *Nonverbal communication* (pp. 671–696). The Hague, The Netherlands: DeGruyter-Mouton. http://dx.doi.org/10.1515/9783110238150.671

Dovidio, J. F., Penner, L. A., Albrecht, T. L., Norton, W. E., Gaertner, S. L., & Shelton, J. N. (2008). Disparities and distrust: The implications of psychological processes for understanding racial disparities in health and health care. *Social Science & Medicine, 67,* 478–486. http://dx.doi.org/10.1016/j.socscimed.2008.03.019

Durrazzo, T. S., Frencher, S., & Gusberg, R. (2013). Influence of race on the management of lower extremity ischemia: Revascularization vs. amputation. *Journal of the American Medical Association Surgery, 48,* 617–623.

Epstein, R. A. (2005). Disparities and discrimination in health care coverage: A critique of the Institute of Medicine study. *Perspectives in Biology and Medicine, 48*(Suppl. 1), S26–S41. http://dx.doi.org/10.1353/pbm.2005.0023

Gaertner, S. L., & Dovidio, J. F. (2012). Reducing intergroup bias: The common ingroup identity model. In P. A. M. Van Lange, A. W. Kruglanski, & E. T. Higgins (Eds.), *Handbook of theories of social psychology* (Vol. 2, pp. 439–457). Thousand Oaks, CA: Sage.

Gerber, J. S., Prasad, P. A., Localio, A. R., Fiks, A. G., Grundmeier, R. W., Bell, L. M., . . . Zaoutis, T. E. (2013). Racial differences in antibiotic prescribing by primary care pediatricians. *Pediatrics, 131,* 677–684. http://dx.doi.org/10.1542/peds.2012-2500

Griggs, J. J., Culakova, E., Sorbero, M. E., van Ryn, M., Poniewierski, M. S., Wolff, D. A., . . . Lyman, G. H. (2007). Effect of patient socioeconomic status and body mass index on the quality of breast cancer adjuvant chemotherapy. *Journal of Clinical Oncology, 25,* 277–284. http://dx.doi.org/10.1200/JCO.2006.08.3063

Griggs, J. J., Sorbero, M. E., Stark, A. T., Heininger, S. E., & Dick, A. W. (2003). Racial disparity in the dose and dose intensity of breast cancer adjuvant chemotherapy. *Breast Cancer Research and Treatment, 81,* 21–31. http://dx.doi.org/10.1023/A:1025481505537

Hagiwara, N., Penner, L. A., Gonzalez, R., Eggly, S., Dovidio, J. F., Gaertner, S. L., . . . Albrecht, T. L. (2013). Racial attitudes, physician–patient talk time ratio, and adherence in racially discordant medical interactions. *Social Science & Medicine, 87,* 123–131. http://dx.doi.org/10.1016/j.socscimed.2013.03.016

Hagiwara, N., Slatcher, R., Eggly, S., & Penner, L. A. (2014, January). *Are racially discordant medical interactions stressful for physicians? Analysis of their linguistic patterns.* Annual Meeting of Society of Personality and Social Psychology, Austin, TX.

Institute for Ethics. (April, 2005). *Physicians are becoming increasingly engaged in addressing disparities: Preliminary survey brief.* Retrieved from http://www.ama-assn.org/ama/pub/physician-resources/public-health/eliminating-health-disparities/commission-end-health-care-disparities/quality-health-care-minorities-understanding-physicians.page

Kawakami, K., Dovidio, J. F., Moll, J., Hermsen, S., & Russin, A. (2000). Just say no (to stereotyping): Effects of training in the negation of stereotypic associations on stereotype activation. *Journal of Personality and Social Psychology, 78,* 871–888. http://dx.doi.org/10.1037/0022-3514.78.5.871

Kuppens, T., & Spears, R. (2014). You don't have to be well-educated to be an aversive racist, but it helps. *Social Science Research, 45,* 211–223. http://dx.doi.org/10.1016/j.ssresearch.2014.01.006

LaVeist, T. A., Nuru-Jeter, A., & Jones, K. E. (2003). The association of doctor–patient race concordance with health services utilization. *Journal of Public Health Policy, 24,* 312–323. http://dx.doi.org/10.2307/3343378

McConnell, A. R., & Leibold, J. M. (2001). Relations among the Implicit Association Test, discriminatory behavior, and explicit measures of racial attitudes. *Journal of Experimental Social Psychology, 37,* 435–442. http://dx.doi.org/10.1006/jesp.2000.1470

Moskowitz, D., Thom, D. H., Guzman, D., Penko, J., Miaskowski, C., & Kushel, M. (2011). Is primary care providers' trust in socially marginalized patients affected by race? *Journal of General Internal Medicine, 26,* 846–851. http://dx.doi.org/10.1007/s11606-011-1672-2

Moskowitz, G. B., Stone, J., & Childs, A. (2012). Implicit stereotyping and medical decisions: Unconscious stereotype activation in practitioners' thoughts about African Americans. *American Journal of Public Health*, *102*, 996–1001. http://dx.doi.org/10.2105/AJPH.2011.300591

National Cancer Institute. (2008). *Cancer health disparities*. Retrieved from http://www.cancer.gov/cancertopics/factsheet/disparities/cancer-health-disparities

National Center for Health Statistics. (2014). *Health, United States, 2013: With special feature on prescription drugs*. Hyattsville, MD: U.S. Government Printing Office.

Neville, H. A., Awad, G. H., Brooks, J. E., Flores, M. P., & Bluemel, J. (2013). Color-blind racial ideology: Theory, training, and measurement implications in psychology. *American Psychologist*, *68*, 455–466. http://dx.doi.org/10.1037/a0033282

Pearson, A. R., West, T. V., Dovidio, J. F., Powers, S. R., Buck, R., & Henning, R. (2008). Delayed audiovisual feedback in intergroup and intragroup interaction. *Psychological Science*, *19*, 1272–1279.

Penner, L. A. (2014, November). *Disparities in healthcare: The potential role of race-related thoughts and feelings*. Detroit, MI: Grand Rounds, Karmanos Cancer Institute.

Penner, L. A., Dovidio, J. F., Edmondson, D., Dailey, R. K., Markova, T., Albrecht, T. L., & Gaertner, S. L. (2009). The experience of discrimination, and Black–White health disparities in medical care. *Journal of Black Psychology*, *35*, 180–203. http://dx.doi.org/10.1177/0095798409333585

Penner, L. A., Dovidio, J. F., West, T. V., Gaertner, S. L., Albrecht, T. L., Dailey, R. K., & Markova, T. (2010). Aversive racism and medical interactions with Black patients: A field study. *Journal of Experimental Social Psychology*, *46*, 436–440. http://dx.doi.org/10.1016/j.jesp.2009.11.004

Penner, L. A., Eggly, S., Griggs, J. J., Underwood, W., III, Orom, H., & Albrecht, T. L. (2012). Life-threatening disparities: The treatment of Black and White cancer patients. *Journal of Social Issues*, *68*, 328–357. http://dx.doi.org/10.1111/j.1540-4560.2012.01751.x

Penner, L. A., Gaertner, S., Dovidio, J. F., Hagiwara, N., Porcerelli, J., Markova, T., & Albrecht, T. L. (2013). A social psychological approach to improving the outcomes of racially discordant medical interactions. *Journal of General Internal Medicine*, *28*, 1143–1149. http://dx.doi.org/10.1007/s11606-013-2339-y

Penner, L. A., & Hagiwara, N. (2014). Racism and health. *The Wiley-Blackwell encyclopedia of health, illness, behavior, and society*. New York, NY: Wiley-Blackwell. Retrieved from http://onlinelibrary.wiley.com/doi/10.1002/9781118410868.wbehibs290/abstract;jsessionid=ED8B21CF56C767EDDF56186C704F5293.f04t01

Penner, L. A., Hagiwara, N., Eggly, S., Gaertner, S. L., Albrecht, T. L., & Dovidio, J. F. (2013). Racial healthcare disparities: A social psychological analysis. *European Review of Social Psychology*, *24*, 70–122. http://dx.doi.org/10.1080/10463283.2013.840973

Richeson, J. A., & Shelton, J. N. (2005). Brief report: Thin slices of racial bias. *Journal of Nonverbal Behavior*, *29*, 75–86. http://dx.doi.org/10.1007/s10919-004-0890-2

Sabin, J. A., & Greenwald, A. G. (2012). The influence of implicit bias on treatment recommendations for four common pediatric conditions: Pain, urinary tract infection, attention-deficit/hyperactivity disorder, and asthma. *American Journal of Public Health, 102*, 988–995. http://dx.doi.org/10.2105/AJPH.2011.300621

Sabin, J. A., Nosek, B. A., Greenwald, A. G., & Rivara, F. P. (2009). Physicians' implicit and explicit attitudes about race by MD race, ethnicity, and gender. *Journal of Health Care for the Poor and Underserved, 20*, 896–913. http://dx.doi.org/10.1353/hpu.0.0185

Sabin, J. A., Rivara, F. P., & Greenwald, A. G. (2008). Physician implicit attitudes and stereotypes about race and quality of medical care. *Medical Care, 46*, 678–685. http://dx.doi.org/10.1097/MLR.0b013e3181653d58

Saha, S., Jacobs, E. A., Moore, R. D., & Beach, M. C. (2010). Trust in physicians and racial disparities in HIV care. *AIDS Patient Care and STDs, 24*, 415–420. http://dx.doi.org/10.1089/apc.2009.0288

Salami, M. A., Etukakpan, B., & Olapade-Olaopa, O. (2007). Update on prostate cancer in Black men. *Journal of Men's Health & Gender, 4*, 456–463. http://dx.doi.org/10.1016/j.jmhg.2007.07.041

Smedley, B. D., Stith, A. Y., & Nelson, A. R. (2003). *Unequal treatment: Confronting racial and ethnic disparities in health care*. Washington, DC: National Academies Press.

Stewart, M., Brown, J. B., Donner, A., McWhinney, I. R., Oates, J., Weston, W. W., & Jordan, J. (2000). The impact of patient-centered care on outcomes. *The Journal of Family Practice, 49*, 796–804.

Thompson, H. S., Valdimarsdottir, H. B., Winkel, G., Jandorf, L., & Redd, W. (2004). The Group-Based Medical Mistrust Scale: Psychometric properties and association with breast cancer screening. *Preventive Medicine, 38*, 209–218. http://dx.doi.org/10.1016/j.ypmed.2003.09.041

Venkat, A., Hoekstra, J., Lindsell, C., Prall, D., Hollander, J. E., Pollack, C. V., Jr., . . . Gibler, W. B. (2003). The impact of race on the acute management of chest pain. *Academic Emergency Medicine, 10*, 1199–1208.

Vorauer, J. D., Gagnon, A., & Sasaki, S. J. (2009). Salient intergroup ideology and intergroup interaction. *Psychological Science, 20*, 838–845. http://dx.doi.org/10.1111/j.1467-9280.2009.02369.x

Vorauer, J. D., & Sasaki, S. J. (2009). Helpful only in the abstract? *Psychological Science, 20*, 191–197. http://dx.doi.org/10.1111/j.1467-9280.2009.02265.x

17

RACIAL COLOR BLINDNESS IN COUNSELING, THERAPY, AND SUPERVISION

ALAN W. BURKARD, LISA M. EDWARDS, AND HADIYA A. ADAMS

Race is perhaps one of the most difficult topics to discuss in contemporary society. Although race influences so many aspects of everyday life, we are often hesitant and sometimes afraid to broach, openly discuss or acknowledge the impact of racial issues in our daily lives. As such, race and how it affects society holds power over people in complex and sometimes insidious ways.

Counselors feel this same tension. Some counselors believe that openly including discussions of racial concerns is vital to the counseling and therapy process (e.g., Burkard & Knox, 2004; Day-Vines et al., 2007). Others, however, have argued that such discussions are unnecessary (e.g., Abramowitz & Murray, 1983; Garb, 1997) and perhaps even a distraction from important clinical issues (e.g., Garb, 1997). The latter perspectives are consistent with *color-blind racial ideology* (CBRI), which has emerged as a critical variable in psychology and counseling (Neville, Awad, Brooks, Flores, & Bluemel, 2013). CBRI is the denial of racial differences and racism by emphasizing that everyone is the

http://dx.doi.org/10.1037/14754-018

The Myth of Racial Color Blindness: Manifestations, Dynamics, and Impact, H. A. Neville, M. E. Gallardo, and D. W. Sue (Editors)

same or has the same life opportunities (Neville et al., 2013). We agree with others (e.g., Neville et al., 2013) that a growing body of evidence indicates CBRI is detrimental to clients and counseling processes as well as the overall supervision and education of future practitioners. As such, we contend that decreasing CBRI and working to directly address race and power in therapy has benefits in counseling, supervision, and preprofessional education. Consider the following case example, which highlights the potential impact of addressing these issues in therapy:

> An African American man sought counseling for depression and for interpersonal difficulties in a romantic relationship. During the intake, the client described an incident in which he was surrounded by police and eventually was taken into custody. The client disclosed that his White partner had called the police, indicating there was a Black man in a car outside of her apartment building. The White therapist asked if the client had considered how race may have been a factor in this situation, and he admitted he had not considered that possibility. The therapist encouraged the client to reflect on how race may have influenced the situation with police and the interpersonal conflict between the client and his partner. Acknowledging the potential role of race in this situation led to an expanded discussion of the conflict, helped the client gain new perspectives they had not considered, and appeared to deepen the working alliance between client and counselor. After discussing some of the implications of the client's race in the conflict and police incident, the therapist asked what it was like to discuss the role of race in this situation with a White therapist, which also led to a productive discussion about the working relationship between counselor and client.

Consider what may have happened if the counselor had not raised race as an area of concern with this client. What opportunities for deeper exploration and understanding might have been missed? What critical issues might have been ignored? Particularly relevant, then, is what happens when a counselor maintains a CBRI and a color-blind approach in counseling and supervision in contrast to a racially conscious and inclusive perspective.

We address these issues in this chapter. We review conceptual associations between CBRI and other multicultural counseling constructs that are specific to counseling practitioners and trainees, examine the current empirical findings specific to racial color blindness in counseling and supervision processes, offer comment on possible implications for counseling and supervision, and conclude with suggestions for future research. Throughout this chapter, we use the terms *counselor* and *counseling* to refer broadly to mental health practitioners (e.g., counselors, psychologists, therapists) and their related clinical and counseling processes and practices.

As discussed throughout this book, defining racial color blindness is important to furthering our understanding of its effects on society and relationships; in particular, clearly operationalizing this concept for research is essential to move empirical work forward. For this chapter, we rely on Neville et al.'s (2013) proposed definition of *color blindness*, which comprises two dimensions: *color evasion* and *power evasion*. We refer readers to Neville et al.'s (2013) article and the chapters in this book for further clarification. It is also important to consider an alternative ideology to color blindness. In other words, how would we describe an alternative worldview to CBRI? A common perspective in the counseling literature has been a *multicultural* approach that emphasizes the recognition, understanding, and celebration of differences (Neville et al., 2013; Plaut, Thomas, & Goren, 2009; Sasaki & Vorauer, 2013). As an expansion of this multicultural approach that incorporates both color and power (e.g., Neville et al., 2013), we propose that a *multicultural ideology* (MCI) may provide an alternative worldview to CBRI. An MCI would include both *race consciousness* and *oppression consciousness*. A counselor or supervisor who uses a race-conscious approach actively seeks to understand the racial heritage of his or her clients and supervisees through active discussions of race and the meaning of race for the client or supervisee. The oppression-conscious counselor or supervisor embraces an awareness of power differences, discrimination, and oppressive systems (Appiah & Gutmann, 1996). As such, racism is acknowledged, particularly the implications of systemic oppression as well as the individual and collective actions intended to address racial inequities. The earlier vignette reflects a counselor using an MCI approach, in that the counselor questioned the African American client about how race was manipulated by the girlfriend in calling the police, and the counselor's attempt to explore the meaning of race for the client–counselor relationship.

COUNSELING CONSTRUCTS ASSOCIATED WITH RACIAL COLOR BLINDNESS

Although CBRI research is emerging in the broad field of psychology, color-blind and multicultural ideologies have been a focus of basic research in counseling and mental health practice for a few decades. Much of the recent research in this area has been facilitated by the availability of the Color-Blind Racial Attitude Scale (Neville, Lilly, Duran, Lee, & Browne, 2000). Overall, the collective evidence on preprofessionals and counselors suggests clear associations among CBRI, multicultural counseling competency, and counselor empathy that would be indicative of potentially poor services to clients. Here, we examine this extant research or, more specifically, the empirical relationships between CBRI and multicultural counseling concepts that have emerged among a sampling of counselors and preprofessionals.

A strong relationship continues to emerge empirically between racial color blindness and multicultural competency. For instance, early research found a relationship between lower counselor ratings of multicultural competency and less developed racial identity attitudes that are believed to represent a color-blind perspective (Constantine, 2001; Constantine, Juby, & Liang, 2001). Perhaps supporting this perspective, Gushue and Constantine (2007) found that higher levels of racial color blindness were associated with less integrated forms of White racial identity and were inversely related to higher levels of White racial identity among counseling and clinical psychology trainees. Relatedly, evidence has also indicated that high racial color blindness attitudes are associated with lower self-reported ratings of multicultural counseling competence among preprofessionals (Spanierman, Poteat, Wang, & Oh, 2008) and counselors (Chao, 2006; Neville, Spanierman, & Doan, 2006). As such, perhaps preprofessionals and counselors who are less self-aware of their racial identity development and their CBRI are more likely to struggle to exhibit multicultural competency in their practice.

Related to multicultural counseling competency is the concept of empathy, which some believe may be a determining factor to client perceptions of counselor competence in multicultural counseling (Ridley, Ethington, & Heppner, 2008; Ridley & Lingle, 1996). In fact, Constantine (2001) found that counselors high in empathy were more aware of racial factors when conceptualizing clients concerns and in integrating race and culture into client treatment conceptualizations than counselors low in empathy. Furthermore, in an investigation of licensed psychologists from the American Psychological Association Practice Directorate, Burkard and Knox (2004) found that psychologists' empathy ratings of clients were lower when color-blind attitudes were high, regardless of the race of the client (i.e., African American or White) or the focus of the client's presenting concern (i.e., depression or discrimination). Such preliminary findings indicate that racial color blindness may generally limit counselors' capacity for empathy, a concern that may adversely affect work with clients whether the counseling occurs in interracial situations or not.

It may be important to note that much of the research on racial color blindness just noted consisted of samples of predominately White participants. Neville et al. (2013) indicated that color-blind ideology may be present for both racial minorities and Whites, but their reasons for adopting this ideology may be quite different. For instance, in noncounselor samples, research consistently shows that CBRI is higher in Whites than in people of color (Neville et al., 2000); however, color-blind racial attitudes are also used by members of racial minority groups to manage interracial relations (Chen, Lephuoc, Guzmán, Rude, & Dodd, 2006; Neville, Coleman, Falconer, &

Holmes, 2005). CBRI research is more prevalent among Whites in counseling than racial or ethnic minorities in counseling. Such findings indicate that White counseling trainees have a number of strong emotional reactions to race-related materials, such as sadness and disgust (Ancis & Szymanski, 2001); anger and frustration (D'Andrea & Daniels, 2001); and anxiety, discomfort, and agitation (Utsey, Gernat, & Hammar, 2005). CBRI may help to reconcile such diverse reactions from White trainees to racial issues. For instance, in a recent investigation of White counseling preprofessionals, lower levels of racial color blindness were found to be associated with higher levels of White empathy and guilt (i.e., compassion costs) and lower levels of fear of interracial group contact (i.e., White fear; Spanierman et al., 2008). Furthermore, these emotional reactions were found to mediate between racial color blindness and multicultural counseling competency, suggesting that ideology and emotional reactions are linked and perhaps important to address in an integrated manner during multicultural counseling education.

EFFECTS OF CBRI ON COUNSELING AND SUPERVISION PROCESSES

Although the initial research noted here may illuminate important empirical associations between constructs, there is a growing body of evidence that focuses on racial color blindness in applied counseling and supervision settings. As such, these investigations address client, counselor, preprofessionals, and supervisor experiences or decisions when racial issues are addressed or ignored in such applied settings. The current evidence overwhelmingly points to deleterious effects when race is ignored and quite positive effects when race is integrated into applied work. In fact, some believe that race should be explicitly addressed in cross-racial counseling because the absence of race in counseling results in a loss of depth to the counseling process (Qureshi, 2007). Of note here is that much of this research focuses on color-evasive strategies, and little research addresses power-evasive interventions. Although the reasons for this focus on color evasion that has emerged are not entirely clear, it may be that color-evasion approaches occur more frequently in applied settings and are easier to research. Additionally, this research is applied and focused on actions that reflect color-blind and multicultural approaches in counseling, and as such, few studies incorporated a measure of racial color blindness in the research.

Counseling Processes

Counselors and researchers have long wrestled with whether racial differences between counselors and clients mattered in counseling (e.g., Abramowitz

& Murray, 1983; Atkinson & Lowe, 1995). Early research yielded inconsistent findings in addressing this question, leaving practitioners and researchers puzzled regarding the meaning of results and how to best serve clients in cross-racial counseling (Atkinson & Lowe, 1995). As the multicultural movement emerged in psychology, new models emerged that had the potential to explain prior findings and perhaps move future counseling practice and research forward. One important advance in theory from the multicultural movement was the notion that individual differences in counselor racial attitudes, cultural worldview, and cultural competency could profoundly influence the counseling process when client and counselor were racially and culturally different (Helms, 1995). Emerging evidence on CBRI and multicultural ideology in counseling suggests these worldviews may have profound effects on counseling processes and perhaps help explain what may be most helpful in working with racially different clients.

With a few exceptions, much of the research on racial color blindness in counseling focuses on White counselors working with African American clients. Here, researchers sought to understand the experience of White counselors when they reluctantly discuss or do not discuss racial backgrounds (i.e., color evasion) or oppression experiences (i.e., power evasion) with clients of color. In counseling overall, analogue research suggests clients of color (i.e., African American, Asian American, and Mexican American) perceive counselors who openly address and acknowledge race in counseling as more credible and culturally competent in counseling than when race was avoided. In fact, when White counselors were responsive to racial issues (i.e., client concerns about racism, racial differences between client and counselor, client racial identity attitudes), African American clients were more likely to return to counseling for future sessions and to report higher levels of satisfaction with counseling (Wade & Bernstein, 1991).

Although counselors' addressing of racial issues appears to lead to positive outcomes, research has also identified specific interventions that might be important for use within sessions. For example, female African American clients were found to disclose more intimately regardless of the counselor's racial background (i.e., African American or White) when the counselors asked about their experiences of being a Black woman (Thompson, Worthington, & Atkinson, 1994). In fact, female African American clients became more frustrated and exasperated with counselors who avoided or withdrew from racial content in counseling (Thompson & Jenal, 1994). Furthermore, African American clients identified counseling as more successful when racial issues were addressed early in counseling as opposed to when they were avoided. These findings may suggest that when color-blind approaches to race are used in counseling, African American clients are unable to share and work through the meaning of their racial experiences, which may lead to their overall negative emotional reactions regarding the counselor and counseling. Perhaps these experiences are the reason that clients of color perceive that the counseling alliance with their counselor is stronger when the latter is responsive to their racial concerns and background than when race is ignored in counseling (Zhang & Burkard, 2008).

One particular qualitative investigation directly explored counselor discussion or avoidance of racial issues in cross-racial counseling (Knox, Burkard, Johnson, Suzuki, & Ponterotto, 2003). It is important to note that African American counselors were more likely to directly address racial concerns with African American clients than with White clients, whereas White counselors acknowledged they would not normally discuss such concerns with any clients and would only address racial issues when clients felt it to be relevant. African American counselors believed that race was always relevant in counseling, often addressed racial issues with White clients because they perceived client discomfort interpersonally with their race, and they felt comfortable doing so. As such, African American counselors took a racially inclusive approach to counseling with White clients, which they believed had positive effects, often increasing client trust and security in the counseling relationship. For these African American counselors, a racially color-blind approach to counseling was not an option. Although most White counselors did not approach race issues in counseling with African American clients, some did and experienced emotional discomfort while doing so. Although White counselors experienced discomfort in addressing racial issues with African American clients, they also reported that doing so had positive effects on the counseling relationship and also increased client trust and security in the relationship. Interestingly, most White counselors elected to use a color-blind approach unless African American clients voluntarily raised racial information. When racial issues were addressed, White counselors again experienced emotional discomfort. Perhaps relatedly, others have also noted these negative emotional costs (i.e., guilt, fear) among Whites seeking to maintain positive interracial relations while also holding a color-blind ideological perspective (e.g., Spanierman et al., 2008); furthermore, such approaches also lead to undesirable nonverbal behaviors (Devine, Evett, & Vasquez-Suson, 1996; Dovidio, Gaertner, Kawakami, & Hodson, 2002) and a depletion in the ability to process information cognitively (Richeson et al., 2003; Richeson & Trawalter, 2005).

Interestingly, clients of color appear to not only expect that counselors are interested in their racial experiences but that their counselors are not color blind to their own racial attitudes and beliefs. For instance, several researchers have found that therapist self-disclosure of their racial attitudes and beliefs is critical to overall self-disclosure on the part of clients of color (La Roche & Maxie, 2003; Thompson & Jenal, 1994; Thompson et al., 1994). One qualitative study by Burkard, Knox, Groen, Perez, and Hess (2006) examined the use of self-disclosure by White counselors in addressing racial issues in cross-racial counseling. They found that White counselors self-disclosed their cognitive and emotional reactions (e.g., validated the experiences, disclosed feeling similarly upset) to acknowledge client experiences of racism and oppression after clients disclosed these events and their effects. In these situations, maintaining a racially inclusive approach that acknowledged power and discrimination, rather than a color-blind and power-evasive approach, improved the counseling relationship and appeared to help clients integrate their experiences and move on to other important concerns. Such findings suggest that counselors need to avoid being color blind when asking about client experiences and also in disclosing their own racial beliefs.

Supervision Processes

Interestingly, multicultural education has been found to be associated with lower self-ratings of racial color blindness (Spanierman et al., 2008) and to actually reduce color-blind attitudes to race (Colvin-Burque, Zugazaga, & Davis-Maye, 2007). In this sense, color-blind ideology may be malleable, and exploring the role of color blindness in supervision practice is important to understand. As such, researchers have examined when racial issues are addressed or incorporated into supervision in contrast to when they are not, which would seem to be reflective of color-blind practices. Additionally, research on color blindness in supervision is more complex, for the focus could be on how race is addressed between supervisee and client and how race is addressed between supervisor and supervisee.

Although it has been over a decade since Duan and Roehlke's (2001) study, these authors found that 93% of supervisors had not experienced supervising trainees who were racially different from themselves. When racial differences were present, Gatmon et al. (2001) found that supervisors and supervisees discussed racial differences about 32% of the time and supervisors initiated these discussions only 48% of the time. It is unclear how far we have come since this research was completed, but these findings indicate that discussions regarding racial issues in supervision have traditionally been infrequent. Interestingly, when supervisors and supervisees discuss racial issues in supervision, supervisees rate the supervisory alliance and satisfaction with supervision higher than when racial issues are avoided (Gatmon et al., 2001). These early investigations suggest that racial issues appear to be infrequent focuses in supervision. Although this finding may be reflective of the few number of cross-racial supervision experiences that occur in supervision, it may be important to offer that discussions of racial issues in supervision should be occurring in all supervision experiences.

More recently, a few qualitative investigations have yielded findings contradictory to the Gatmon study and directly related to color-blind and multicultural approaches in supervision. This research suggested that when racial issues were avoided in supervision, both supervisees of color and White supervisees reacted negatively (Burkard, Johnson, et al., 2006); however, supervisees of color had much stronger reactions to the exclusion of racial issues, including feeling offended, distressed, uncomfortable, and scared. The effects of these events on supervision were different along racial lines. White supervisees felt they learned that supervisors of color were unwilling to explore cultural issues in supervision; in contrast, supervisees of color hid their emotional reactions from White supervisors and became distrustful, guarded, and minimized their disclosures. Supervisees of color were commonly concerned about the negative effect on client treatment when supervisors ignored racial issues in supervision, believing that client needs were not well met. By contrast, all supervisees regardless of race had positive perceptions of supervision when racial issues were included: The supervision relationship improved, they felt satisfied with supervision, and they also believed that client treatment was improved by including racial issues in supervision discussions.

While exploring ruptures in cross-racial supervision with a racially mixed sample of supervisees (i.e., African American, Asian American, White), Lubbers (2013) found that ruptures emerged when supervisors were critical of supervisees' inclusion of racial concerns in counseling, and often they specifically directed supervisees to ignore racial concerns. In these situations, supervision relationships immediately became unstable. Supervisees came to view supervisors as oppressive and lost trust in them, feeling distressed when their supervisors encouraged these color-blind approaches. In response, many supervisees attempted to resolve their conflict and address racial issues in supervision by identifying their reasons for addressing race issues with clients. Additionally, supervisees expressed their distress that supervisors requested that they ignore the concerns and move on. In response, supervisors continued to dismiss supervisees' concerns, and the supervision relationship continued to deteriorate. The collective findings from the Burkard, Johnson, et al. (2006) and Lubbers studies highlight the value of addressing racial issues in supervision and the potential costs of a color-blind approach within cross-racial supervision and for supervisees of color.

Supervisees appear to have specific reactions to color-blind approaches in supervision, and some initial evidence suggests that supervisors may also have to contend with supervisees who struggle with color blindness. In a qualitative study of difficult feedback events (i.e., supervisors were hesitant to offer feedback) in cross-racial supervision by Burkard, Knox, Clarke, Phelps, and Inman (2014), White supervisors found that supervisees of color initially struggled to understand the difficult feedback regarding cultural issues during supervision but then eventually engaged in supervision to learn more. By contrast, supervisors of color (SRCs) had significant struggles with White supervisees. Here, SRCs provided some difficult feedback regarding racial issues in client care, and White supervisees reacted negatively and sought to minimize the importance of race in such discussions. They often questioned SRCs' competence and challenged their reasoning for including racial issues. Ruptures emerged in these instances that developed into impasses. SRCs felt disturbed by their White supervisees' reactions and struggled to address these concerns in supervision. Although prior evidence has consistently suggested that supervisees often struggle with supervisors who appear unprepared to contend with racial issues in supervision, these recent findings suggest the picture may be more complex and that supervisors may also need support in contending with supervisees, particularly White supervisees who may embrace a color-blind racial perspective.

LOOKING FORWARD:
APPLICATIONS AND FUTURE DIRECTIONS

Perhaps the conclusion from the literature is that race matters in counseling and supervision and that CBRI among counselors and supervisors has the potential to be harmful to clients and supervisees. Within counseling, the preponderance of research is focused on White counselors and clients of color, and the outcomes from this research indicate that counselors who interact from a CBRI perspective have clients who are less satisfied, disclose less, and are unlikely to return, particularly when clients of color are working with White counselors. The outcomes in supervision are similarly negative and harmful for supervisees. For many years, the counseling literature has espoused a multicultural perspective that would support counselors, supervisors and instructors acknowledging and addressing race, racial prejudice, and oppression in their respective professional roles (e.g., Ponterotto, Casas, Suzuki, & Alexander, 2010). Indeed, as noted earlier in this chapter, approaches that are both race and oppression conscious (e.g., grounded in multicultural ideology) have promise for decreasing CBRI and promoting more positive outcomes within counseling.

Given that CBRI encourages counselors to ignore race in counseling, perhaps more attention should be given to encouraging counselors to develop skills in talking about race with clients (Neville et al., 2013). More recently, *broaching* has emerged as a useful framework for conceptualizing a group of behaviors or styles for addressing and discussing race, ethnicity, and culture during the counseling process (Day-Vines, Bryan, & Griffin, 2013; Day-Vines et al., 2007). This continuum suggests that professionals might have five orientations regarding broaching: avoidant, isolating, continuing/incongruent, integrated/congruent, and infusing. The *avoidant* therapist espouses a color-blind approach to race, whereas the *infusing* therapist demonstrates an understanding of the effect of sociopolitical influences on clients' lives and the importance of advocacy (Day-Vines et al., 2013). With the availability of a scale and preliminary validation of the broaching construct (e.g., Day-Vines et al., 2013), it is hoped that professionals might be able to assess broaching orientation in themselves and their supervisees and intervene to work toward a more adaptive approach.

Within counseling and supervision, we have also found that practicing asking questions about race or role-playing interactions, such as those in Cardemil and Battle's (2003) article "Guess Who's Coming to Therapy: Getting Comfortable With Conversations About Race and Ethnicity in Psychotherapy," can be particularly helpful. For example, these authors include specific questions that can be used to gain more information about cultural identity and the role that racial/ethnic differences might play on clients' or supervisees' sense of comfort with addressing culture in psychotherapy or supervision.

Finally, several strategies can be integrated into multicultural practice and assessment to learn more about clients' identities and the meanings these identities have in their lives. For example, the ADDRESSING framework proposed by Pamela Hays (2008) provides a tool for conceptualizing identities across multiple life domains. Each of the letters in the acronym ADDRESSING represent a facet of identity (e.g., Age, Developmental disability) that the counselor can explore with respect to its influence on the client and his or her experiences. Another useful tool, the community genogram (Ivey & Ivey, 1999), provides the opportunity for the client and counselor to generate a narrative about the client within a community context, integrating cultural data relevant to the client's life. It should be noted that the community genogram is intended to help focus on positive resources and cultural strengths, so that clients might be able to use past successful strategies to address current concerns.

In addition to the strategies noted here that counselors and supervisors can use to diminish color- and power-evasive ideology, we also believe that increased attention should be given to the role of the trainee and professional as advocate. The American Counseling Association's Advocacy Competencies (Lewis, Arnold, House, & Toporek, 2003) provide a useful framework to consider how advocacy can be integrated into work with clients at client–student, school–community, or public arena levels. In this model, professionals can work with clients or on behalf of clients at the various levels. For those working with clients on a micro (client/student) level, providing empowerment and helping clients realize their power to challenge racial inequalities is an important goal (Neville et al., 2005). This might include helping a student identify external barriers affecting her development as well as her strengths. On a macro level, professionals might engage in social-political advocacy or disseminate information publicly to lobby for legislation and policy change to combat racial inequities (Lewis et al., 2003). Each of these levels provide unique opportunities for counselors to advocate for clients and bring about increased positive change.

FUTURE DIRECTIONS FOR RESEARCH

We hope that this chapter begins to address the research on color-blind racial attitudes in counseling and supervision. Working within the recently expanded definition of CBRI (Neville et al., 2013), which is composed of two main components, color evasion and power evasion, as well as the alternative ideology of multiculturalism (i.e., race consciousness and oppression consciousness), many new questions may arise for future research. Although the potential list of directions could be expansive, the following three areas seem particularly salient. Perhaps the first area to consider is the evolving definition of racial color blindness. Neville et al.'s (2013) recent synthesis of research and literature on this topic offers an important extension of previous work, and they suggest that further work is needed that operationalizes both the color- and power-evasive aspects of racial color blindness in a measure. Additionally, research suggests that Whites (Richeson & Nussbaum, 2004) and people of color (Chen et al., 2006; Neville et al., 2005) both use color-blind approaches, but the reasoning for using such an approach varies greatly across racial and ethnic groups. As such, we need to know more about how to operationalize and measure color blindness in various racial and ethnic groups.

The second area of potential research is translating the meaning of recent research, particularly from social psychology, within counseling and supervision processes. For instance, research suggests that Whites high in racial color blindness appear to experience cognitive depletion in interracial relations (Richeson et al., 2003; Richeson & Trawalter, 2005). Such a finding has important implications for counseling, for it may suggest that White counselors or supervisors high in CBRI may be preoccupied with managing their thoughts during cross-racial counseling and supervision in such a way that it makes them less available and present when working with clients. As another example, Apfelbaum, Sommers, and Norton (2008) found that Whites are prone to acknowledging race less frequently then African Americans and were perceived as less friendly by African American partners. Furthermore, Norton, Sommers, Apfelbaum, Pura, and Ariely (2006) found that when Whites avoided racial topics in interracial social situations, African Americans perceived them to have insensitive nonverbal behavior. Here again, these findings may have important implications for counseling and supervision, and as such, future counseling researchers may want to explore whether these findings are applicable to counseling and supervision processes.

One final area to continue to investigate is how CBRI affects clients and supervisees. Preliminary research in supervision (Burkard, Johnson, et al., 2006; Lubbers, 2013) suggests that color blindness or avoiding racial discussions may have adverse consequences for clients and supervisees. This research needs to be extended, perhaps to investigate different outcomes, such as satisfaction with therapy, the working alliance in therapy and supervision, and longer term effects on client well-being. Furthermore, research is warranted on how the dynamics between therapists/supervisors from the same ethnic group as their clients/supervisees (e.g., a Latina/Latino supervisor with a Latina/Latino supervisee) influence outcomes. Clearly more study is needed to better understand the role of CBRI within the clinical realm.

REFERENCES

Abramowitz, S. I., & Murray, J. (1983). Race effects in psychotherapy. In J. Murray & P. R. Abramson (Eds.), *Bias in psychotherapy* (pp. 215–255). New York: Praeger.

Ancis, J. R., & Szymanski, D. M. (2001). Awareness of White privilege among White counseling trainees. *The Counseling Psychologist, 29*, 548–569. http://dx.doi.org/10.1177/0011000001294005

Apfelbaum, E. P., Sommers, S. R., & Norton, M. I. (2008). Seeing race and seeming racist? Evaluating strategic color blindness in social interaction. *Journal of Personality and Social Psychology, 95*, 918–932. http://dx.doi.org/10.1037/a0011990

Appiah, K. A., & Gutmann, A. (1996). *Color conscious: The political morality of race*. Princeton, NJ: Princeton University Press.

Atkinson, D. R., & Lowe, S. M. (1995). The role of ethnicity, cultural knowledge, and conventional techniques in counseling and psychotherapy. In J. G. Ponterotto, J. M. Casas, L. A. Suzuki, & C. M. Alexander (Eds.), *Handbook of multicultural counseling* (pp. 387–414). Thousand Oaks, CA: Sage.

Burkard, A. W., Johnson, A. J., Madson, M. B., Pruitt, N. T., Contreas-Tadych, D., Kozlowski, J. M., . . . Knox, S. (2006). Supervisor cultural responsiveness and unresponsiveness in cross-cultural supervision. *Journal of Counseling Psychology, 53*, 288–301. http://dx.doi.org/10.1037/0022-0167.53.3.288

Burkard, A. W., & Knox, S. (2004). Effect of therapist color blindness on empathy and attributions empathy in cross-cultural counseling. *Journal of Counseling Psychology, 51*, 387–397. http://dx.doi.org/10.1037/0022-0167.51.4.387

Burkard, A. W., Knox, S., Clarke, R., Phelps, D., & Inman, A. (2014). Supervisors' experiences of providing difficult feedback in cross-ethnic/racial supervision. *The Counseling Psychologist, 42*, 314–344. http://dx.doi.org/10.1177/0011000012461157

Burkard, A. W., Knox, S., Groen, M., Perez, M., & Hess, S. A. (2006). European American therapist self-disclosure in cross-cultural counseling. *Journal of Counseling Psychology, 53*, 15–25. http://dx.doi.org/10.1037/0022-0167.53.1.15

Cardemil, E. V., & Battle, C. L. (2003). Guess who's coming to therapy? Getting comfortable with conversations about race and ethnicity in psychotherapy. *Professional Psychology: Research and Practice, 34*, 278–286. http://dx.doi.org/10.1037/0735-7028.34.3.278

Chao, R. (2006). Counselors' multicultural competencies: Race, training, ethnic identity, and color-blind racial attitudes. In G. R. Walz, J. C. Bleuer, & R. K. Yep (Eds.), *Vistas: Compelling perspectives on counseling 2006* (pp. 73–76). Alexandria, VA: American Counseling Association.

Chen, G. A., Lephuoc, P., Guzmán, M. R., Rude, S. S., & Dodd, B. G. (2006). Exploring Asian American racial identity. *Cultural Diversity and Ethnic Minority Psychology, 12*, 461–476. http://dx.doi.org/10.1037/1099-9809.12.3.461

Colvin-Burque, A., Zugazaga, C. B., & Davis-Maye, D. (2007). Can cultural competence be taught? Evaluating the impact of the soap model. *Journal of Social Work Education, 43*, 223–242. http://dx.doi.org/10.5175/JSWE.2007.200500528

Constantine, M. G. (2001). Multicultural training, theoretical orientation, empathy, and multicultural case conceptualization ability in counselors. *Journal of Mental Health Counseling, 23*, 357–372.

Constantine, M. G., Juby, H. L., & Liang, J. J.-C. (2001). Examining multicultural counseling competence and race-related attitudes among White marital and family therapists. *Journal of Marital and Family Therapy, 27*, 353–362. http://dx.doi.org/10.1111/j.1752-0606.2001.tb00330.x

D'Andrea, M., & Daniels, J. (2001). Expanding our thinking about White racism: Facing the challenges of multicultural counseling in the 21st century. In J. G. Ponterotto, J. M. Casas, L. A. Suzuki, & C. M. Alexander (Eds.), *Handbook of multicultural counseling* (2nd ed., pp. 289–310). Thousand Oaks, CA: Sage.

Day-Vines, N., Bryan, J., & Griffin, D. (2013). The Broaching Attitudes and Behavior Survey (BABS): An exploratory assessment of its dimensionality. *Journal of Multicultural Counseling and Development, 41*, 210–223.

Day-Vines, N. L., Wood, S., Grothaus, T., Craigen, L., Holman, A., Dotson-Blake, K., & Douglass, M. (2007). Broaching the subjects of race, ethnicity, and culture during the counseling process. *Journal of Counseling & Development, 85*, 401–409. http://dx.doi.org/10.1002/j.1556-6678.2007.tb00608.x

Devine, P. G., Evett, S. R., & Vasquez-Suson, K. A. (1996). Exploring the interpersonal dynamics of intergroup contact. In R. M. Sorrentino & E. T. Higgins (Eds.), *Handbook of motivation and cognition: The interpersonal context* (Vol. 3, pp. 423–464). New York, NY: Guilford Press.

Dovidio, J. F., Gaertner, S. L., Kawakami, K., & Hodson, G. (2002). Why can't we just get along? Interpersonal biases and interracial distrust. *Cultural Diversity and Ethnic Minority Psychology, 8*, 88–102. http://dx.doi.org/10.1037/1099-9809.8.2.88

Duan, C., & Roehlke, H. (2001). A descriptive "snapshot" of cross-racial supervision in university counseling center internships. *Journal of Multicultural Counseling and Development, 29,* 131–146. http://dx.doi.org/10.1002/j.2161-1912.2001. tb00510.x

Garb, H. N. (1997). Race bias, social class bias, and gender bias in clinical judgment. *Clinical Psychology: Science and Practice, 4,* 99–120. http://dx.doi.org/10.1111/j.1468-2850.1997.tb00104.x

Gatmon, D., Jackson, D., Koshkarian, L., Martos-Perry, N., Molina, A., Patel, N., & Rodolfa, E. (2001). Exploring ethnic, gender, sexual orientation variables in supervision: Do they really matter? *Journal of Multicultural Counseling and Development, 29,* 102–113. http://dx.doi.org/10.1002/j.2161-1912.2001.tb00508.x

Gushue, G. V., & Constantine, M. G. (2007). Color-blind racial attitudes and White racial identity attitudes in psychology trainees. *Professional Psychology: Research and Practice, 38,* 321–328. http://dx.doi.org/10.1037/0735-7028.38.3.321

Hays, P. A. (2008). *Addressing cultural complexities in practice, second edition: Assessment, Diagnosis, & Therapy.* Washington, DC: American Psychological Association.

Helms, J. E. (1995). An update of Helms's White and people of color racial identity models. In J. G. Ponterotto, J. M. Casas, L. A. Suzuki, & C. M. Alexander (Eds.), *Handbook of multicultural counseling* (pp. 181–198). Thousand Oaks, CA: Sage.

Ivey, A. E., & Ivey, M. B. (1999). *Intentional interviewing and counseling: Facilitating client development in a multicultural society* (4th ed.). Pacific Grove, CA: Brooks/Cole Publishing Company.

Knox, S., Burkard, A. W., Johnson, A. J., Suzuki, L. A., & Ponterotto, J. G. (2003). African American and European American therapists' experiences of addressing race in cross-racial psychotherapy dyads. *Journal of Counseling Psychology, 50,* 466–481. http://dx.doi.org/10.1037/0022-0167.50.4.466

La Roche, M. J., & Maxie, A. (2003). Ten considerations in addressing cultural differences in psychotherapy. *Professional Psychology: Research and Practice, 34,* 180–186.

Lewis, J., Arnold, M., House, R., & Toporek, R. (2003). *Advocacy competencies.* Retrieved from http://www.counseling.org/Resources

Lubbers, L. M. (2013). *Supervisees' experiences of ruptures in multicultural supervision: A qualitative study* (Doctoral dissertation). Retrieved from http://epublications.marquette.edu/dissertations_mu/295/

Neville, H. A., Awad, G. H., Brooks, J. E., Flores, M. P., & Bluemel, J. (2013). Color-blind racial ideology: Theory, training, and measurement implications in psychology. *American Psychologist, 68,* 455–466. http://dx.doi.org/10.1037/a0033282

Neville, H. A., Coleman, M. N., Falconer, J. W., & Holmes, D. (2005). Color-blind racial ideology and psychological false consciousness among African Americans. *Journal of Black Psychology, 31,* 27–45. http://dx.doi.org/10.1177/0095798404268287

Neville, H. A., Lilly, R. L., Duran, G., Lee, R., & Browne, L. (2000). Construction and initial validation of the Color-Blind Racial Attitudes Scale (CoBRAS). *Journal of Counseling Psychology, 47,* 59–70. http://dx.doi.org/10.1037/0022-0167.47.1.59

Neville, H. A., Spanierman, L., & Doan, B. T. (2006). Exploring the association between color-blind racial ideology and multicultural counseling competencies. *Cultural Diversity and Ethnic Minority Psychology, 12,* 275–290. http://dx.doi.org/10.1037/1099-9809.12.2.275

Norton, M. I., Sommers, S. R., Apfelbaum, E. P., Pura, N., & Ariely, D. (2006). Color blindness and interracial interaction: Playing the political correctness game. *Psychological Science, 17,* 949–953. http://dx.doi.org/10.1111/j.1467-9280.2006.01810.x

Plaut, V. C., Thomas, K. M., & Goren, M. J. (2009). Is multiculturalism or color blindness better for minorities? *Psychological Science, 20,* 444–446. http://dx.doi.org/10.1111/j.1467-9280.2009.02318.x

Ponterotto, J. G., Casas, J. M., Suzuki, L. A., & Alexander, C. M. (Eds.). (2010). *Handbook of multicultural counseling* (3rd ed.). Thousand Oaks, CA: Sage.

Qureshi, A. (2007). I was being myself but being an actor too: The experience of a Black male in interracial psychotherapy. *Psychology and Psychotherapy: Theory, Research and Practice, 80,* 467–479. http://dx.doi.org/10.1111/j.2044-8341.2007.tb00425.x

Richeson, J. A., Baird, A. A., Gordon, H. L., Heatherton, T. F., Wyland, C. L., Trawalter, S., & Shelton, J. N. (2003). An fMRI investigation of the impact of interracial contact on executive function. *Nature Neuroscience, 6,* 1323–1328. http://dx.doi.org/10.1038/nn1156

Richeson, J. A., & Nussbaum, R. J. (2004). The impact of multiculturalism versus color blindness on racial bias. *Journal of Experimental Social Psychology, 40,* 417–423. http://dx.doi.org/10.1016/j.jesp.2003.09.002

Richeson, J. A., & Trawalter, S. (2005). Why do interracial interactions impair executive function? A resource depletion account. *Journal of Personality and Social Psychology, 88,* 934–947. http://dx.doi.org/10.1037/0022-3514.88.6.934

Ridley, C. R., Ethington, L. L., & Heppner, P. P. (2008). Cultural confrontation: A skill of advanced cultural empathy. In P. B. Pedersen, J. G. Draguns, W. J. Lonner, & J. E. Trimble (Eds.), *Counseling across cultures* (6th ed., pp. 377–393). Thousand Oaks, CA: Sage. http://dx.doi.org/10.4135/9781483329314.n22

Ridley, C. R., & Lingle, D. W. (1996). Cultural empathy in multicultural counseling: A multidimensional process model. In P. B. Pedersen, J. G. Draguns, W. J. Lonner, & J. E. Trimble (Eds.), *Counseling across cultures* (4th ed., pp. 21–46). Thousand Oaks, CA: Sage.

Sasaki, S. J., & Vorauer, J. D. (2013). Ignoring versus exploring differences between groups: Effects of salient color blindness and multiculturalism on intergroup attitudes and behavior. *Social and Personality Psychology Compass, 7,* 246–259. http://dx.doi.org/10.1111/spc3.12021

Spanierman, L. B., Poteat, V. P., Wang, Y., & Oh, E. (2008). Psychological costs of racism to White counselors: Predicting various dimensions of multicultural counseling competence. *Journal of Counseling Psychology, 55,* 75–88. http://dx.doi.org/10.1037/0022-0167.55.1.75

Thompson, C. E., & Jenal, S. T. (1994). Interracial and intraracial quasi-counseling interactions when counselors avoid discussing race. *Journal of Counseling Psychology, 41*, 484–491. http://dx.doi.org/10.1037/0022-0167.41.4.484

Thompson, C. E., Worthington, R., & Atkinson, D. R. (1994). Counselor content orientation, counselor race, and Black women's cultural mistrust and self-disclosures. *Journal of Counseling Psychology, 41*, 155–161. http://dx.doi.org/10.1037/0022-0167.41.2.155

Utsey, S. O., Gernat, C. A., & Hammar, L. (2005). Examining White counselor trainees' reactions to racial issues in counseling and supervision dyads. *The Counseling Psychologist, 33*, 449–478. http://dx.doi.org/10.1177/0011000004269058

Wade, P., & Bernstein, B. L. (1991). Culture sensitivity training and counselor's race: Effects on Black female clients' perceptions and attrition. *Journal of Counseling Psychology, 38*, 9–15. http://dx.doi.org/10.1037/0022-0167.38.1.9

Zhang, N., & Burkard, A. W. (2008). Client and counselor discussions of racial and ethnic differences in counseling: An exploratory investigation. *Journal of Multicultural Counseling and Development, 36*, 77–87. http://dx.doi.org/10.1002/j.2161-1912.2008.tb00072.x

INDEX

priming with CBRI and recognition of discrimination, 128

racial socialization of, 61–62

in yes–no task studies, 131

Choi, C. C., 194

Choi, J., 221

Chow, R. M., 150

Christ, O., 235

Chung, A. H., 150

Chung, Y. B., 197

Clarke, R., 303–304

Class. *See also* Socioeconomic status (SES)

discussions of, 98–99

identity and, 108

Clegg, Roger, 53

CoBRAS (Colorblind Racial Attitudes Scale), 143, 145–146, 152

in evaluating diversity courses, 229

initial validation of, 194

in recent research, 297

Cognitive ability tests, stereotype threat and, 252

Cognitive depletion, in interracial interactions, 75, 306

Cognitive dissonance, 192–193

Cognitive empathy, 178

Cokley, K. O., 197

Cole, E. R., 229

Coleman, M. N., 195

Collectivism, 179

Colleges. *See* Higher education

Color-blind mind-set

in interracial relationships, 71–75

multicultural mind-set vs., 70–71

Color blindness

as medical condition, 39

polyculturalism vs., 148–149

racial. *See* Racial color blindness

Colorblind Racial Attitudes Scale. *See* CoBRAS

Color-blind racial ideology (CBRI), 39–50, 158–161. *See also individual topics*

among people of color, 191, 194–196. *See also* Internalized racism

beliefs in, 40–41

color evasion in, 41. *See also* Color evasion

definitions of, 5–7

detrimental effects of, 45–46

differing conceptions of, 125–126

in education system. *See* K–12 schools

examples of, 39–40

and explanations for workplace disparities, 249–250

impossibility of, 42–45

and institutional racism, 41

main tenets of, 158–159

and more effective intergroup bias reduction approach, 49–50

power evasion in, 41. *See also* Power evasion

preferential, 177

racelessness in, 41–42, 47–49

and racialized hierarchy, 40, 106

reasons for endorsing. *See* Endorsement of color blindness

strategic, 177

as a system justification theory, 192–194

U.S. historical ideas underlying, 209

Color-blind racism, 29–31. *See also* Racial color blindness

Color consciousness, 64, 250. *See also* Race consciousness

in Brazil, 92

contingent, 107

counterpublics' perspective on, 90. *See also* Counterpublics

cultural assumptions impeding, 100

in K–12 teacher education, 220–222

and racial literacy, 98

White resistance to, 99

Color-conscious teacher training, 220–221

Color evasion, 6, 8–9, 41, 142, 297

in CBRI in schools, 209

in counseling, 299

measuring, 147, 149–152

race consciousness vs., 297

and workplace disparity, 250–251

workplace diversity policies for, 262

Color insight, 107n3

Common ingroup identity model, 288

Community genograms, 305

Competitive racism, 29

Concealed stories, 109–110, 112–113, 115

and contemporary racial attitudes, 278–279

and health of U.S. Blacks and Whites, 276–277

and patients' racial attitudes, 279, 282–284

and physicians' racial attitudes, 279–284

Health inequalities, 8
in Brazil, 93
in United States, 276–277

Hehman, E., 57

Henderson-King, D., 230

Henry, P. J., 142

Hernandez, Jessica, 5

Hess, S. A., 301–302

Hierarchy, racialized, 40, 106

Higher education, 227–238
diversity courses in, 229–230
extracurricular learning in, 235–236
increasing learning and awareness in, 232–235
learning process in, 230–232
liberalizing effect on racial attitudes in, 228–229

Hiring decisions, 244–245

Hispanics. *See also* Latinos; *specific topics*
as CEOs, 246
on corporate boards, 246
household income of, 25
median weekly earnings of, 246
occupational status of, 245
unemployment rate for, 244

Hoffman, M. L., 178, 185

Hogan, C. M., 150

Hogan, D. E., 229–230

Holoien, D. S., 76

Homeless families with children, 207

Home ownership, 109–110

hooks, b., 100

Housing inequality, 26, 109–110

Humanism, 48, 100–101

Hunt, Darrien, 4

Iacoboni, M., 187

Identity
common ingroup identity model, 288
intersecting aspects of, 108
racial. *See* Racial identity

Identity management, 261–271
benefits of, 268–269
challenges in addressing discrimination, 264–265
and color-blind workplace diversity policies, 261–264
costs of, 269–271
strategies for, 265–268

Identity recategorization, 266

Identity redefinition, 267, 270

Identity regeneration, 266–268, 270

Identity safety, 64

Identity switching, 265–267

Ignoring race, 8–10, 54, 58, 106. *See also* Color-blind racial ideology (CBRI)

Implicit prejudice, 59–63

Implicit racial bias, 181, 279–288

Impossibility of color-blind approach to race, 42–45

Impression management
by minorities, 75
by Whites, 72–73

Incarceration, racialized, 113

Inclusion, microaggressions undermining, 111

Income inequality, 25, 246

Individualism, 179

Infusing therapists, 305

Inherited silence, 61–62

Injustice, perpetuation of, 109

Inman, A., 303–304

Institute of Medicine, 281

Institutional racism, 27, 41

Integrated/congruent therapists, 305

Intent, shifting focus to outcomes from, 113–114

Intergroup empathy, 176

Intergroup Ideologies Measures: Color-blindness subscale, 144, 148–149

Intergroup learning about race, 232–233

Internal traits framework (workplace disparities), 247

Internalized racism, 191–202
and CBRI as system justification theory, 192–194
and critical consciousness as corrective to CBRI, 199–202
defined, 196
and impact of minimizing race, 198–199

Occupational inequality, 26. *See also* Unemployment
Occupational status, disparities in, 245–247
Ogbu, John, 90, 91
Oh, E., 194
Oppression consciousness, 297
Organizational climate, 134–135. *See also* Corporate cultures/climates
Outcomes, shifting focus from intent to, 113–114
Outgroup bias, 46, 129
Outgroups
  dehumanization of individuals from, 182
  perceived interpersonal similarity, 80–81
  perceived outgroup variability, 80
  prejudice and amount of contact with, 235

Palmer, B., 230
PALS (Portrait of American Life), 149–150
Pappas, G., 215
Parents Involved in Community Schools v. Seattle School District No. 1, 58–59
Park, B., 45, 149
Parker, Tiana, 198
Parks, Rosa, 114
Partner effect, 70, 73, 75
Pascarella, E. T., 230
Patients' racial attitudes, 279, 282–284
Pauker, K., 128
Pedagogy of the Oppressed (Freire), 93, 199
Pedersen, P. B., 178–179
Penner, L. A., 282, 283, 288–289
Perceived interpersonal similarity, 80–81
Perceived outgroup variability, 80
Perez, M., 301–302
Performance outcomes, improving, 268–269
Perry, Rick, 125, 126
Personal interactions
  of Americans, 69
  interracial, 59. *See also* Interracial interactions/relationships
Perspective taking, 178
Peter, Laurence J., 192

Peter's Quotations (Peter), 192
Pettigrew, T. F., 235
Pettijohn, T. F., II, 229–230
Pew Research Center, 183
Phelps, D., 303–304
Physicians' racial attitudes, 279–284
Pickett, K. M., 236
Pierson, C. T., 230
Plata, M., 210
Plaut, V. C., 45, 60, 135, 149
Plessy v. Ferguson, 95
Police officers, people of color attacked/killed by, 3–5, 180, 181
Political race, 108
Politicians, minority, 32
Politics of accountability, 115
Polyculturalism, 148–149
Ponterotto, J. G., 301
Portrait of American Life (PALS), 149–150
Positive verbal/nonverbal behaviors, 76–77
Postracial society
  importance of race in, 32–35
  racial domination in, 29
  rationalization for, 105–106
  viewing United States as, 26, 101, 158
Poverty, 7, 207
Power and privilege awareness, 250, 255
Power evasion, 6, 9–10, 41, 142, 297
  in CBRI in schools, 209
  in counseling, research on, 299
  measuring, 145, 151, 152
  oppression consciousness vs., 297
  and workplace disparity, 250
  workplace diversity policies for, 262
Prasad, P. A., 278
Pratto, F., 57
Praxis, 200
Precedents, 113
Preferential CBRI, 177
Prejudice
  camouflaging, 59–63
  with color-blind approach, 46, 71, 130, 180
  concerns about appearance of, 130–132
  fear of exhibiting, 72
  implicit and explicit, 59–63

Prejudice, *continued*
  new form of, 159
  racism as, 27, 33
  reduced with perceived outgroup
    variability, 80
  in students paired with Asian Ameri-
    can roommates, 235
Prescriptive stereotypes, 269–270
Prevention focus, 46
Prilleltensky, I., 202
Priming studies, 127–130, 134
Privilege, 27, 28
  camouflaging, 57–59
  legitimization of, 126
  resistance to dealing with, 100
  and system justification, 193
Privilege evasion, 250
Probst, T. M., 229
Procedural contexts, CBRI in, 126
Psychological perspectives, on empathy,
    177–180
Psychological well-being
  racelessness and, 48–49
  and system-justifying beliefs, 47
Psychopaths
  cultural, 184
  lack of empathy response in, 182
Pura, N., 59–60, 72, 130, 306
Purdie-Vaughns, V. J., 44, 46
Pygmalion effects, 210

Qualitative research, 160–161

Race, 6
  as automatically activated social
    category, 285
  brain processes activated by, 43
  categorizing people by, 43
  divergent community views of, 5
  minimizing, 198–199
  as national division, 25–26
  Obama's comments on, 33
  and other aspects of identity, 108
  racial disparities in United States,
    7–8
  roles and influence of, 64
  stories we tell about, 108–111
  talking about, 10, 63–64
Race ambivalence, 107
Race cognizance, 107n3

Race consciousness, 105–118. *See also*
    Color consciousness
  as active state, 107
  agenda for developing, 111–117
  as alternative to racial color blind-
    ness, 106–108
  concerns about, 107–108
  defined, 111
  in multicultural ideology, 297
  scope of, 108
  and story metaphor, 108–111
Race matters argument, 42–45
Racelessness
  in color-blind approach to race,
    41–42, 47–49
  defined, 47
Racelessness Scale (RS), 48–49
Racial apathy, 168
Racial color blindness, 5–6. *See also*
    Color-blind racial ideology
    (CBRI)
  among people of color, 191,
    194–196. *See also* Internalized
    racism
  approaches to, 39
  and attacks on counterpublics, 90
  in Brazil, 92
  debunking myth of, 8–10
  as dominant organizational diversity
    philosophy, 243
  election of Obama as indication of,
    3, 10
  failure of, 106–107
  instrumentalist assumptions about,
    100
  interpretations of, 63
  and lack of empathy, 180
  and multicultural competency,
    298–299
  multiculturalism compared to, 60–61
  proponents' arguments for, 106
  race consciousness as alternative to,
    106–108
  reasons for endorsing. *See* Endorse-
    ment of color blindness
  strategic, 59–60, 130–133, 185
  varying definitions of, 6
Racial domination system, 27–29
Racial group membership, perspective
    created by, 218–219

Racial identity
    absence of, in Brazil, 92
    Cross Racial Identity Scale, 197
    and impact of minimizing race,
        198–199
    as means of avoiding problems, 98
    Multidimensional Inventory of Black
        Identity, 48
    and personal psychological function-
        ing, 48–49
    White, multiculturalism as threat
        to, 77
Racial literacy, 98, 99
    cultural assumptions impeding, 100
    as essential in a democracy, 116–117
Racial socialization
    of children, 61–62
    protective messages about, 195
    of White middle-school children,
        165–167
Racial stereotypes, 179. See also Stereo-
        type threat
    and academic achievement, 211–212
    automatic activation of, 56
    and CBRI in middle schools,
        214–215
    and dual-identity approach, 79
    in health care, 281
    judgments affected by, 44–45
    literature on, 47
    of males of color, 5
    in organizational decision making,
        251
Racial stories, 30, 31. See also Stories
Racial worldviews, 5. See also Worldviews
Racialized hierarchy, 40, 106
Racism
    and attacks on counterpublics, 90
    in Brazil, 94, 96–97
    contemporary forms of, 10, 28–29.
        See also New racism
    as danger to democracy, 116
    defining, 26–28
    differing conceptions of, 26–28
    divergent community views of, 5
    eliminating, 106
    internalized. See Internalized racism
    in law enforcement and criminal
        justice, 3–5
    liberal, 99–101

modern, 142
Obama's view of, 33
symbolic, 142
White accountability for interrupt-
        ing, 115
Racism Without Racists (Bonilla-Silva),
        30
Racist groups, growth of, 26
Reddock, Lisa, 198
Reframing, 79. *See also* Framing
Republican Party, 26
Research, need for change in, 34. *See
        also specific types of research and
        specific topics*
Residential segregation, 28–29, 158
Resilience to stereotypes, 254–255
Resistance movements, 114
Resistance stories, 110
Reverse racism, 33
Rice, D., 224
Richeson, J. A., 46, 213
Rifkin, J., 182
Right-wing authoritarians,
        multiculturalism and, 77
Rios, D., 229
Roberson, L., 247, 255
Roberts, John, 105–106
Roberts, R. A., 111, 213
Robinson, Eugene, 92
Robinson, Max, 41
Rodriguez, C., 79
Roediger, David, 94
Roehlke, H., 302
Rogers, Renee, 197
Roommates, 235–236
Rosenthal, L., 148–149, 152
Rosenthal, R., 210
RS (Racelessness Scale), 48–49
Ruble, D. N., 79
Rudman, L. A., 230
Ryan, C. S., 148, 152

Saguy, T., 57
Sameness, myth of, 100–101
Sasaki, S. J., 46, 74, 77, 285
Scheepers, D., 79
Scheindlin, Shira, 9
Schniedewind, N., 221
Schofield, J. W., 214–215
School climate, 212–213, 219

School life. *See also* Higher education;
    K–12 schools
    negotiating race in, 162–164
    racial socialization of White middle-
        school children, 165–167
School segregation, 30, 158, 1210
Scott, Walter, 5
Sears, D. O., 142
Segregation
    counterpublic formation and, 95
    history of, 111
    of schools, 30, 110, 158
Self-disclosure of attitudes/beliefs, by
        therapists, 301–302
Self-esteem, protecting, 268
Self-hatred, racelessness as precursor to,
        47–48
Self-presentation, color-blind mind-set
        and, 72–73
Self-report measures, 142
Sellers, R. M., 48
Senior leadership positions, disparities
        in, 246–247
Sensitivity training, 220
Serrano-Garcia, I., 200
SES. *See* Socioeconomic status
Sex-blind (term), 262
Sexuality
    discussions of, 98–99
    identity and, 108
Shared meaning-making processes, 162
Shelton, J. N., 73–74, 76, 236
Sheriff, Robin, 92
Shooter bias, 45
Sidanius, J., 150, 228–229, 235
Silence, inherited, 61–62
Silent stoning, 182–183
Silverstein, J., 184
Similarity, perceived interpersonal, 80–81
Singh, A. A., 197
Slater, R. B., 90–91
Slavery
    in Brazil, 94, 95
    in United States, 27, 28, 94, 95
Social dominance, 134, 196–198
Social inequality, 79
Social justice, 108, 126
Social movements, need for, 34
Social neuroscience, on empathy,
        180–182

Social psychology research, 125–137
    correlational field studies, 134–135
    future possibilities for, 136
    measures used in, 151
    priming studies, 127–130, 134
    student roundtables, 132–133
    yes–no group tasks, 127–128,
        131–132
Socialization, racial, 61–62, 165–167,
        195
Sociocultural organizational context
        framework (workplace disparities),
        249
Sociocultural phenomenon, internalized
        racism as, 196–198
Socioeconomic status (SES)
    and health care disparities, 278
    and health disparities, 277
    and implicit/explicit prejudice, 279
Sociopolitical development (SPD), 200,
        201
Sommers, S. R., 58–60, 72–74, 128,
        130, 131, 306
Sotomayor, Sonia, 106n1
Spanierman, L. B., 194–195
SPD (sociopolitical development), 200,
        201
Status quo
    and architected stereotypes, 192
    cognitive dissonance and maintenance
        of, 192–103
    protecting, 57
    stock stories rationalizing/justifying,
        109, 111
Steele, C. M., 46
Stereotype reassociation, 266
Stereotype regeneration, 266
Stereotype threat, 211–212
    creating conditions for, 251–253
    defined, 252
Stereotypes
    architected, 192
    changing, 268–269
    descriptive, 269, 270
    prescriptive, 269–270
    racial. *See* Racial stereotypes
Stevenson, H., 146
Stock stories, 109, 111, 112
    interrupting, 114–115
    neoliberal ideas in, 116

Van der Pole, Johann (aka Frei Chico), 93–94
Van der Toorn, J., 192, 201–202
Vargas, N., 150
Variability, perceived outgroup, 80
Vianna, H., 96
Voight, A., 199–200
Vorauer, J. D., 46, 74–77, 129, 285

The Wages of Whiteness (Roediger), 94
Wagner, U., 235
Walzer, A. S., 229–230
Wang, D. C., 195
Wang, Y. F., 194–195
Warren, J. W., 91
Watts, R. J., 199–200
Watts-Jones, D., 196
Wealth inequalities, 7, 25–26, 109–110
Weinstein, R. S., 211–212
Wenglar, K., 210
West, T. V., 80, 236
White Americans. See also specific topics
    as CEOs, 246
    on corporate boards, 246
    discrimination against, 58
    encouraging antiracist community
        in, 34
    health of. See Health care disparities
        (Black–White)
    homeownership by, 109
    homicide rates for, 93
    household income of, 25
    impression management by, 72–73
    incarceration of, 7, 8
    income level of, 93
    job offers for, 245
    median weekly earnings of, 246
    mortality rate for, 276
    occupational status of, 245
    racial socialization of, 165–167
    resistance to color consciousness
        in, 99
    unemployment rates for, 7, 244
    wealth of, 7

White identity, multiculturalism as
        threat to, 77
White supremacy
    in Brazil, 100
    CBRI as pillar of, 159
    in Latin America, 101
    negative consequences of, 99
    new face of, 32
Whiteness
    "burden of 'acting White,'" 90
    as foundational idea of CBRI, 209
Williams, P., 208–209
Williams, W. S., 197
Wilson, Darren, 3–4, 181
Wingate, K., 207, 208
Wittenbrink, B., 45
Wolski, C., 129, 149
Workplace disparities, 243–256
    breaking cycle of, 255–256
    CBRI and explanations for,
        249–251
    creating conditions for stereotype
        threat, 251–253
    cultivating awareness of diversity
        dynamics, 253–255
    existence of, 244–247
    frameworks for understanding,
        247–249
Workplaces with CBRI policies. See
    Identity management
Worldviews, 5
    in counseling processes, 300
    cultural, of teachers, 217–218
Writing answers to learn, 232
Wynne, J., 210

Yes–no group tasks, 127–128, 131–132
Yoshino, K., 197–198

Zatick, C. D., 246
Zero-sum beliefs, 57–58
Zigler, E., 48–49
Zimmerman, George, 63–64, 125, 180,
    184

ABOUT THE EDITORS

Helen A. Neville, PhD, is a professor of educational psychology and African American studies at the University of Illinois at Urbana–Champaign. She is a past associate editor of *The Counseling Psychologist* and of the *Journal of Black Psychology*. Her research on race, racism, and color-blind racial ideology has appeared in a wide range of peer-reviewed journals. For her research and mentoring efforts Dr. Neville has received the American Psychological Association (APA) Graduate Students Kenneth and Mamie Clark Award, the APA Division 45 Charles and Shirley Thomas Award for mentoring and contributions to African American students and community, and the APA MFP Dalmas Taylor Award for Research. She was honored with the Association of Black Psychologists' Distinguished Psychologist of the Year Award and the Winter Roundtable Janet E. Helms Mentoring Award.

Miguel E. Gallardo, PsyD, is an associate professor of psychology and director of Aliento, The Center for Latina/Latino Communities at Pepperdine University. He maintains an independent, consultation practice in which he conducts therapy with adolescents and adults and consults with organizations and universities on developing culturally responsive systems. He teaches courses on multicultural and social justice, intimate partner violence, and professional practice issues. Dr. Gallardo's areas of scholarship and research include the psychotherapy process when working with ethnocultural communities, particularly the Latina/Latino community, and the processes by which individuals develop cultural awareness and responsiveness. Dr. Gallardo is currently director of research and evaluation for the Multiethnic Collaborative of Community Agencies, a nonprofit organization dedicated to serving monolingual Arab, Farsi, Korean, Vietnamese, and Spanish-speaking communities. He has published refereed journal articles, books, and book chapters in the areas of multicultural psychology, Latina/Latino psychology, and ethics and evidence-based practices.

Derald Wing Sue, PhD, is a professor of psychology and education in the Department of Counseling and Clinical Psychology at Teachers College and the School of Social Work, Columbia University. He received his PhD from the University of Oregon and has served as a training faculty member with the Institute for Management Studies and the Columbia University Executive Training Programs. He was the cofounder and first president of the Asian American Psychological Association, past presidents of the Society for the Psychological Study of Culture, Ethnicity and Race (Division 45), and the Society of Counseling Psychology (Division 17). Dr. Sue is a member of the American Counseling Association, fellow of the American Psychological Association, the American Psychological Society, and the American Association of Applied and Preventive Psychology. Dr. Sue has served as editor of the *Personnel and Guidance Journal* (now the *Journal for Counseling and Development*), associate editor of the *American Psychologist*, and editorial member for the *Asian Journal of Counselling*; he serves on the Council of Elders for *Cultural Diversity and Ethnic Minority Psychology* and has been or continues to be a consulting editor for numerous journals and publications.